# Standard Grade

# COMPUTING STUDIES

John Walsh



Hodder & Stoughton

A MEMBER OF THE HODDER HEADLINE GROUP

*To Helen, Peter John, Mary, Sarah, Siobhan and Cecilia*


## Acknowledgements

The author and publishers would like to thank everyone who helped in the production of this book, especially J.J. Timmons and Christine Peace of the Bank of Scotland, Suzanne Yager of Channel Four Productions and Peter Beverley of New Prestel.

We would like to thank the following companies, individuals and institutions who have given permission to reproduce photographs in this book:

Ann Ronan picture Library (309 top); Argos (3); Bank of Scotland (187, 190); Charles Babbage Institute, University of Minnesota (311); Eolas (103); E.Y.P (100); Glasgow Herald and Evening Times (40); Holme Partnership (144); Roddy Paine (4, 8, 89 both, 90, 99, 110, 120 both, 121 both, 141, 148, 145, 158, 169, 184, 199, 199, 206, 208, 211, 222, 224, 232, 232); Scotsman Publications (247); Spreckly Pittam Ltd (226, 242); Science and Society photo Library (308 both, 309 bottom, 310 both); Visa (193);

We would also like to thank the following who gave permission to reproduce copyright material:

Glasgow Herald (21, 103, 176); Scotland on Sunday (17); The Scottish Daily Express (189); The Sunday Post/D.C. Thomson Ltd (202); The Weekly News/D.C. Thomson Ltd (193);

The illustrations were produced by GDN Associates, Hastings.

*British Library Cataloguing in Publication Data*
A catalogue for this book is held with the British Library

First published 1994
Impression number 10 9 8 7 6
Year 2000 1999 1998 1997





Printed in Great Britain for Hodder and Stoughton Educational,a division of Hodder Headline Plc, 338 Euston Road, London NW1 3BH by Scotprint Ltd, Musselburgh, Scotland.

# Contents


| | | Page |
|---|---|---|
| 1 | General purpose packages | 1 |
| 2 | Word processing | 28 |
| 3 | Databases | 39 |
| 4 | Spreadsheets | 51 |
| 5 | Graphics | 65 |
| 6 | Integrated packages | 73 |
| 7 | Desktop publishing | 80 |
| 8 | Viewdata and Teletext | 88 |
| 9 | Electronic mail | 103 |
| 10 | Automated systems | 120 |
| 11 | Computers in design and manufacture | 141 |
| 12 | Commercial data processing | 153 |
| 13 | Banking | 183 |
| 14 | Electronic point of sale | 198 |
| 15 | Airline reservations | 211 |
| 16 | Hardware | 222 |
| 17 | Systems software | 250 |
| 18 | Operating and filing systems | 259 |
| 19 | Low level machine | 270 |
| 20 | Programming | 284 |
| | Appendix 1 Glossary of terms used in the book | 301 |
| | Appendix 2 History of computers | 308 |
| | Index | 313 |

# Preface

This book is intended to act as a valuable resource for both pupils and teachers by providing a concise set of notes which closely follow the syllabus for the Scottish Certificate of Education Standard Grade Computing Studies to be examined in and after 1994.

Each chapter in the book matches a syllabus topic, covering all the compulsory application areas and the systems topic. In addition to this, in separate chapters we look at case studies of particular application areas.

The book covers programming, but does not refer exclusively to any particular software or hardware.

The main part of the text in each chapter is tailored to the needs of foundation and general pupils, while the 'More to do' sections and 'Extra Questions', set against a tinted background, offer opportunities to take concepts further and will be invaluable to those working for credit level. Throughout the text there are questions designed to help reinforce knowledge and understanding and problem
solving skills. Although the questions are divided into these two categories, some questions may not 'fit' precisely into a particular category. All the answers to the knowledge and understanding questions can be found within the text of that chapter.

Suggestions for **practical activities** are included in certain chapters, and appendices provide additional background on

- The **historical aspects** of the development of computer hardware
- A short **glossary** of computing terms, which is designed to be used frequently throughout the book.

Bold type has been used in the text to indicate that a term or phrase is new, and that an explanation can be found either in the following text, or in the glossary, or in both. The terminology used throughout the book is designed to relate extremely closely to the terminology around which the document **Standard Grade Amended Arrangements in Computing Studies, in and after 1994** is structured. Indeed, the book as a whole is designed to completely fulfil the requirements of that document.

The order of chapters in the book is not intended to be a recommended order in which to teach or learn the syllabus topics. Teachers and pupils may prefer to follow an entirely different order, and will certainly find it useful to dip into different parts of the book, as required, for reference or revision.

# 1 General purpose packages

## Introduction

Computers store and handle information. Information is handled by a computer in the form of **data**. Computers control the storage of information and can change the way it is presented to the user. They can control the way data is moved from one place to another and they can change data from one form to another by using the rules that are stored in a computer program.

There are many different types of information stored on a computer as data.

**DATA**

a general term for numbers, characters and symbols which are accepted and processed by a computer system

- **NUMBERS**
  e.g. 0, 1, 2, 3, 4, 5, 6, 7, 999, 0.976, –123 are all **numbers**
- **TEXT**
  e.g. ABCDEFGHIJKLMNOPQRSTUVWXYZ and abcdefghijklmnopqrstuvwxyz are **text**
- **GRAPHICS**
  The diagrams and other pictures in this book are **graphics**
- **SOUND**
  Music or any other noise produced by a computer is **sound**

**GRAPHICS**

pictures or charts on a computer screen

Computers store data as a series of numbers, so any information that can be translated or coded as a series of numbers can be stored as data and processed by a computer.

## Information and data

What is the difference between information and data? **Information** has a meaning. For example, '1 October 1995' is information, meaning the first day of the month of October, in the year 1995. Computers store information as a series of numbers. These numbers are **data**, which don't mean anything on their own. Only if you know how the computer has organised the information as data does it mean anything to you. For example 951001 ... is data.

If you know that the computer puts the last two digits of the year as the first two digits of this data, and the number of the month as the third and fourth digits and the day of the month as the last two digits, then you understand that these numbers mean the same as the information above.

**EXAMPLE**

When people apply for a driving licence they are given a personal identification number. This is used to help identify a person's details. Part of this number refers to the person's date of birth – but the figures are arranged differently from the way we normally write a date.

For example, if the person was born on 12 October 1978, this would normally be written as 12.10.78 (where 12 is the day of the month; 10 refers to October as the tenth month and 78 is the year 1978).

On the driving licence the computer records the date as 710128. This is simply a string of digits, or a piece of data, unless you know how to 'decode' the data to make the date. When you can do this, the digits become information.

So we can say that

| |
|---|
| *Information (for people) = data (for computers) with structure.* |

Data becomes information when you understand what it means. Computers process data, people use information.

## Application packages

The most common method of processing data with a computer system is by using the series of instructions stored in a **computer program** called an **application package**. There are a huge number of application packages, from games like Super Mario Bros. to spreadsheets like Excel.

## General purpose packages

There is an important difference between Super Mario Bros. and Excel. The game application has only one purpose – for the user to play a game. It is a single purpose package. You cannot add any information to the game. When you start playing all you can do is to follow the instructions and play it. On the other hand, you can use a spreadsheet application like Excel for many different purposes, but you must supply your own information to the spreadsheet before it is of any use to you. Application packages that require you to provide your own information like this are called **general purpose packages.**

Examples of general purpose packages:
- word processors
- spreadsheets
- databases
- graphics programs
- desk top publishing programs.

## Computer hardware

The basic **hardware** needed to run a general purpose package is a computer system consisting of a processor, monitor, keyboard, disk drive and printer. Some general purpose packages need particular input devices (like a mouse, graphics tablet, or scanner) and output devices (like a plotter).

Complete systems may be specially designed to perform a particular task like word processing. These are called **dedicated systems** because they can only perform one task. The word processor in the photo can't be used to produce graphics, because the program is designed for word processing alone, and cannot be changed.

*Dedicated word processors*

Computers using general purpose packages have a number of advantages over using paper, ink and human brain power alone:

- information can be processed more speedily and accurately
- changes are easily made to the information and to the layout of any particular document
- information can be got at more easily when it is stored in electronic form than information stored in filing cabinets, for example
- it is easier for many people to access the same information when computers are networked.

**NETWORK**

a number of computers joined together so that data can be transferred between them

*A selection of general purpose packages*

### *What does a general purpose package consist of?*

If you said that a general purpose package was a computer program then you would be very close to the correct answer, but a general purpose package is more than just a computer program. When you buy a general purpose package it includes one or more disks containing the program, but it also has quite a lot of paperwork with it. At the very least there will be a book of instructions (a manual) on how to use the program. There may also be a tutorial guide (a book containing a series of lessons which teach you how to use the package), and perhaps a quick reference guide or function keystrip – there is often also a demonstration program to teach you how to use the package. This is usually easier to follow and much quicker than reading the manual!

You will use many different general purpose packages during your Computing Studies course. Which ones you use will depend on what is available in your school or college.

### *General purpose commands*

Many general purpose packages use the same commands, such as:

- **RUN (OPEN APPLICATION)**
  This is the command that you give to the computer to start the program running
- **NEW**
  This command creates a new, empty **file**, ready for you to put in your own information
- **LOAD**
  This command reads a particular file from **backing storage**, for example a hard disk
- **SAVE**
  With this command the computer writes a file to backing storage so that you can use it again later
- **PRINT**
  Using this command you can produce a **hard copy** (or **printout**) of your file. In some cases you may wish to print only some of the file, perhaps only page two out of a three-page document.

**FILE**

a collection of data or a program held on backing storage or in memory

**BACKING STORE**

a system for permanently holding the contents of memory on disk or tape

**HARD COPY**

A printed copy of your work, usually on paper

### *Common features of general purpose packages*

Many operations are also the same for different packages, for example:

- **INSERT**
  Put additional information in – perhaps insert an extra row or column of numbers into a spreadsheet
- **AMEND**
  Change or correct spelling – for example, change their to there
- **DELETE**
  You may remove material – for example, by deleting a paragraph from a document
- **CHANGE TEXT APPEARANCE**
  Most packages allow you to change the way your text looks by using italics, bold, underlining or other styles. You can also usually change the typeface, or font
- **COPY**
  Using COPY you can take a copy of part or all of your document and duplicate it somewhere else in the same document – or even in another document
- **MOVE**
  You can take out part of the document and put it somewhere else in the same (or another) document

## QUESTIONS

### Knowledge and understanding

1 Explain in your own words the difference between data and information. Give one example of each.

2 Ask your teacher to show you a general purpose package such as Pagemaker, Excel or Word. Make a list of all the books and other materials that come with it.
Try to identify
- the manual
- the tutorial guide
- the quick reference guide
- the function keystrip or keyboard template
- the software licensing agreement
- the registration document.

Look at the disk(s). If there is more than one what do they all contain?

3 When you buy a new software package you probably want to start using it straight away. What should you do with the original disks *before* you use the program?

4 Why are general purpose packages sometimes described as being 'content free'?

### Problem solving

1 Here are the parts of four people's driving licence identification numbers which refer to their dates of birth.

What are the dates of birth of these people?
(a) Alex Jones 712119
(b) Mary Campbell 511254
(c) Miriam Horowitz 408309
(d) Joseph Timmons 704192
What would the code numbers be for
(e) 15 October 1976
(f) 27 June 1959
(g) 7 March 1936
(h) 11 February 1908
(i) your own birthday?

**2** Think about postcodes. What is your home postcode? What is the postcode for your school? Look up a local telephone directory which gives a list of all the postcodes in your town or district (like Thomson Local). What do the different parts of your postcode mean? Try to translate the data contained in your postcode into information.

# The human computer interface

**FIGURE 1.1** *The human computer interface?*

The **human computer interface** (usually shortened to HCI) is the way the user and the program communicate with each other. Many different things could be regarded as part of the HCI, like the way the screen looks, or whether the program makes it clear to the users what they have to do next. An example of the HCI is shown in figure 1.1. Programs that are easy to learn to use and help you understand as you are using them are called **user-friendly** programs.

## EXAMPLE OF A USER-FRIENDLY PROGRAM

You are working on a computer and want to save your text. The instruction your system needs to do this (the correct syntax) is
SAVE 'TEXT'
but perhaps you are not really familiar with this system, or make a mistake or press the wrong key and instead type
SAVE 'TEXT
You have missed out the final ' – you have made a **syntax error**.

A non-user-friendly system would not save your text with this message – in fact it would probably give you an error message, which you'd have to look up in the manual to explain. But a user-friendly system would probably not give you an error message – it would go ahead and save the text or would display a helpful message on the screen to ask you to confirm that you really do want to save the text.

Some systems (like the RISC OS system that is used by the Archimedes and BBC A3000/A5000/A4 computers) allow you to choose the type or complexity of the messages that are displayed on the screen.

**SYNTAX ERROR**

a mistake in a programming instruction – for example typing PTRIN instead of PRINT

**ON LINE**

connected to a computer system

## On-line help and on-line tutorials

Some systems have **on-line help** which you can call up while you're working on the program – there is nothing more annoying than having to stop and find a manual to look up commands when you are very busy!

Many packages also have an **on-line tutorial** which will teach you enough about the basic features of the package or system you're using to get you started. (Examples of these are Macintosh Basics Tour, Welcome disk for BBC, WORKS Tutorial on the Nimbus)

## Menu-driven and command-driven systems

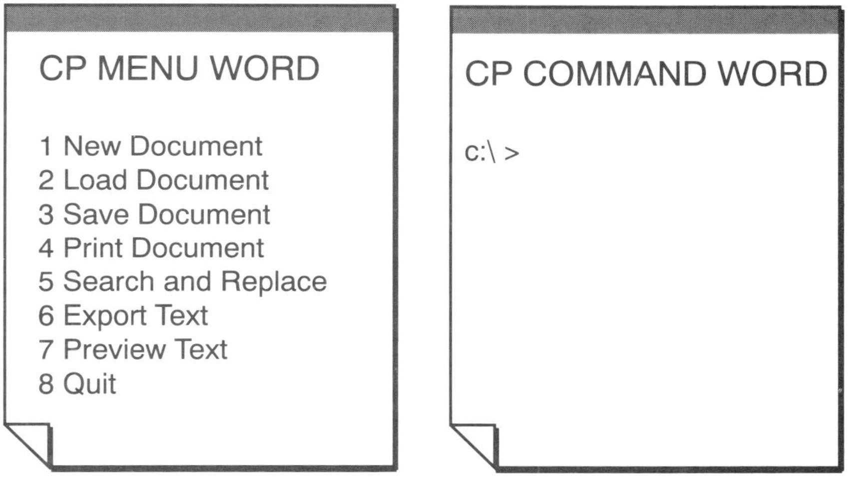


**FIGURE 1.2** *Menu-driven and command-driven software. Which is the more user friendly?*

**MENU**

a list on screen for the user to choose from

Look at figure 1.2. The screen on the left shows a list of items that the user can choose from (a menu) to make the computer do something – this is a **menu-driven program**. The screen on the right has no such list. On this system, the user has to know which instruction to type in, by remembering it correctly or by referring to the manual – this is a **command-driven program**.

- VIEW, VIEWSHEET, WORDSTAR and QUEST are command-driven programs
- WORDWISE, INTERWORD, WORD and WORKS are menu-driven programs

Menu-driven systems are usually more user-friendly than command-driven systems, because you are less likely to make mistakes if you don't have to remember all the commands.

# WIMP systems

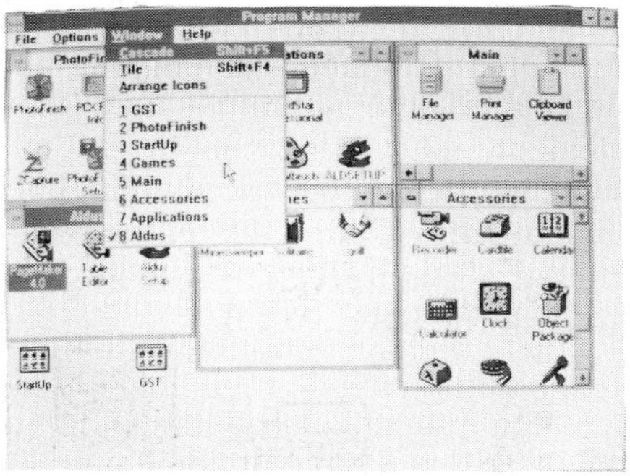

*A typical WIMP screen display*

To try to make computers easier to use, a specialised program has been developed which makes the computer screen more like an ordinary office with a desk. The idea is that you have a 'filing cabinet' (backing store hard disk) which holds your data, a hand (pointer) to use to select and move things, and a bin to throw things out. This system is known as WIMP:

- **W**indow
- **I**con
- **M**enu (or **M**ouse)
- **P**ointer (or **P**ull down/**P**op up menu)

An example of a WIMP system is shown in the photograph.

## Windows

A **window** is an area of the computer screen where you can see the contents of a directory, a document or a program. Some systems allow several windows on the screen at the same time, and windows can overlap each other. To help you keep track of what is going on at any time, the window on top is the one which is 'active' (you can see an example of this in figure 1.3). Some computers allow you to have more than one active window and to have programs running in each.

**FIGURE 1.3** *Overlapping windows. The window in front is the 'active' window – the one that's being worked on*

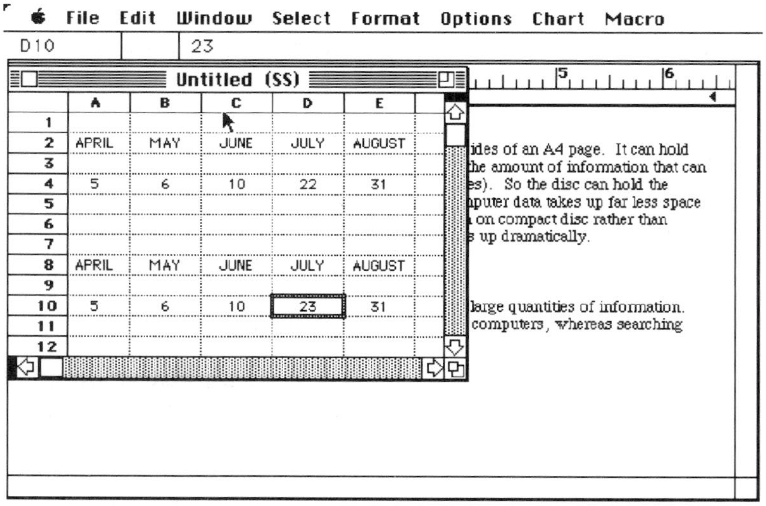


**PERIPHERAL**

any device that may be attached to a computer system for input, output or backing storage

**UTILITY**

A program which helps you to perform a task, for example delete a file

## Icons

An **icon** is a small picture that appears on the screen to represent a file, an application program, a directory or a **utility** like the bin (you can see some icons in figure 1.4). Some systems have a special area of the screen on which icons appear. **Peripherals** such as disk drives or particular **interfaces** like

**FIGURE 1.4** *A selection of icons you might see in a WIMP system*

Econet or other networks may also be shown by icons. WIMP systems which use icons to represent different things on the screen are often called **Graphical User Interfaces** (or GUIs).

### Menus

A **menu** is another feature that WIMP systems offer. Menus can be 'pop-up' or 'pull-down' depending on the system you are using, but whichever system you use, the menu is operated by pressing or releasing one or more buttons on the mouse. People who are familiar with a system often prefer to use a sequence of key presses (keyboard commands) for some operations instead of selecting an option from the menu because they find it faster than using the mouse.

**MOUSE**

an input device (with a ball underneath and one or more buttons on top) used to control a pointer on screen

### Pointers

You use a **pointer** on a WIMP system to select icons or to choose options from a menu. You move the pointer across the screen with the mouse or a tracker ball (this is really an upside-down mouse). The mouse and its uses are explained in more detail in Chapter 16. If you wish, you can use certain keys on the keyboard instead of a mouse to move the pointer. Usually, the keys you would use are the cursor (arrow) keys.

## QUESTIONS

**Knowledge and understanding**

1 Why are menu-driven programs easier to use than command-driven programs?
2 What does WIMP stand for?
3 Name three items that can be represented by icons.
4 Describe in your own words what you understand by a user-friendly system.
For any programs you have used, choose one that you think is user-friendly and one that is not. Give reasons to justify your choice.
5 Asfal has lost the manual for his spreadsheet program and cannot remember how to print, but the program has an on-line help system. How will this help him?

## *More to do*

In addition to the features already mentioned, general purpose packages often allow you to place some information at the top and the bottom of each page of your document – these are known as the **header** (top) and the **footer** (bottom). Most of the pages in this book have a header (containing the chapter name and number) and a footer (with the page number). The header and footer are typed only once at the start, when you are setting up the document, and will be printed on all the pages. The program will automatically put the correct number on each page.

### *RAM and ROM*

**RAM (random access memory)**

a microchip that stores data temporarily. The data is lost when the computer is switched off

**ROM (read only memory)**

a microchip in which data is permanently stored and is not lost when the computer is switched off

**Software** can be found in one of two forms:

- stored on disk or tape
- on a ROM (stands for Read Only Memory) chip.

Software that is stored on disk or tape must be loaded into the computer's RAM (Random Access Memory ) before it can be run. Software stored on ROM does not need to be loaded from backing storage, but is available for use as soon as the computer is switched on. General purpose packages are available on disk, tape and ROM. The software of dedicated computer systems is often stored in ROM. You will find more information on RAM and ROM in Chapter 16.

The commands that you use to operate any of the features depends on the type of HCI your system has. It may be a dedicated system which only performs one type of application and has its software stored on ROM, or it may be running a WIMP program and you should use the mouse to select an application by its icon.

## EXTRA QUESTIONS

**Knowledge and understanding**

1 Explain why headers and footers may be useful when
(a) printing a book
(b) printing a data(base) file.

2 For any general purpose packages you have used, name one that is menu-driven, one that is command-driven and one that has a WIMP interface.
Which of these do you think would be easiest
(a) for a beginner to learn to use
(b) to use now that you know how to use it (how does it help your productivity?)
Give your reasons in each case.

3 Name two of the common forms in which software is distributed.
Choose one form and give one advantage and one disadvantage for this method of distribution.

# *Software integration*

**Integrated packages** combine two or more general purpose packages (perhaps word processing, spreadsheet and database) in a single package. Integrated packages have a number of advantages over using the general purpose packages separately.

### Advantages of using integrated software

- The HCI is the same for each part of the package. This means that the keys you have to press for an operation in one program in the package will be the same for the same operation in another part. For example 'command – L' will load a document whether you're using the word processor or the spreadsheet program.
- Different types of documents can be open at the same time. You can switch between them by pressing a key, choosing from a menu, or clicking the mouse. If you are using a windows system, you can have the different documents open in separate windows.
- It is easy to transfer data between different parts of the package. For example, you can move a table from a spreadsheet to a word-processed document.

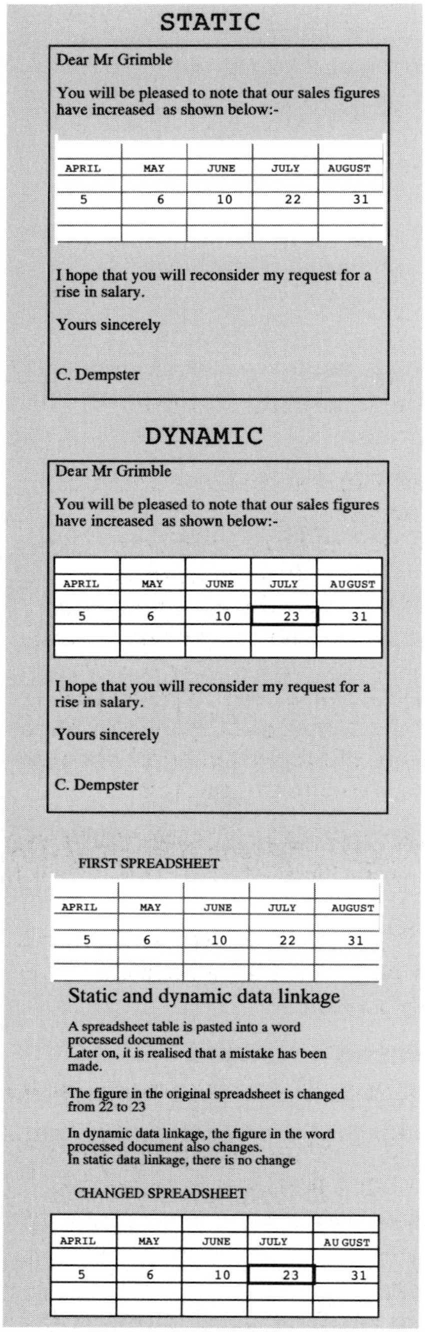

STATIC
Dear Mr Grimble
You will be pleased to note that our sales figures have increased as shown below:-
APRIL MAY JUNE JULY AUGUST
5 6 10 22 31
I hope that you will reconsider my request for a rise in salary.
Yours sincerely
C. Dempster
DYNAMIC
Dear Mr Grimble
You will be pleased to note that our sales figures have increased as shown below:-
APRIL MAY JUNE JULY AUGUST
5 6 10 23 31
I hope that you will reconsider my request for a rise in salary.
Yours sincerely
C. Dempster
FIRST SPREADSHEET
APRIL MAY JUNE JULY AUGUST
5 6 10 22 31
Static and dynamic data linkage
A spreadsheet table is pasted into a word processed document
Later on, it is realised that a mistake has been made.
The figure in the original spreadsheet is changed from 22 to 23
In dynamic data linkage, the figure in the word processed document also changes.
In static data linkage, there is no change
CHANGED SPREADSHEET
APRIL MAY JUNE JULY AUGUST
5 6 10 23 31


## Disadvantages of integrated packages

- The individual programs that make up the different parts of the integrated package are less powerful or have fewer features than separate general purpose packages, which means that you can't do quite as much with them.
- The integrated package may be larger (that is, take up more of the computer's memory) than the packages are if stored separately. This leaves less room in the memory to store documents.

### Dynamic and static linkage

Data in the various parts of the integrated software can be linked together in one of two ways:

- dynamic links
- static links

**Dynamic linkage** means that if the same data is used in different parts of the package and you change it in one part, the change will be carried by the computer over into all the programs using that data.

**Static linkage** means that the data in each part of the package is separate and changing it in one part will not affect any other files using that data.

**EXAMPLE**

Look at figure 1.5.
Later on, the sales sales figures change – the sales figure for July is now 23. In dynamic data linkage, changing the number in the spreadsheet automatically changes the figure in the word-processed document. In static linkage, changing the original spreadsheet would have no effect on the copy in the word-processed document, and Mr or Ms Dempster would have to retype the letter.

**Figure 1.5** *How static and dynamic links work*

# *Choosing a software package*

Here are the most common types of software package and their main features:

- **WORD PROCESSING**
  Production of text

- **SPREADSHEET**
  Numbers/calculations
- **DATABASE**
  Storing/sorting/searching/organising data
- **GRAPHICS**
  Drawing pictures, graphs or charts
- **DESKTOP PUBLISHING**
  Making up pages (as in a book)
- **PRESENTATION**
  Production of slides – for example, making overhead projector transparencies for lectures

There are a huge number of packages available – which one should you choose for a particular task?

You may find that a package which is sold as a word processor will have features that overlap with other general purpose package functions – you may be able to produce a chart from within a spreadsheet or carry out a mail merge operation using only the data contained in your word processor. These extra features are often included by the manufacturer to make their program appear more powerful than a rival package which does the same job. In fact, very few users of modern general purpose packages use all of the features available in the package.

## QUESTIONS

**Knowledge and understanding**

1 What is an integrated package? Find out about one integrated package that is used in your school. What applications does it contain?

2 Give two advantages and two disadvantages that an integrated package has over a separate general purpose package.

## *More to do*

When you are considering the most appropriate package to carry out a particular task you must also bear in mind what hardware and software you have available.

**EXAMPLE**

You have data on a spreadsheet which needs to be charted and printed out in colour. The hardware you have available is

- Blurb computer, with Blurbsheet (spreadsheet package) and Blurbplot (charting package), and a colour printer
- Quack computer with Extoll (spreadsheet) and a black and white laser printer.

Doing the task on the Quack would be very simple, with its easy-to-use HCI and quick plotting facilities, but you could only print it out in black and white.

The Blurb software, although it is less easy to use (because you have to transfer data between packages before you can plot it) may be the only solution since it is running on the system linked to the colour printer.

An alternative solution would be to do the work on the Quack and save the file to disk. You could then transfer the file to the Blurb computer (using a file transfer utility package such as Blurb>>Quack) and print it out from there on the colour printer. This solution would take some time and effort, but the chart production would be quicker, and overall might save you time.

## EXTRA QUESTIONS

**Problem solving**

Here are some more scenarios where you might need to consider which package to use.

You do not need to actually design or implement a solution to these problems. Analyse each one, and choose the appropriate hardware and software for this task. Justify your choice in each case.

**1** Producing a club newsletter six times a year.
**2** Compiling a list of names and addresses for festive greetings cards.
**3** Sending the same letter to six different people.
**4** Producing a monthly rota for playgroup duty.
**5** There is to be a survey of club membership in school. The survey response form has ten check boxes – one for each club in the school – and everyone has to fill in his or her name and class on the response sheet and put a tick in the box for each club they belong to. After you have collected the replies, you must produce a report which lists every person's name and class under every club that they say they belong to.

# *Storage of information*

Manual storage usually involves using a filing cabinet or a card index. The cards or files have to be placed into the filing system in a certain order (usually alphabetically) so that

> **BACKUP**
>
> a copy of a program or data made in case the original is lost or destroyed

they can be retrieved easily. Electronic methods of storage involve using computers to store data on disk or tape. It is important that all the information stored on a computer system is regularly copied to **backup** disks or tape. If this is not done, one mistake could mean that all of the information is lost.

### Storage capacity

If you cover both sides of an A4 page of paper with normal typing you will have produced about 8000 characters (this is nearly 8 kilobytes of computer storage). Compare this with the amount of information that a 3.5 inch floppy disk will hold (about 800 kilobytes). The disk can hold the equivalent of 100 pages of A4 paper – so it is easy to see why computer data takes up far less space than data on paper. If we go one step further, and store our information on compact disc rather than magnetic disk, the amount of information we can store goes up dramatically – one 12 cm compact disc can hold 600 000 kilobytes. How many pages of A4 paper would that be?

### Protecting data stored on computer systems

Computer systems are being used to store, process and retrieve large amounts of information for several reasons.

- The computer can process the data very quickly, but searching through manual filing systems can take a very long time.
- Manual files take up much more space than computers to store the same amount of information.
- The amount of cross-referencing between various files (linking together pieces of information which are stored separately) within an organisation is very limited with manual files. Cross-referencing becomes almost impossible if the information you are looking for is stored in a different organisation. For example, if you wanted to find out about your bank account and your building society account you would have to visit each place and look through a card index or filing cabinet if it was stored manually.
- For manual filing systems you must be near a file to look at it, so you may not be able to look up cross-references easily if the files are stored some distance apart.

Computerised filing systems overcome all of these limitations.

- Processing and cross-referencing is fast and powerful using modern database packages.
- They can store large quantities of information on a single disk.
- Databases held by different organisations can be linked by a

network system, and accessed from anywhere in the world by telephone.

Because of this, more and more organisations are using computers to store and process records about you and millions of other people. This can help you to get the goods and services you want and can lead to better services (for example by improving medical care or helping the police to fight crime).

The growth of computerised record-keeping brings dangers. The information may be entered wrongly, get out of date or it may be mixed up with information on someone else. The effects can be very serious – people can be refused jobs, housing, benefits or credit, be overcharged for goods or services or even wrongfully arrested. If an organisation holds any records about you, you have a right to see a copy of that information, to check that it is **accurate**, **complete** and **up to date**. Organisations which hold this type of information are expected to make sure that it doesn't get lost, stolen or changed by system failures or mistakes.

There are exceptions to your right to see the information held about you, but they only apply if allowing you to see the data would be likely to (for example) prevent the police from catching a criminal, and the person preventing you from seeing the information would have to be able to justify their decision. You may not see information about you if it is kept in order to

- prevent or detect crime
- catch or prosecute offenders
- collect tax
- carry out health and social work.

## QUESTIONS

### Knowledge and understanding

1 What precautions would you advise an organisation which held personal data on magnetic disk to take?

2 Personal data is information about *you* held on computer. Make a list of organisations or people who may have information about you. Compose a letter to one of these organisations, asking to see what information they have.

3 It is important that the information stored on a computer system is accurate, complete and up to date. If the information is not kept in this way, then it can lead to inconvenience, and can have very serious consequences.
Give examples of what could happen if information in any of the following systems was not accurate, complete and up to date.
(a) an airline's booking system
(b) the police national computer
(c) an employee's tax return.

## More to do

### Data protection

The **Data Protection Act** allows you

- to check if any organisation keeps information about you on computer
- to see a copy of this personal data

These rights are called **subject access rights** because people about whom information is held are called **data subjects**. The person or organisation holding the data is called a **data user**.

Under the Data Protection Act data users must

- obtain and process the information fairly and lawfully
- register the purposes for which they hold it
- not use or disclose the information in a way contrary to these purposes
- hold only information which is adequate, relevant, and not excessive for the purposes
- hold only accurate information, and, where necessary, keep it up to date
- not keep the information any longer than necessary
- give individuals access to information about themselves, and, where appropriate, correct or erase the information
- take appropriate security measures

Figure 1.6 shows a newspaper article about data held on computer.

**FIGURE 1.6** *This article (from Scotland on Sunday, October 1991) shows how you can find out about data held on computer about you*

**Personal secrets on sale for £1**

Detailed financial information on tens of thousands of Scots is available for £1 and the cost of a stamp. Information on bank accounts and balances, charge and credit cards, mail order payments, catalogues and even TV and video rentals is held on credit reference agency databases —and is easily available.

Files are stored on computer by address and under the provisions of the consumer protection and data protection acts are meant to be secret. But the system is open to widespread abuse. Individuals can request information held on them by credit reference companies, but when it comes from someone living in a block of flats, information on the whole block is sent.

Last week Robert Hainsworth of Northumberland Place, Edinburgh, demonstrated how easy it was to get sensitive information on his neighbours. He had approached his branch of the Royal Bank of Scotland for an Access card. Although he had never had any court judgment for debt against him he was turned down. The bank said that he had the right to request information held on him by the credit checking agency, Equifax Europe.

"I sent off the fee of £1 and back came the report on me. There was no check that I was who I claimed to be; I didn't even have to prove I was Robert Martin Hainsworth. I could have been anyone."

Hainsworth discovered an incorrect entry claiming he had a court judgment against him for bad debt. But what appalled him was the dossier on all the people who had lived at his present and previous home over the last six years. It also included bank details on neighbours, including account numbers and balances, as well as extensive details on month-by-month transactions on things such as Marks & Spencer charge cards, Grattan catalogues, Visionhire rentals and RoyScot credit cards.

In August last year the registrar for data protection, who polices the collection and storage of electronic information, served notices on the major credit reference agencies requiring them to change their system so that files were held on person rather than on property. The three principle agencies have lodged appeals in the High Court in London. No date has been set for a hearing and until the court decides the outcome, the present system will remain.

Richard McCrohan, a director of Equifax, said he was satisfied with the precautions his company took to avoid private information being sent to a third party."Our check is that people usually send their cheque for £1, which is some kind of proof. And we always send the report to the address we hold on our file. It is what our customers want and it has proved to be predictive of future debt."

Rosemary Jay, legal officer with the Registrar of Data Protection, said that it was precisely because of the way that companies insisted on compiling their records that indiscriminate information was given out. "If anyone has a complaint they should certainly write to us," she added.

Three main agencies, each of them holding details on up to 60 million financial transactions a year, dominate the market. Equifax Europe is a joint venture between Next, the retail chain, and Equifax of the United States, the biggest provider of financial information in the world with a turnover last year of 1.2bn.

Almost all of Britain's major companies provided one of the three databases with credit information on their customers.

*—Ron McKay,*
*Scotland on Sunday 6/10/91*

## *Misuse of computers*

The **Computer Misuse Act** is intended to protect all types of information (not just personal) stored on computer systems. Like the Data Protection Act, it has been drawn up because of the growth in the use of computers and the need to change the law to stop people abusing them.

### 'Hacking'

One area which is covered by this act is unauthorised access to computer files or '**hacking**'. One of the most widely publicised cases of computer 'hacking' in the UK was in the 1980s when Steve Gold and Robert Schifreen gained access to Prince Philip's PRESTEL mailbox.

### Computer viruses

Another area is the writing and distribution of computer '**viruses**' and other pieces of code which destroy data and cause computers to crash unpredictably, or take up processor time in meaningless calculations. Viruses are usually spread by people copying disks from unofficial sources. In the USA in 1990, a virus created as an experiment spread into a continent-wide computer network and destroyed vast amounts of data.

Chapter 12 has more information about computer crime.

## EXTRA QUESTIONS

**Knowledge and understanding**

1 What is
(a) a data subject?
(b) a data user?

2 What rights are given to a data subject by the Data Protection Act?

3 Find out about
(a) the United States Freedom of Information Act
(b) the film War Games, which showed what could happen when a hacker gained access to the computer controlling the US strategic nuclear missile defences
(c) the way your computer system can protect your files from being deleted accidentally or infected by a virus.

# Effects of computers on jobs and careers

People employed in all levels of commerce and industry are expected to be familiar with computer systems.

### EXAMPLE

A recent television advertisement for a particular computer system showed a businessman complaining to another that his staff could not work their new computers even after six weeks training. The other businessman (whose staff were using a different system) didn't have that problem. The point that the advert was trying to make was that the second computer system (which the advertisement was for) was so easy to use that people don't need to go on extensive training courses to use it. Even so, any employer who introduces a computer system into the workplace will have to spend a lot of money to train their staff to operate it.

School Business Studies departments do not use manual typewriters any more – even the name of the skill that they teach has changed from 'typewriting' to 'keyboarding'. Job advertisements no longer ask for 'typists' – they ask for 'word processor operators'. The expression 'words per minute' is being replaced by 'key depressions per hour'. Perhaps this is because word processors have editing and spell check facilities so first time accuracy is less important, and it is easy to change the layout of a document once the text has been entered.

The development of word processors has reduced the size of the typing pool (see the photos below) because word processor operator can do the work of at least three typists. Skilled typists are not needed to operate word processors because typing mistakes can be corrected easily. When electronic mail (mail sent directly from one computer to another down the telephone line) becomes more popular, the 'ordinary' mail will be used less, and workers in the Post Office could lose their jobs.

*Offices in 1940 and 1994*

More and more people have personal computer systems on their desks or in their briefcases. They can call up databases, type their own memos or send letters by electronic mail using built-in modems – doing away with the need for an assistant or secretary.

Are there any office activities that could not be done by computer?

# *Effect of computers on working conditions*

## Advantages

In many offices the working conditions have improved because general purpose packages such as word processing programs have been introduced.

- The office is less noisy because typing on an electronic key board is quieter than a typewriter.
- The office may be cleaner, because the computers can be located separately from a printing works, for example.
- Standards of work can be higher because correction and amendment is easier.
- Tasks can take less time to do so staff are not overloaded and feel less stressed.
- Links between packages on a computer mean that responses to changes can be very quick - for example if prices change a new price list can be produced easily.

## Disadvantages

Some aspects of work have got worse because of computers. A secretary's job used to have quite a lot of variety in it – typing, filing, taking shorthand. But a word processor operator doesn't need to file or take shorthand, and the job can become very boring

Find out what happened when computers were introduced to the newspaper industry in the 1980s.

### *Changing from a manual system to a computerised system*

Setting up a computer system and training staff to use it is expensive and takes time. Also, people almost always underestimate the time it takes to transfer all the data that is held on paper onto the computer system – which can cause a lot of stress.

What precautions should a business take to reduce the effects of the computer system crashing and all the data being lost?

### Effects on health

Computer systems themselves can affect your general health, depending on the amount of time that you use them.

- The glare from a computer screen can damage your eyesight if you look at it for long. You can cut down the glare by fitting a screen in front of the computer screen or by wearing specially coated spectacles.
- Radiation from the computer screen is also thought to be unhealthy. Users can wear a special garment to protect them from this radiation.

The EC has developed strict laws about the health and safety of business users of computers. They cover all aspects of the use of computers, from the lighting in the office to the design of the chair that the operator uses. These laws came into effect in the UK in 1993.

What effect will these new laws have on businesses which use computer systems?

## *The 'paperless office'*

The increase in the use of computers has made it easy to prepare and distribute circular letters or **mail shots** to people – you only need to look at your letters each morning to see the amount of correspondence which has originated from a word processor. By combining computerised mailing lists with a **standard letter**, mail shots become very easy to produce. Most people treat these letters as junk mail and throw them out, often without bothering to read them. Look at the newspaper articles in figure 1.7 – and the cartoon in figure 1.8.

> **MAIL SHOT**
>
> letters prepared by mail merge and sent out to individuals on a mailing list – also called direct mail or junk mail

> **STANDARD LETTER**
>
> a general letter which contains spaces for personal details (such as a person's name) to be inserted. Used in mail shots

**How to put a stop to direct mail**

People fed up with receiving personally addressed direct mail advertisements will get new help to control their post bag from January 1.

For the first time, the Advertising Standards Authority will regulate the use of computerised lists of names and addresses so that individuals' rights to privacy are respected.

Companies breaking the new rules could ultimately lose their Royal Mail discounts, a sanction which could put them out of business.

"These rules will go a long way to solving a lot of the problems we see with direct mail," said association spokeswoman Caroline Crawford.

Junk mail, which includes door-to-door leaflet drops and letters simply addressed to the "householder" or "occupier," are not covered by the rules.

Instead, the regulations will cover direct mail, the personalised letters whose names are compiled on computerised lists using increasingly sophisticated selection technique.

Under the rules, advertisers collecting names and addresses should make clear if the information is to be used for direct mail.

If the names and addresses are to be passed to someone else, such as another mail order firm, the individual must have the opportunity to opt put and be able to stop such a move.

If any one asks for their name to be corrected or removed from a mailing list the advertiser must comply.

The rules boost codes of practice already being operated by the £7 billion a year direct marketing industry, which employs 25,000 people.

But with the Advertising Standards Authority now becoming involved, people should find it much easier to raise complaints about direct mail.

The authority stressed that an effective way to stop unwanted direct mail was to contact the senders and ask them to halt further letters. Advertisers are usually keen to delete what they call "negative names from their lists.

Another tactic is to write to the Mailing Preferences Service, Freepost 22, London W1E 7EZ and ask it to stop unrequested mail being sent. This body covers 90% of the industry but it can take several months for names to be deleted from the computer lists.

*—Glasgow Herald 27/12/91*

**FIGURE 1.7** *What some people in the media think about junk mail*

FIGURE 1.8

This mail shot facility is one reason why computers, which were expected to reduce the amount of paper we use, have actually caused it to increase. A phrase that has been used often in the last ten years is 'the paperless office', which means that all our data would be stored on disk or tape and the amount of paper we use would be less. But this has not happened – paper usage has increased. Vast quantities of paper are being churned out by computer printers and facsimile (fax) machines. Most people like to have a hard copy of their letters as well as storing it on disk, because they feel that even the poorest quality printout is much easier to read than a document on a computer screen. And there are a few things that you cannot do to an electronic document that you can to one on paper – for example sign it. Though you can scan your signature and add it to a document this is not acceptable legally. Can you think why a scanned signature is not acceptable?

FIGURE 1.9

# Computers in communication

Electronic communication is the way that data is sent from one computer to another. The data is usually sent along a wire, but it may also be sent by radio waves or by light – along a fibre optic cable perhaps. Electronic communications are described in more detail in Chapter 9.

## Networks

When computers are linked they are said to be part of a network. There are two types of network, depending on the distance between the computers making up the network.

- **Local area networks** (LANs) cover a small area – a single room, a whole building or a factory. An example of a LAN is shown in figure 1.10
- **Wide area networks** (WANs) cover larger areas – a town, country or a whole continent.

## Local Area Networks

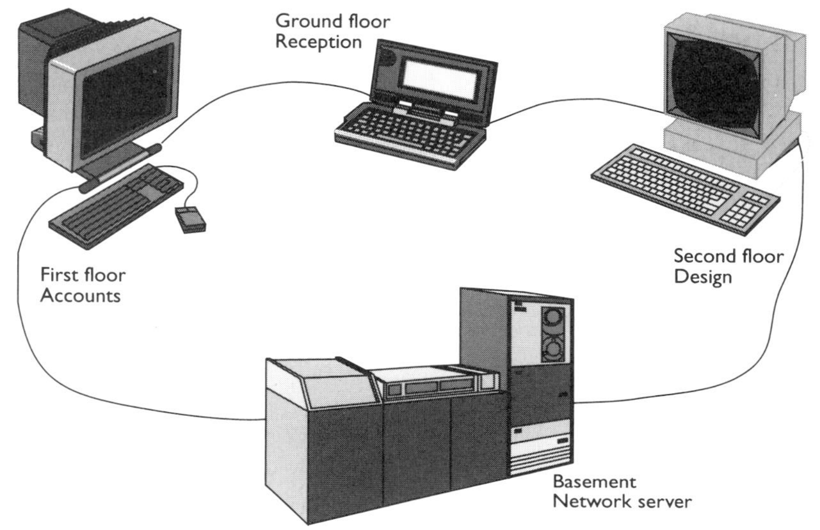


**FIGURE 1.10** *A local area network in an office building. You can see how all the terminals are attached to the main computer*

> **FILE SERVER**
>
> A station on a local area network which holds files which the users can access

> **OFF LINE**
>
> not connected to a computer system

Each computer on a LAN is called a station. The different stations on a network don't have to be the same – one may have a disk drive or a printer, or may only have a computer screen and keyboard. Usually one station on the network is set aside as the **file server**. On the file server station all the programs available are stored, together with a list of names of authorised users. Before you can use a network system, you have to identify yourself to the file server – this is called 'logging on'. To log on to any network you usually have to type in your user identity (which might be your name or a code – but it is personal to you) and then a password. When you have done this correctly the file server allows you access to the network – you are now on line to the network and can load programs or look at files. When you have finished using the network, you should 'log off', or go 'off line'. This means that the network will no longer accept any of your commands until you log on again.

LANs have several advantages

- You can transfer data and programs between stations.
- Everyone on the network can share just a few expensive peripherals such as disk drives and printers, which makes the system cheaper to set up than if every station had its own printer and storage device.
- A mailing service can be operated.
- By using passwords your data can be kept secure.
- Unauthorised interference can be reduced by allowing different users different levels of access.

## Wide Area Networks

WANs have most of the advantages of LANs, but you should remember that they are used differently. LANs are usually used every day for a relatively long period of time, but WANs are used only occasionally to share data or send electronic mail. They are not normally used for sharing peripherals – there would be very little point in printing out your latest masterpiece if you had to travel to the other side of the Atlantic Ocean to collect it! One of the most popular uses of a WAN is to send electronic mail. You can type a letter at one station and send it instantly to any number of users anywhere in the world. If the person at the other end is not using the network when you send the letter, the computer will store it until they are on line, and are able to read it.

### *Modems*

When a computer uses a telephone line to connect to another computer, a **modem** is needed at each end of the link. Computers can only understand digital signals (which are made up of a series of zeroes and ones – see Chapter 10), but ordinary telephone lines (which are used for voice transmission) can't transmit digital signals. The modem changes the digital signals from the computer at one end of the link to sounds (which can be sent along the telephone line). The modem at the other end of the link changes the sounds back to digital signals, which the receiving computer can understand. Telephone lines are being developed that will carry digital signals, and in the future modems will not be needed.

## Data link

The method used to send data from one computer to another is called the data link. In an electronic mail system the data link could be the telephone line, in a Teletext system it could be the television signal. Sometimes the data is accidentally changed or corrupted by interference from outside – for example, an owl sitting on your TV aerial will affect the picture quality. The less chance there is of interference affecting the data link, the more **reliable** the data transmission will be. An optical fibre data link is very reliable because it is not affected by electrical interference.

## Network security

The information on a network must be guarded carefully so that users can see only the data they're meant to see. Different users on a network are allowed different levels of access so that they can look at, store, or load information, depending on their need.

In a school network, the class teacher would have a higher level of access (be allowed to access more data) than a pupil so that she can examine and change the files belonging to any individual in the class. The level of access (also called network privileges) given to any network user is determined by the person in charge of the network – the network manager – who gives each user a special user identity and password to allow her or him to log on.

If you use a network, you should change your password regularly so that no one else can discover it, and you shouldn't choose a password which would be easy for someone else to guess – like a family name or your birthday. If someone discovers your password, they could delete your files, read your private electronic mail, or (on a chargeable system like PRESTEL) run up a large bill in your name – which you'd have to pay! Some individuals ('hackers') take great pleasure in trying to outwit network security systems. 'Hacking' usually involves gaining unauthorised access to data belonging to someone else and is illegal.

## *Multi access*

A multi access system is made up of a large central computer with many terminals linked to it. The central computer constantly checks each of the terminals in turn. If a terminal wants access to the central computer, data is sent very quickly to it and returns from it at the same high speed. This fast response gives the user of each terminal the impression that they are the only one using the system. Multi access systems are used for

- airline reservations
- the police national computer
- automated telling (cashcard) machines.

### Teletext

**Teletext** is an information service which is transmitted as part of the ordinary television signal. To receive Teletext you must have a TV aerial and a special television set or an adapter connected to your computer. Teletext consists of pages of information which can be text and low-resolution block graphics. It is a one way system – the user can't **interact** with it or send messages back to the television company. Teletext is said to be non-interactive.

Examples of Teletext services are CEEFAX, Teletext on 3, Teletext on 4.

**INTERACTION**

a way of using a computer in which the operator's instructions are processed continuously – like a conversation

### Viewdata

**Viewdata**, like Teletext, holds pages of information, but it is a two-way or interactive system – users can both send and receive messages. To use Viewdata, you must have a telephone link and a computer system or a special keypad with a television set.

Examples of Viewdata services are PRESTEL (UK) and TELETEL (France).

Chapter 8 will give you more information on Teletext and Viewdata.

### Fax machines

A **facsimile** (**fax**) machine can send documents along the telephone line to another fax machine. First it scans the document (like a photocopier does) and changes the information into data which is then transmitted. The fax at the other end changes the data into a document and prints it out.

## QUESTIONS

**Knowledge and understanding**

1 What is the difference between a LAN and a WAN?

2 Describe two advantages that a LAN has over a set of stand-alone computer systems.

3 What hardware do you need to receive Teletext? Name three Teletext services.

4 What hardware and software do you need to receive Viewdata?
Name two Viewdata services.

5 Give one difference between Teletext and Viewdata.

6 If your school has a network, describe what you would have to do to
(a) log on to your own directory or workspace
(b) open a word processing package and obtain a hard copy.

7 Why do users on a network need passwords?

**Practical activities**

1 Count the number of junk mail items that your household receives in a week.

2 Check the amount of paper that is wasted in your computer class, for example during a word processing exercise or a programming lesson. What can the class do to reduce this waste? Find out from your teacher the cost of printer paper. Go to the library and find out how many sheets of A4 paper can be made from one tree.

How many trees and how much money is wasted by your class in a year?

Extend this calculation to all the computer printers in the school, and to the school office.

What could you do with the paper instead of throwing it away?

3 Repeat this calculation for the junk mail you counted earlier.

## KEY POINTS

- Information (for use by people) = data (for use by computers) with structure
- Application packages may be single or general purpose
- General purpose packages need to have information put in before they can be used
- General purpose packages share common features – like load, run, open
- The human computer interface is the way that the user and the program communicate with each other
- Integrated packages combine two or more general purpose packages (like a word processor, a spreadsheet and a data base) in a single package
- Manual storage of data usually involves using a filing cabinet or a card index
- Electronic methods of storage involve using computers to store data on disk or tape
- All information that is stored on a computer system should be regularly copied to backup disks or tape
- Personal information stored on a computer system must be accurate, complete and up-to-date
- Information held on a computer system is covered by the Data Protection Act
- Computers have made it easy to prepare and distribute mail shots
- Local area networks cover a small area – a single room, a whole building or a factory
- Wide area networks cover a large area – a town, country or a continent
- Teletext consists of pages of information which are transmitted alongside a television signal
- Viewdata consists of pages of information and is a two-way system

# 2 Word processing

Most people who use a computer for anything other than playing games use it as a word processor. People use their word processors for many different tasks. At present I am using mine to write this book. Tomorrow I may use it to produce a new rota for the Playgroup, and the day after for a letter to my local newspaper.

One advantage of producing your own documents on a word processor is that you can type the letter straight in at the keyboard. If you make a mistake, you can easily change it on the screen before printing the final version.

## *What is a word processor?*

A word processor is a computer that you use for writing, editing and printing text. A **dedicated word processor** is a system that can **only** be used for word processing. A word processing package is an example of a general purpose package (these were discussed in Chapter 1).

## *Why use a word processor?*

Instead of writing a letter by hand and then typing out one copy of the final version, with a word processor you can type the letter at the keyboard straight away and print it out when you need it (this printout is called a **hard copy**). You can save the letter to disk so that if you want to use it again you will not have to type it again. You can simply load the letter into the word processor and make whatever changes are needed.

## *Features commonly found on word processors*

Word processors have all the features that are found in all general purpose packages. They also have features special to word processing, such as:

- wordwrap
- formatting
- search and replace
- spelling checker
- word count
- standard paragraphs.

Let us look at each of these features in a bit more detail.

## Wordwrap

With a word processor, when you reach the end of a line of text you do not need to press the return key to take a new line. A word processor will take a new line automatically and will move partly completed words at the end of one line to the start of the next line.

## Formatting

A word processor allows you to change the way your page is laid out by **formatting** the text.

### *Line length*

You can change the length of each line of the text, making it shorter or longer, by altering the text margins in the document. In some word processors, the text margins are controlled by the settings on a 'ruler' at the top of each page. Figure 2.1 is an example of a typical word processor screen display showing a text ruler.

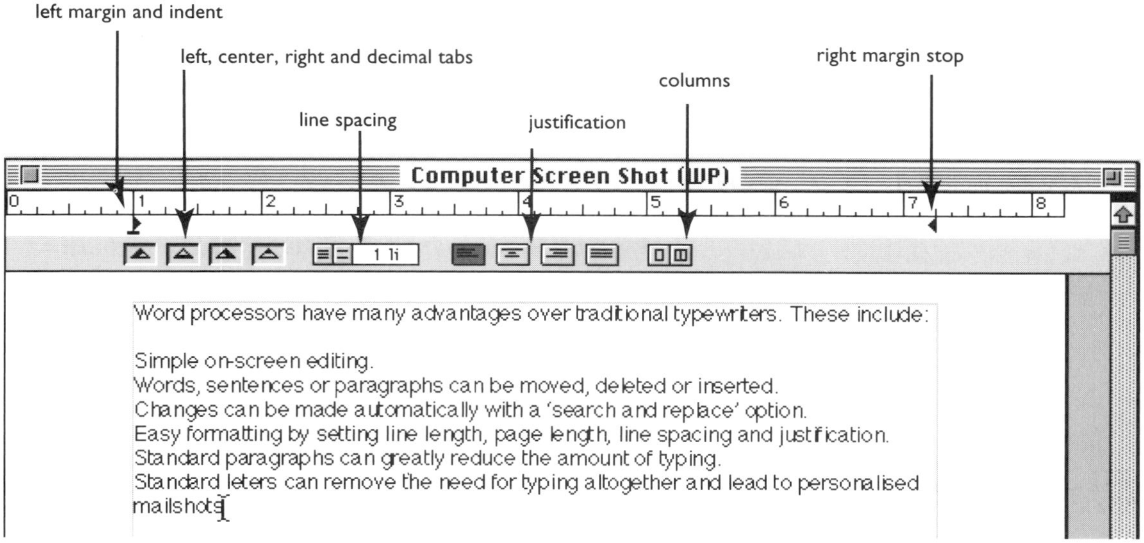


**FIGURE 2.1** *A typical word processor screen display, showing a text ruler*

### *Page length*

Using a word processor you can alter the length of your page – that is, the number of lines of text printed before the document takes a new page.

### *Line spacing*

If you need more space between each line of text, you can set it automatically by choosing double spacing. You can see how different they look in the examples here.

The quick brown fox jumped
over the lazy dog.

This text is single spaced.

The quick brown fox jumped

over the lazy dog.

This text is double spaced.

### *Justification*

Any text in a document can be justified or centred. When you *centre* text it is placed in the middle of the page, with both ends uneven – like this:

The quick brown fox jumped
over the lazy dog.

This text is centred

Justifying text means that the machine adjusts the spacing between the words to make the ends even. If you *right justify*, the text at the right-hand ends will line up but the left-hand ends will be uneven, like this:

The quick brown fox jumped
over the lazy dog.

This text is right justified.

Left justifying makes the left-hand edges even, but the right-hand ends will be uneven. To make both edges even you can *fully justify* the text. The text of this book is set left justified.

### *Tabulation*

By placing the tab stops along the text ruler at any position you want you can produce tables. A special key on the keyboard, called the TAB key, is used to move the cursor to each tab stop in turn.

## Search and replace

The search and replace facility means that you can instruct the word processor to replace one word with another wherever it occurs in a document. Most word processors carry out search and replace in two ways, **globally** and **selectively**.

### *Selective search and replace*

The selective search and replace choice shows you each word

before changing it and asks you to confirm that you want it changed by pressing a key before going on to the next word.

### *Global search and replace*

Global search and replace means that every occurrence of the word is replaced throughout the whole document without asking you to confirm that you want each change. This is a very powerful feature but it must be used carefully, otherwise you could make unexpected changes and ruin your document. For example, if you choose to globally change 'is' to 'are' you could end up with Brit*are*h instead of Brit*is*h!

To help avoid mistakes like this, you can search for whole words only, or you can put a space after the word you are looking for (the search string). Some word processors offer extra facilities within their search and replace, such as upper and lower case matching. For example, choosing to replace 'There' with 'Their' would not change 'there' to 'their' because the program is looking specifically for a capital letter at the beginning of the word and will ignore each word that doesn't begin with a capital T.

## Spelling check

Spell checking used to be an extra feature on many word processors, but now all but the most simple packages include this facility. This book has been written on a word processor with a spelling check facility, so there should be no mistakes in the spelling!

You would normally spell check a document once you have finished entering it into the word processor but before you print out the final version. Spelling checkers have a very large **dictionary** of correctly spelled words stored on disk. When you run a spell check it compares all the words in the document with the words stored in the dictionary and highlights any words that it can't find in the dictionary. However, this does not mean that the words you have typed are misspelt – they may be proper names, such as Harjinder or Siobhan, or simply words it doesn't know.

When it highlights a word as unknown, the spell checker will probably offer you an alternative word from its dictionary. At this point in the check, you can choose to move to the next word, accept the change the spell checker has suggested, correct the word by retyping it or have the spell checker 'learn' the unknown word. If you choose the 'learn' option, then the new word is added to a new user dictionary, not to the main dictionary. This allows you to build up specialised user dictionaries containing for example, technical, medical, legal, or scientific words as required. Specialised dictionaries can often be bought already made up for particular subjects.

### CARE!

A spelling checker is not infallible. If you use the wrong word in your document (for example, 'their' instead of 'there') but you have spelt it correctly, the spell checker will ignore it. You could end up with some rather odd phrases.

You must stay alert when spell checking a document. If you hit 'yes' when the program suggests an alternative, but you meant to leave it alone, it will replace your word with the one it wants – again producing some very odd phrases!

### Grammar checking

A spelling checker program does not check the grammar of your document. For example, 'Their is two cows in that field' is incorrect English grammar, but the sentence does not contain any misspelt words, and so would pass a spelling check.

You can buy grammar checking software. It works in a similar way to a spelling checker, by highlighting sentences that it thinks contain grammatical errors and suggesting alternative words or phrases. This type of software usually comes as a separate program, and is not a standard feature of most word processing packages.

### Word count

This is very useful, particularly if you have to write an essay or an article containing an exact number of words. Some word processing packages will give you a constant readout on the screen of the number of words you have typed. Other packages will give you the total words when you ask them to.

A spelling checker will usually count the number of words in the document, and give you the result when it has finished. This is useful but it means that you must run the spelling checker each time you want to count the words, and this can waste time if you have a long document to go through.

### Thesaurus

This is sometimes known as a **word finder**. If you type a word, you can ask the thesaurus program to produce a list of words with the same meaning (synonyms). This can be very useful if you do not want to use the same word twice.

### Standard paragraphs

You may find that you want to use the same paragraph in several documents (perhaps you're typing a party invitation). It would be very time-consuming to type this paragraph in each letter.

> **STANDARD PARAGRAPH**
>
> a piece of text which can be combined with others like it to make up a complete document

You can save time (and typing!) by making up a **standard paragraph** and storing it to disk. You can then make up a letter by loading a number of such paragraphs from the disk, and placing them into your document. Standard paragraphs are typically used in solicitors offices because legal contracts often have many long and complicated paragraphs which do not change from one contract to another. To make up a contract, the correct paragraphs are inserted into the new document and the names of the persons involved are added. Figure 2.2 shows how you can produce a contract using standard paragraphs.

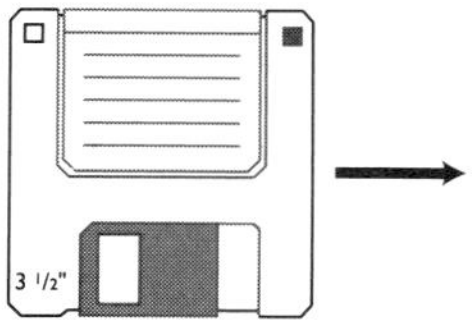


**Contract for the hire of plant machinery**

| |
|---|
| The period of this loan shall be for no shorter than six months as per our standard contract. |
| The items on loan will be those as specified in appendix D (attached). |
| The party of the first part, notwithstanding the use to which the equipment should be put, can at any time during the aforesaid period, recoup any losses due to malfunction. |
| Any losses which are payable will be honoured on the third of each month preceding the annual claim period. |
| This agreement may be cancelled at any time by giving one month's notice in writing to both parties involved. |
| This contract is invalid unless signed by the Managing director of Pugloan PLC. |

**FIGURE 2.2** *How to produce a contract using standard paragraphs. Each paragraph is selected from a list on the disk. The paragraphs are loaded into the word processor.*

# Printer quality

The various types of printer that are used with computer systems are described in detail in Chapter 16. Different types of printer will give different quality of hard copy. For example, you may use either a dot matrix or a laser printer. Dot matrix printers are less expensive than laser printers, but the printout is not of such good quality. Many businesses use paper with the name and address (and sometimes the logo) of the firm already printed on it. A laser printer, with its capability to print high-quality graphics, could be used to produce the complete letter including the logo. This would save the business money because it would not have to purchase specially printed paper with the logo on.

## QUESTIONS

**Problem solving**

1 Make up a checklist of the features of a word processor that have been described in this chapter.
Circle each of the features that a word processing package you have used possesses.
Make a list of any features in your package which are not in the checklist.
Write a sentence to describe the purpose of each of these features.

2 Consider what would happen if a document was to be searched to replace every occurrence of 'he' with 'she'. Describe how you would do this with the word processing package that you have used. What might happen to the document if you are not careful?
What type of search and replace should you use to avoid this?
Is there any other way to avoid mistakes like this?

3 Why don't spelling checker programs automatically correct every mistake they find? Give an example of a type of mistake which would not be highlighted by a spelling checker.

**Knowledge and understanding**

1 Name two types of business that could use standard paragraphs.
2 What is wordwrap?
3 What is the difference between a dedicated word processor and a computer system running a word processing package?
4 Look through magazines or catalogues for advertisements for electric typewriters and dedicated word processor systems. Compare the features that they offer. What is happening to typewriters? What are typewriter manufacturers having to do to make sure that they sell as many machines as possible?

## *More to do*

### *Standard letters*

There are many instances where standard letters can be used to save typing basically the same letter again and again. Here are just a few examples:

- A letter offering someone a job interview, or even a job.
- Legal documents in a solicitor's office – contracts or deeds of covenant.
- Summonses and notifications of court appearances sent out by the police.

These documents can be produced quickly and easily using a word processor. Each letter or document is typed, and blanks are left for items like name and address (which will be inserted later) and the file is stored on disk. This file can be loaded from disk when needed and the missing dètails can be added to produce a personalised letter.

**MAIL MERGE**

the process of automatically loading personal details from a separate mailing list and placing them into the correct places in a standard letter

## *Mail merge*

If the standard letter has to go to many different people, the list of names and addresses (the mailing list) can be stored on a database. Using a mail merge facility, each name and address on the mailing list will automatically be loaded into the correct places in the standard letters when they are printed. Figure 2.3 shows how this is done. Circular letters (often called 'junk mail') are usually produced using mail merge (Chapter 1 contains more information about junk mail and circular letters). Mail merge is an example of dynamic data linkage between the word processor and the database. Many modern word processing packages have a database facility, which lets the user do a mail merge without having to use a separate database package.

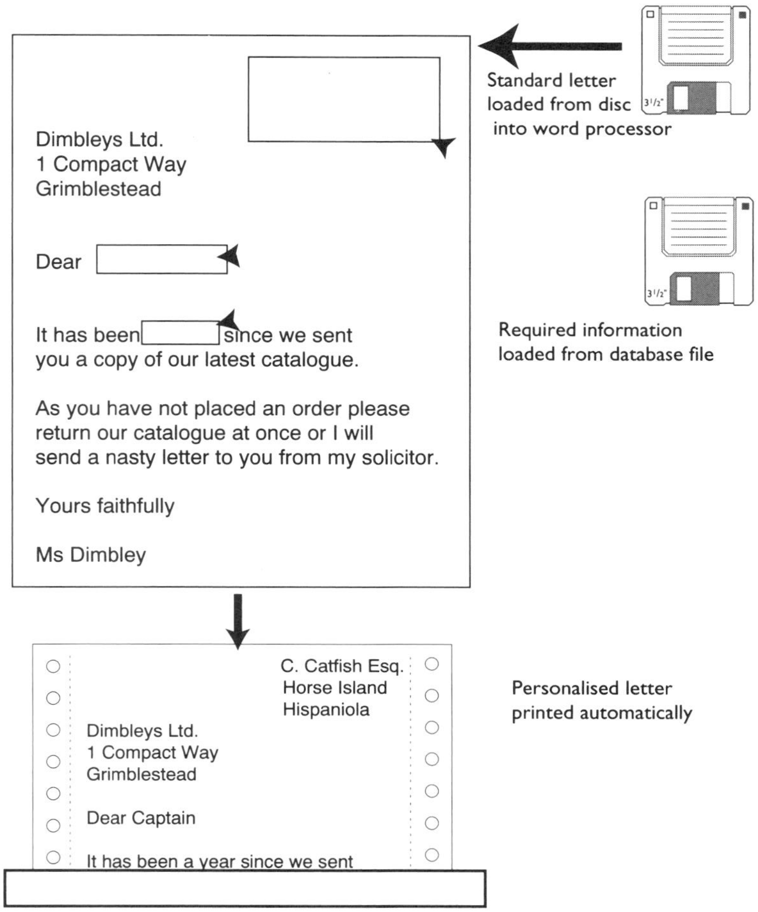


**FIGURE 2.3** *Mail merge using a standard letter*

## *Printer drivers*

Printers are able to produce many different printing styles, like <u>underline</u>, **bold**, *italic*. Some printers can also produce different typefaces – here are a few:

Times
Helvetica
Courier
Σψμβολ.

But before a printer can do this the computer must send it the correct code for the effect wanted. The codes used by different printers will not be the same – on an Epson daisy wheel printer, for example, 27,71 may produce bold print but the same code could tell a Suzulu dot matrix printer to produce italic print.

This causes quite a problem for companies who write word processing packages, because they know that all the users of their package are unlikely to use the same printers. The people who use the program want simply to enter one code for (say) underlining in their document and have it printed out the way they want regardless of the printer they're using.

To make life simpler for the user, software manufacturers have developed **printer driver** programs (see figure 2.4). These special programs take the special codes used in the word processing document, and translates them into the appropriate code for the printer being used. So, if you had a Qume laser printer in your office and an Integrex ink jet printer at home, then all you need to do is load a different printer driver program (rather than change the codes in the word processed document) to get the same effects.

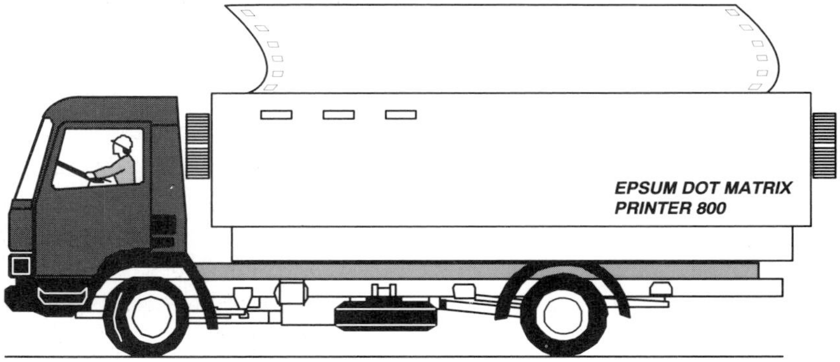


**FIGURE 2.4** *A printer driver*

## *Importing and exporting text*

One feature of word processing packages that is becoming more important is their ability to share data with other word processors running on different computer systems – sending text via electronic mail is a good example of this. Receiving text from another word processing package is known as **importing** text. Producing text in a form that can be transferred to a different package is known as **exporting** text.

When you export text you could lose some of the formatting – and your beautifully laid out paragraphs, tab stops or special typefaces could disappear. If your document has text and graphics in it, you probably won't be able to transfer the graphics and the text together. You will have to create a text-only document and transfer the text and graphics files separately. This often happens if you are sending text to a different computer system – perhaps from an IBM-compatible laptop to an Apple Macintosh.

Many computer companies have developed software that allows documents to be transferred from one machine to another while keeping the formatting. An example is VIEW >> MAC, which lets you convert documents that you have created using FIRST WORD PLUS (on the Archimedes), VIEW, WORDWISE or INTERWORD (on the BBC) into MACWRITE (on the Macintosh) and back again.

# EXTRA QUESTIONS

**Problem solving**

1 Why can't you transfer a document from one word processing system to another simply by saving the document on a floppy disk and using it with the other system?

2 Why do we sometimes need to use a printer driver program?

3 Describe the steps in preparing and sending a personalised circular letter to the parents of all the pupils in the first year at your school.

4 Collect examples of personalised circular letters that have been sent to your home.
Why do businesses take the trouble to send letters like this, rather than sending the same letter to everyone?

5 Why is the ability to import and export text desirable on a word processing system?
What disadvantages can be associated with this process?
What are computer companies doing to solve this problem?

## KEY POINTS

- A word processor is a computer used for saving, editing and printing text
- A dedicated word processor is a system that can only be used for word processing
- A typical word processor also has the following features: wordwrap, alter line length, change page length, change line spacing, justification, tabulation, search and replace
- Most word processors allow you to search and replace globally and selectively
- Spelling checkers work by comparing all the words in the document with the words stored in a dictionary
- Spelling checkers do not check the grammar in your document
- You can compose a letter by loading a number of standard paragraphs from disk and placing them into a document.
- A standard letter has blanks left for details, such as name and address, to be inserted later
- Mail merge is the process of automatically loading personal details from a separate mailing list and placing them into the correct places in a standard letter
- A printer driver program may be needed to translate the formatting codes in a document into the appropriate code for the printer being used.
- Most word processing packages can import and export text

# 3 Databases

## What is a database?

Any large amount of information must be stored in some sort of order so that it can be accessed easily and quickly – a filing system is ideal for the job. Everyone uses filing systems, but they may not always be aware of them – cups, saucers and plates are probably 'filed' in a kitchen cupboard, newspapers might be 'filed' under a coffee table, socks might be 'filed' in a drawer in your bedroom.

A **database** is a structured collection of similar information which you can search through. Databases can be stored manually (in a filing cabinet, or on index cards) or electronically using a computer system. (Chapter 1 gives more explanation of manual and electronic filing systems.) Keeping your database on computer means that you can access the information much more easily and quickly than if you used a manual system–but the data must be organised in a way that allows speed of access. A program that is used for organising data on a computer system is called a **database package**. A database package is an example of a general purpose package. (General purpose packages are described in Chapter 1.)

Data in a database is organised into data files, records and fields. A **data file** is a collection of structured data on a particular topic. The file can be held in the computer's memory or in backing storage on a disk. Individual files are made up of records. A **record** is a collection of structured data on a particular person or thing. Each record is made up of one or more fields. A **field** is an area on a record which contains an individual piece of data. Figure 3.1 shows more clearly how a database is structured.

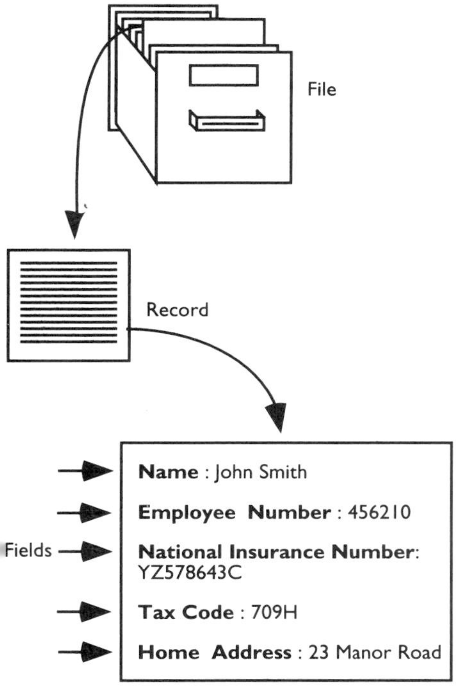


**FIGURE 3.1** *An example of a manual database. Computer databases use the same principles, storing individual items in fields, which together make up a record. A group of records is a file*

### EXAMPLE

Look at a telephone directory. Each separate area in the directory – name, address, town and telephone number – is a *field*. The set of fields (that is, the whole address and phone number) for one person is a *record*. The set of records together – the whole directory – is a *file*. There is now a computer database (called Phonebase) which you can access to obtain someone's telephone number.

# What are databases used for?

*Mr Lang's prints are taken at Strathclyde Police headquarters by Fife Chief Constable William Moodie*

Databases are used in many applications by many different organisations. Here are a few:

- The telephone directory
- The Police National Computer
- The Inland Revenue
- The Driver and Vehicle Licensing Centre
- A personal Christmas card list
- A magazine's mailing list.

A company may create a database with many files and arrange it so that the files can be accessed in different ways for use in different applications. The same data is stored only once but it can be manipulated by the application program so that the data files can be shared by various pieces of software. An example is a database that contains three files – names and addresses of customers, customer orders and details on types of business. A user could find information from all three files for a particular company by using that company's name or their address.

**EXAMPLE**

The fingerprints of people who have been convicted of an offence or who are awaiting trial are now stored on computer databases. The first fingerprint database to be used in the UK was installed in October 1991 by the Scottish Criminal Records Office in Glasgow at a cost of £1.5 million. It is called The Automatic Fingerprint Recognition System and stores 260 000 fingerprints. The operators can make six complete searches of the system in a day – much better than the two searches a day that was possible when all the fingerprints were stored manually. Its probable effect on catching criminals is outlined in the photograph!

Using computer databases means that records can be processed quickly and accurately, making information available at a speed which is impossible using a manual system.

# Features of databases

Databases, like word processors (described in the last chapter) have all the features common to general purpose packages. The following features are special to databases.

- Create fields
- Add and alter records
- Search
- Sort

Searching and sorting records are the two main reasons for using a database package.

Let us look at each of these features separately.

## Create fields

When you start a database application, the first thing you must do is to create one or more fields to hold the information which you want to store. Some programs also ask you to choose the size of the field and the type of information that you wish to store.

### *Types of field*

- A **text field** is used to hold only letters.
- A **numeric field** only stores numbers.
- An **integer field** stores only whole numbers.
- **Date** and **time** fields also contain numbers, but organised in a particular way.

### *Choosing the size of the field*

If you have to decide on the size of the field you want, remember to allow for spaces, because a space is counted as a character and will take up the same amount of room as any other character (letters, numbers, punctuation). It is probably better to choose a field that is bigger than you expect to use, because you may not be able to change it later on without creating a new database.

## Add and alter records

Once you have created the basic record structure by deciding on the fields, the next step is to use the database package to enter information. At this point the database is empty and you must create a new record for each item that you are going to enter. Some database applications allow you to alter the record format, that is, you can add new fields or delete existing ones. You can also change the type or size of the fields.

## Search

The search facility allows you to look through the database for information. To do this, you must enter the field or fields that you want to search and the details that you want to find. This is called to **'search on a field'** using whatever **conditions** you require. To give an example, you might be looking for items on your database with 'height in metres greater than 5000 – here the field that you would be searching on is 'height in metres' and the condition you want is 'greater than 5000'. Figure 3.2 shows how a simple search on one field can be carried out.

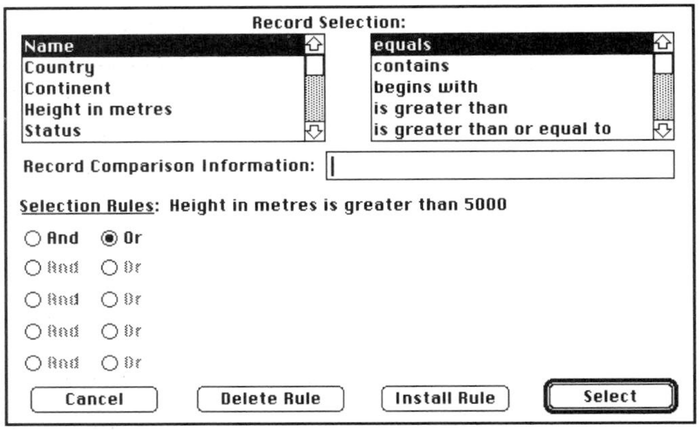


| Name | Country | Continent | Height in metres | Status |
|---|---|---|---|---|
| Cotopaxi | Ecuador | South America | 5978 | active |
| Popocatapetl | Mexico | Central America | 5452 | active |
| Sangay | Ecuador | South America | 5410 | active |
| Tungurahua | Ecuador | South America | 5033 | active |
| Kilimanjaro | Tanzania | Africa | 5889 | dormant |
| Misti | Peru | South America | 5801 | dormant |
| Aconcagua | Argentina/Chile | South America | 6960 | believed extinct |
| Chimborazo | Ecuador | South America | 6282 | believed extinct |
| Orizaba | Mexico | Central America | 5700 | believed extinct |
| Elbrus | USSR | Asia | 5647 | believed extinct |
| Demavend | Iran | Middle East | 5366 | believed extinct |

**FIGURE 3.2** *Simple searching on one field in a database*

### *Linking search options*

You can link the conditions of search in a field. At the end of the search all the records which match the set of conditions you have put in will be displayed. If no records match the required conditions, then you can choose to change the conditions or abandon the search.

#### EXAMPLE

In figure 3.3 you can see a search through three fields on a database. The fields are occupation, sex and age, and the conditions are scholar, female and greater than 12. A successful search will give you a list of girls on your database over 12 who are still at school.

### Sort

Sorting allows you to arrange the records in a database in **alphabetic** or **numeric** and **ascending** or **descending** order. Ascending numeric order would be 1, 2, 3, 4 ..., descending alphabetic order would be Z, Y, X, W ... To start the sort, you must choose a field (like 'height in metres' in the last example) on which to sort the database, or the records will stay in the order in which you typed them, not the order you want.

You should use sorting whenever you have changed the database by adding or deleting information.

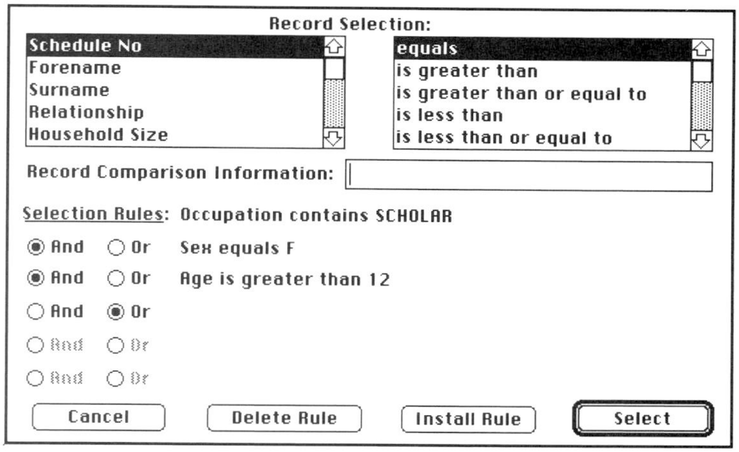


| Forename | Surname | Relationship | Family Size | Sex | Age | Occupation | Town of Birth |
|---|---|---|---|---|---|---|---|
| Charlotte | Page | D | 4 | F | 14 | scholar | Datchworth |
| Louisa | Skeggs | D | 7 | F | 15 | scholar | Datchworth |
| Philadelphia | Colborn | N | 3 | F | 13 | scholar | Littlehampton |
| Lucy M | Chalkley | D | 8 | F | 13 | scholar | Aston |
| Mary J | Shadbolt | D | 8 | F | 13 | scholar | Tewin |
| Dinah | Cutts | D | 6 | F | 13 | scholar | Tewin |
| Jane | Brownsell | D | 9 | F | 13 | scholar | Datchworth |
| Emma M | Collins | D | 4 | F | 14 | scholar | Datchworth |

**FIGURE 3.3** *A search on three fields in a database*

## EXAMPLE

A club membership list is stored in a database. The list is stored in alphabetical order by member's name and a new person joins the club. Once you have added the new member's details you must sort the database to make sure that the records are still in alphabetical order.

# QUESTIONS

### Knowledge and understanding

1 Write down the types of information each of the following databases are likely to contain
  (a) Police National Computer
  (b) Inland Revenue Office
  (c) Driver and Vehicle Licensing Centre
  (d) Your Christmas card list
  (e) The mailing list of a magazine.

2 Explain in your own words what is meant by data file, record and field.

3 Make up a manual database on one of the following
  (a) a list of telephone numbers
  (b) a Christmas card list
  (c) each person in the class's favourite pop group, video and television programme
  (d) a birthday list.

### Practical activities

1 Using a computer and a database package that you are familiar with, type in the details of the manual database(s) you created in (3).
  (a) Sort the entries in alphabetical order on the name field.
  (b) Print out your own record.
  (c) Print out the records of the people whose name begins with the same letter as yours.
  (d) Search for the people who were born in the same month as you.
  What other information could you find out from this database?

# More to do

## Reports

Any information on your database that you print out is a report. When you select information from a database you may search and sort to find the records you want and to get them into the correct order. Once you have done this, you must decide which fields you want to print and in what order. By making these decisions you are setting up a report definition. Of course, you could choose simply to print the complete contents of the database.

## Computed fields

A **computed field**(sometimes called a **calculated field**) can be included in a database or as part of your report definition. A computed field will carry out a calculation on another field or fields and give you an answer (like a **cell** in a spreadsheet). To explain this, think of a database that contains two fields, called total pay and total deductions. You could set up a third field (called net pay) with the formula (= total pay – total deductions). This is a computed field. By including it in your report definition it would be printed out along with the report.

Other examples of computed fields used in reports include column totals and sub-totals.

Figure 3.4 shows a database that uses computed fields.

**CELL**

a box on a spreadsheet that can contain text, numbers or formulas

1 =Length*Width

| Name | Founded | Stadium | Gr Capacity | Length | Width | Pitch Area | T |
|---|---|---|---|---|---|---|---|
| Aberdeen | 1903 | Pittodrie Stadium | 24000 | 110 | 71 | 7810 | A |
| Airdrieonians | 1878 | Broomfield Park | 26000 | 112 | 68 | 7616 | A |
| Albion Rovers | 1881 | Cliftonhill Park | 10000 | | | 0 | C |
| Alloa Athletic | 1878 | Recreation Ground | 9000 | 110 | 75 | 8250 | A |
| Arbroath | 1878 | Gayfield Park | 15000 | | | 0 | A |
| Ayr United | 1910 | Somerset Park | 18500 | 111 | 75 | 8325 | A |
| Berwick Rangers | 1881 | Shielfield Park | 10673 | 112 | 76 | 8512 | E |
| Brechin City | 1906 | Glebe Park | 7500 | 110 | 67 | 7370 | E |
| Celtic | 1888 | Celtic Park | 67500 | 115 | 75 | 8625 | C |

**Football (Database)**

**Football Report 1**

Selection Rules: Founded is less than 1890
and Gr Capacity is greater than 30000

| Name | Founded | Stadium | Gr Capacity | Length | Width | Pitch Area |
|---|---|---|---|---|---|---|
| Celtic | 1888 | Celtic Park | 67500 | 115 | 75 | 8625 |
| Partick Thistle | 1876 | Firhill Park | 36000 | 110 | 71 | 7810 |
| Queen's Park | 1867 | Hampden Park | 75000 | 115 | 75 | 8625 |
| Rangers | 1873 | Ibrox Stadium | 44000 | 115 | 75 | 8625 |

**FIGURE 3.4** *At the top you can see a computed field in a database. The bottom part of the figure is a report prepared by selecting records and a computed field*

## *Altering input and output formats*

You can choose how the information in your database is presented to you by altering the format. Some applications allow you to alter both the way the screen looks (the input format) and how the report looks (the output format). In figure 3.5 you can see one of many possible database input formats. You can set up screen input formats to ease the problems associated with data collection, for example, by making the screen less cluttered or by increasing the size of the text. By using only selected fields in the printout and rearranging the position of the fields you can alter output formats. This means that you can prepare documents like invoices on your database and print them directly from the database without having to retype them on to pre-printed forms.

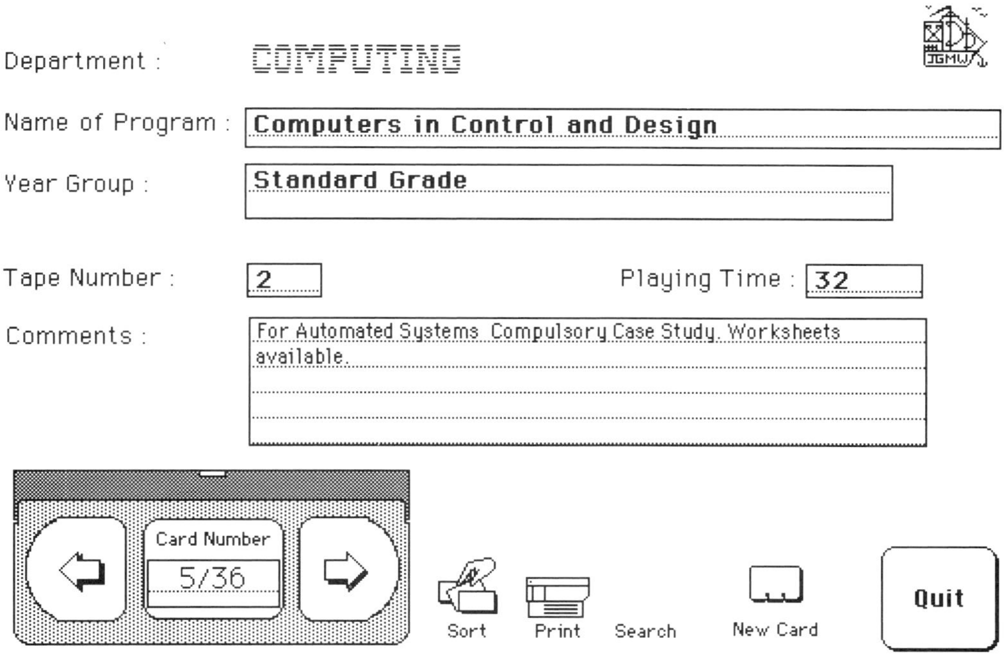


**FIGURE 3.5** *An example of a screen input format on a database*

## *Use of keywords*

The text that you use to search a file for a particular entry or part of an entry is called a **keyword**. Some systems use the term search string instead of keyword. By choosing your keywords carefully you can save a lot of time when using databases.

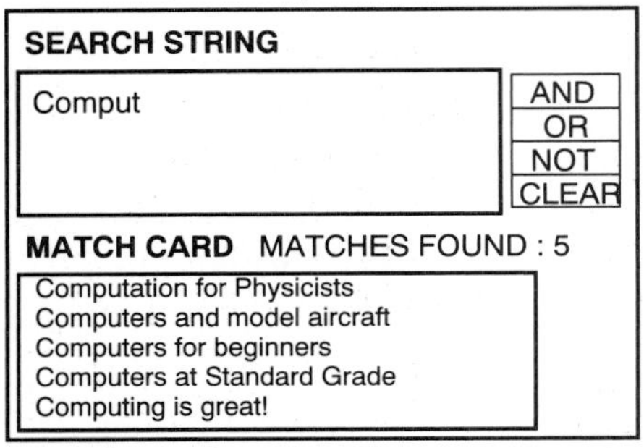


**FIGURE 3.6**
*Searching a database using a partial search string. In this figure the search will find all the titles which start with 'Comput''*

**EXAMPLE**

You might wish to search a large database such as the British Telecom Directory enquiries service (Phonebase) or the Electronic Yellow Pages for someone's phone number or address. You can narrow down the search by entering the person's full name. However, you must be careful how you enter the name – a search for 'John Harold Greaves' may be unsuccessful because the database file contains the name only as 'John H. Greaves'. Unless the name you're searching for is very common (like Smith), you would probably be more successful by simply searching for the family name ('Greaves' in our example).

If you are not sure how a word in the database is spelt, you may enter only part of it as the keyword and the database will match all items with that set of characters. You can also select 'start of string' or 'whole word' (compare this with the search and replace facility described in Chapter 2), to help your search. In figure 3.6 the user has searched a software database using only part of a word, and it has come up with several items to choose from.

## *Key fields*

A **key field** is a field which is used to identify a particular piece of information on the database so that you can find a particular record in a file as quickly as possible. The Scottish Examination Board has a computer database of all the candidates for the Standard Grade examinations. Two or more candidates at the same school with the same name can be distinguished because the database also stores everyone's date of birth. In this case, the key field would be date of birth because it is very unlikely that people with the same name were also born on the same day.

What other information could be stored on this database that we could use as a key field? Why is the date of birth information the best choice here?

## *More sorting*

You can sort on more than one field. For example, if you had an address database with first name and last name stored on separate fields you might wish to sort in ascending alphabetical order so that Janet Smith comes before John Smith. Some database applications will let you choose to sort on last name followed by first name in a single operation but others will make you sort on first name, wait until the records have been sorted, and then sort them again on last name. The second database type means that you have to perform two operations, which takes longer than the first type – but it will produce the same result in the end.

## *Verification and validation*

You *must* ensure that the information you hold in a database is accurate (remember the Data Protection Act described in Chapter 2?).

To **verify** data means to check that it has been entered correctly. One way of verifying data is to ask the user if what has been typed in is correct. Some applications ask you to enter the data twice. If the data you put in the second time is different from the first time the application will warn you – it uses the second time to verify the data.

To **validate** your data means to check that it is allowable and sensible, that you have used the correct type of data or that it is within acceptable limits. As data is input, the computer program will check it using a series of validation checks. A validation check would not allow

- a numeric field to contain text
- the date 30. 2. 97 to be accepted (it knows that February never has 30 days) or
- ages more than 110 or less than 0.

## *Expert systems*

The database packages described so far allow users to store data and retrieve it as they need to, but they cannot make any intelligent decisions based on the data they contain. An **expert system**, on the other hand, is a system that does make intelligent decisions.

An expert system is a program that has access to a huge database of knowledge about one particular subject. It can draw conclusions, make decisions and even offer advice based on the knowledge it has. It is called an 'expert' system because in a sense it has the knowledge of a human expert.

An expert system is made up of three parts.

1 The facts and rules, known as the **knowledge base.** This is like a giant database, but is more flexible in that it contains rules as well as facts. It is the job of the **knowledge engineer** to extract these facts and rules from the human experts and put them into a form that the computer is able to understand.
2 The coding or program. This is known as the **inference engine** or **expert system shell**. The program uses special languages (like PROLOG) to compare the new information with its knowledge base and draw inferences until it reaches a conclusion or can go no further.
3 The screen – the **explanatory interface**. This is used to display the questions it asks the user, but can also display how the system makes its conclusions. The expert system can also use the screen to explain its reasoning to the user, rather than simply to present an answer.

**EXAMPLE**

MYCIN is an expert system used in medical diagnosis. The program asks patients questions about their illness and they can type in their responses. The program analyses these responses using the rules that have been programmed into it. The conclusions that the program draws could be used to help the doctor discover the illness or condition which the patient is suffering from. Figure 3.7 is a look at what a visit to the doctor could be like in the future!

By using the same program (the expert system shell) with a different knowledge base we could develop an expert system to find out what is wrong with a car when it breaks down.

The computer will see you now!

**FIGURE 3.7** *The future of doctors' surgeries?*

## *Artificial intelligence*

Expert systems are part of the larger field of **artificial intelligence** (or **AI**), which started in the 1950s when people started programming computers to play chess and other games. A games program can be called intelligent if it can learn from its mistakes and plays better the next time. We are still trying to develop machines which could display some of the characteristics of human intelligence (like being able to understand natural language).

## EXAMPLE

The computer program Eliza was written in 1965 as an experiment to find out if computers could be programmed to make human conversation. Eliza works by recognising patterns in the sentences typed in by the user and responds mechanically with preset adapted responses. In figure 3.8 someone is trying to hold a conversation with the Eliza program.

```
HELLO. MY  NAME IS ELIZA. WHAT'S YOURS?
JOHN
ALRIGHT, JOHN,WHAT WOULD YOU LIKE TO TALK
ABOUT TODAY?
ARTIFICIAL INTELLIGENCE
ALL RIGHT, CAN YOU TELL ME MORE?
COMPUTERS THAT CAN THINK LIKE HUMANS
WHAT DO YOU THINK MACHINES HAVE TO DO WITH
YOUR PROBLEM?
DO YOU THINK YOU ARE A HUMAN?
DO YOU HAVE MANY RESTLESS NIGHTS?
NO
WELL, WHY NOT?
I SLEEP WELL
MANY PEOPLE HAVE MILD INSOMNIA.
DO YOU HAVE A BRAIN?
NO ONE REALLY KNOWS.
ARE YOU KIDDING?
APPARENTLY YOU THINK THAT I AM KIDDING.
YES
```

```
YOU SEEM QUITE POSITIVE
I'M POSITIVE
DO YOU THINK IT IS NORMAL TO BE POSITIVE?
IT IS BETTER THAN BEING NEGATIVE
IN YOUR OPINION, HOW FREQUENTLY IS IT
 BETTER THAN BEING NEGATIVE?
ABOUT 75%
WHAT DOES THAT SUGGEST TO YOU?
MOST PEOPLE ARE POSITIVE
I'M NOT SURE I UNDERSTAND YOU FULLY.
ARE YOU ALIVE?
IT'S HARD TO SAY, JOHN
DO YOU THINK ABOUT WHAT TO SAY?
ACTUALLY I DO THINK ABOUT WHAT TO SAY
THAT IS VERY INTERESTING
THAT IS VERY INTERESTING?
THANK YOU FOR TALKING TO ME
GLAD TO BE OF ASSISTANCE.
THAT'S ENOUGH FOR TODAY.
GOOD BYE
```

**FIGURE 3.8** *A dialogue with Eliza*

## EXTRA QUESTIONS

### Knowledge and understanding

1. Describe the three main parts of an expert system.
2. Find out the names of two expert systems other than those mentioned in this book and describe how they are used.
3. What is meant by validation?
   Why is validation necessary in a database system?
4. What is meant by verification?
   Why is verification necessary in a database system?

### Problem solving

1. Calculate the storage requirements for an address book database containing 300 records. Use your own name and address as a typical entry.
   How large would the file be if you included each person's telephone number as well?

**Practical activities**

1 If you have access to a copy of the Eliza program, try it out by typing in the same responses shown in figure 3.8.
Does Eliza sound like a real person?

## KEY POINTS

- A database is a structured collection of similar information which can be searched
- Databases can be stored manually on filing cards or electronically using a computer system
- A database package is a program that is used for organising data in a structured way on a computer system
- Data in a database is organised into data files, records and fields
- A data file is a collection of structured data on a particular topic
- Individual data files are made up of records
- A record is a collection of structured data on a particular person or thing
- Each record may consist of one or more fields
- A field is an area on a record which contains an individual item of data
- In addition to the features that all general purpose packages have, a database also allows you to create fields, add and alter records, search and sort
- Sorting allows the records in a database to be rearranged in a given order
- You can search a database for information which matches the conditions you have entered
- To search a file for a given entry or part of an entry you can use keywords
- A key field is a field used to identify a particular piece of information
- To verify data means to check that it has been accurately entered
- To validate data means to check that it is allowable and sensible
- An expert system is able to draw conclusions, make decisions and offer advice based on a large database of knowledge

# 4 Spreadsheets

## *What is a spreadsheet?*

A spreadsheet package is an example of a general purpose package (see Chapter 1) that is mostly used for calculations. A page of a spreadsheet looks like a sheet of paper which is divided into vertical **columns** and horizontal **rows**. Each column has a letter at the top and each row has a number at the side. Lines between the columns and rows divide the page up into boxes, which are usually called **cells**. Cells are identified by their column letter and row number, for example the cell in the third column and seventh row down is called C7. This is known as the **cell reference**. If you know the reference of a particular cell, then you will know where you are on the page. You can put numbers (values), text or formulas (calculations) into cells, or simply leave them empty. Any text that is in a cell has no effect on the calculations the spreadsheet will carry out, but will be printed along with the figures when you obtain a hard copy. In figure 4.1 you can see a spreadsheet page, with some cell references.

**FIGURE 4.1** *A spreadsheet page, showing some cell references*

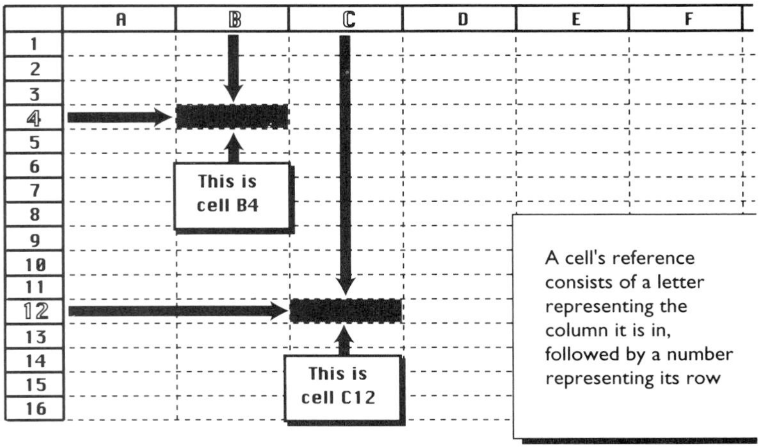


> **SCROLLING**
>
> moving the display on the screen, usually by using the cursor keys or the mouse

There are usually too many cells in a spreadsheet for them all to be displayed on a screen at once (you can use as many as you want), so the screen acts as a window to look at selected parts of the spreadsheet. You can move round or **scroll** the window when you want.

# What are spreadsheets used for?

You can use a spreadsheet for all types of calculations involving numbers – from very simple calculations like working out the weekly takings from the school tuckshop to the complete finances of a multinational company. A typical spreadsheet, with a simple calculation, is shown in figure 4.2.

Row numbers — Column letters — Text — Value

| | A | B | C | D | E |
|---|---|---|---|---|---|
| 1 | School | Tuckshop | Takings | | |
| 2 | | | | | |
| 3 | | Mars Bars | Coke | Crisps | Kit Kat |
| 4 | Monday | 32 | 44 | 57 | 89 |
| 5 | Tuesday | 12 | 22 | 23 | 48 |
| 6 | Wednesday | 56 | 76 | 73 | 67 |
| 7 | Thursday | 23 | 19 | 34 | 43 |
| 8 | Friday | 16 | 20 | 12 | 31 |
| 9 | | | | | |
| 10 | Total items | 139.00 | 181.00 | 199.00 | 278.00 |
| 11 | | | | | |
| 12 | Unit Cost | £0.37 | £0.23 | £0.19 | £0.20 |
| 13 | | | | | |
| 14 | Cash Total | £51.43 | £41.63 | £37.81 | £55.60 |
| 15 | | | | | |
| 16 | WeeklyTotal | £186.47 | | | |

| | A | B | C | D | E |
|---|---|---|---|---|---|
| 1 | School | Tuckshop | Takings | | |
| 2 | | | | | |
| 3 | | Mars Bars | Coke | Crisps | Kit Kat |
| 4 | Monday | 32 | 44 | 57 | 89 |
| 5 | Tuesday | 12 | 22 | 23 | 48 |
| 6 | Wednesday | 56 | 76 | 73 | 67 |
| 7 | Thursday | 23 | 19 | 34 | 43 |
| 8 | Friday | 16 | 20 | 12 | 31 |
| 9 | | | | | |
| 10 | Total items | =Sum(B4:B8) | =Sum(C4:C8) | =Sum(D4:D8) | =Sum(E4:E8) |
| 11 | | | | | |
| 12 | Unit Cost | .37 | .23 | 0.19 | 0.20 |
| 13 | | | | | |
| 14 | Cash Total | =B10*B12 | =C10*C12 | =D10*D12 | =E10*E12 |
| 15 | | | | | |
| 16 | WeeklyTotal | =Sum(B14:E14) | | | |

**FIGURE 4.2** *A typical spreadsheet display. At the top is a simple example and underneath is you can see the same spreadsheet with the formulas visible*

Spreadsheets are particularly useful for solving problems, planning and making models or **simulations** of events that happen in real life. By using a spreadsheet you can look at the effects that changing something will have on the final results. This is called looking at a 'what if' situation. Look at figure 4.3. If John Grimes' sales go up in March, then the monthly total will also change.

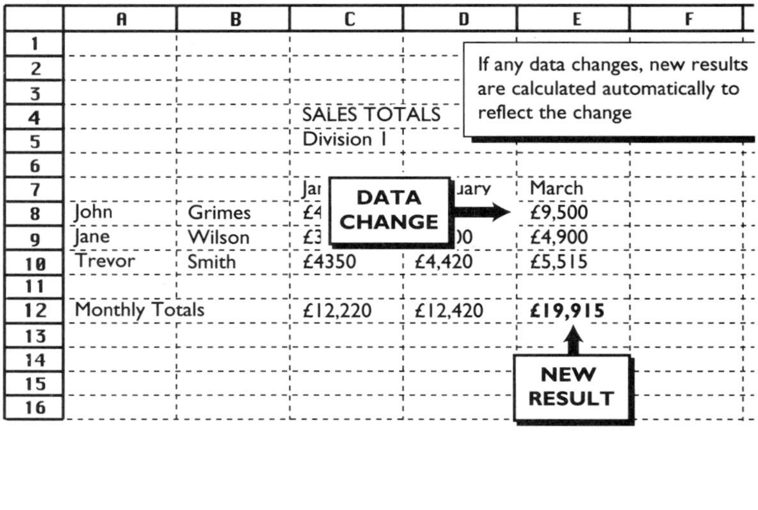
A
B
C
D
E
F
If any data changes, new results are calculated automatically to reflect the change
SALES TOTALS
Division 1
March
John
Grimes
£9,500
Jane
Wilson
£4,900
Trevor
Smith
£4350
£4,420
£5,515
Monthly Totals
£12,220
£12,420
£19,915
DATA CHANGE
NEW RESULT

**FIGURE 4.3** *Changing data in a spreadsheet*

**EXAMPLE**

Figure 4.3 shows a very simple change, but we could look at a much more complex example. A large company uses a spreadsheet with 10 000 cells with many complex formulas to model the company's performance on the stock market. The managing director could find out how changing the annual sales from one branch would affect the overall profits simply by changing a value in one part of the spreadsheet document. This would save her a lot of time and would be very helpful in making management decisions.

The spreadsheet data could be made more interesting to look at if it is displayed in the form of a chart (you will see an example of a chart in figure 4.8). Many spreadsheets have built-in charting functions or are linked to other graphics programs that can generate charts.

# *Features of spreadsheets*

Spreadsheets have all the features common to general purpose packages. The list below gives the features that are special to spreadsheets.

- Formulas
- Formatting
- Insert rows and columns
- Replication
- Calculation
- Charting

Let us look at these features more closely.

## Formulas

You can carry out calculations on the spreadsheet by entering formulas into the cells. A simple formula is

[= A3 + B9]

This formula means 'add the contents of cell A3 to the contents of cell B9 and place the answer in cell ...' (here you should give the reference of the cell you want it to go in). Always remember that the formula refers to each cell by its cell reference rather than by its contents.

Symbols that are often used in spreadsheets are

+ (add)
– (subtract)
* (multiply by)
/ (divide by).

Using formulas, you can choose to total, divide, average or express as percentages the figures in rows and columns. If you change the number in a particular cell, the instructions contained in the formulas will change any related figures automatically throughout the whole sheet, so you don't have to go through the whole sheet yourself.

What do these formulas mean?

[= A5 + B2]
[= A10 * P12]
[= D15 – A3]
[= K11/E4]

## Sum

Because we use spreadsheets mostly for calculations, they often have extra functions built in. One operation that is commonly done on spreadsheet is totalling a column of figures. To do this, the program uses the sum function. For example, the formula

[= SUM (B6:B14)]

will tell the program to add together all the values in column B between cell B6 and B14. Instead of having to write out

[= B6 + B7 + B8 + B9 + B10 + B11 + B12 + B13 + B14]

we can use a **range** for the numbers. In this example the range is B6:B14, but it could be any other range of cells (like C1:C4)

## Formatting

As with word processing, you can format your spreadsheet document to change the way it looks.

### *Column width*

You can make a column as wide or as narrow as you want, so that you can fit in one number or a lot of text into one cell.

### *Justification*

Again, like a word processed document, you can choose to justify the contents of any cell – left, right or centred. For example, you might want to show a column of numbers centred in their respective cells. You can see what these would look like in figure 4.4.

### *Cell attributes*

You can alter the number of decimal places used when a value is displayed (1, 1.0, 1.00 etc.). Some spreadsheets also let you choose from a list of preset configurations for date, currency and

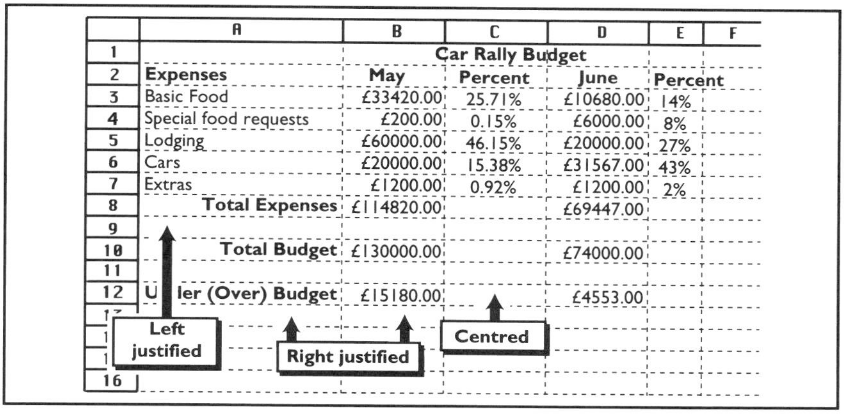


**FIGURE 4.4** *In this figure you can see the various ways of justifying material in columns*

so on. For example, if you select 'currency' from the menu, the computer will automatically fix the number of decimal places for any value in that cell at two, because the spreadsheet expects you to enter the value of the currency as pounds and pence. You can apply a different set of attributes to each cell. In figure 4.5 you can see some of the cell attributes you can alter.

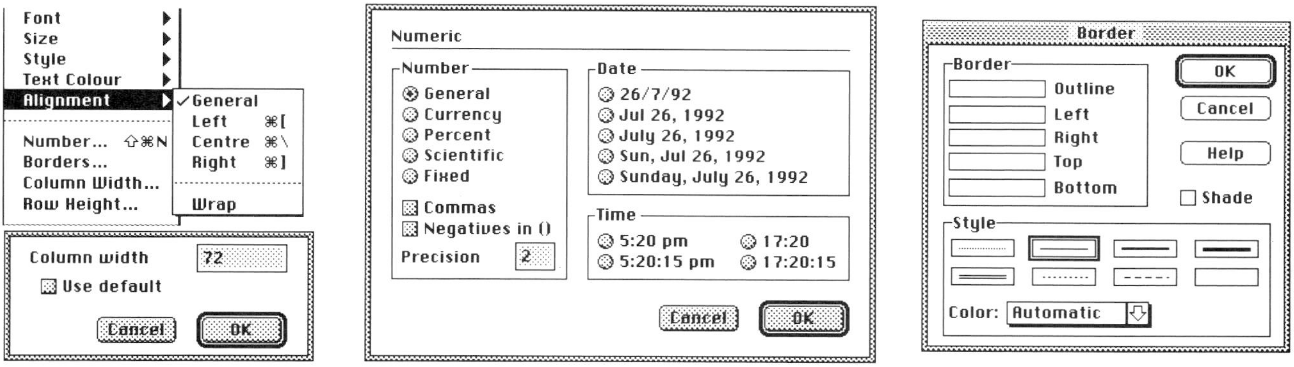


**FIGURE 4.5** *Here are some of the cell attributes that can be altered in a spreadsheet*

## Insert row and insert column

Most spreadsheets will let you add an extra row or column to your document. If you insert the new column or row between two columns or rows that already have data in them, then the data in those columns (or rows), along with any formulas, will be preserved. Any cell references should also be preserved and reorganised automatically. In figure 4.6 you can see a spreadsheet window before and after a new column is added.

## Replication

Replication simply means copying. This is a particularly useful feature of a spreadsheet, especially for copying formulas from one cell to another.

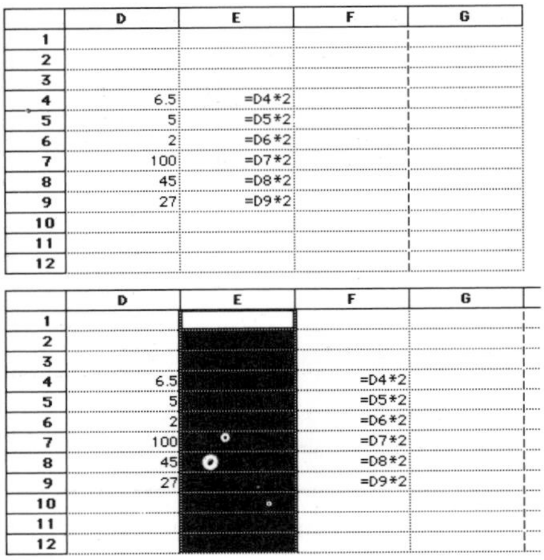
D E F G
6.5 =D4*2
5 =D5*2
2 =D6*2
100 =D7*2
45 =D8*2
27 =D9*2
D E F G
6.5 =D4*2
5 =D5*2
2 =D6*2
100 =D7*2
45 =D8*2
27 =D9*2

**FIGURE 4.6** *A column has been inserted in this spreadsheet. What was in column E is now in column F and a new column E has been created*

Look at the spreadsheet in figure 4.7. The formula [= H17/I17] has been entered in cell J17. If you want this formula in cells J18, J19, J20, and J21 you can copy it from cell J17 into all the other cells instead of typing it in each time. This saves a great deal of time, and reduces your chances of making a mistake. Look at figure 4.7 again. Have you noticed that the cell references in column J have changed automatically to match the calculations – H17 has changed to H18, so that when the calculation is carried out the answer in cells J18 to J21 isn't the same as in J17! This happens because the program has a special feature called referencing. We will come back to this later.

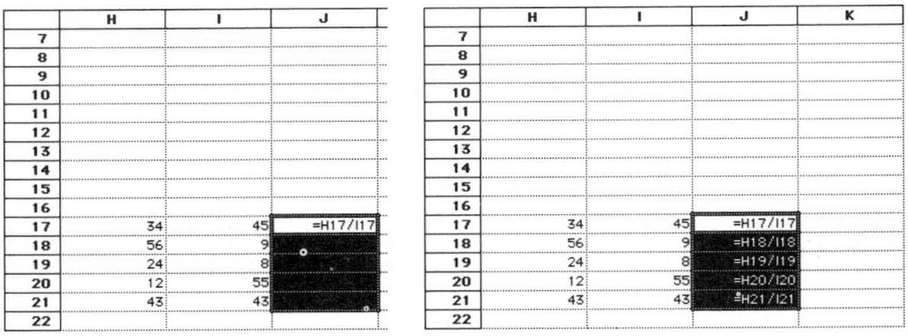
H I J
34 45 =H17/I17
56 9
24 8
12 55
43 43
H I J K
34 45 =H17/I17
56 9 =H18/I18
24 8 =H19/I19
12 55 =H20/I20
43 43 =H21/I21

**FIGURE 4.7** *Relative referencing in a spreadsheet. Note how the numbers in the new cells have changed to keep the calculations right*

## Calculation

When you change a value in a spreadsheet cell any other cells in that document whose values are affected by that value are changed (or updated) automatically. This is known as **automatic calculation**. Some spreadsheets allow you to turn off automatic calculation, preventing this updating until you tell it to. This is called **manual calculation**.

## Charting

A printout of the values in a spreadsheet can be very uninteresting to look at but you can make the figures more interesting if you produce them in the form of a chart. Common types of chart that are used are

- bar charts
- pie charts
- line graphs.

Can you identify examples of each of these in figure 4.8? Powerful spreadsheet packages can produce many kinds of chart, in colour and even in three dimensions. Charts are often used in for writing company reports and can be made into slides for lectures and other presentations.

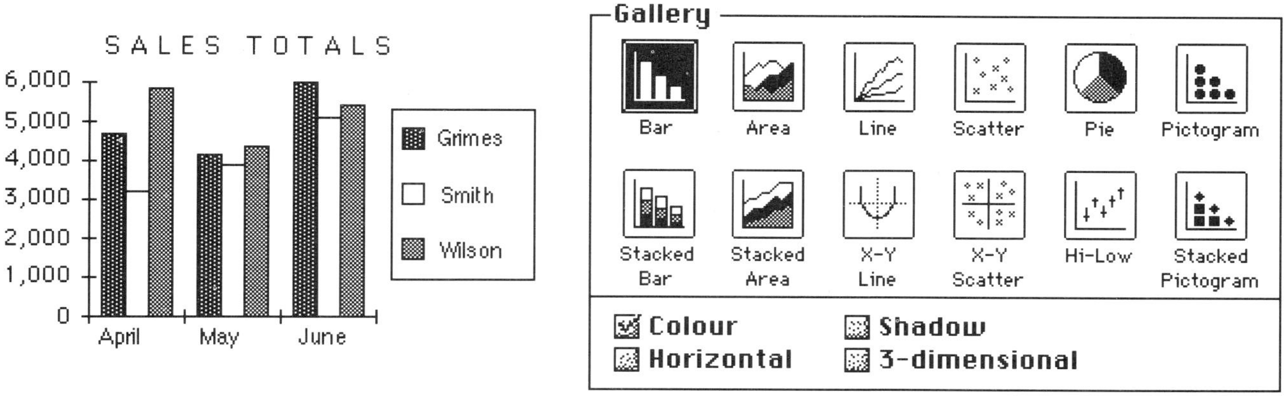


**FIGURE 4.8** *Charts*

## QUESTIONS

### Knowledge and understanding

**1** What types of information can be contained in a spreadsheet?

**2** What makes spreadsheets so useful to businesses?

### Problem solving

**1** Make up a checklist of the features of a spreadsheet described in this chapter.
Underline each of the features that a spreadsheet package you have used possesses.
Make a list of any features in your program not in the checklist.
Write a sentence to describe the purpose of each of these features.

**2** Use a spreadsheet package to construct
(a) The seven times multiplication table.
(b) The school tuckshop spreadsheet shown in figure 4.2.
(c) Your weekly expenses/how you spend your pocket money.
(d) The number of hours of television watched by each of the pupils in your class.
(Work out what you are going to do using squared paper and show the plan to your teacher before you use the computer).
Print out the spreadsheet. Also produce a pie chart or bar chart of your results if your program allows you to.

## *More to do*

### *Functions*

Most spreadsheet packages provide a variety of special **functions**, which can be classified as

- Mathematical (SUM)
- Financial (interest calculations)
- Statistical

- Trigonometric (COS)
- Logical (IF, AND, OR)
- Date and Time (DATE) and
- Special purpose

## *Formulas and conditions*

The IF function is very powerful when you use it in a spreadsheet cell. It allows you to make choices, depending on the values placed in other cells. For example, in cell A10 this formula

[= IF (D5>1200),500,200]

means 'if the value of cell D5 is greater than 1200, then place the value 500 in A10 otherwise place 200 in A10'. You can combine the IF function with the AND and OR logical functions to make the spreadsheet even more versatile. These functions allow programming of spreadsheets in their own **high level language** (these are looked at more closely in Chapter 20). You could even be using a spreadsheet's language to carry out part of the programming requirement of your Standard Grade course!

**HIGH LEVEL LANGUAGE**

a computer language in which instructions are written in normal or everyday language

## *Relative and absolute references*

As we saw earlier, a cell in a spreadsheet is identified by its cell reference (like A4 or Z19). Let's assume that cell A4 contains the value 189. If you write a formula in another cell, maybe cell B4, you will put

[= A4*1.75].

Cell B4 is now said to **refer** to cell A4. Suppose you now wish to copy this formula to another cell, somewhere else in the spreadsheet, maybe B5. You will find that the formula in B5 has changed to

[= A5*1.75].

The spreadsheet has copied the formula **relative** to the original one. This is normal in a spreadsheet, and will always happen unless you tell the program not to do it. Look at the example in figure 4.7. What happened to the formula as it was copied into cells J18, J19, J20 and J21?

Sometimes you may not want the formulas to behave like this. The alternative to relative referencing is called

**absolute referencing**. In the previous example concerning cell B5, if the formula had been copied into cell B5 using an absolute cell reference, then it would have remained as

[= A4*1.75 ].

Spreadsheets sometimes use the $ symbol in the cell reference to show that absolute referencing is in operation.

**EXAMPLE**

You can use absolute referencing in a spreadsheet that calculates the net price of items, to which you must add value added tax (VAT). Suppose you place the current VAT rate in cell B2. Each item, regardless of its position in the spreadsheet, must be multiplied by the contents of cell B2 to give the final price. When you set up the spreadsheet, any formulas will have to refer to cell B2 using an absolute reference. Copy the example in figure 4.9 and try it using a spreadsheet package.

**FIGURE 4.9** *Absolute cell referencing in a spreadsheet. This one helps work out how much things will cost when VAT is added to them*

| | A | B | C | D |
|---|---|---|---|---|
| 1 | | | | |
| 2 | VAT RATE | 17.50% | | |
| 3 | | | | |
| 4 | | | | |
| 5 | | net price | VAT | gross price |
| 6 | | | | |
| 7 | balloons | £ 0.50 | £ 0.09 | £ 0.59 |
| 8 | lollipops | £ 0.12 | £ 0.02 | £ 0.14 |
| 9 | dummys | £ 0.65 | £ 0.11 | £ 0.76 |
| 10 | | | | |

| | A | B | C | D |
|---|---|---|---|---|
| 1 | | | | |
| 2 | VAT RATE | .175 | | |
| 3 | | | | |
| 4 | | | | |
| 5 | | net price | VAT | gross price |
| 6 | | | | |
| 7 | balloons | .5 | =B7*$B$2 | =B7+C7 |
| 8 | lollipops | .12 | =B8*$B$2 | =B8+C8 |
| 9 | dummys | .65 | =B9*$B$2 | =B9+C9 |
| 10 | | | | |

## *Cell protection*

Most spreadsheet packages will allow you to protect or 'lock' the contents of a cell if you don't want them to be changed – perhaps text would end up in a cell containing a formula – and the spreadsheet would give an incorrect answer. This is called **cell protection**. Cell protection is particularly useful if your spreadsheet is going to be used by someone else, perhaps someone who only wants to enter figures and get the answer without understanding how the spreadsheet works. In this case the programmer of the spreadsheet would set cell protection to cover all of the cells that she doesn't want the user to change.

## EXTRA QUESTIONS

### Knowledge and understanding

1 List four groups into which spreadsheet functions may be classified.
2 Name a particularly useful function when programming using spreadsheets.
3 Explain in your own words absolute and relative cell references.
4 Why is cell protection a useful feature of spreadsheets?

### Problem solving

1 Describe a situation when you would use relative referencing in a spreadsheet and one when you would use absolute referencing.

### Practical activities

Carry out the following tasks using a spreadsheet package with which you are familiar

1 Mr Grimble's sweetie shop
(a) The sales for Mr Grimble's sweetie shop are shown below

| Sweet | Monday |
|---|---|
| Humbugs | 23 |
| Mint Imperials | 12 |
| Gobstoppers | 56 |
| **Total** | |

**FIGURE 4.10** *Mr Grimble's sweetie shop*

Enter these headings and figures in a spreadsheet and use the spreadsheet to calculate the total for Monday's sales. Save your spreadsheet as *Grimble1*. Print out your completed spreadsheet. Write a sentence to explain how you got the spreadsheet to do the calculation.

(b) One full week's sales were

| Sweet | Mon | Tues | Wed | Thurs | Fri |
|---|---|---|---|---|---|
| Humbugs | 23 | 1 | 5 | 78 | 123 |
| Mint imperials | 12 | 34 | 7 | 9 | 49 |
| Gobstoppers | 56 | 26 | 2 | 56 | 12 |
| **Daily totals** | | | | | |

Enter these headings and figures in a spreadsheet and use the spreadsheet to calculate the daily sales totals. Add an extra column to the spreadsheet to show the item totals and weekly total. Save your spreadsheet as *Grimble 2*. Print it out. Write down *two* improvements that would make your spreadsheet more useful to Mr Grimble.

(c) Another week's sales for the shop were

| Sweet | Mon | Tues | Wed | Thurs | Fri |
|---|---|---|---|---|---|
| Humbugs | 23 | 1 | 5 | 78 | 123 |
| Mint imperials | 12 | 34 | 7 | 9 | 49 |
| Gobstoppers | 56 | 26 | 2 | 56 | 12 |
| **Daily totals** | | | | | |

Enter these headings and figures in a spreadsheet and calculate the daily sales totals, the item totals and the average sales of each item. If humbugs are 1p each, mint imperials 2p, and gobstoppers 7p, what would Mr Grimble's weekly takings be? Save your spreadsheet as *Grimble3* and print it out. Use the spreadsheet data to produce a pie chart showing the item totals for one week. Print out a copy of the chart.

**2** Children in Need

The Cubs have decided to organise a sponsored swim to raise funds for the Children in Need Appeal. The swimming pool can be hired for £30 an hour on a Saturday, and they have decided to hire it for six hours. The Akela has also decided that it would be a good idea to get some badges printed as awards to people who take part in the swim.

Peter John is working towards his computing Hobbies Badge at Cubs. He has estimated some of the costs and has worked out the following figures on his microcomputer. Figure 4.12 shows the figures if 40 people take part and raise an average of £10 each

| | A | B | C | D | E | F |
|---|---|---|---|---|---|---|
| 1 | | | | | | |
| 2 | Children in Need Appeal | | | | | |
| 3 | | | | | | |
| 4 | | | | | Unit Cost | |
| 5 | Number of People | 40 | | Badges | 0.5 | 20 |
| 6 | Amount raised per person | 10 | | Pool Hire | 30 | 180 |
| 7 | | | | | | |
| 8 | Income Total | 400 | | | Costs Total | 200 |
| 9 | | | | | | |
| 10 | | | | | Profit for Charity | 200 |
| 11 | | | | | | |

**FIGURE 4.11**

(a) Which cells in the spreadsheet contain formulas? Write down what these formulas are, and then type in this spreadsheet and get it working. Save it as *swim*. Print out a copy.
(b) Peter John decides that the Cubs must aim for a higher prof it, and that they must aim for at least 50 people, raising £15 each. Which cells will have to be changed to take account of this? Make these changes and save your new spreadsheet as *swim1*.
(c) Use the spreadsheet to find out how much the Cubs could raise if more people took part in the swim, or if the average amount each of the 50 people raised was more than £15. How many people would have to be sponsored at £20 if the Cubs wanted to raise £1000?

**3 Zoe's chairs**
Zoe works in a shop that sells furniture, but the pay is not very good. She has looked around for a way to add to her wages. She has a home computer and she has designed and built a chair to sit on while using it. Zoe thinks that she could make more chairs and sell them. and sets about using a spreadsheet program on her microcomputer to work out how much the chairs would cost to make using various materials and how much she would have to charge for them to make a profit.

**FIGURE 4.12** *Zoe's chair*

The spreadsheet printout in figure 4.13 shows how much it would cost to make the chair in two types of wood: pine and marante. The PARTS heading covers items like glue, screws and varnish. Zoe decides to pay herself £1.50 an hour. Enter the data into a spreadsheet. Save the spreadsheet as *chair*.

| | A | B | C | D | E | F | G |
|---|---|---|---|---|---|---|---|
| 1 | | | | | | | |
| 2 | Zoe's | Chairs | PLC | | | | |
| 3 | | | | | | | |
| 4 | | COST OF | | TIME | TOTAL | TOTAL | |
| 5 | | WOOD | PARTS | HOURS | LABOUR | COST | |
| 6 | | | | | | | |
| 7 | Pine | 5.50 | 2.00 | 6.00 | 9.00 | 22.50 | |
| 8 | Marante | 10.00 | 2.00 | 6.00 | 9.00 | 27.00 | |
| 9 | | | | | | | |
| 10 | | | | | | | |

**FIGURE 4.13**

(a) After she has worked out her basic costs, Zoe realises that she has to deliver any chair she sells. Her father agrees to deliver the chairs but insists that Zoe pays for the petrol. They agree to a price of £5 per chair. Insert a new column called DELIVERY, and insert £5 for each chair. Change the formula in the TOTAL COST column. Save this new version as *chair1*. Print out a copy.
(b) Zoe's boss says that she has a friend in the timber trade who will supply the wood cheaper – £4 for the pine and £8.50 for the marante. Change your spreadsheet to take account of these new figures. Save this version as *chair2*.
(c) Now Zoe needs to work out how much to charge for the chairs. She decides that she would like a profit of 40%. Add a column to the end of the spreadsheet for SELLING PRICE. Save this version of the spreadsheet as *chair3*. Print out a copy of your spreadsheet and keep it.
(d) What would Zoe have to sell the chairs for if she decided on a 10% profit? What would the price be if her profit was 50%?
(e) With the help of your spreadsheet, work out what Zoe would make in a year, assuming that she makes and sells 50 chairs.

## KEY POINTS

- A spreadsheet is divided into columns and rows
- Each box on the sheet is called a cell
- Each cell is identified by a cell reference – such as B8, Z19
- Cells can contain numbers, text or formulas, or may simply be left empty
- Spreadsheets can show the effects of changing events. These are called 'what if' situations
- Spreadsheets have the features common to all general purpose packages. A spreadsheet also has the following features: formulas, formatting, insert row and column, replication, calculation and charting
- Most spreadsheet packages provide a variety of specialised functions for simplifying complex calculations
- Cell references in a spreadsheet may be relative or absolute
- The contents of a spreadsheet cell may be protected to prevent them from being changed

# 5 Graphics

## What is a graphics package?

A **graphics package** is another general purpose package, one that you use to draw pictures (or **graphics**) on the monitor. Like any other general purpose package, the pictures produced can be saved to backing storage or printed out as hard copy.

## What is a graphics package used for?

The pictures produced by a graphics packages can be used in many ways:

- The pictures may be put with text into a document, like a report or a newsletter – or even a book, like this one
- They may be used in a computer game, like Super Mario Bros
- Pictures from a graphics package may be used for design, if they're imported into a **computer aided design** (**CAD**) package or a **computer aided manufacture** (**CAM**) package
- Computer graphics are used to produce special effects in television programmes and film
- Using a graphics package you can alter photographs before they are printed.

Like any information displayed on a computer screen, graphics are made up of tiny dots called **pixels** (more about these in Chapter 19).

**BACKING STORE**

a system for permanently holding the contents of memory on media such as disk or tape

**IMPORT**

to bring in data from one file into another, sometimes between two different types of package

# Features of graphics packages

**POINTER**

a shape displayed on screen which is used to select from a menu. It is usually controlled by a mouse

**GRAPHICS TABLET**

an input device which allows you to draw freehand using a hand-held pointer on a board

**MOUSE**

an input device (with a ball underneath and one or more buttons on top) used to control a pointer on screen

**TRACKBALL**

an input device consisting of a ball which is turned by hand, used to control a cursor on the screen. Works like an upside-down mouse

In a graphics package you will find all the features possessed by general purpose packages, as well as quite a few features special to producing graphics.

- Draw graphic
- Enter text
- Select tool
- Alter tool attributes
- Scale graphic
- Rotate graphic.

Let us look at each of these features more closely

## Draw graphic

You draw graphics – lines, boxes, circles or whatever – on the screen by moving the **cursor** (this is also called the **pointer**). To draw a shape, you must position the cursor on the screen where the shape is to start and then move it in the directions you require to make the shape. Different programs use different items to control the cursor, and depending on the program you may find yourself using

- the keyboard
- a graphics tablet
- a light pen
- a trackball
- a joystick or
- a mouse

to move the cursor around the screen.

## Enter text

Graphics packages allow you to enter text anywhere on the screen – so that you can label a diagram, for instance. To do this, move the cursor to the position where you want to place the text and type in the words – just as in the example in figure 5.1.

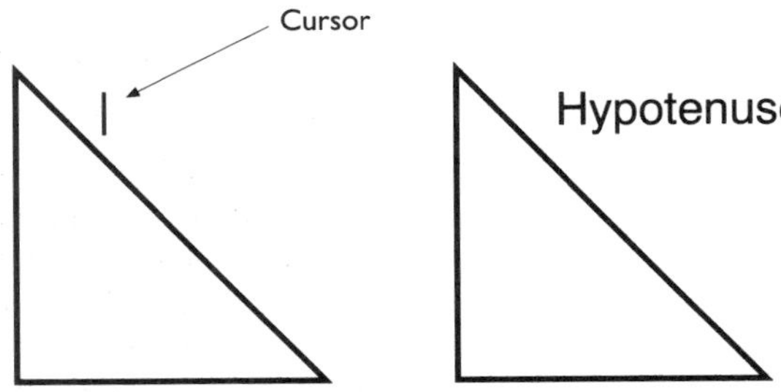


**FIGURE 5.1** *How text can be entered on a graphic*

> **WIMP**
>
> Windows, Icons, Menu (or Mouse), Pointer (or Pull down menu)

> **MENU**
>
> a list on screen for the user to choose from

## Select (change) tool

One of the main features of graphics packages is that they have a set of aids (or **tools**) that you can use for drawing. Each tool in a graphics package has a different function. Try drawing a circle freehand on the screen – it's very difficult! – but the circle tool in a graphics package lets you draw perfect circles every time. As well as the circle tool, there may be tools for drawing a box, a straight line, a triangle, an arc.

Usually a menu of the tools available is displayed on the screen (this is called the **tool palette** – rather like an artist's palette). This may simply be a list of text or a list of icons. In figure 5.2 you can see a selection of the icons that may be used in some WIMP systems. On some graphics packages the cursor will change shape whenever a new tool is selected, so that you can tell which tool you're using. Other packages display a message on the screen or highlight the tool chosen from the menu to remind the user what drawing tool they're using.

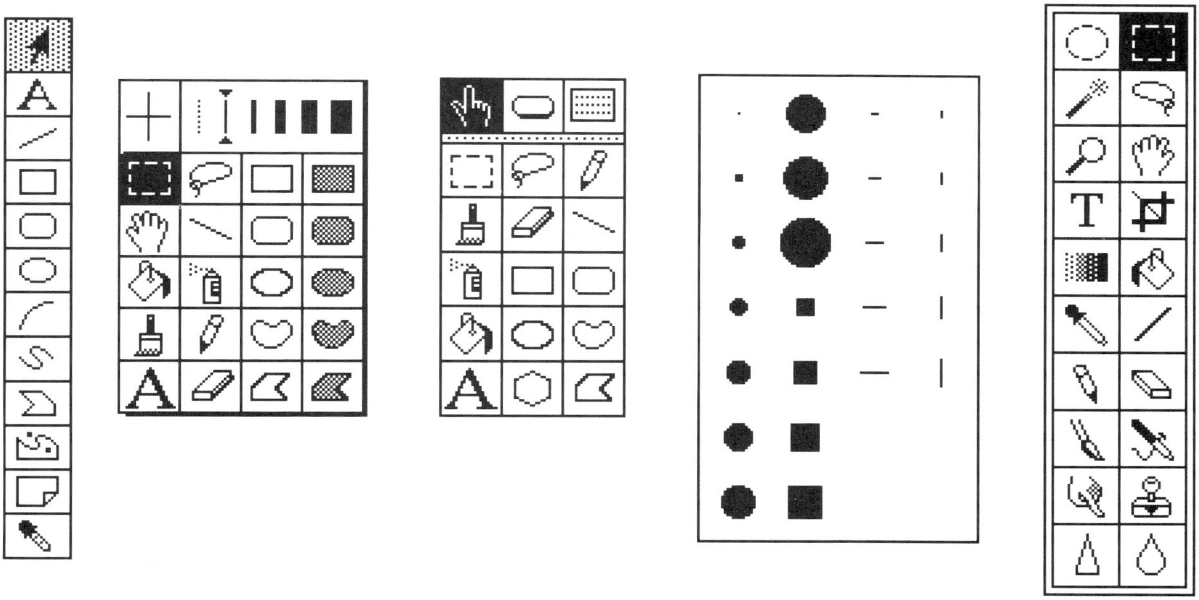

**FIGURE 5.2** *A selection of icon menus*

## Alter tool attributes

Whatever method of tool selection the package uses, it will allow you to change the properties of the tool. This means that you don't have to use different tools to draw lines of different thicknesses, for example, because you can choose the width of the line that the line drawing tool will produce. Or you could change the type of colour or shading you're using simply by choosing a different type of shading for the shading tool to use.

> **ICON**
>
> a symbol or picture on a screen – part of a graphical user interface

### Scale graphic

You can change the size of your picture using a graphics package. The changes can be very precise – by putting in a percentage number you can make tiny changes to the graphic. Or you can resize the picture very roughly by stretching or squashing a picture using the selection tools.

### Rotate graphic

Often you will want to rotate a picture or part of a picture. You can rotate a picture in some programs by choosing the area you want to change using the selection tool and simply turning it in any direction. In other programs, the user must enter the exact number of degrees through which he or she wants to rotate the selected area – this will give a very precise rotation. Using this facility to rotate text can be very useful if you are labelling diagrams. In figure 5.3 you can see some examples of text and graphics that have been scaled and rotated.

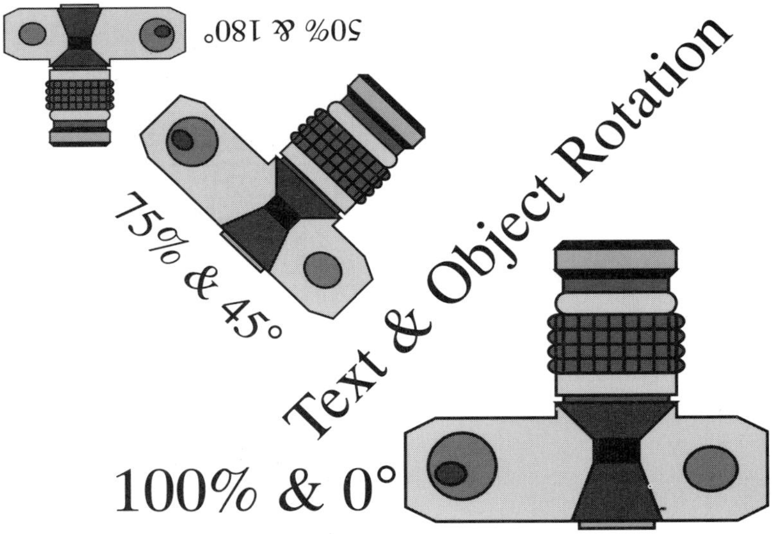


**FIGURE 5.3** *Scaling and rotating graphics*

## QUESTIONS

**Knowledge and understanding**

**1** Make a checklist of the features of a graphics package described in this chapter.
Circle each of the features that are available in a graphics package you have used.
Write down the name of this package.
List any features in your package that are not in the checklist.
Write a sentence to describe the purpose of each of these features.

**2** Why do graphics packages have a selection of tools?

**Problem solving/practical abilities**

1 Collect examples of advertisements from magazines and newspapers which contain graphics. Try to identify which features in a graphics package could be used to produce the effects in the examples you have collected.

2 Use a graphics package to produce a birthday card.

3 Use a Teletext graphics package to produce a page with text and graphics.

## *More to do*

### *Paint and draw*

Graphics packages can be classified into two main types, **paint** and **draw**. Both types of package are used to make pictures, but they work differently.

- Paint packages produce pictures by changing the colour of the tiny dots (called pixels) which make up the screen display. When two shapes overlap on the screen in a paint package, the shape which is on top rubs out the shape underneath.
- Draw packages work by producing objects on the screen. When you overlap shapes in a draw package, the shapes remain separate. They can be separated again and both shapes stay the same.

You can see these effects in figure 5.4

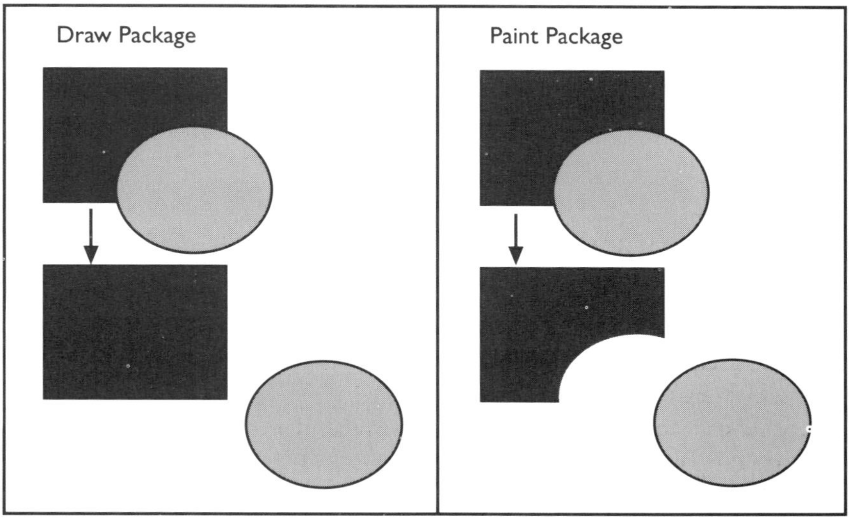


**FIGURE 5.4** *Separating overlapping shapes in paint and draw packages. In a draw package the two items are separate, but in a paint package you can see that there's a bit missing from the underneath part*

## Graphics resolution

The quality of the picture you can produce is determined by the **resolution** of the graphics available. The smaller the size of the pixels the finer the lines that you can display on the screen.

*Small pixels mean high resolution. Large pixels mean low resolution.*

**FIGURE 5.5** *A high-resolution graphic*

A high-resolution graphic is shown in figure 5.5. One way of describing the resolution of the screen is to give the number of pixels horizontally and vertically. Teletext graphics have 75 pixels across and 80 pixels down on each screen – this gives a very low-resolution picture, as you can see in figure 5.6.

Microcomputers often allow you to choose whether you want high or low-resolution graphics – they are said to have different graphics modes. High-resolution graphics usually need more computer memory than low-resolution graphics, and you will need more memory if you want to use more colours on the display.

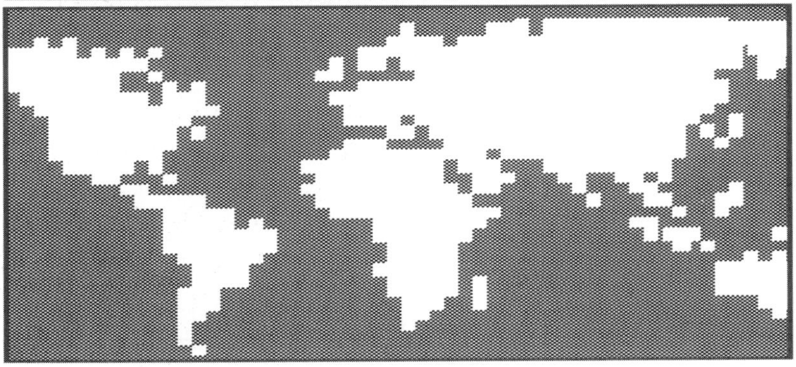

**FIGURE 5.6** *Teletext graphics are low resolution*

## Animation

Many television and film companies use computer graphics to produce their station logos, which often appear to assemble themselves on screen as you watch (like the Channel 4 logo in the illustration). This way of using graphics is called **animation**. Animation is used in games and in tutorial and demonstration programs.

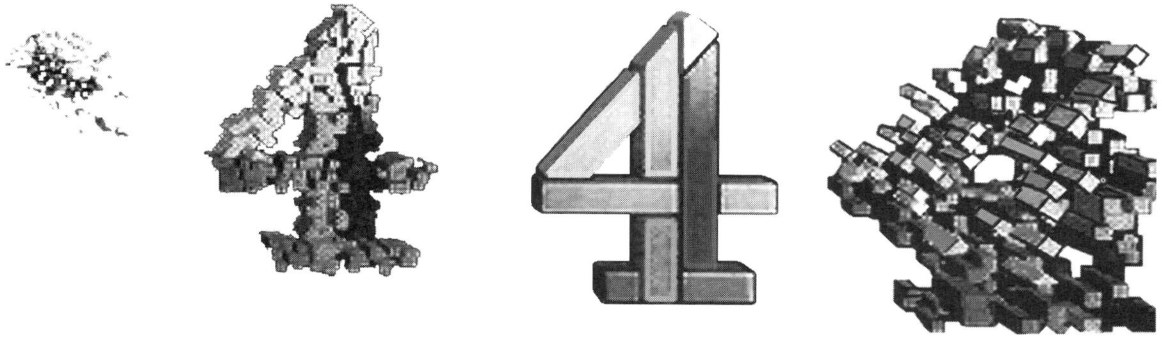

*Animation*

## EXTRA QUESTIONS

**Knowledge and understanding**

1 What do we mean by the term graphics resolution?
Find out the screen resolution obtainable on the microcomputers in your school.
Try to get hold of a printout from two screens with different resolutions, like Teletext graphics and one other.

2 What is animation?
Ask your teacher if any of the graphics packages available in your school are capable of producing animation.
If you have access to such a package, design your own animated logo and try to reproduce it on the computer screen.
If you can't get hold of one of these packages, run a demonstration disk like the ones for Pagemaker or Lotus 1-2-3 and watch the animation used.

**Problem solving**

1 Which type of graphics package – paint or draw – would be suitable to
(a) draw your self-portrait?
(b) draw a plan of the school?
(c) produce a logo for your club?
(d) design a greetings card?
Give your reasons in each case.

## KEY POINTS

- A graphics package is a program that allows the user to draw pictures
- Graphics, like any information displayed on a computer screen, are made up of tiny dots called pixels
- A graphics package has the features common to all general purpose packages, and has the following too:
  - draw graphic
  - enter text
  - select tool
  - alter tool attributes
  - scale graphic
  - rotate graphic
- Graphics packages can be classified into two main types: paint and draw
- Paint packages produce pictures by changing the colour of the pixels that make up the screen display
- Draw packages work by producing objects on the screen
- High-resolution graphics are made up from a large number of small pixels
- Low-resolution graphics are made up from a small number of large pixels
- The process of moving graphics on screen is called animation

# 6 Integrated packages

In Chapter 1 we mentioned integrated packages. Let us now look at them in more detail.

## *What is an integrated package?*

**APPLICATIONS PACKAGE**

a piece of software (together with its accompanying disks and manuals) that performs a particular task

**HUMAN COMPUTER INTERFACE**

the way the computer and its user communicate

Integrated packages combine two or more different application packages in a single package – for example, a word processor, a spreadsheet, a database and a graphics package.

Integrated packages may be very useful because

- all the applications have a common human computer interface (or HCI)
- you can have several different documents open at once
- transferring data between applications is easy.

But

- integrated packages don't have all the features that the separate applications have
- integrated packages use up more memory.

## *Advantages of integrated packages*

**PROMPT**

a character which appears on screen to tell the user that the computer wants you to do something

### Common HCI

This means that each separate part of the package communicates with the user in the same way. The commands used, the keys that must be pressed, the menus and the **prompts** that appear on the screen are the same in every application within the integrated package.

### EXAMPLE

Suppose you have to use 'command – L' to load a document in the word processor. By using 'command – L' you will also be able to load a document into the spreadsheet package or the database. This is very useful because the user only needs to learn one set of commands to operate all of the parts of the package.

**WINDOW**

an area of the screen set aside for a particular purpose

## Documents of different types can be open at once

A word processor document can be open at the same time as a spreadsheet and a database and the user can switch between them. A windows system is ideal for this because the different documents can be open in separate screen windows and they can be viewed next to each other. In figure 6.1 you can see several windows open at once.

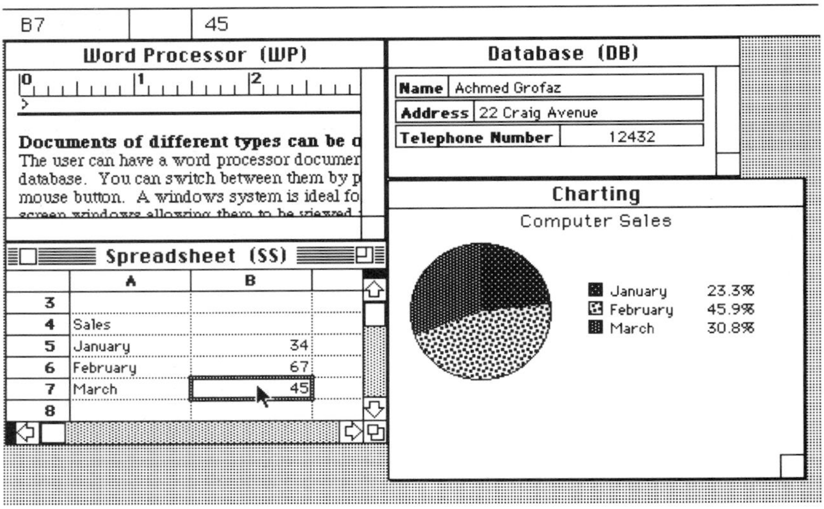


**FIGURE 6.1** *An integrated package. It shows a word processor, a database and a spreadsheet, each in a separate window in the screen. The data from the spreadsheet has been displayed as a pie chart*

## Transfer of data between different types of document

Integrated packages make it easy to produce documents like reports, which need to share data from several applications in an integrated package. You could take the data from a spreadsheet and a drawing you have prepared in the graphics application and insert them in a word processor document.

### *Linking data*

You can transfer data between the separate applications within an integrated package in two ways – statically or dynamically. (Dynamic and static links are explained in Chapter 1.)

**DYNAMIC LINKAGE**

a change to the data in one file will automatically be carried over to the same data in another file

**STATIC LINKAGE**

a change to the data in one file will not affect the same data in other files

### EXAMPLE

Suppose your name, address and telephone number are held in a database document and you have transferred them to a document in the word processor. You move to a new address and your telephone number changes. If the database and word processor were linked dynamically, as soon as you alter the database the data in your word processor document will also change. In static linkage the word processor document is not automatically changed when the database is altered – you have to change it separately.

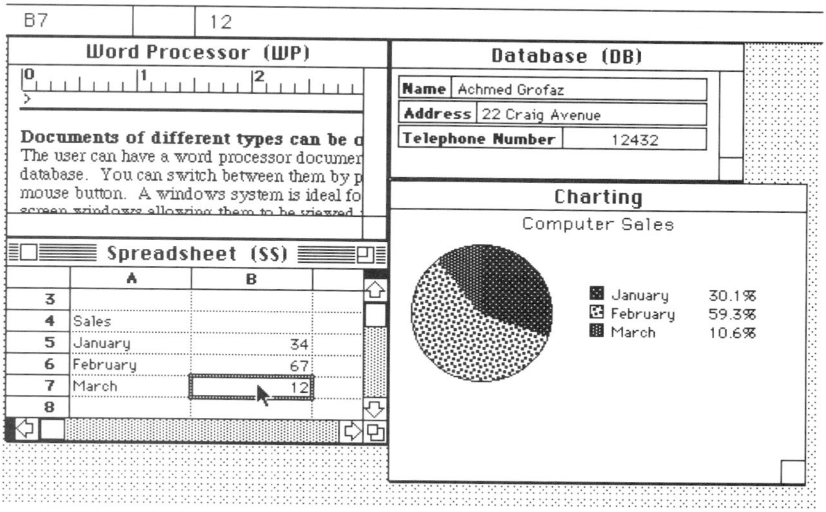


**FIGURE 6.2** *Dynamic linkage. Note the value in cell B7 has changed to 12. What other differences are there between this screen and the one in the previous figure?*

***More dynamic links***

Dynamic linkage is also used in mail merge and to chart data from a spreadsheet.

## MAIL MERGE

The mail merge facility was discussed in Chapter 2. Mail merge uses a dynamic link between a word processor document and a database. The word processor document may be a standard letter with spaces left for the variable data from the database (names, addresses, dates). Before you do a merge, you must select the fields from the database and set up the link with the correct positions in the word processor document. Some packages allow you to check the merged document before you print it, but usually the letters are printed directly as hard copy – which means that if you find a mistake you have to reprint the whole lot.

**FIELD**

a single item of data stored in a record

## CHARTING DATA

To chart the data from a spreadsheet you must identify the area on the spreadsheet that holds the data you want, either by highlighting the appropriate cells or by typing the cell references into a chart definition. The chart is then drawn automatically. Bar charts, line charts and pie charts are the ones used most often. Once a chart has been drawn it can be transferred to the word processor document to form part of a report or to the graphics area to be edited and sized.

# Disadvantages of integrated packages

## Integrated packages lack features

The individual programs that make up the different parts of the integrated package are often not as powerful as the separate application packages, or they don't have as many features. Perhaps a word processing package allows you to compile a table of contents – but the variant of the word processor used as part of an integrated package might not allow you to do that.

Integrated packages are usually a compromise between power and price. Users are unlikely to be willing to pay more for an integrated package than for a separate application. To keep costs down, software companies produce cut-down versions of their existing separate application packages. Cut-down versions are smaller and less powerful than the separate packages. You could find that a spreadsheet in an integrated package will have fewer cells than there are in a separate package, or the database has a fixed record size or format. The dictionary in a word processor in an integrated package may be smaller than in the same word processor if it is used as a separate package, or the thesaurus might not be available.

## Integrated packages use more memory

The integrated package may be larger than each package separately. This would take up more of the computer's memory and leave less room for documents.

Another reason why the individual programs that make up the different parts are smaller is because of memory limitations. A typical integrated package made up of four programs may take up 400 kilobytes on a one megabyte computer, which leaves only 624 kilobytes for data. A separate spreadsheet package will occupy about 300 kilobytes of memory on its own, which leaves 724 kilobytes for data on the one megabyte computer. Because of the size of the integrated package (in our example only 400 kilobytes) each program will be smaller than a separate application package, and so probably has fewer features. So you can see that a program in an integrated package is likely to have fewer features and leaves less room for documents than a separate application.

# Applications of integrated packages

Integrated packages are often used on portable computers. One reason for this is that the integrated package can easily be stored in ROM – which means that the package is available as soon as the machine is switched on. For example, the Cambridge Z88 computer is supplied with the application PIPEDREAM, which is an integrated package consisting of a word processor, database and spreadsheet.

Because integrated packages provide quite a lot of features for a relatively low cost, they are often used by people on a small budget (like schools and small businesses). You can imagine that trying to equip a school's computer room with a complete set of software for each workstation would be very expensive. Schools can save a lot of money by buying an integrated package for each machine rather than separate application packages. You miss out on some extra features, but get three or more applications for the price of one.

## *Integration without an integrated package*

Many stand-alone packages have some of the features that have been described as special to integrated packages. For instance, you might be able to transfer data from one package to another. Certain **operating systems** (the program which runs the computer system itself) allow you to work on more than one program at the same time in separate windows (this is called **multi-programming**) – perhaps a spreadsheet in one window and a word processing package in another. At present, though, the two different packages are not likely to have a common HCI, which means you'd have to use two different sets of commands – and could make mistakes. New computers are being developed with new operating systems and integration of programs without an integrated package will probably become more common.

## QUESTIONS

### Knowledge and understanding

1 What is an integrated package?
2 Give three advantages that an integrated package has over separate application packages.

### Problem solving

1 Refer to an integrated package that you know, and list the steps you would take to
   (a) carry out a mail merge
   (b) chart data from a spreadsheet.

# EXTRA QUESTIONS

**Problem solving**

**1** Why are integrated packages often chosen by
(a) users on a limited budget?
(b) people who haven't used computers before?

**2** What is meant by static and dynamic data linkage?

**3** Many integrated packages also contain a communications program.
(a) What could this part of the package be used for?
(b) Suggest a task which would be easier using an integrated package containing a communications program.

**4** Read the advertisement below and answer the questions which follow.

> **GRANDWORKS**
>
> – is the ideal companion for the new Big Book portable computer. Big Book has four megabytes of random access memory, a 40 megabyte hard disk and a built-in modem. Grandworks contains six applications: Word processor, Database, Spreadsheet, Graphics, Charting and Communications, yet occupies only 700 kilobytes! Ideal for report writing! All the computer you'll ever need – All the applications you ever wanted.

How many applications does Grandworks contain?
How much memory will be left for data if you used Grandworks on the Big Book computer?
Which part of the Grandworks would use the Big Book's built in modem?
Why is Grandworks advertised as 'ideal for report writing'?

## KEY POINTS

- Integrated packages combine a number of different application packages in a single package – you could have a word processor, a spreadsheet, a database and a graphics package in an integrated package
- Integrated packages have several advantages:
  - All the parts use the same HCI
  - Documents of different types can be open at the same time
  - It is easy to transfer data between different types of document
- Integrated packages also have some disadvantages:
  - Integrated packages have fewer features than separate application packages
  - Integrated packages use more memory than a single application package

# 7 Desktop publishing

## *What is desktop publishing?*

> **PERIPHERAL**
>
> any device that may be attached to a computer system for input, output or backing storage

> **SCANNER**
>
> an input device which allows printed text or graphics to be displayed on the screen. Usually used with OCR software

Desktop publishing is producing professional looking reports, newsletters, newspapers, booklets and magazines on a microcomputer and peripherals. It is known as **desktop publishing** (this is often shortened to DTP) because the whole process takes place within the computer system sitting on the user's desk.

A DTP system usually consists of

- a computer system
- a high-quality printer (usually a laser printer)
- a specialised DTP software package
- many DTP systems also include a scanner (this will be explained in Chapter 16) so photographs and diagrams can be put directly into the system.

A DTP package is not designed to be used as a word processor, or as a graphics package – any text or graphics that are used in the final publication should have been prepared separately in their specialised packages. The already-prepared material is imported into the DTP package and placed on the page where it is needed. DTP packages are sometimes called **page make-up packages**, because they are used to arrange (make up) each page of the publication.

## *The traditional publishing process*

In the traditional publishing process (you can see an outline of this in figure 7.1) the author types the text of the book (this is called the **copy** or the **typescript**) on a typewriter or word processor and supplies rough drawings and photographs for illustrations. The copy is then typed into a special machine called a typesetting machine, which has all the right typefaces and styles needed. Once the text has been put into the typesetting machine (it has been typeset), it is printed out (this printout is called a **proof**) and someone has to check it for mistakes. The corrections must be entered on the text held on

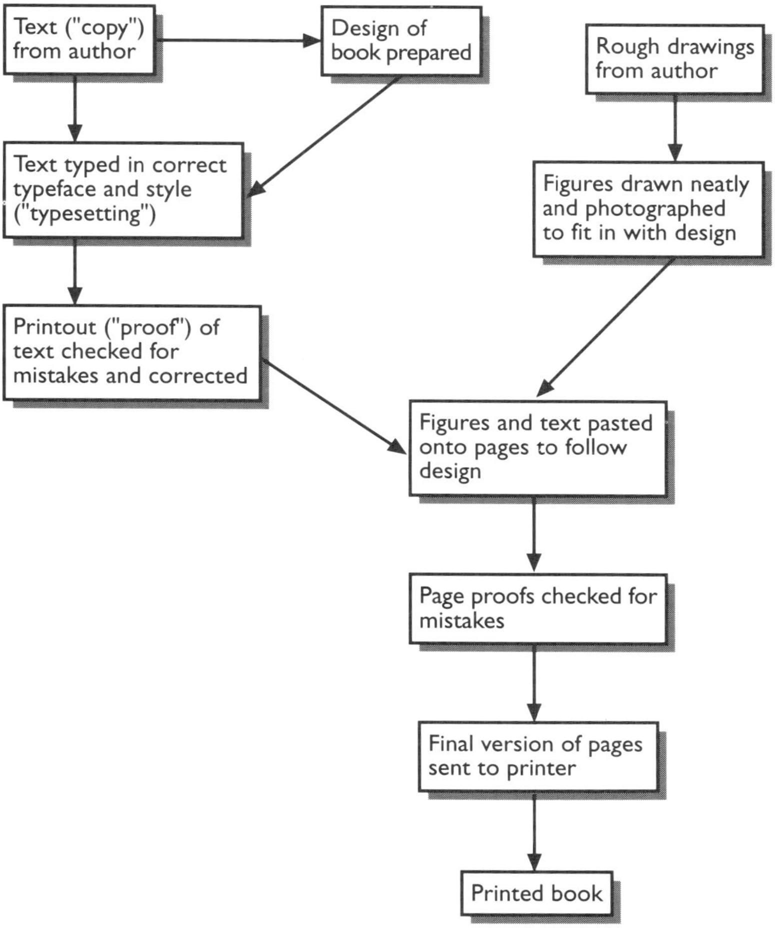


**FIGURE 7.1** *A rough outline of the traditional publishing process*

the typesetting machine. At the same time as the text is being typeset, the pages are designed and any pictures needed are drawn and photographed so that they can be reproduced. The corrected text and the pictures are then pasted onto the pages to fit the page design and another proof, this time of the whole page, is printed and must be checked. The pages are corrected again, printed out and checked again. Any more mistakes are corrected. Once everyone involved is happy with the way the pages look they are sent to the printer.

## The desktop publishing process

In figure 7.2 you can see the main features of DTP. Here are the typical steps that you would use to create a publication using a DTP package

1 The text is written on a word processor.

2 The graphics are created using a graphics package, or are imported using a scanner.
3 Templates for the document are designed. The template will include the number of columns of text that will go on a page, where the graphics will go and page numbers. This operation involves the same skills as page design in the traditional process.
4 The text is imported from the word processor and placed on the page where needed. The text should already have been checked for mistakes using the spelling checker in the word processor. If there is too much text to fit on a single page it will run on to the next page, and you can set the text to flow around the places reserved for graphics.
5 Data from other programs can also be imported – like a table or a chart that you created in a spreadsheet package.
6 The graphics are inserted into the places reserved for them. You may have to cut the picture to fit (this is called cropping) or scale it to suit the space available on the page.
7 The final document is printed. This can be done on a high-quality laser printer, but if you want a really high-quality printout or a large number of copies (for example when printing a book, a magazine or a newspaper) printing can be done by a professional printer. The pages that you have created are saved on a disk which you would send to the printer. If the printer has a computer system compatible with yours and a modem then you could send the disk file containing the pages directly to the printer via electronic mail (more about this in Chapter 9). Writers who prefer to work from home often use electronic mail to send their material to the printer.

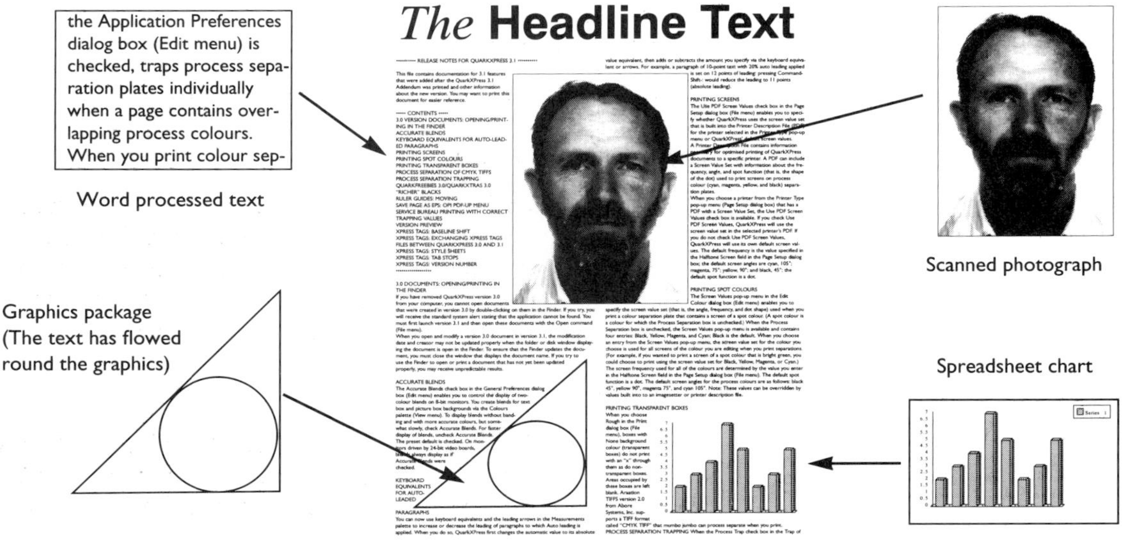


**FIGURE 7.2** *The main features of DTP*

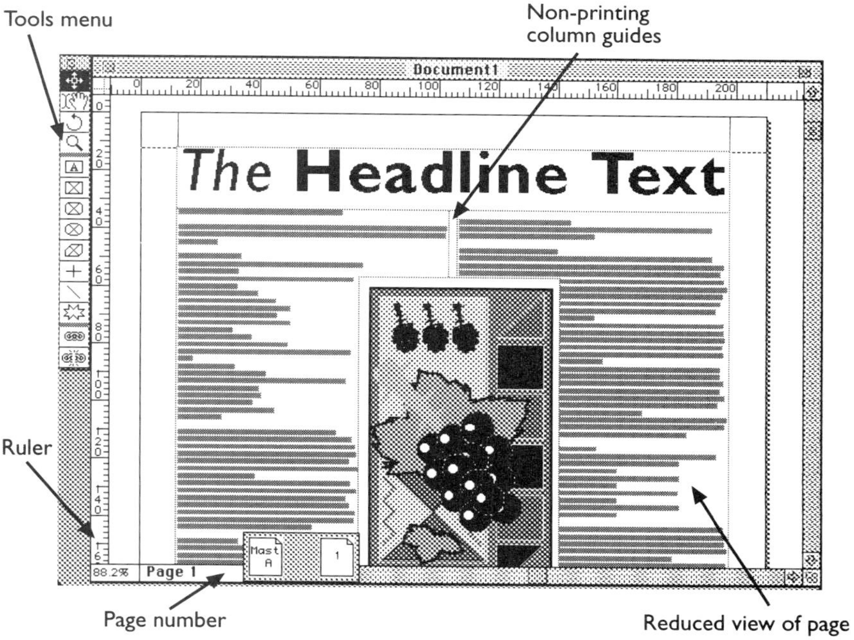


**FIGURE 7.3** *A DTP package in action*

# Features of DTP packages

DTP packages have all the features of general purpose packages, but also have some special features, like

- text columns
- banner headlines
- drop capitals
- templates
- text flow around graphics.

Let's look at these features more closely.

## Columns of text

In many publications (such as magazines and newspapers) the text is laid out in columns rather than across the whole page. With a DTP package you can set out the text in columns. Some word processors also let you do this, but what you can produce is very limited compared with a DTP package.

## Banner headlines

A banner headline is text set in a large typeface and arranged across the whole page – it is not included in the main body of the text. A banner headline is also often called a **masthead**.

### Drop capitals

A drop capital is a large initial letter at the beginning of a paragraph of text. Drop capitals are often used to draw the reader's attention to the beginning of an article. You will see these in most newspaper and magazine articles.

### Templates

On a DTP system you can create **templates** or **master pages**. The templates can be used to mark out standard layouts for a number of pages. For example, in a newsletter you might want to use two columns of text on editorial pages, three columns for features pages, and four columns for news pages. Using the template you can create as many different master pages as you want – one for each kind of page layout you want. Some DTP packages will give you some ready-made templates that you can use for different types of publication. Using these ready-made templates can speed up the process of laying out a page, especially if you haven't used a DTP package before.

### Text flow around graphics

You can choose to flow the text round a graphic, rather than have to leave, say, half a page for a picture. This can give a very pleasing effect and can save space on the page from being wasted or unused.

If you look back at figure 7.2 you will see many of these features being used.

## QUESTIONS

### Knowledge and understanding

1 Name three features of a DTP package and explain what each is used for. Cut out and collect examples of these features from newspapers or magazines.
  Make a poster for the classroom.
2 What are the main steps involved in the desktop publishing process?
  Which skills are needed both in DTP and traditional publishing?

### Problem solving

1 Many newspapers are printed far from the journalist's office where the articles are written. Suggest how computers could be used to communicate with the printing works.
  What hardware would you need to do this?
2 Obtain a copy of a newspaper or magazine which was produced using a DTP package. Try to find out which package was used, and some details about the hardware used.

## *More to do*

DTP packages have even more features than those already described

### *Typefaces*

A DTP package allows you to vary the typeface more than a word processor does. A **typeface** is the design of a set of characters (letters or numbers). It is also called a **font**. There are many fonts. Here a few:

Times
Helvetica
Σψμβολ

The style of a typeface is the kind of character in a font which is used. Normal type (like most of the text in this book) is called roman or regular – you could also use *italic* or SMALL CAPITALS.

The size of a typeface (how big it is) is measured in points. There are 72 points in an inch. Most of the text of this book is 12 point – it is one-sixth of an inch high.

The weight of the text is the blackness of the characters – for example **bold** text is more black than roman.

### *Style sheets*

In any publication you should be very careful to be consistent in the way you use the typographical style – changing heading style or text size every couple of pages

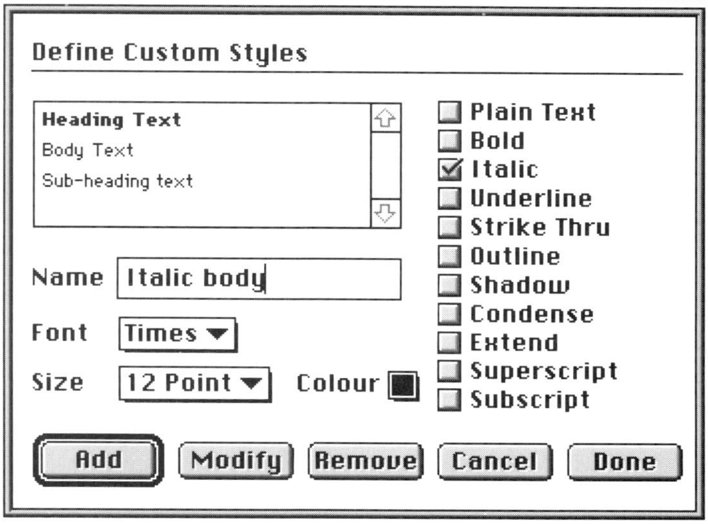


**FIGURE 7.4** *Here is a simple style sheet that you might use in a DTP package*

can be very confusing for the reader! Some DTP packages allow you to create a style sheet to specify text attributes such as

- the size and weight of the typeface
- the line and character spacing
- the tab settings and
- the page length.

In figure 7.4 you can see a simple style sheet for a DTP package. Once you have created a style sheet you can apply the same style to many features of a document, without having to set the typeface individually for each one.

## *Differences between packages*

As microcomputer systems become more powerful and software packages offer more features, the differences between different packages are becoming less distinct. Many word processing packages now offer most of the features described here for DTP packages. Many graphics drawing packages can now be used for page layout. Many DTP packages now offer word processing and spell checker facilities, so you can create your text directly in the DTP package rather than typing it into a word processor and importing it.

# EXTRA QUESTIONS

### Knowledge and understanding

1. Describe the three features of a typeface
2. Why is the ability to create a style sheet particularly useful in a DTP package?

### Problem solving

1. Look at some advertisements for DTP and word processing packages.
   Make a list of any features that are used by both types of packages.
2. Jane has just bought a word processor which allows her to put text into columns. She says that she can use it as a DTP package.
   Do you agree with Jane?
   What features is she unlikely to find in her word processor that she may need for desktop publishing?

## KEY POINTS

- Desktop publishing is a way of producing professional quality printed material on a microcomputer system
- Desktop publishing leaves less room for mistakes than traditional publishing because there are fewer stages and fewer people involved in DTP
- Desktop publishing packages have features such as columns, banner headlines, drop capitals, templates, text flow around graphics, different typefaces, style sheets

# 8 Teletext and Viewdata

## *What is Teletext?*

Teletext is the name given to the information services that the television companies provide in the form of pages which they send with the television signal. You can only use Teletext when television programmes are being transmitted. Figure 8.1 gives you a brief outline of how Teletext is transmitted.

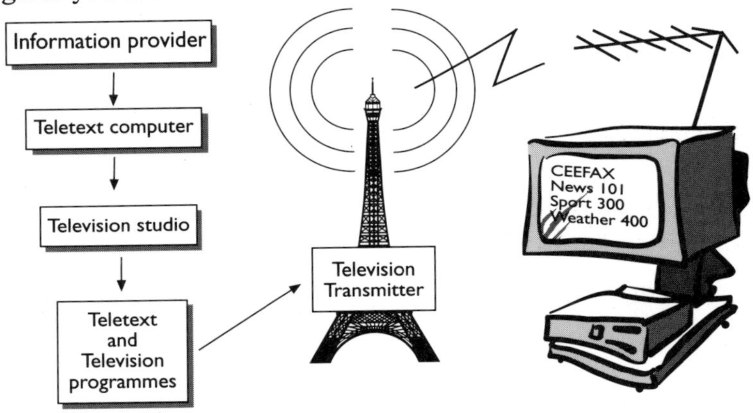


**FIGURE 8.1** *Teletext transmission*

### Teletext services

There are several Teletext services:

- The BBC Teletext service is called CEEFAX
- ITV provides Teletext on 3
- Other television channels like satellite television have their own Teletext services.

The photograph on the next page shows you some of the services that TV companies provide.

### Information on Teletext

Companies store the information on the Teletext pages in a database on a large computer system.

The sorts of information you can access on Teletext include

- news
- sport
- travel

**DATABASE**

a structured collection of similar information which can be searched

- weather
- stock market prices
- television programme listings
- children's pages
- cinema
- hobbies
- recipes.

The information on Teletext is generally more interesting to users at home than to businesses. Teletext pages are changed or updated regularly throughout the day.

### Costs of Teletext

Because the pages are sent with the television signal, Teletext is free – provided you've bought a television licence! Once you have bought the Teletext television or the adapter and a TV licence then you do not need to pay any more.

### Limitations of Teletext

Teletext is only a one-way system. You can receive pages, but can't send any information back to the television company that provides the service. You can't use Teletext to send messages to another user.

## *Hardware*

Not every television set is able to receive Teletext – you need special hardware.

- The television must be fitted with a decoder so that it can decode the Teletext signals. Teletext televisions are about 20 per cent more expensive than ordinary television sets because they are fitted with this decoder.
- You need a keypad or remote control handset so you can select the pages.
- If you want to use your computer to receive Teletext it must be fitted with a Teletext adapter. When a computer is used with an adapter, it will only receive Teletext. You won't be able to look at television pictures and sound unless your monitor also has a television tuner.
- Whether you use your TV or a computer, you need a TV aerial.

## *Pages and frames*

Teletext information is sent out in **pages**. Each page has a page number. Three numbers are used to identify each page. The lowest number used is 100 and the highest is 999, so there are up to 900 different page numbers possible. This might seem a bit limited for all the information that is put out, but the actual number of screens of information (these are called frames) has no limit – a page may consist of any number of frames.

Each channel holds about 300 pages of information. More pages being transmitted means there are more to scroll through, and it takes longer for the particular page you want to come round.

# How to operate Teletext

*A Teletext TV handset*

To operate Teletext you need a keypad or remote control handset. You can see a typical handset that you would use to operate Teletext in the photograph.

## Choosing a page

To choose a page, key the number in to the television remote control handset, or type it on the computer keyboard. The page number at the top left of the screen will automatically change as you type the numbers. This gives useful feedback – it lets you check that you haven't made a mistake. Once you have entered all three digits, the system cycles through the pages from the page currently being transmitted to the one you want, and you must wait until the page you want appears on the screen. The time between requesting a page and the page arriving is called the **response time**.

The top line of a typical Teletext page looks like this

P100 CEEFAX 100 Thu 26 Dec 14.54/34

This shows the page number you have selected (P100), the name of the service (CEEFAX), the page currently on display (100), the date (Thu 26 Dec) and the time, including seconds. The frame number is usually displayed on another line. It lets you know what frame number you're on and how many frames there are on the current page (like 2/5 or 4/8).

## Choosing a frame

The page you have chosen might contain a number of frames. These frames cycle in the same way that the pages do. You have no way of selecting a particular frame, so if the display arrives at frame 10 of 14 and you want frame 7, you will have to wait for it to cycle round to frame 7.

To stop a page from cycling to the next frame before you are ready, press the hold button on the handset. If you have not finished reading frame 2/5 then pressing the hold button will stop the next frame (3/5) being displayed until you press hold again and release the frame.

**LOCAL AREA NETWORK (LAN)**

a network confined to a single room or building

## Making your own pages

A piece of software called a **Teletext editor** allows you to make up your own Teletext pages. Some schools use a Teletext editor to produce a daily magazine of Teletext pages which can be displayed throughout the school on a local area network by software such as COMMUNITEL.

## QUESTIONS

### Knowledge and understanding

1 What is Teletext?
2 What hardware do you need to access Teletext?
3 What is the difference between a page and a frame on Teletext?
4 What costs are involved in receiving Teletext?
5 How does a user operate Teletext?

### Problem solving

1 Why is Teletext called a one-way system?
2 What must you do to stop a Teletext page from cycling through frames?

### Practical activities

1 Design a frame of information for Teletext on a topic of your choice.
Use a Teletext screen planning grid or a piece of squared paper (40 x 25 squares).
Use colour and graphics to brighten up your frame.
If you have access to a Teletext editor, transfer the frame to the screen, save it to disk and print it out.
2 Look at the questions below. For each question, write down the channel, page and frame number where you found the answer. (You will need access to a Teletext television or a computer with a Teletext adapter to answer these questions.)

(a) Which page contains instructions on how to use Teletext?
(b) What channel has information on air quality?
(c) What is the top video this week?
(d) What films are on at the Odeon in Glasgow?
(e) How many different sports are covered by Teletext pages?
(f) Name two firms who advertise on Teletext.
(g) How many football matches has East Stirling drawn this season?
(h) How many points has Queen's Park Football Club?
(i) What is the highest page number on CEEFAX? On Teletext on 3?
(j) What is on the pages in the last question?
(k) How much does an ounce of gold cost?
(l) What is the weather like today in Peking? In Toronto? In Karachi?
(m) What is on Radio 4 at 8.30 tonight?
(n) How many films are on BBC this week?
(o) What is the weather forecast for your area tomorrow?
(p) What is the current exchange rate for US dollars?
(q) List two competitions that are on this week.

## *More to do*

**KILOBYTE (k)**

1024 bytes

### *Extra facilities available on Teletext*

- Each Teletext page is made up of characters and low-resolution (block) graphics.
- Each page can hold 25 lines of 40 characters, which takes about 1 kilobyte to store.
- The colours available are white, red, yellow, green, blue, cyan and magenta.
- Special codes can be used to make the characters on the screen flash, or become invisible until you press a button (these facilities are called **conceal** and **reveal**).

- **ALARM**

  Because the time is transmitted as part of the Teletext signal, most Teletext televisions allow you to set a time for an alarm message to be displayed on the screen.

- **SUBTITLES**

  Teletext is often used to display **subtitles** for television programmes. The dialogue is superimposed on the picture at the bottom of the screen when you select a particular page (on CEEFAX page 888 gives subtitles). This is particularly helpful for hearing-impaired people. Subtitles are also often shown for a film or TV programme being transmitted in a foreign language.

- **RESIZING THE SCREEN**

  Any Teletext page can be enlarged on the screen. The **size** facility will display the top or bottom of the page in double height characters (the whole page won't fit!). This facility is especially useful for visually impaired users.

- **MOVING AROUND TELETEXT QUICKLY**

  Some Teletext TV handsets let you store the next page in a sequence and then display it immediately instead of having to type in the number. For example, if you choose page 103, page 104 would be stored and all you have to do to display it is to press the 'next page' button.

  The handset may have coloured buttons that take you to menu pages in the system, allowing you to move very quickly to the correct page without having to key in or remember individual page numbers. This facility is sometimes advertised as 'Fastext'.

## *Teletext adapters*

Users of Teletext adapters can access some additional features which someone using a Teletext TV set can't.

- Individual frames can be saved and printed out.
- You can select individual frames from a page, but this is not automatic – you may have to write a computer program to do it.
- If you have suitable software, you can use the adapter as a **Teletext file server** on a local area network. This allows several users at different stations on the network to access Teletext, as if each one had an adapter at their own computer.
- You can receive computer programs.

## *Telesoftware*

The name given to computer programs that are transmitted as Teletext or Viewdata pages is Telesoftware. Receiving telesoftware is called **downloading** it.

The BBC was the first company to distribute software by Teletext. They originally set up the service as part of the BBC computer project and it was funded by a premium on sales of Teletext adapters for the BBC model B computer. Channel 4 also provided a limited telesoftware service. The service closed in 1989, but it was sending out a wide range of software, for both BBC and IBM computers.

Many independent organisations and individuals run Viewdata bulletin boards which distribute telesoftware for many computer formats. The most well known of these formats was MICRONET on PRESTEL, which sadly was closed in October 1991.

## *Speed of Teletext transmission*

Teletext data is broadcast at about 4000 characters per second. This is equivalent to four pages of information each second. A transmission speed of one character per second is called one **baud**. For one channel to broadcast 300 pages will take 75 seconds (300 divided by four), so any single page is transmitted once every 75 seconds. This could be the longest you would have to wait for the page you want. What actually happens is the pages used most often (like menu page 100 on CEEFAX) are broadcast more than once during a cycle of pages so you don't have to wait too long for it to come around.

## EXTRA QUESTIONS

**Knowledge and understanding**

1 What additional features do you get if you use a Teletext adapter?
2 What is telesoftware?
3 How much storage space (in kilobytes) is needed for a Teletext page ?
4 Describe some of the features provided by Teletext.

**Problem solving**

1 What is the longest time you would have to wait for a page on Teletext if the channel was broadcasting
(a) 200 pages?
(b) 500 pages?
2 Select an item from the news on Teletext. Compare the information with the information from other sources – newspapers, television and radio news reports. Did you get the same information from each source? Which source was easiest to understand? Which account was most interesting?

# *What is Viewdata?*

**WIDE AREA NETWORK (WAN)**
a network which covers a large geographical area like a country. Used for long-distance communication via satellite, radio or telephone line

Viewdata is the name given to the pages of information sent over a computer network, down the telephone system. The computer receiving the pages is linked via a wide area network to a large computer holding the database of information. Figure 8.2 is a brief outline of how Viewdata is transmitted.

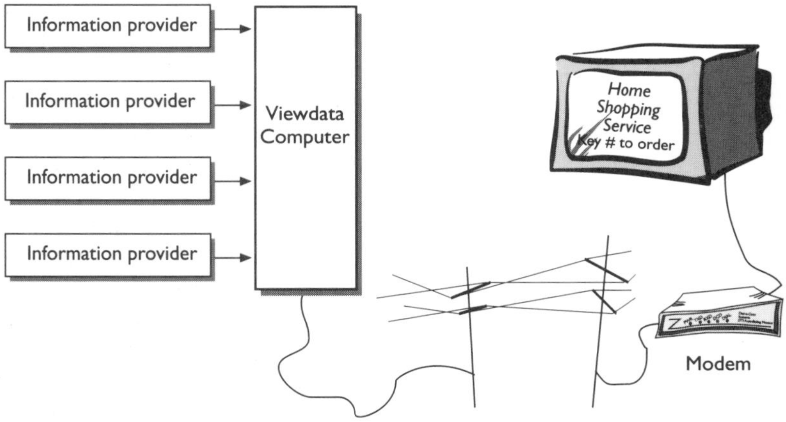


**FIGURE 8.2** *Viewdata transmission*

**ON LINE**

connected to a computer system

### Two-way communication

Viewdata communication is two way – you can send as well as receive messages. Because of this, Viewdata is sometimes called **interactive** communication. Viewdata is also known as an on-line system because the user is connected to the main computer directly by the telephone line.

### Viewdata pages

Like Teletext, Viewdata is transmitted as pages and frames. The pages and frames in Viewdata don't cycle around automatically like Teletext – they appear when you ask for them.

The number of pages in Viewdata is very large – PRESTEL has over 300 000 pages of information, and it is only one Viewdata system. A PRESTEL page can contain up to 26 frames – for example page 3000 will have frames 3000a, 3000b and so on up to 3000z. You cannot see PRESTEL frames out of sequence. When you select a page, you always see frame 'a' first.

## *Hardware*

- To receive Viewdata you need a computer system with a modem (for more information on modems look back to Chapter 1).
- To receive Viewdata on an ordinary television set you need a special keypad or a dedicated Viewdata terminal (one of these is shown in the photograph).
- Whether you use a computer or a TV set, you must be connected to a telephone line.

## *Operating a Viewdata system*

### Logging on

To access a Viewdata system, you must connect to the Viewdata computer by dialling a telephone number. You can program your communications software and modem to dial the number automatically. You must then log on to the system by typing a user identity and password. (Remember these terms? They are explained in Chapter 1.) Your user identity tells the computer who you are and your password (which you should keep secret) proves to the computer that you are who your user identity says you are. Once the computer is sure of you it will log you on, and usually responds to a successful log on by printing an appropriate message on the screen. You can't change your user identity, since it is given to you by the system, but you should change your password frequently so that no-one can discover it. No-one can log on without the right password for that user identity. Keeping your password secret stops people accessing the system who aren't supposed to.

Once you have logged on, the system will present you with a menu screen like the one in the photo.

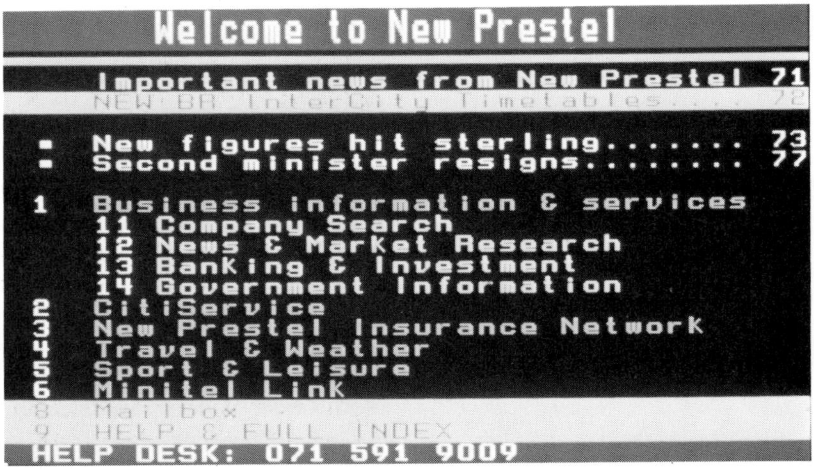


*PRESTEL's main menu*

## Choosing a page

The way you select a page depends on the particular Viewdata service you are using, but three methods are commonly used.

**1 Choosing from a menu**

The most straightforward method is to choose a page from a menu pressing the number shown will take you to the page you want.

The top line of a typical Viewdata page looks like this

CITISERVICE 881a

Premium Time charge 31p/min

This shows the name of the organisation who produced the page – the information provider (CITISERVICE), the page number (881), the frame letter (a) and the charge. If a service carries a premium charge this is shown on the page. In this case the charge is 31p per minute. Page charges on PRESTEL can range from 0p to 45p on average. The system will always warn you if the page you are about to see has a charge.

### MENUS ON PRESTEL

Because the PRESTEL database is so large, you may have to go through several menus to find the page you want. If you are not familiar with the information available, start at the main menu on page 1. If you want details about train times go to the British Rail main menu, then to the regions sub-menu and so on until you find what you want.

2 **Remembering the page number**
If the user knows the page number, he or she can key it in and will be taken directly to that page. An example would be *88801345#, where the # symbol means press the <RETURN> or <ENTER> key.

3 **Keyword routing**
Some systems have a third method of finding information. This is called keyword routing. To find a particular page you can key in a keyword (like *TRAVEL#). The system will then take you to an appropriate page (*TRAVEL# would take you to a page about travel, *WEATHER# would take you to a page about the weather *PROFILE# would take you to *The Financial Times* profile directory).

## *Messaging*

Because your terminal is connected directly to the main computer, you can send messages to other Viewdata users using the mailbox facility. A **mailbox** is an area on the main computer where messages are stored until they are read. All the users of a Viewdata service have their own **mailbox number**. To send a message, use a blank page (called a message frame), type the mailbox number of the person you want to mail and then type the message. The message will be sent immediately into the recipient's mailbox. The next time he logs on, he will be told that a new message is waiting for him. Once he has read it, the message can be stored, printed out or deleted from the mailbox. You can send the same message to several users at the same time. Viewdata systems have colour graphics, and you can send greetings using ready made frames.

Messaging is one form of electronic mail which is explained in Chapter 9.

## QUESTIONS

### Knowledge and understanding

1 Describe the three methods of finding a page using a Viewdata system.
2 What is a mailbox?
3 Which service, Teletext or Viewdata, is interactive?
Describe three other differences between Teletext and Viewdata.

### Problem solving

1 Why does a Viewdata service need a password when Teletext does not?
What could happen if someone discovers your password?
2 How would you send a message to another user on a Viewdata system?

## More to do

### Closed user groups

Some areas of the PRESTEL database are private, and you can only access them by paying an extra subscription. You then become a member of the **closed user group**. When you log on to PRESTEL, the computer can tell from your user identity which user group(s) you belong to and it will normally direct you straight to your user group. If you do not belong to a closed user group, the computer will send you to the main PRESTEL menu after logging on.

### Response frames

A **response frame** can be used for replying to an advertisement, to order goods or to take part in a survey. Instead of a blank message frame, the information provider generates a response frame which consists of a series of questions only requiring short answers. This means that users find it easy to complete and have less chance of making mistakes. If you are ordering goods you can pay for them immediately by entering your credit card number on part of the response frame. Only the information provider can generate response frames. The system manager then loads the response frames onto the Viewdata service.

### Hosts and gateways

The Viewdata computer that has the database of information is known as the **host computer** and is linked to other host computers by a **gateway**. A gateway is a link between two different computers.

When someone logs on to PRESTEL the PRESTEL computer is the host. If the user wants to access the careers computer, the PRESTEL computer will pass her to it through the careers gateway, and the careers computer becomes the host. When the user has finished with the careers computer it passes her back through the gateway to the PRESTEL computer, which becomes the host computer again.

### Speed of Viewdata transmission

Viewdata is sent out from the host computer at a speed of 1200 characters per second (or 1200 baud). Each Viewdata page is the same size as a Teletext page

(1kilobyte), so it should take just under one second to transmit a Viewdata page. When you type data in a Viewdata response frame, it is transmitted back to the main computer at a speed of 75 baud. Viewdata has a faster response time than Teletext because there is no cycling of pages.

## *Costs of using Viewdata*

Users of any Viewdata service will have to pay the cost of the telephone call. Users must also pay

1 a subscription to the particular service
2 time charges when on line
3 a subscription to any of the closed user groups they belong to
4 premium service charges for using certain parts of the database

## *Some Viewdata services*

### Phonebase

Phonebase is provided by British Telecom. It contains the complete telephone directory for the whole United Kingdom, organised into a database system. Phonebase is connected to the British Telecom computer which handles the normal directory enquiries service. This means that you can search the database instead of having to look through a book, which can save time. Using Phonebase can be cheaper than telephoning Directory Enquiries.

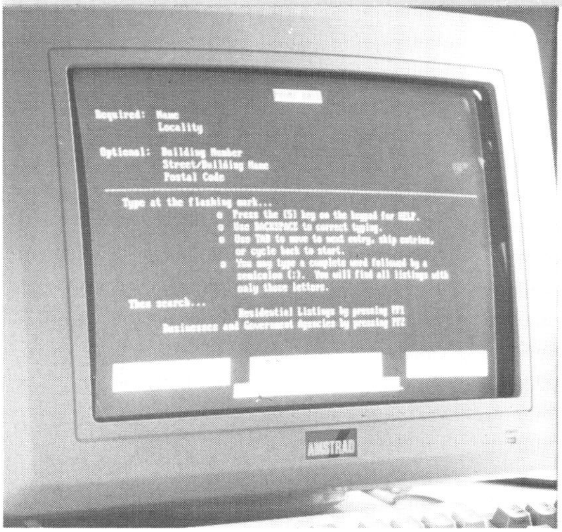


*Phonebase*

### Electronic Yellow Pages

Electronic Yellow Pages is also provided by British Telecom. It is set up in a similar way to Phonebase.

*Electronic Yellow Pages*

### Teleshopping

You can use Viewdata to purchase goods or services from the comfort of your own home using your television and Viewdata keypad (or home computer and modem) – this is called **teleshopping**. Interflora is one of the organisations which provides a teleshopping service that you can access through the PRESTEL gateway. You may select flowers and other gifts from lists on screen and pay for them using your credit card.

## EXTRA QUESTIONS

### Knowledge and understanding

1 Compare these features of Teletext and Viewdata
  Availability
  Costs
  Speed of transmission and response
  Quantity of information provided
  Communication with other users
  The help facilities on each service.
2 Find out what is meant by the term videotex.
3 What is a gateway?
4 Find out if any other countries have Teletext or Viewdata services. Give the names of the countries and the services they provide.

**Problem solving**

1 A new company which repairs vacuum cleaners wishes to advertise.
Which type of service, Teletext or Viewdata would you advise the company to choose and why?
Which service would you recommend for use at home?

2 Teleshopping is buying goods or services using Viewdata.
Some people think that teleshopping will replace visiting shops in person. Do you agree with this idea?
Give two advantages and two disadvantages of teleshopping.

3 One Teletext service used to be advertised as 'The ultimate newspaper'.
Will Teletext replace newspapers?
Give a reason for your answer.

4 Approximately how many pages of information are available on PRESTEL?
What amount of storage space would be needed to hold all of this information?
What type of backing storage device (disk or tape) would you recommend for PRESTEL?
Why?

**Practical activities**

1 If you have access to VIEWDATA, try out some of the databases listed in this chapter.
Try to find another two databases and explain what information they provide.

## KEY POINTS

- Teletext is information services provided by the television companies
- Teletext pages are sent along with the television signal
- To receive Teletext, you must have a special TV set or a computer with an adapter
- A Teletext page may be made up of one or more frames
- You can make up your own Teletext pages using a program called a Teletext editor
- Teletext is a one-way system
- Computer programs received via Teletext are called telesoftware
- Viewdata is information sent over a computer network.
- To receive Viewdata, you must be linked to the remote computer via the telephone system
- To receive Viewdata you need either a computer system and modem or a Viewdata terminal
- Viewdata is a two-way (interactive) system
- A user identity and a password are normally required to enter Viewdata
- Viewdata systems charge for the information they provide
- Messages can be sent on Viewdata using a response frame
- Messages are stored in an area called a mailbox until they are read
- A Viewdata system may allow you access to other systems through a gateway
- You can do your shopping from home by ordering goods through Viewdata

# 9 Electronic mail

## What is electronic mail?

**NETWORK**

two or more computers joined together so that data can be transferred between them

**WIDE AREA NETWORK (WAN)**

a network which covers a large geographical area like a country. Used for long-distance communication via satellite, radio or telephone line

Electronic mail is a way of sending messages from one computer to another, usually over telephone lines. You could type a letter on a word processor and send it from your terminal to another one on the network. Electronic mail is most useful when the two terminals are part of a wide area network and a long way apart. You will often hear people talking about 'e-mail', which is what 'electronic mail' is usually shortened to.

Instead of writing a document or letter on a word processor and posting it, you send it via the telephone to another terminal. You don't need to print your letter on paper, no envelopes or stamps are needed, and no postman delivers the letter. If the person at the other end isn't using the system (if they're not logged on) when the message arrives, the computer stores it until they're ready to read it. This means information can be passed from one place to another straight away.

Electronic mail is used a lot for sending letters, but anything which can be saved to disk can be sent by electronic mail – a data file, a computer program, a file containing a newspaper produced by a desktop publishing package, a graphics file.

If you live in a remote area you might be able to work from home and communicate with your office using electronic mail. This is known as **teleworking**, and several companies have tried it – like British Telecom and the company in the photograph.

*Teleworking*

### Gaelic line from Lewis

THE Gaelic language boom is offering even more possibilities to the growing number of "teleworkers" already attracted to the Highlands and Islands the spread of high-tech communications, writes **COLIN McSeveny.**

A loose network of around 100 people in the remotest parts of Scotland now use the telephone, fax, and personal computer to run their businesses, normally dealing with clients hundreds of miles away.

Annie MacSween is one Lewis native who has not been forced to follow in the footsteps of so many of her ancestors and leave the islands.

Her clients range from television companies, which have committed an unprecedented level of funds to help revive interest in the language, to educational institutes and specialist publishers.

"I am limited only by how many commissions I have to turn down for time reasons and it is clear that there is a lot of scope for expanding this kind of work throughout the Highlands, particularly given the current upsurge in interest in the language," she said.

"The advantages to businesses are obvious in that the overheads in using me for such services are virtually nonexistent," she added.

Regional officials agree that the establishment of digital communications — Highland and Islands Enterprise has invested £16m with BT — should lead to further expansion in the next few years.

"There is now a growing army of teleworkers in the region, ranging from people providing a basic secretarial service or software problem-solving to consultancy and translation," HIE's John Lough said.

Western Isles Enterprise chief executive Donnie MacAulay also welcomed the trend, saying it allowed people the ideal mix of rural life and highly-skilled employment. "Much of this knowledge-type work is ideally suited to the Western Isles and we are keen to back individuals with good commercial projects in this sector," he said.

*—The Herald 31/3/1992*

**PASSWORD**

a secret code that you use to access private information on a computer system or to log on to a network

### Electronic mail services

One of the largest electronic mail services in the United Kingdom is Telecom GOLD, which was launched by British Telecom in March 1982. More than 105 000 people subscribe to Telecom GOLD. Each one has their own user identity and password. The Telecom GOLD user's user identity is the same as their mailbox number (for example, 01:PVE001 or 01:TCD001). A version of Telecom GOLD is used for schools and educational purposes. It is called CAMPUS 2000.

CAMPUS 2000 has quite a few facilities especially for educational use. These include

- Electronic mail
- Conferencing
- A directory of users
- Access to specialised educational databases and many other services like INTERNET, DIALOG and JANET.

**GATEWAY**

a link between two different host computers

You can access the above services from CAMPUS 2000 through a gateway which allows the system to connect to different computers.

## *The equipment you need for electronic mail*

The hardware you need depends on whether the electronic mail service is operating on a local area network or on a wide area network. You can see the kind of hardware you need for electronic mail and Viewdata in Figure 9.1.

**LOCAL AREA NETWORK (LAN)**

a network confined to a single room or building

**HARDWARE**

the physical parts or devices which make up a computer system

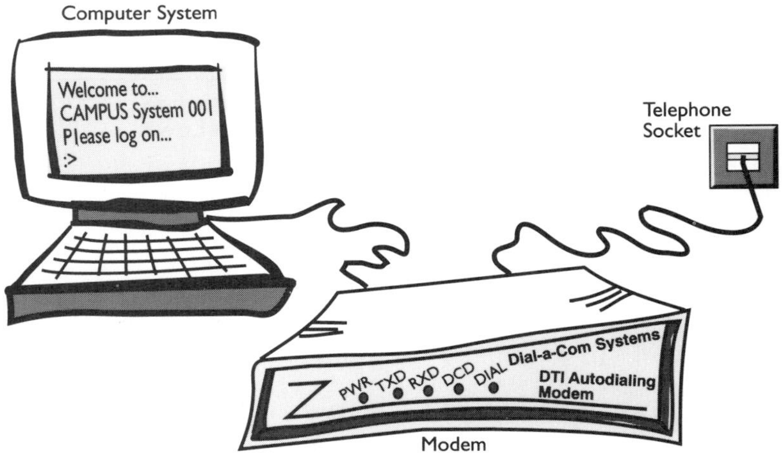


**FIGURE 9.1** *The hardware you need to use electronic mail and Viewdata*

**MODEM**

a device used to connect a computer system to a telephone line. Modem is short for **mo**dulator–**dem**odulator

**SOFTWARE**

the programs that the hardware of the computer runs

- If it is on a local area network, then all you need is a computer system connected to the network and suitable communications software.
- If the electronic mail service is operating on a wide area network, you need a modem and a subscription to the service as well.

### Software

- Two examples of electronic mail packages suitable for use on a local area network are MACEMAIL (for Acorn computers) and TOPMAIL (for Apple Macintosh computers).
- Communications software you'd need to work on a wide area network are HEARSAY and DIALUP (for Acorn computers) and RED RYDER and VICOM (for the Macintosh). Many integrated packages, like MICROSOFT WORKS have communications software suitable for accessing electronic mail on a wide area network.

## Using electronic mail on CAMPUS 2000

Here is an example of an electronic mail session on CAMPUS 2000 where messages are going between two schools in Scotland. Really it doesn't matter how far apart the two users are – they could be in the next room or another continent. The text in bold shows what the user has to type in.

```
Welcome to the CAMPUS System 01
Please Log on
> id pve061
Password:
The Campus 2000 System 19.4Q.106(01)
On At 21:44 30/12/94 GMT
Last On At 20:41 29/12/94 GMT

Mail call (14 Read, 2 Unread, 1 Unread express,
Total 17)

>mail read

To: ST.ANDREW'S.ACAD.AYR (PVE061)
From: DUNROAMIN.HIGH (DUN007) Delivered:Fri 30-Dec-
94 22:05 GMT Sys 10001 (7)
Subject: SHUG MEETING NEXT WEEK
Mail Id: IPM-10001-941230-198870826
```

```
Dear John

Please note that the next meeting of the Strathdon
Higher User Group (SHUG) will take place on Tuesday
and not Wednesday of next week.

Please reply

Jemima


Action Required: reply
Text:

Dear Jemima

Thank you for letting me know
See you on Tuesday

Regards

John
.send

Mail Id: IPM-10001-941230-199030218

DUNROAMIN.HIGH -- Sent

Action Required:
```

Did you notice that when the user logs on at the beginning the password doesn't appear on the screen. Why, do you think?

## More features of electronic mail

- The user could set up the system to automatically acknowledge the letter as soon as they've read it.
- Individual letters can be protected by a password, so only the person who was sent the letter can read it. This is particularly useful if the electronic mailbox belongs to an organisation (such as a school) rather than to one person.
- If the message is urgent, it can be sent 'express'. Express messages don't get there any faster, but they go to the top of the person's list of messages to be read.
- Also, if the receiver is using their electronic mail system while you're sending them an express message, the system will alert them that urgent mail has arrived for them.

### On and off line

When the user is connected to the electronic mail system, he or she is *on line*. When they're not connected they're *off line*. When you're on line you are charged the cost of the telephone call to the electronic mail computer. You'll quickly find that it's cheaper to write a letter off line on a word processor, save it to disk, and send it later than to write it while you're on line. If you are replying to letters sent to your mailbox and the reply is short, it is quicker to reply while you're on line but if your reply is more than a few lines long it is much better to type it off line. Typing the letter off line also means you can keep a copy on disk.

## Using electronic mail on Prestel

You can see how this works in Figure 9.2. Comparing PRESTEL and CAMPUS 2000
The basic process is the same on both systems.

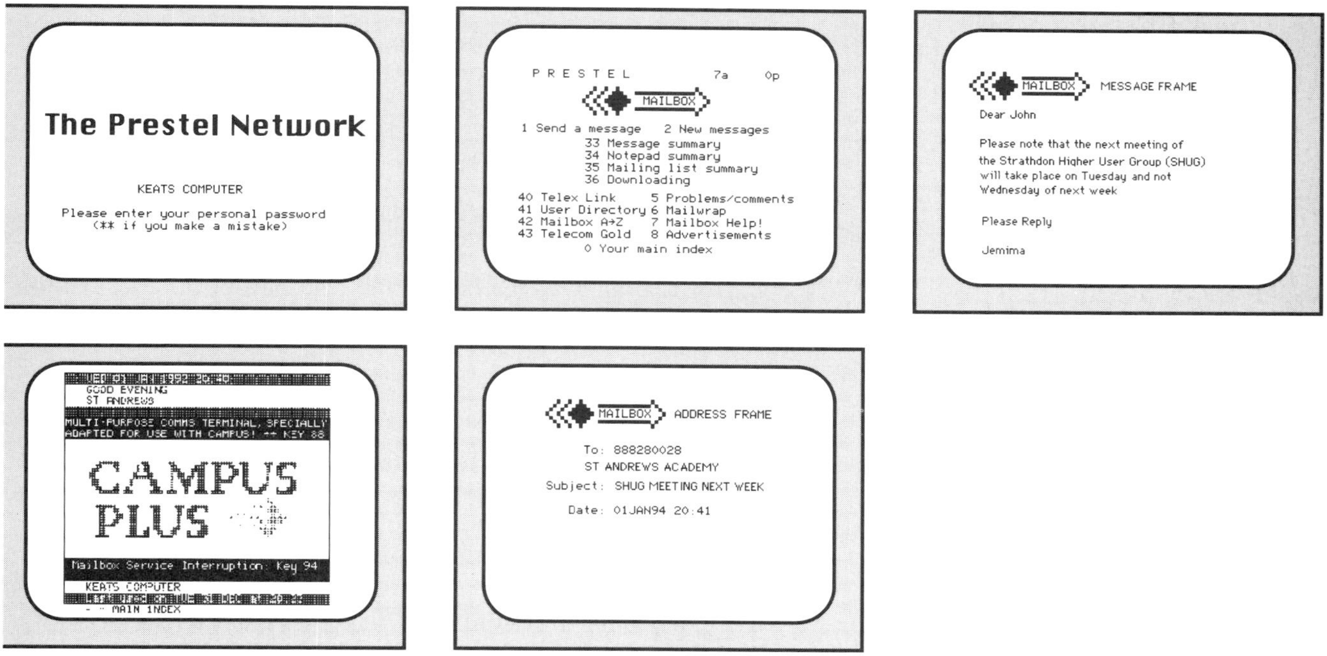


**FIGURE 9.2** *The opening log on screens and part of the PRESTEL messaging system. Replies are sent by moving to another frame and choosing reply from the menu. The user is then given another blank message frame to type the text of the reply*

1 Log on
2 Select the electronic mail facility
3 Select the function (for example send a message)
4 Type in mailbox number of recipient
5 Type your message
6 Log off.

The two systems are also quite different in some ways.

- PRESTEL is a Viewdata system and is therefore based on individual frames of text with colour and simple graphics (remember Viewdata? We looked at it in Chapter 8). When a PRESTEL message frame has been filled with text and the user wants to move on, the whole screen is cleared.
- The PRESTEL messaging system is operated by making choices from a menu.

- CAMPUS 2000 isn't based on frames – the screen scrolls or moves up as new information is added at the bottom. It is therefore called a scrolling system.
- Users of CAMPUS 2000 can choose to use menus or type in commands.
- Since CAMPUS 2000 is a scrolling system (not based on frames), it is more suited to electronic mail than PRESTEL, especially if long messages have to be transmitted, saved to disk, or printed.
- Sending messages from a word processor directly from disk is also more straightforward on CAMPUS 2000 than on PRESTEL.

**ON-LINE HELP**

help in the form of information screens available when using a computer program

Both systems provide on-line help. This means that if you forget the commands or don't know what item to choose from a menu, the system will give you instructions and advice while you're on line.

## Advantages and disadvantages of e-mail

Electronic mail systems have good and bad points. Let's look at some of these and compare electronic mail with sending a letter by post or making a telephone call.

### Advantages

- Electronic mail is much faster than sending a letter by post, since the message takes only seconds to arrive instead of days.
- Electronic mail is accurate. You are less likely to misread a letter than to misunderstand someone's voice on the telephone.
- The message may be shorter and more to the point because you don't have to waste time by saying your name (on electronic mail the name of the sender is on the header), and you can't make conversation so easily (electronic mail is less interactive than the telephone).
- Electronic mail is very accessible, since you can check electronic mail from any suitable computer anywhere in the world. If you are travelling around, you can check your mail box by logging on to the system anywhere where there is a telephone line or a satellite link.

- Electronic mail cuts across time zones, for example, between Scotland and Singapore. If the time in Scotland is 10.00 a.m. it is about 7.00 p.m. (later the same day) in Singapore and the offices in Singapore will probably be closed. But your electronic mail will be delivered to the office's mailbox just the same.
- There is no need to worry whether the person you're mailing is there to read the message because it will be stored by the system until it is read and deleted. Contacting someone during office hours by telephone can be quite difficult.
- Electronic mail is usually cheaper than sending a letter by post.
- Less paper is usually involved, because messages can be stored on disk. If you need a paper copy you can print it out.

### Disadvantages

- You must check your mailbox regularly for the system to work. You'd never think of not looking in your letterbox at home every day, yet some users of electronic mail *never* check their mailboxes. This is where the system can break down. To make efficient use of the system you should check your mail box at least once a day.
- Electronic mail can be expensive if you use it at peak periods because telephone calls cost more at peak times. But for most users connection to the system is charged at local call rates.
- The person you're mailing needs a mailbox on the system. If he doesn't have a mailbox, then you can't send electronic mail to him.
- Every letter you send will look the same on the screen and when printed out on the same printer. You can't use company letterheaded paper to impress the recipient.
- Electronic mail can be pretty impersonal because there is much less interaction between callers than there is when you're speaking on the telephone.
- Electronic mail is not yet as secure as the postal system. If someone finds out your password he might read your mail. Worse, he could change your password so you can't access the system. He could send out false mail in your name. There are no 'clues' like handwriting or a signature to prove that the message is actually from you or is a forgery. All electronic mail messages do, however, contain the time and date when they were sent so you might be able to trace a forgery.

## Facsimile transceivers

You are probably more familiar with the term fax machine than facsimile transceiver. Fax machines work like long-distance photocopiers. Text and diagrams on paper can be fed

**FACSIMILE (FAX) MACHINE**

a machine that scans a document and changes it into a signal that can be sent along a telephone line. The document is printed on another fax machine somewhere else

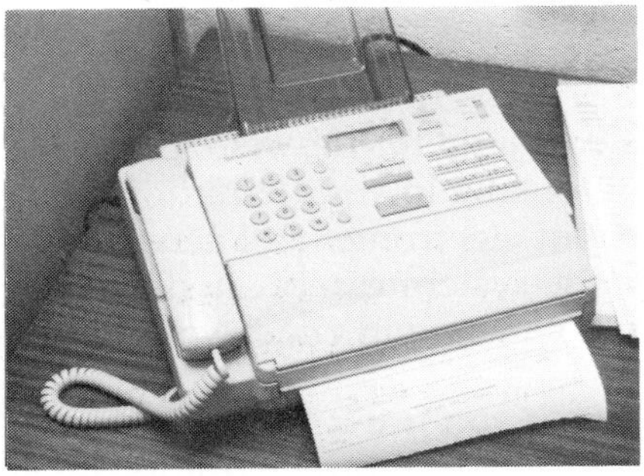

*A fax machine in operation*

into the fax machine in one place and a copy appears on a machine in another place, which may be hundreds or thousands of miles away.

### How a fax machine works

The fax machine works by scanning the paper and converting the patterns of text or diagrams into signals. These are sent along telephone lines or via satellites to another fax machine which converts the signals back into text or diagrams so you can read them. The receiving fax machine must be switched on and connected to the telephone system or the fax won't work. Usually it prints out a hard copy immediately, though on some systems you can look at the message on screen first or store it on disk if you want.

### Fax modems

You can buy a fax to add on to some computer systems. These are called **fax modems**. If you use one of these you can fax anything you've created on your computer to another fax machine (it doesn't have to be another fax modem). Some systems can receive as well as send faxes. Having a fax modem does have its disadvantages, though. It can be difficult to send something you haven't created on your computer – like a photograph or a page from a book! How could you get that type of information into your computer? Having a fax modem also means you have to leave your computer on all the time in case someone wants to fax you.

### Diskfax

A diskfax is a machine which will copy a whole diskful of data to a blank disk in a similar machine any distance away. In some instances this may be quicker and cheaper than sending the files as electronic mail. Like using a fax machine, you don't have to be very skilled at using this system to send material (compared to using electronic mail, when you do need some skill).

## *Social effects of electronic mail*

As the use of electronic mail goes up, it could have several effects on the way we work.

- Jobs involved in connecting and maintaining telephone lines, cables and satellites are likely to increase as the amount of electronic mail increases.
- Related industries (such as modem manufacturers) may increase trade and need to take on more staff.

- Jobs in the postal and messenger services could be at risk, since electronic mail is cheaper, faster and more efficient.
- However, people are unlikely to stop sending letters and cards altogether, because they are much more personal than electronic mail.
- Some official documents will probably always have to be written down or printed on paper and delivered in the traditional way. Electronic mail won't completely remove the need for this.

## QUESTIONS

### Knowledge and understanding

1 What is electronic mail?
2 What hardware and software is required to access an electronic mail service
  (a) on a local area network?
  (b) on a wide area network?
3 What is teleworking?
4 What effect might an increase in the use of electronic mail have on
  (a) postmen?
  (b) stamp collectors?
  (c) modem manufacturers?
5 What is meant by scrolling?

### Problem solving

1 Why is it cheaper to prepare electronic mail messages off line before sending them?
2 What would you need to know and what questions would you ask to find out if electronic mail is cheaper than the post?
3 Why doesn't your password come up on the screen while you're logging on to an electronic mail service?
4 What are the main steps involved in sending an electronic mail message on a wide area network?
5 Give three advantages and three disadvantages of electronic mail compared with using the post and the telephone.

### Practical activities

1 If your school has access to CAMPUS 2000 or PRESTEL, prepare a letter off line on a word processor, then upload it on to the system and send it to a nearby school.

## *More to do*

### *More facilities available on CAMPUS 2000*

**DATA FILE**

a file containing data on backing storage or in memory. Normally organised as a set of records

#### Mail reference files

A **mail reference file** is a data file which you can store in your mailbox. It may contain lists of people you can send mail to (these are called distribution lists). For example, you could set up your mail reference file to know that 'Jimmy' is mailbox number TCP009 and 'Jemima' is mailbox number DUN007. You can send mail to Jimmy or Jemima simply by typing in their name instead of their mailbox number. Using a mail reference file is like storing someone's telephone number in the memory on a telephone.

**DATABASE**

a structured collection of similar information which can be searched

A mail reference file can also hold lists of user identities grouped together under single headings. For example a group AYR could have the mailbox numbers of all the schools in Ayrshire. To send the same message to all the schools in Ayrshire all you have to do is to send the message once, and address it simply to AYR. Or you could set up groups containing individual mailbox numbers, for example PROJECT-TEAM, and send the same message to everyone in the group in one operation.

## Using the directory of users on CAMPUS 2000

One of the databases on CAMPUS 2000 you can search is the system's User Directory (it is called ENQUIRE). ENQUIRE has details of everyone who subscribes to CAMPUS 2000. Here is an example of what happened when someone used the directory to search for a school called St Andrew's. The user first typed 'andrew', but didn't get the answer he was looking for. He had to change the search string to 'st andrew' to get the information he wanted. You can search the ENQUIRE database on fields other than name. As in the last example, the words in bold are what the user typed in.

```
          ***********************
                 * CAMPUS *
           * Directory of Users *
               * (ENQUIRE) *
           *********************

Help is available at any prompt by entering .HELP
Enter DIR.INFO at the system prompt to request your
entry to be altered.

Directory Read or Scan: scan
N(ame), T(ype), L(ea), C(ontact), M(ailbox) or
.H(elp):name
Institution name: andrew
30/12/91

1 ANDREW EWING SCHOOL      PRIM HOUNSLOW  01:YOB022
2 ANDREW'S ENDOWED PRIMARY SCHOOL     PRIM HAMPSHIRE
01:YDO243
```

```
Produce labels: n
Create MAIL.REF: n
Directory Read or Scan: scan
N(ame), T(ype), L(ea), C(ontact), M(ailbox) or
.H(elp):name st andrew
30/12/91

ST ANDREW'S ACADEMY SECO STRATH AYR 01:PVE061
ST ANDREW'S ACADEMY SECO STRATH RENFREW 01:PVE198
ST ANDREW'S BOOTHSTOWN C.E.P.S PRIM SALFORD 01:YPN034
ST ANDREW'S HIGH SECO STRATH DUNBARTON 01:PVE082
ST ANDREW'S HIGH SECO STRATH LANARK 01:PVE170
ST ANDREW'S SECONDARY SECO STRATH GLASGOW 01:PVE124
ST ANDREW'S C.E. INFANTS PRIM CALDERDALE 01:YLR119
ST ANDREW'S C.E. JUNIOR PRIM CALDERDALE 01:YLR106
ST ANDREW'S COLLEGE POLY STRATH DUNBARTON 01:PVE484
ST ANDREW'S COMPUTER CENTRE ADVS GWENT 01:YMR048
ST ANDREW'S HIGH SECO CROYDON 01:YMZ040
ST ANDREW'S PRIMARY PRIM STRATH ARGYLL 01:PVE505
ST ANDREW'S UNIT SPEC CHESHIRE 01:YLU006
```

## Conferencing

CAMPUS 2000 provides the Caucus conferencing system. This system allows any number of users to take part in a discussion on line without having to meet face to face. In fact they might be in different countries thousands of miles apart. The person organising the conference starts it off by entering an item (or list of items) for discussion. The people involved can state their views by responding to the item. Everyone's responses appear on all the terminals (with their names) for everyone else to see. Each user can also send private messages during the conference, which will be seen only by the one person they're being sent to.

A conference on CAMPUS 2000 can be public or private. A public conference is open to anyone on the system. A private conference is like a closed user group on PRESTEL, and only a named group of people can take part.

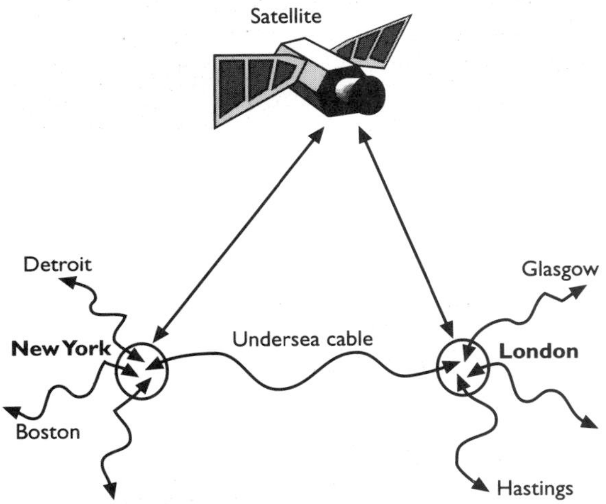


**FIGURE 9.3** *A wide area network linked by satellite and cable*

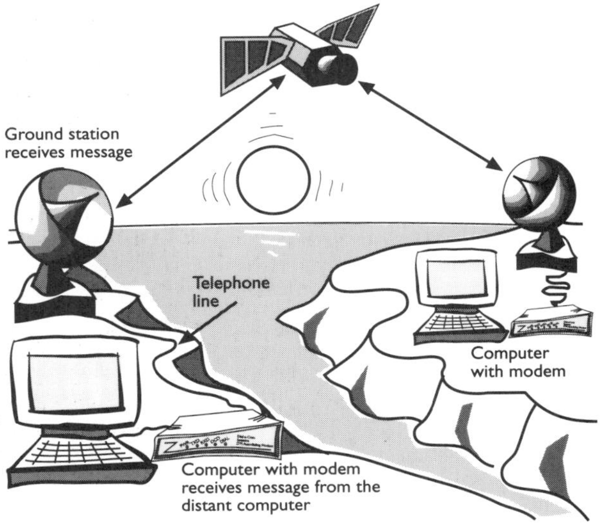


**FIGURE 9.4** *Satellite communication*

## *Electronic Data Interchange*

Electronic Data Interchange is a system used by businesses to send data files from one computer system to another. Electronic Data Interchange is sometimes called 'paperless trading'. The data is set out in a common format, to agreed standards. A central computer agency handles the transfer of data between the parties involved. This system can save huge sums of money – one company using it has seen the cost of transferring 1000 documents drop from £1510 to £325 (an 80% saving)! Electronic Data Interchange also has many of the other advantages of electronic mail.

## *More about modems*

You need a modem for electronic mail because the data from the computer is in the form of digital signals but the telephone system can only carry analogue information. In figure 9.5 you can see how a modem changes digital signals from a computer into analogue signals in a process called **modulation**. When the signals are changed back, this is called **demodulation**. Can you see where a modem gets its name?

Future telephone systems will operate using digital signals and there will be no need for modems, because computers can be connected directly to the telephone system.

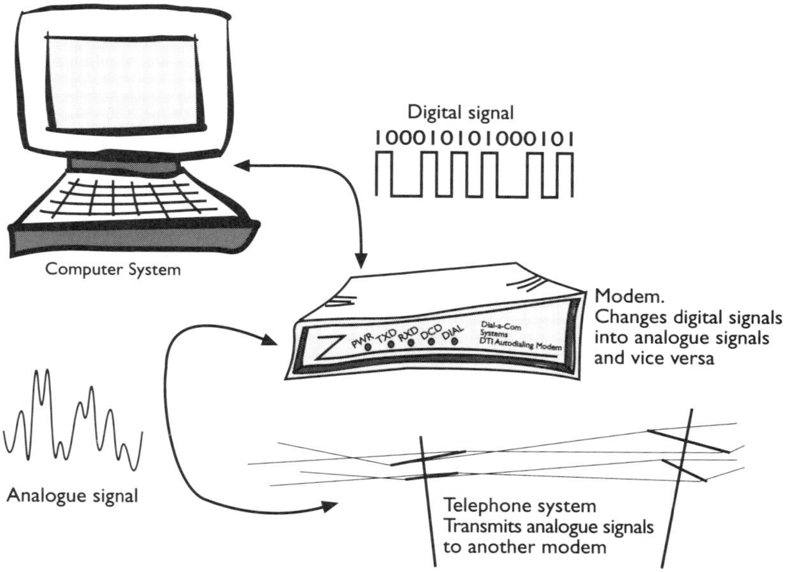


**FIGURE 9.5** *How a modem works*

## *Speed of access*

You can use Electronic Mail at a variety of speeds, depending on the speed of the modem. This may be important for businesses who use electronic mail a lot, since they can send data at higher speeds, saving telephone charges and time charges for using the system. Some electronic mail services base their charges on the amount of data sent rather than time spent on line. This means that users who send data faster would only save on telephone charges.

## EXTRA QUESTIONS

### Knowledge and understanding

1 Name a searchable database on CAMPUS 2000.
  What would you enter to search for your school's mailbox number using this system?
2 How does a fax machine work?
3 What is Electronic Data Interchange?
  How is it different from electronic mail?

**4** How can a wide area network be used for conferencing?

**5** Here is an extract from the MICRONET News Service. Read it and answer the questions that follow.

> **SATELLITE E-MAIL**
>
> SkyWord, a new service that sends messages from computers to people on roaming basis via satellite has been introduced by SkyTel.
>
> 'Now a message can be sent from a personal computer to a portable messaging unit in someone's jacket pocket or purse in seconds,' said David Garrison, president of SkyTel. 'By enabling users to send a message from a keyboard to a roaming subscriber, SkyWord extends the computer into a form of personal communications that is no longer location dependent. In short, it's E-mail for people on the move.'
>
> The new service sends messages of between 40-80 characters or up to 20 average length words in alphanumeric format.
>
> SkyWord relies on the computer-to-computer dial-up capability of personal computers and on-line computers using electronic mail systems, as well as laptop computers with telephone modems.
>
> To send a message, the user inputs the text of the message along with the SkyWord subscriber's personal identification number. The user then sends the message via his or her E-Mail system which automatically dials SkyTel's messaging control computer.
>
> From there, the SkyWord message is sent to a satellite uplink and then to the Westar IV satellite orbiting the earth. The message returns to a satellite downlink and is then sent to SkyTel's transmitters. The entire procedure usually takes less than 30 seconds.

(a) How might a message be sent using Skytel?
(b) How long does it take to send a message?
(c) What is the longest message that can be sent on this system?
(d) Give one advantage and one disadvantage of Skytel compared with the other electronic mail systems described in this chapter.

**Problem solving**

**1** How would you send a letter on electronic mail if
(a) it was two lines long?

(b) it was a whole page long?
(c) you had to send the same letter to two people?
(d) you had to send the same letter to all the schools in Edinburgh?

**2** Read the following carefully and answer the questions which follow.

```
Connecting to ECCTIS ...

Welcome to the new ECCTIS database
Number of records ... 83745

                                              Key
The ECCTIS courses database                    1
excluding Teaching courses
Teaching courses                               2
Leave ECCTIS                                   3

Enter 1, 2, 9 or 3: 1

SUBJECT ENTRY

Enter a Subject: computing

.ITEMS.    terms

A     2  SUB=COMPUTER-AIDED CHEMISTRY
B    22  SUB=COMPUTERISED ACCOUNTING
C    36  SUB=COMPUTERS
D   145  SUB=COMPUTERS IN EDUCATION
E     2  SUB=COMPUTERS IN SCIENCE
***** YOUR TERM *****
F    31  SUB=COMPUTING FOR INDUSTRY
G     2  SUB=COMPUTING FOR WOMEN
H    17  SUB=COMPUTING MATHEMATICS
I  85    SUB=CONCRETE
J 124    SUB=CONFECTIONERY

More terms are available
M: More Y: New Search Z: Leave ECCTIS

Enter M,Y,Z or (A-J): g

                   SEARCH RESULT
                   -------------

Courses retrieved:           2

All Levels:                  A
```

```
Non Advanced Courses:       B
Advanced Courses:           C
Postgraduate Courses:       D
First Degree Single:        E
First Degree Combined:      F

Display Courses:            X
New Search:                 Y
Leave ECCTIS:               Z

Enter ONE option from (A-F) or (X-Z): x

COURSES RETRIEVED .... 2
Item 1
Inst. name      Dudley College of Technology
Course title    Computing for Women
Item 2

Inst. name      Dudley College of Technology
Course title    Access to Computing and Higher
                Education for Women

For further details of a course enter the item
number

P: Print Y: New Search Z: Leave ECCTIS

Enter P, Y, Z or (1-2): z

Thank you for using this system

Your session with ECCTIS has now been closed.
Thank you for using Telecom 2000's Gateway
service.

Hit RETURN or ENTER key to return to menu:
```

(a) What was the user searching for using ECCTIS?
(b) What is the total number of records ECCTIS contains?
(c) What type of information does ECCTIS contain?
(d) What two unexpected terms appeared when the database was searched? Why?
(e) How many entries were there under the term COMPUTERS IN EDUCATION?

**Practical activities**

1 If your school has access to CAMPUS, use one of the on-line databases to find out about a subject that interests you. Get a hard copy of the details of your chosen subject.

2 Advertise on CAMPUS for electronic mail pals.
3 Find out (from computer magazines or from an on-line database) about other electronic mail services like DIALOG, COMPUSERVE, CIX, THE SOURCE, INTERNET, JANET.

## KEY POINTS

- Electronic mail is a way of sending messages from one computer to another, usually over the telephone
- Any computer data can be sent using electronic mail
- All types of electronic mail need communications software
- Electronic mail sent on a wide area network also needs a modem and might need a subscription to an on-line service
- CAMPUS 2000 provides a scrolling page service for electronic mail
- PRESTEL uses response frames for electronic mail
- Electronic mail is faster than sending a letter by post
- An electronic mail message is stored in the user's mail box until it is read and deleted
- Users must check their mailbox regularly for the system to work
- Using electronic mail, you can send the same letter to many different users at once
- The person you are trying to send a message to must also have a mailbox on the system
- Fax machines work like long-distance photocopiers
- Fax machines can be used to send diagrams and photographs as well as text

# 10 Automated systems

## What is an automated system?

An automated system is a system where you provide the **input**, the machine or computer carries out the **process** and provides you with the **output**. See if you can identify the input, process and output for each of the examples given in the next few pages.

## Automated systems in everyday life

You see and use automated systems in your everyday life, but you might not know them. Here are a few examples.

- A washing machine is an example of an automated system. Water is put in, together with washing powder and dirty clothes. The machine contains a number of stored programs. By setting the controls of the washing machine, you can select the program you want for the clothes you've put in. You don't have to do anything else.

*An automatic washing machine*

*An automatic camera*

*A video handset*

- Using an automatic camera you get perfect(!) photographs every time. A window in the front of the camera senses the amount of light around and the computer inside the camera sets the shutter speed, aperture and flash automatically to give the right exposure. All you have to do is point the camera and press the button.
- You can use a central heating programmer for heating or hot water continuously or at any time of the day.
- You can program a compact disc player to play your favourite music over and over again.
- You can program a video recorder to record a series of television programmes. Each programme is called an event. A small computer in the video recorder takes in the start and stop times, the date and channel for each event. Once you have programmed it correctly, the recorder will switch itself on at the right time and off again when the programme is finished. Some video recorders have a bar code reader built into their handset or remote control to help speed up the programming. Other video recorders can take their programme information directly from the Teletext pages (Chapter 8 told you all about Teletext) – all you have to do is choose the programme you want from a list on the screen. A third type of video recorder uses special numbers called Videoplus codes, which are published along with the TV listings.
- A vending machine can make up a selection of hot and cold drinks, supply you with a can of drink or a packet of crisps, depending on the buttons you press.

Can you think of any more examples of automated systems in your home?

# Automated systems in industry

Industrial processes use automated systems – here are some examples.

- Car manufacture is almost completely automated. A few years ago a television advert for a family car claimed that its product was 'Designed by computer, built by robots, driven by the intelligent'. The centre of every car manufacturing plant is the **assembly line**, where the cars are put together. The assembly line uses a conveyor belt to move the parts from one part of the factory to the next. A fully automated

**MAINFRAME COMPUTER SYSTEM**

a computer system that can carry out a very large amount of work at high speed. It usually occupies a whole large room

**ROBOT**

a device which can carry out repetitive tasks under the control of a computer program

production line is controlled by a mainframe computer which is linked to individual robots and machines that assemble the components. A typical robot on an assembly line will have a movable, jointed arm with a specialist tool (like a spray gun) attached to it. Figure 10.1 shows how a computer-controlled robot is used to paint a car. The assembly line control program is designed so that the components from other parts of the factory are sent to the right place at the right time – for example so that the right colour of paint goes to the automated paint shop in time for the body panels reaching it to be painted.

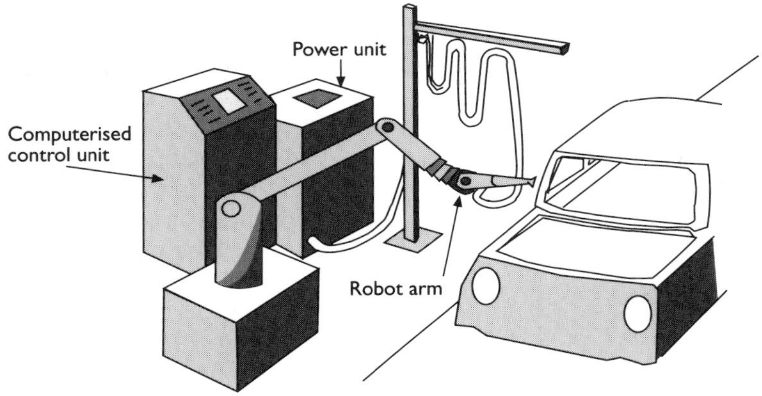


**FIGURE 10.1** *Spray painting on a car assembly line. The robot's arm has a spray jet as its end effector*

- Mushrooms grow very quickly, and will double in size in 24 hours. Figure 10.2 shows you how an automated system can help the mushroom grower to make sure that only mushrooms of the right size are picked to be sold. The system uses a television camera linked to a computer. The grower programs the computer with the size of mushroom that she wants to be picked. The trays holding the mushrooms pass along the conveyor belt, where they are scanned by the camera, which sends information about the size and position

**FIGURE 10.2** *Automatic harvesting of mushrooms*

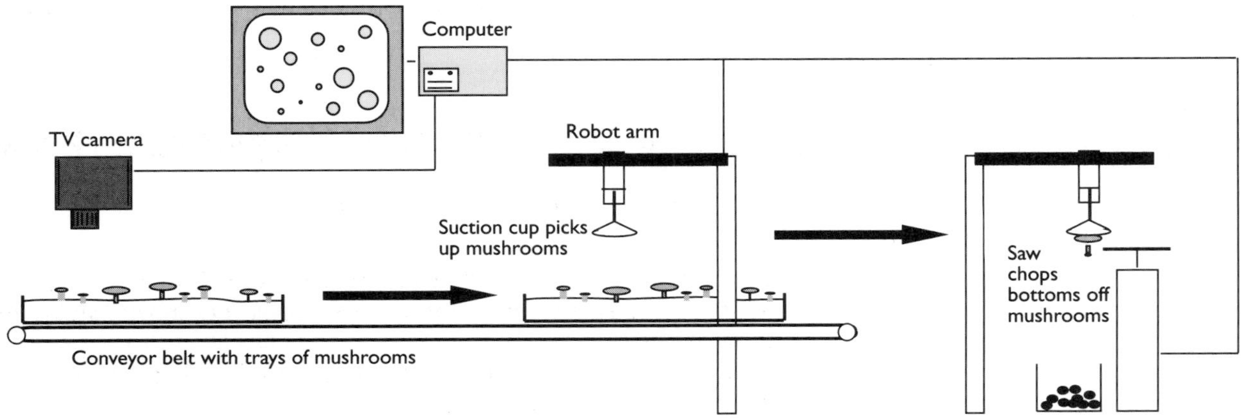

of all the mushrooms in the tray to the computer. When the tray moves into a particular position, the robot arm lifts each correctly sized mushroom out using a suction cup and passes the mushroom over a circular saw blade. This cuts off the end of the stalk. The prepared mushroom is then packed for sale. The tray containing the rest of the mushrooms is left to grow for another day, and the process is repeated. By using this system, the grower can be confident that the mushrooms are picked at the best time, the time which will give them the biggest profit.

- In a large bakery, bread making is completely automated although it is monitored by a human operator. The carefully measured ingredients (flour, water, salt, yeast, conditioner) are mixed in a huge bowl. The operator watches the display on a computer screen which shows a diagram of the measuring and mixing process (like the one in figure 10.3). This type of display is called a **mimic controller**, because it shows the exact details of the process on the screen. The display keeps the operator informed of the weights and temperatures of the ingredients so they can adjust the process if they need to using the control panel.

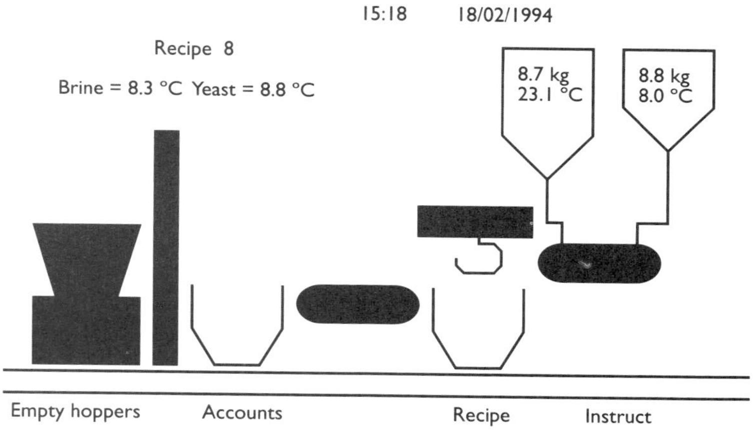


**FIGURE 10.3** *An example of a mimic display during bread making*

# Why do we use automated systems?

Automated systems are used because

- They can carry out the process much faster than a human can
- The tasks that they are programmed to do are often boring or repetitious
- They can be used in places where it would be harmful or dangerous for people

- They are more efficient than people because they can work all day without a break
- They are flexible because they can be programmed to carry out different tasks
- They are more accurate than people and can do finely detailed work without getting tired and making mistakes.

# Types of control

There are two types of control which can be used on any automated system, **open loop** and **closed loop**.

## Open loop control systems

**OPEN LOOP SYSTEM**

a (control) system which does not involve feedback

In an open loop control system the processor is instructed to perform a task and it doesn't stop until it has finished the task.

Examples of open loop control systems:

- a toaster
- a washing machine.

Open loop systems are used for repetitive tasks (like a dishwasher).

Figure 10.4 shows an example of an open loop control system for traffic lights. The traffic lights follow a pre-programmed set of instructions from the control computer. The sequence won't change, no matter how many cars are waiting at the junction, if none of the bulbs are working or even if a lorry crashes into the lights and breaks them.

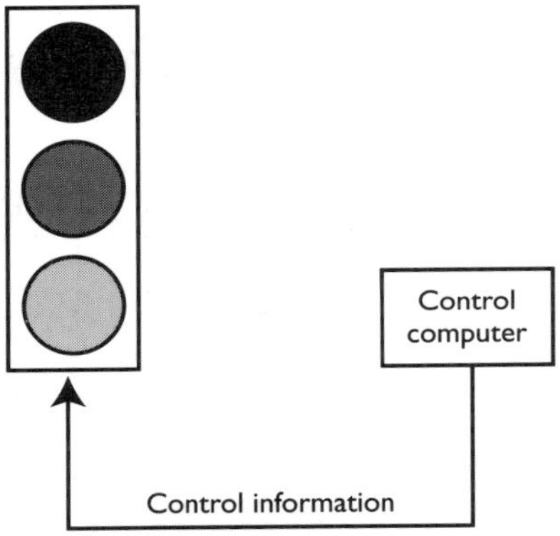


**FIGURE 10.4** *An open loop control system for traffic lights*

## Closed loop control systems

**CLOSED LOOP SYSTEMS**

a (control) system which uses feedback

**SENSOR**

a device which detects something and provides input to a computer system. A bump sensor is an example

A closed loop control system uses one or more sensors to detect what is going on around it, and it can change what it's doing depending on the information it gets from the sensors. This method of passing information from a sensor to a control system is called **feedback**.

A simple way of thinking about closed loop control is

SENSE ⟶ DECISION ⟶ ACTION (with a line from ACTION back to SENSE)

Examples of closed loop systems are

- an automatic kettle
- an oven
- a refrigerator.

Closed loop systems are used for tasks where different actions have to be performed depending on the feedback from the sensors (like a heater controlled by a thermostat).

Figure 10.5 shows how a closed loop control system is used

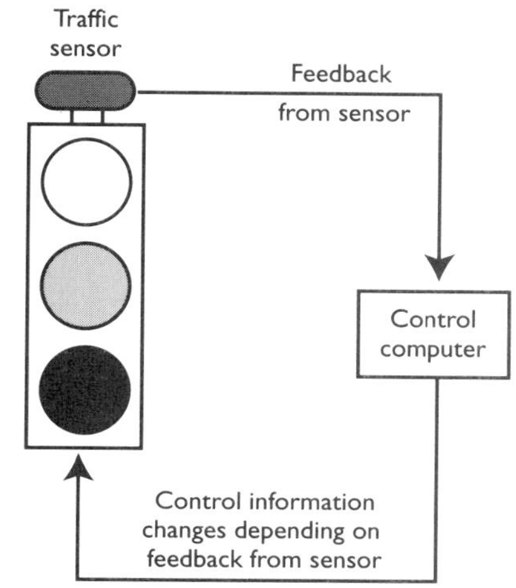


**FIGURE 10.5** *A closed loop control system for traffic lights*

for traffic lights. The traffic lights are following a pre-programmed sequence of instructions from the control computer, just like the ones in figure 10.4, but in a closed loop system if the traffic sensor detects cars waiting at the junction it passes the information to the control computer, which changes the traffic lights. Sometimes the traffic sensor is a loop of wire buried in the road surface. When cars are on the road above the wire the sensor sends the information to the control computer.

### The difference between open and closed loop systems

A closed loop control system uses feedback and an open loop control system doesn't.

It may help you to remember the difference if you think about these two phrases:

'Carry on regardless' is what happens in an open loop control system.

'Hang on. Let's see what is happening in the outside world before I do anything else' is what happens in a closed loop control system.

## *Implications of using automated systems*

Automated systems have taken over many of the jobs that people used to do, and they have had effects on many aspects of our lives. Let us look at the main effects.

### Social implications

Automating operations at work affects people in many ways:

- Quite a few workers will lose their jobs because a computer can do it quicker and cheaper.
- Some of these people will be retrained to do other jobs – like maintain the automated systems.
- This means the skills which these people have will have to change.
- Early computers needed a lot of people (like systems analysts, programmers, computer engineers and data preparation staff) to build and maintain them. Modern computers need fewer people to look after them since they are now more reliable, and much less time is needed to key in data. So more people will be made unemployed.
- The people who used to do boring, repetitive and dangerous jobs will have more leisure time because computers have taken over these jobs. Hopefully these people will use their extra free time to develop their talents and improve their

quality of life. The time allowed for holidays will increase, and the time you have to spend working during a single day will decrease.

- This promise of more leisure time hasn't always worked out – some people have found that the new technology has made life more hectic than it was before!
- Nowadays you can do certain jobs from a computer terminal at home (using networks – see Chapter 9). Fewer people working in potentially dangerous factory conditions means there will be fewer industrial accidents.
- Using a computer keyboard and mouse for long periods of time can be dangerous – you can develop repetitive strain injury in your wrists and hands and you can get severe eye strain by looking at a screen for hours.

## Technical implications

### *Safety*

- The moving parts of a machine must be covered so that no-one can be hurt when they're operating the machine.
- People who work alongside robots must take care that the robot doesn't injure them when it moves.
- Robot vehicles are programmed to move slowly so that people can get out of their way.
- Robot vehicles are also fitted with sensors to detect collisions. If the robot bumps into something, it should instantly stop moving, preventing any damage from being done. This is another example of feedback from a sensor being relayed to a computer which then makes a decision. This is closed loop control. What could happen if the robot was controlled by an open loop system?
- Robot arms which carry out tasks like paint spraying on an assembly line should *only* operate when a component is in position.

### *Quality control*

Using automated systems the quality of a product can be kept consistent. For instance, the automated system in a bakery is continuously checking loaves from each batch to make sure that their weight is within a set range of values. It will produce a printout of the results which the bakery manager can use to monitor the efficiency of the production process. He or she can then change the process as they need to.

## Economic implications

Automated systems are expensive to install a completely automated production line can cost many millions of pounds to set up. Many businesses have changed to automated systems in spite of the costs involved – why?

Unlike people, automated systems don't demand wage rises or costly facilities (like a canteen) while they are working, or go on holiday, so the employers hope that by reducing the number of employees they will save money in a few years. If the automated system works properly, the employers will also gain because more goods will be manufactured in the same time and for the same cost. This is known as **increased productivity**.

## WHEN AUTOMATED SYSTEMS GO WRONG

This automated system didn't work in the way it was supposed to …

In 1987 a computer-controlled traffic system in Melbourne turned into a headache for Australian police. The system had minimum speed signs which instructed motorists to drive at speeds which would take them through traffic lights while they were green. When the system was first installed, the signs in Melbourne were flashing a minimum speed of 75 kilometres per hour – until the local police realised that the city's maximum speed limit is 60 kilometres per hour!

## QUESTIONS

### Knowledge and understanding

1 Give three examples of automated systems.

2 Explain the difference between open and closed loop control.

3 Give two examples of occupations or jobs which have been changed because automated systems have been installed
Will these people need to be re-trained?
What new skills will they need?

4 If automated systems are expensive to install, why are so many businesses using them?

5 Describe two advantages of automated systems to
(a) the employer
(b) the employee

6 What types of business are likely to increase as a result of the introduction of automated systems?

### Problem solving

1 Study the mushroom harvesting example shown in figure 10.2.
(a) Why must the grower tell the computer what size of mushrooms to pick?
(b) Why does the grower not have to tell the computer where the mushrooms are in the tray?
(c) What would happen if none of the mushrooms in a tray were the right size?
(d) Why is there a connection on the diagram between the computer and the circular saw?

2 A pelican crossing is operated by pedestrians pushing a button beside the traffic lights. Draw a diagram similar to the one in figure 10.5 to show a pelican crossing and explain how the control system operates.

3 Look at figure 10.6.
Explain what happens to the valve when
(a) the tank is empty?
(b) the tank is full?
Is this an example of open or closed loop control?

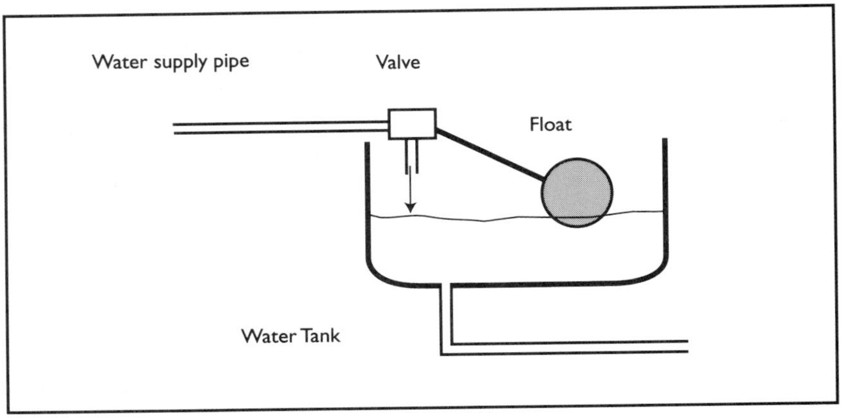


**FIGURE 10.6** *A central heating header tank*

## *More to do*

### *Systems analysis*

Before designing a new automated factory or introducing new technology to a manual system, a **systems analysis** needs to be carried out. A **systems analyst** looks at how various jobs are done manually, and sees if any of these jobs could be done by computer. If a company decides to introduce a computer, the systems analyst may have to design the computer system that will be used. Once the computer has been installed, the systems analyst will monitor the process and try to find ways to improve its performance. See Chapter 12 for more information on the job of a systems analyst.

### *The factory of the future*

Automated systems have changed the way the workplace is designed. Since many large factories now have very few people working in them, architects have designed these factories to suit the way the machines operate. Automated warehouses have products stacked on very high shelves on fork lift pallets – no-one could lift or move these pallets without using a machine.

There are some things that human workers would need on an assembly line which robots wouldn't.

- The workplace would have to be at the right temperature – if it was too cold or too hot the workers would be uncomfortable and wouldn't work as well. Robots can work all day without being affected by the cold.

- Humans also require frequent breaks, canteens and rest rooms.
- If there were no human workers on the assembly line the amount of noise in the factory wouldn't matter.
- In an automated factory, the few human technicians could be confined to the control room, which could be well sound proofed and at a comfortable temperature.

Industries in developed countries have been finding that the costs of employment have been rising very fast, making their prices uncompetitive compared with less well developed nations where the factories are much more labour intensive (less automated) and the workers are paid less. The less developed countries can produce similar goods much more cheaply than western industries can. Manufacturers in the developed countries have introduced automation to reduce their costs and to make their prices competitive.

# *Robotics*

## Robot anatomy

Some robots have parts that resemble human limbs. It is not surprising therefore that these parts are called after the human parts they resemble. A jointed arm robot (like the one in figure 10.7) has a **waist, shoulder**, **elbow** and **wrist**. The part on the end of the arm (the 'hand') is specialised to suit what ever task the robot is programmed to do. This could be a gripper (as in figure 10.7), a suction cup, a paint spray or a welding electrode. Figure 10.8 shows a few of these **end effectors**, as they are called.

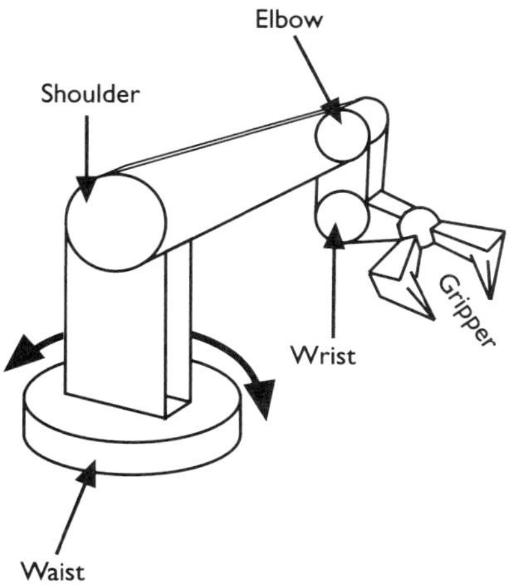


**FIGURE 10.7** *Anatomy of a jointed arm robot. You can see how the various parts resemble (and are named after) parts of the human body*

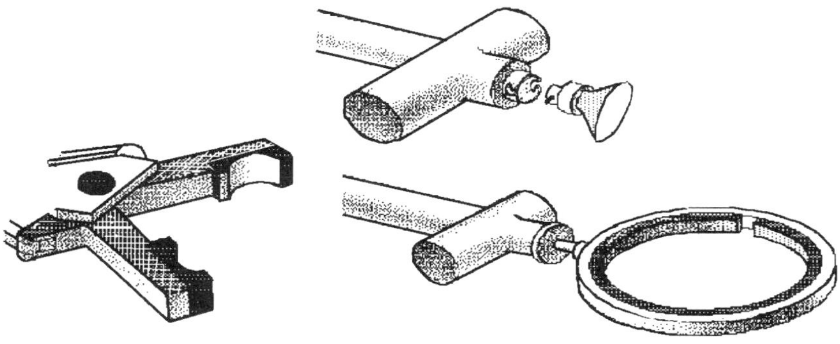

**FIGURE 10.8** *Types of end effectors – you can see a gripper for thin cylindrical objects, a paint spray and a circular collar which can be inflated to grip objects inside it*

Each movable part of the robot arm is powered by an **actuator**. Actuators can be electrical, hydraulic (work by liquid pressure) or pneumatic (work by air pressure).

Robots are connected to a computer by a device called an **interface**. The job of the interface is to make sure that the right signals are sent between the computer and the robot.

Robots which stay in one place all the time, for example at a fixed point on an assembly line, are called **stationary** robots. Robots which move are called **mobile** robots.

## *More to do*

### *Analogue and digital signals*

Most electrical signals, like the output from a microphone, are analogue signals. **Analogue** signals can vary continuously between two limits. If you could see an analogue signal it would look roughly like the shape a skipping rope makes when you hold the ends and shake it up and down (something like figure 10.9).

Computers can only work with **digital** signals, which have only two values – on or off. A digital signal therefore consists of a series of 'ons' and 'offs'. An 'on' signal is represented by a 1 and an 'off' by a 0. When used like this, 0 and 1 are binary numbers, and a series of 0s and 1s are called **bits**. A sequence of these bits sent to the computer gives the required instruction. Figure 10.10 shows what a digital signal would look like if you could see it. You will find out more about 'on' and 'off' signals, binary numbers and bits in Chapter 19.

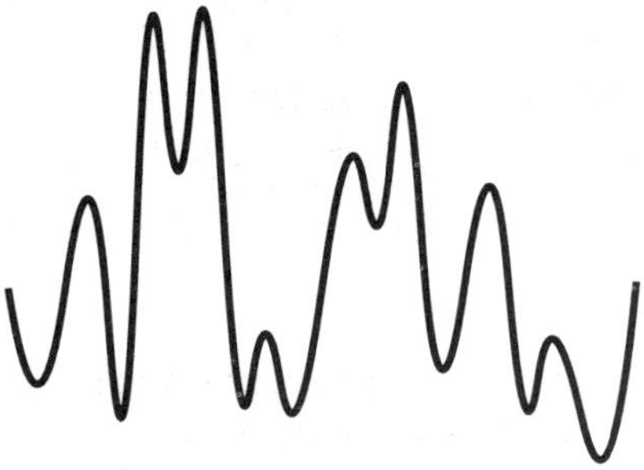

**FIGURE 10.9** *An analogue signal*

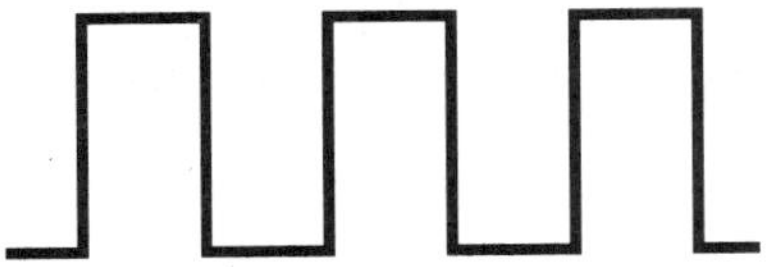

**FIGURE 10.10** *A digital signal*

### *Signal converters*

A computer is connected to another device (a printer, a disk drive, a robot or another **peripheral**), by a circuit called an interface. Usually this interface has to be able to change the digital signals from the computer to an analogue signal that the other device can understand. This is done by a **digital to analogue converter**. Signals can be changed in the other direction by an **analogue to digital converter**. Digital to analogue and analogue to digital conversion is illustrated in figure 10.11. An analogue to digital converter samples the incoming analogue signal at regular intervals, changes the continuously varying voltage to binary numbers, and sends the bits to the computer.

**PERIPHERAL**

any device that may be attached to a computer system for input, output or backing storage

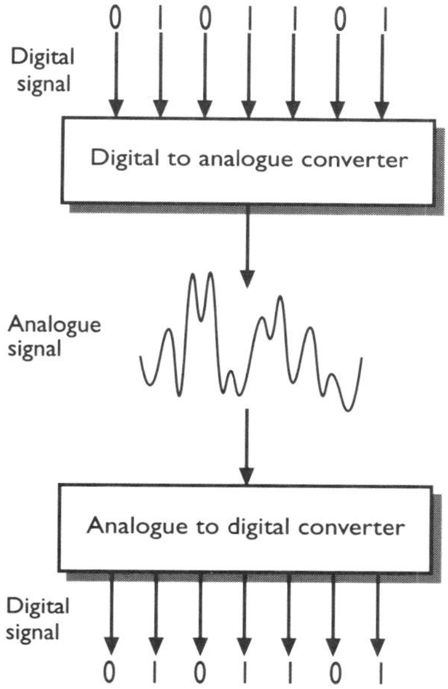


**FIGURE 10.11** *Conversion from digital to analogue signals and back again*

In a closed loop control system signals need to be sent in both directions – to and from the computer – so it will need both types of converter.

## *Transducers*

A **transducer** is a device which changes an external physical input (temperature, pressure or light) into an analogue signal. This signal can be fed into a computer via an interface. Temperature sensors, strain gauges and photocells are all transducers.

### Digitisers

A **digitiser** converts a visual image from a video or television camera into a digital form that the computer can process. Modern video cameras use a special integrated circuit or 'chip' that is sensitive to light. This is another example of a transducer.

## Programming robots

Robots are normally controlled by a computer program which is made up of instructions written in a **high level language** (programming languages are described in much more detail in Chapter 17).

Robots that work on different assembly lines sometimes need to be reprogrammed to carry out different tasks. This could be done by writing a new program for the new task, but some robots can be 'taught' exactly what movements you want them to make.

### TEACHING ROBOTS

To teach a robot to do paint spraying, the human operator will spray one item using the end of the robot's arm. The positional sensors in the arm tell the control computer about the sequence of movements of each joint that are involved in the process and the central computer stores this information. The arm's actuators can then repeat the stored sequence of movements to spray an item on its own. This is called **programming by example** or **lead-through programming**.

If the robot arm is too large or heavy for the operator to move like this he will use a device called a teach pendant. He controls the arm with the buttons or a joystick on the pendant and sets the computer up to learn or copy each movement of the arm. The Fischer Technik model shows in figure 10.19 a robot arm which can be 'taught' using a series of switches on its baseboard.

**PROGRAM**

a list of instructions which tell the central processing unit what to do

**HIGH LEVEL LANGUAGE**

a computer language with instructions written in normal or everyday language

## More to do

**READ ONLY MEMORY (ROM)**

a microchip that stores data permanently. The data is not lost when the computer is switched off

### ROM software

Stationary robots which are linked directly to a computer store their control programs on magnetic tape or disk, especially those which can be 'taught'. Mobile robots, on the factory floor or in outer space, have control programs that are fixed and are not changed easily. Their programs are stored on **Read Only Memory** (**ROM**) chips. ROM chips are a more expensive way of storing software than disks, but they retain their information if the power is switched off, and a program contained in ROM can be loaded many times faster than from disk (see Chapter 16 for more about ROM).

### Degrees of freedom

The part on the end of the robot arm that carries out a specialised task is called the end effector (you saw some of these in figure 10.8). One of the most important specifications of a robot arm is the number of **degrees of freedom** it has. The number of degrees of freedom is the number of ways the arm can move (these are called the axes of movement) – the movable joints of an arm. The number of degrees of freedom a robot has governs the range of movements it can perform. If a robot is to work in three dimensions, it must have at least three degrees of freedom. The human arm has at least eight degrees of freedom.

- The wrist joint can move in two planes – up and down, and side to side – giving two degrees of freedom.
- The elbow joint can only move in one plane, but the forearm bones can cross over – giving two degrees of freedom.
- The shoulder joint can move in three planes, and the shoulder itself can move up and down (shrug) – giving four degrees of freedom.

If you have ever tried to retrieve an object which has fallen into a confined space, you will appreciate what a versatile limb the arm is!

The terms roll, pitch and yaw are used to describe different types of movement.

- **Yaw** is movement from side to side.
- **Pitch** is up and down motion.
- **Roll** is rotation.

**FIGURE 10.12** *The end effector on a jointed arm robot, showing roll, pitch and yaw*

## Autonomous guided vehicles

In a modern fully automated factory the problem of keeping the production line supplied with parts can be solved by using a different type of robot called an autonomous guided vehicle. One of these is shown in figure 10.13.

**FIGURE 10.13** *An autonomous guided vehicle. Note the front and rear bumpers which are used to detect objects in the vehicle's path. The sensor underneath the vehicle lets it follow a pre-programmed path*

Autonomous guided vehicles do all the fetching and carrying of parts from the warehouse to the assembly line. They are controlled by computer during their journey, and can find their way from one place to another by following wires buried in the factory floor. This is an example of a **magnetic guidance system**. In some factories the vehicle follows a painted line on the factory floor. This system is called a **light guidance system** and is more flexible than magnetic guidance, since it is much easier to paint a new line than it is to dig up the floor and bury a wire. However, the light guidance system can be affected by dirt on the floor covering the paint.

All vehicles are fitted with front and rear sensors to detect unexpected objects in their path (like people, or other vehicles which have broken down). If anything touches these sensors, the vehicle will stop instantly so that it doesn't hurt someone or break something. The control program on the autonomous guided vehicle has to interact with the computer and receive the output immediately – it must be a **real time system**. This means that the program must be constantly operating and ready to take action. If the vehicle doesn't stop immediately when it meets an obstruction people could be hurt or costly equipment damaged.

## Remote-controlled vehicles

Remote-controlled vehicles are used in places where it is not safe for people to go.

Figure 10.14 shows a remote-controlled vehicle being used by a bomb disposal expert to examine a suspicious device on the underside of a car. The vehicle is equipped with a television camera which relays a picture to the operator controlling it at a safe distance. The end effector of the vehicle is a grab that the operator can use to remove the bomb from the car.

**FIGURE 10.14** *How a bomb disposal expert can use a remote-controlled vehicle*

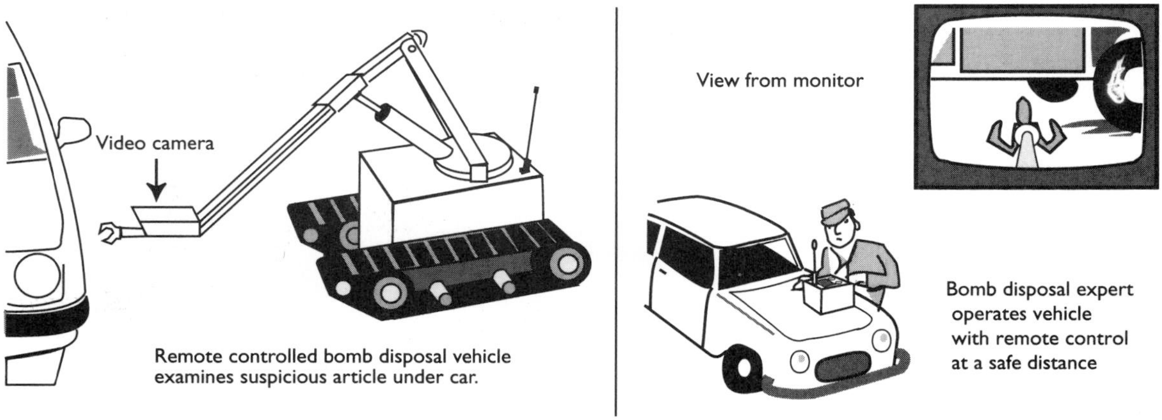
Video camera
Remote controlled bomb disposal vehicle examines suspicious article under car.
View from monitor
Bomb disposal expert operates vehicle with remote control at a safe distance

## Educational robots

### *Floor turtle*

The turtle (you can see two examples in figure 10.15) was one of the first educational robots to be developed. It is made of a plastic dome which covers two large wheels. Each wheel has a motor attached. The turtle has a device that raises and lowers a pen through an opening underneath. Some turtles also have a small hooter which can make sounds. You can connect the turtle directly to the computer via a cable, or operate it by infrared remote control (like the remote controller on a television set).

Floor turtles can draw shapes by moving in a pattern over a piece of paper with the pen held down. They are programmed using a language called Logo.

**FIGURE 10.15** *Turtles*

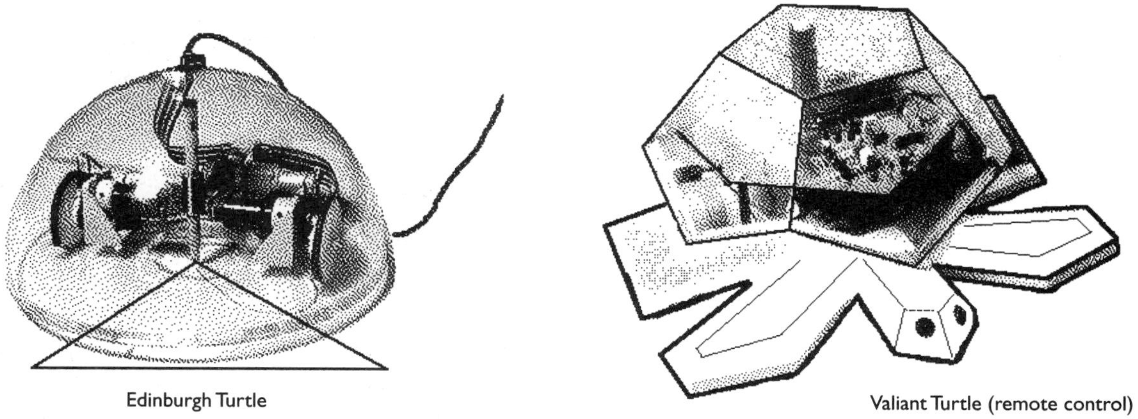
Edinburgh Turtle
Valiant Turtle (remote control)

### BBC Buggy

The BBC Buggy has the same features as the floor turtle. It also has two flat plates which stick out from the front (you can see these in figure 10.16). The flat plates are connected to microswitches and the Buggy can be programmed to detect objects in its path. If you fit the Buggy with light detectors it can read bar codes, follow a line or detect a light source.

**FIGURE 10.16** *BBC Buggy*

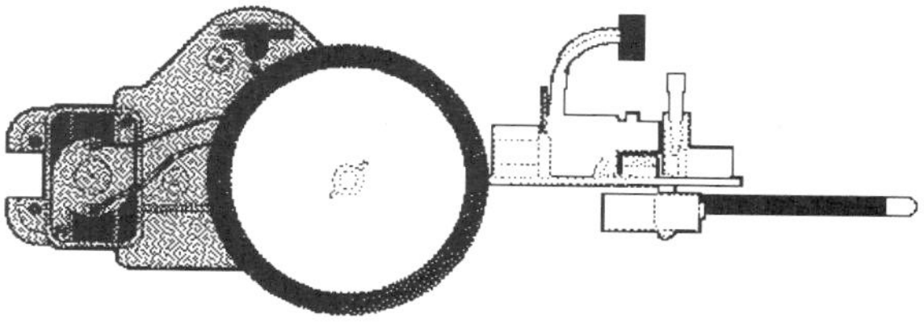

**FIGURE 10.17** *The Trekker*

### Trekker

The Trekker is very like a BBC Buggy, and it has a magnetic reed switch. Trekker is shown in figure 10.17.

### Robot kits

You can use modelling kits like Lego Technic and Fischer Technik to make a variety of robotic devices like those in figures 10.18 and 10.19. You can interface your device to a computer system and program it using a special control language (such as Control Logo).

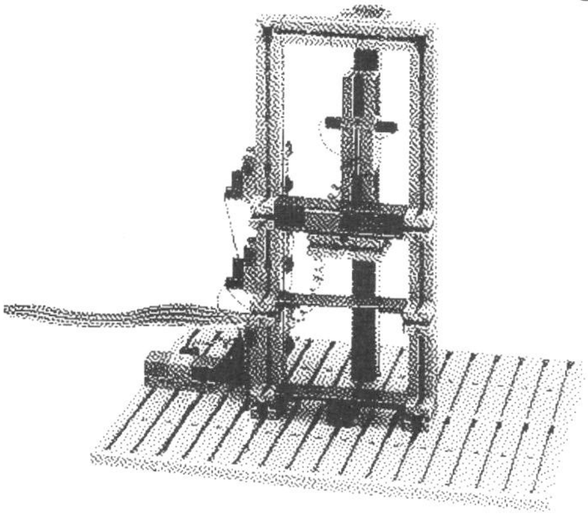

**FIGURE 10.18** *An automatic lift designed by Fischer Technik*

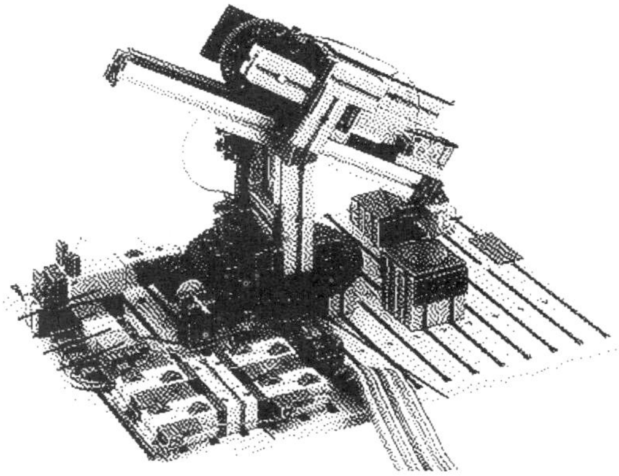

**FIGURE 10.19** *A programmable arm designed by Fischer Technik. The switches on the baseboard are used to 'teach' the robot to do a sequence of movements*

## More to do

### Control languages

Computer programs are always written in a programming **language**. There are many programming languages. Here are a few:

- BASIC
- FORTRAN
- COMAL
- Pascal

Some languages, called high level languages, are similar to English and therefore are easy for us to read and understand. The higher the level of the language, the closer it is to English and therefore the easier it is for someone to read a **program listing** and understand what it is performing.

Some robots are programmed in languages like the four we just mentioned, others are programmed in languages specially designed for robot control. These are called control languages, and the commands they use (like GRASP, MOVE, WAIT, TURN ,SPEED) are related directly to the robot world.

Control Logo is a language that allows programmers to define their own high level commands. To do this the programmer uses simple **routines** such as TURNON, TURNOFF, WAIT, PULSE and incorporates them into higher level **procedures** such as MOVE_BUGGY. Here is an example of a Control Logo command:

```
TO MOVE_BUGGY
TURNON 1
WAIT 100
TURNOFF 1
END
```

**PROGRAM LISTING**

a hard copy or a screen display of the instructions making up a computer program

**ROUTINE**

a programming instruction which carries out a particular task

**PROCEDURE**

part of a computer program which is identified by name (like TAKE_IN_WORDS or MOVE_BUGGY)

### Expert systems

An **expert system** is a special computer program which can apply hundreds of rules that it has learnt from a human expert, within a particular field of knowledge. Expert system programs can diagnose your health problems, give you legal advice or help you to find out what is wrong with your car when the engine won't start! (For more details, go back to Chapter 3.)

Expert systems can apply human-generated rules more consistently than humans do, and can explain how they came to any conclusions. This means that any mistakes they make can be corrected easily.

In the future, expert systems will be combined with robots. This means that remote controlled vehicles used in space or on the sea bed could be replaced by autonomous robots with expert systems to control their navigation and the work that they are doing.

## More to do

Here is an article from PRESTEL about robots (1991).

### Let the robot do it

'Nope, too risky. Let the robot do it.' Japanese experts, who have just unveiled three robot prototypes capable of replacing humans, predict that this will be the catchphrase of tomorrow's workplace. After seven years of work financed by the Japanese government in collaboration with private industry, the Advanced Robot Technology Research Association (ARTRA) recently presented its work to the general public in Tsurumi, outside Tokyo.

On display were three robots designed to perform various tasks in situations dangerous to humans: in radioactive areas inside nuclear power plants, under the sea or in extraordinarily high temperatures. Tokyo's investment in the project totalled £70 million. Billed as the most sophisticated systems yet built anywhere, the exhibition drew only 300 curious spectators.

But their interest to the 20 companies that took part in the project, including some of the country's biggest robot manufacturers, was obvious. 'The companies can now use and develop our technology,' said ARTRA secretary general Takayuki Tsunemi. The robot designed for nuclear power plants resembles a centaur, the mythical half-man, half-horse, with four legs, two arms, two 'eyes' and the capacity to move at 300 metres per hour and hurdle obstacles in its path. It could be on the market in four to five years, Mr Tsunemi said, after the prototype which weighs 1700 pounds is made smaller and lighter. Activated from a command centre outside a radioactive zone, the robot could conduct security checks in Japan's 40 operating nuclear plants and the 15 more to be built by the year 2000. The other prototypes are a tiny submarine with four arms and another centaur like creature with six legs and the capacity to withstand temperatures of up to 800 degrees Celsius. They should also find practical applications fairly quickly, in submarine oil exploration or fighting fires in petrochemical complexes.

With an unprecedented shortage of manpower, Japan is likely to automate its economy further. 'Japanese people don't want to do dirty, tiring and risky work,' said Mr. Tsunemi, who is already thinking of 'intelligent' fourth-generation robots. Those, he said, would not be controlled by computers but, endowed with 'fuzzy logic', could increasingly imitate human reason. At the end of last year, Japanese companies were already using more than 250,000 industrial robots (that's about 60% of the world market) against only 37,000 in the United States at the end of 1989. The Japanese Industrial Robot Association (JIRA) estimates that the figure will rise to 900,000 by the year 2000.

The automobile machine tool sector currently uses nearly 70% of Japan's industrial robots. But for JIRA vice president Kanji Yonemoto, the future belongs to the social robot, capable of helping the blind, elderly or handicapped and to those designed for the building industry whose manpower shortage has already reached 400,000 people.

## QUESTIONS

### Knowledge and understanding

1 Name three parts of a robot arm.
2 Draw up a table with two columns. Head the columns Stationary and Mobile. Look at the pictures of the robots in this chapter and write the name of each robot in the correct column.
3 What is an expert system? What can expert systems do?
4 What is the purpose of an interface?

### Problem solving

1 Why would dirt on a factory floor have no effect on a magnetic guidance system on an autonomous guided vehicle?
2 Explain how a programmer could teach a robot to weld two parts of a car door together.

**FIGURE 10.20** *Daleks*

## EXTRA QUESTIONS

### Knowledge and understanding

1 What is meant by the term degrees of freedom?
How many degrees of freedom has
(a) the Fischer Technik robot arm shown in figure 10.19?
(b) your leg?

2 Describe the types of end effectors which the Daleks in figure 10.20 have.

3 Why does an interface contain an analogue to digital converter?

4 What advantages do control languages have over other high level languages?

5 Why is some robot control software stored on ROM?

6 Read the PRESTEL article on page 137.
(a) Give three examples of where robots can work and humans can't.
(b) How many robots were being used in Japanese companies by the end of 1991?
(c) Why does Japan wish to further automate its economy?

### Problem solving

1 What device would you use to connect a computer to a robot
(a) if feedback was required?
(b) if no feedback was required?

2 Find out how a video camera, a digitiser and a computer may be used to provide pattern recognition.

## KEY POINTS

- In an automated system you provide the input, the machine or computer carries out the process and provides you with the output
- Automated systems can work much faster than humans
- Automated systems may be programmed to do repetitious tasks, in places that are harmful or dangerous for people
- Automated systems are more efficient and more accurate than humans
- Automated systems are flexible because they can be reprogrammed to carry out different tasks
- Two types of control can be used on any automated system – open loop and closed loop
- A closed loop control system uses sensors to detect what is going on around it
- A closed loop system can change its action depending on feedback from the sensors
- An open loop control system carries out its task regardless of what is going on round about it
- A jointed arm robot is said to have a waist, shoulder, elbow and wrist, like the parts of the human body
- Robots that stay in one place all the time are called stationary robots
- Robots that move are called mobile robots
- Robots are connected to a computer by an interface
- Many of the signals that robot sensors output are analogue signals
- Computers can only work with digital signals, which have only two values – on or off
- An interface between a computer and a robot arm may need a digital to analogue converter
- A transducer changes an external physical input (like temperature) into an analogue signal
- A digitiser converts a visual image into digital form
- Robots are normally under the control of a program written in a high level language
- A control program for a mobile robot must work in real time
- The end effector of a robot arm carries out a task
- Robot vehicles in a factory may use magnetic guidance or light guidance systems

# 11 Computers in design and manufacture

## What is computer aided design?

*A CAD station*

> **MENU**
>
> a list on screen for the user to choose from

> **PLOTTER**
>
> an output device which draws on paper using pens. Used mainly for CAD

**Computer aided design** (usually shortened to **CAD**) is a way of using a computer to design the structure or appearance of an item on the screen. The operator of a CAD system can create and manipulate images on a high-resolution screen. A designer often uses a digitising tablet (this is also called a **graphics tablet**) as an input device to a CAD workstation. A digitising tablet allows the designer to draw in the usual way, using an electronic pen. The photo shows you what a graphics tablet looks like. The menu for the graphics tablet may be displayed on the screen or on the surface of the tablet itself. The graphics tablet menu will look something like the one in figure 11.1. Sometimes the design is output in a form suitable for transfer to a computer-controlled machine, ready to start the manufacturing process. If a high-quality printout is required a plotter may be used as the output device.

Using a CAD system can greatly reduce the amount of work a designer has to do by making all the necessary calculations and by allowing her to change the design many times on the

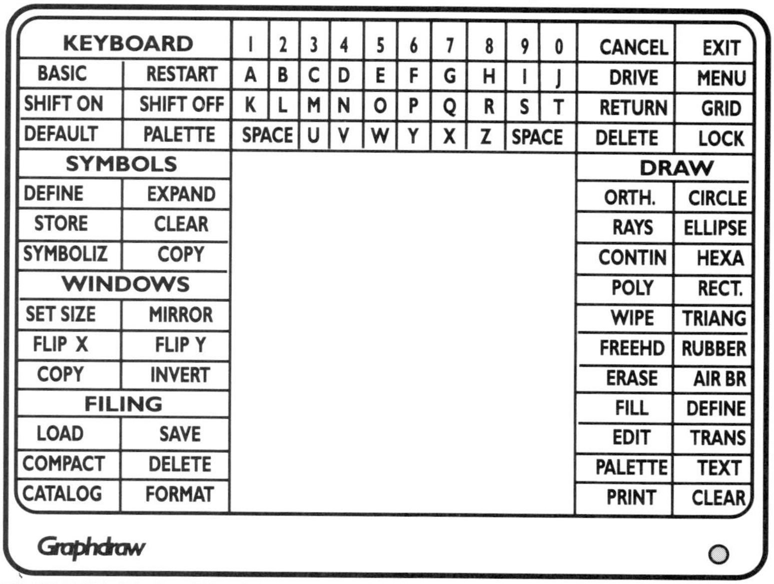


**FIGURE 11.1** *The kind of menu that a graphics tablet has*

computer screen before it is printed. Using CAD, a picture on a computer screen can be turned around and viewed from any angle. The operator can input any changes to the design to the computer and see its effect straight away on the screen. Also, the computer can enlarge any part of the picture so that very small details are visible.

## Uses of CAD

The use of CAD is growing rapidly and computers are now being used to help design anything from postage stamps to motorways. Here are a few examples.

### Car design

CAD may be used to design the shape of a car body. The designer tries to produce a shape which looks good and people will want to buy. At the same time she must make sure that the shape of the car is streamlined so that it will have a low petrol consumption and so on. You can see a car designed by computer in figure 11.2.

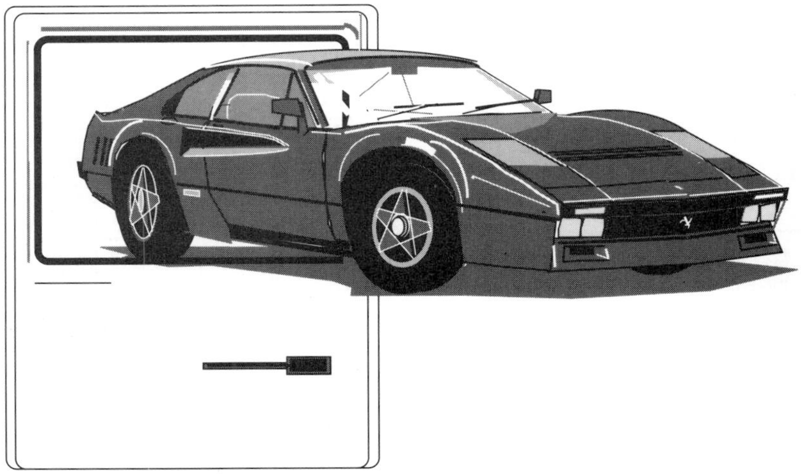

**FIGURE 11.2** *A car designed by CAD*

### Kitchen units

Many DIY stores sell kitchen units. Some of these stores offer a free kitchen planning service. The customer measures the dimensions of their kitchen and draws it out on squared paper. The figures are input to a special computer program together with details of any doors and windows in the room. The operator uses the computer program to plan the kitchen by placing kitchen units (held on memory) onto the plan. A hard copy of the plan is printed out for the customer. A kitchen planned by computer is shown in figure 11.3. The computer can also be used to calculate the cost of the kitchen by adding together all the prices for the units which have been selected. A list of the separate kitchen units may be printed to simplify ordering.

**FIGURE 11.3** *A kitchen planned by computer*

## Road design

Road designers use CAD. A new road must be safe to drive along. A driver must have a good view of the road at every bend and junction. The designer can use the computer to plan the route the road will take and to show how the road will appear as you drive along it even before it has been built. By using CAD, mistakes can be corrected before any money is spent on the road.

## Housing

A computer can be used to design a housing estate. The appearance and location of each house can be adjusted to give the best appearance and the most economical use of the available land. The local authority planners, who must approve the design, can be shown how each street on the proposed estate will appear – to pedestrians, to drivers or from the air. Prospective house buyers don't need to imagine the view from the windows of their new house – they can see it on the computer screen. Look at the article in the photograph over the page.

*A computer-generated office development*

# What is computer aided manufacture?

**Computer aided manufacture** (usually shortened to **CAM**) is using a computer to control the production process – like making a part for a car or cutting cloth to make an item of clothing. The details about a particular product are stored, and can be changed or added to later. Using CAM means that products can be consistently made very accurately.

# Uses of CAM

Like CAD, CAM systems are being used more and more, in many different situations. Here are two examples.

### Postage stamp manufacture

One method of making postage stamps involves taking a photograph of the original stamp design and using a process known as chemical etching to transfer the design to a copper cylinder which is then used in the printing press.

This chemical etching of the printing cylinder has recently been replaced by a computer-controlled process:

1 First, the original design of the stamp is scanned and a digitised image is produced and stored on the computer.
2 Next, the cylinder is placed in a special lathe, called a computer numerically controlled (CNC) lathe.
3 Using the digitised image the computer tells the lathe to engrave the design on to the cylinder. This process uses a very high resolution – 117 lines per centimetre (or 300 lines per inch).

**DIGITISE**

converting an analogue quantity to a digital one. Digitising a picture breaks it into dots and each dot is given a digital value for brightness and colour

*A CNC lathe in action*

This new process means that corrosive chemicals are no longer needed, and the copper removed from the cylinder during engraving can be recycled. The whole process is therefore much friendlier to the environment than the old method.

### A CAM assembly line

One of the most important factors keeping a completely automated assembly line running is making sure that all the parts needed are quickly available. Computers are used to control cranes that pick up the parts and store them or put them on the conveyor ready to be assembled. When the parts arrive at the stores from other factories, a computer weighs them to check that they are the correct weight. At the start of each shift, the operators tell the computer how many finished products it has to make. The computer then works out how often the parts will be needed and will order them when they're needed. The computer can be programmed to give priority to certain lines that may be running short of parts.

### Flexible manufacturing system

A **flexible manufacturing system** is a special type of CAM system used in some factories. Using this system the manufacturing process can be easily changed around to make completely different products. This would be an advantage to factories in that they would be able to alter the items they produce quickly in response to consumer demand.

## Computer integrated manufacture

In **computer integrated manufacture** (usually shortened to CIM) CAD and CAM systems are combined to design and manufacture a particular product. This combination of CAD and CAM becomes CIM when the original drawing on the CAD system is transformed into the finished product with little or no human intervention.

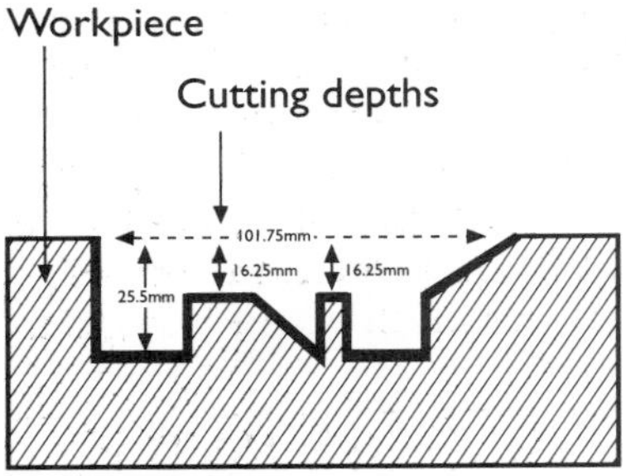


**FIGURE 11.4** *A drawing produced by a tool simulation program*

### MAKING CAR ENGINE COMPONENTS

Components for a car engine can be produced using CIM. A CAD system is used to design the component by drawing it on the screen in three dimensions. When the design is complete, all the measurements needed to produce a particular part are calculated.

Before manufacture starts, a special piece of software called a tool simulation program is run. This program shows the operator how deep the machine will have to make cuts to produce the finished component. A drawing produced by a tool simulation program is shown in figure 11.4. If the tool simulation program produces a component that looks the way it was designed, then the data that was needed to produce the component is stored on tape, ready for the next stage in the process, which is also under computer control.

A blank piece of metal of the right size (this is called the workpiece) is inserted into a computer-controlled milling machine. The instructions for producing the component are fed into the machine from the tape. The milling machine follows the instructions precisely, cutting away the exact amounts of metal needed to produce the finished component.

The advantage of computer control is that once the machine has been programmed to make a component, the process can be repeated over and over again. The operator only has to fit and remove the workpiece or check for any faults. The machine will continue to produce components as long as it is supplied with workpieces and the tape containing the instructions.

Once the component has been made, its measurements are checked very accurately. These measurements are then checked against the original design to make sure the finished component matches the specifications. If there are any inaccuracies, a new set of instructions is produced and the process is repeated until the component is correct. When the instructions are finally right they are used to make many thousands of components.

## Advantages of using CIM

The use of computer-controlled equipment has increased productivity and competitiveness of manufacturing in several ways.

1 Computer-controlled methods are faster and more accurate than older methods. A CNC machine drilling holes in printed circuit boards can produce the same output per hour as four human operators each working an eight hour shift. The machine can work to an accuracy of thousandths of an inch

for each component, which even the most skilled human operator would find impossible to do for any length of time.

2 Waste can be minimised. The designer uses a computer to draw the shape of the pieces to be cut out. The computer can produce a cutting plan by arranging several pieces together so that they fit or 'nest' together, thus reducing the amount of waste. this nesting is important in the clothing industry. Skilful use of nesting will reduce the overall size of the piece of cloth that the pattern is cut from (like that shown in figure 11.5). This is especially important in mass manufacture of clothes, when a large number of pieces of cloth are being cut together.

**FIGURE 11.5** *A dressmaking pattern, showing nesting*

3 A single operator can see a complete job through from start to finish using computer-controlled equipment. This also increases job satisfaction.

4 Computer-controlled systems are simpler to operate and demand less skill of the operator. A CNC machine may be programmed to change its tools automatically. This helps keep the production rate high, and minimises the amount of intervention by the operator.

5 However, manual equipment is still needed in the workplace, mainly for small jobs which are needed immediately and for which it would be uneconomic to program a CNC machine.

## *Effects of computer-controlled systems*

The introduction of new technology has caused major changes in employment patterns. Machines have replaced people on the production line so fewer people are needed. This has caused great concern about job losses. On the other hand, many people think that not to introduce new technology could make their firm less competitive and even put them out of business.

Companies which introduce new technology need to retrain their workers to operate it and people are still needed to program and maintain the computers. Some of the skills which were needed before the introduction of new technology are still needed today so the operator can see if the new technology is working correctly. For example, a person who operates a CNC lathe needs the same basic skills as a manual lathe operator does, but must also understand what part the computer plays in the operation.

Studies into the effect that new technology has had on the work force have shown that generally people enjoy using the new systems. Some workers were even more enthusiastic about the technology than the management who introduced it.

## CAD packages

A professional CAD system consists of

- a computer
- one or more terminals with large high-resolution colour monitors
- high-quality colour plotters and
- a range of specialised software packages to drive the system.

In a commercial CAD system, a graphics tablet is often used as the input device (like the one in the photograph). A graphics tablet allows the operator to draw in a natural way and also to choose from a menu using an electronic pen.

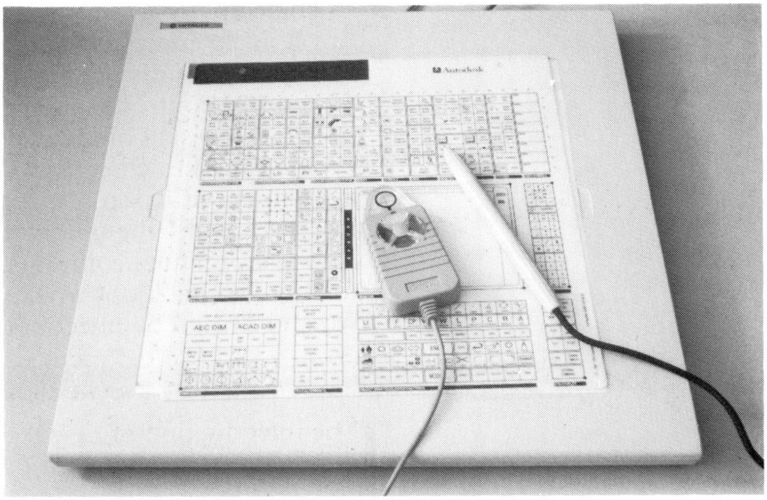

*A graphics tablet*

The hardware and software used for CAD ranges from large systems costing several hundreds of thousands of pounds (like the systems used in the car and aircraft industries) to relatively inexpensive systems which are designed specifically for microcomputers.

### MACDRAW™

**WIMP**

Windows, Icons, Menu (or Mouse), Pointer (or Pull down menu)

MacDraw is a drawing package which may be used for CAD. MacDraw runs on the Macintosh range of computers and is WIMP based. (For an explanation of WIMP systems see Chapter 1). MacDraw has these features:

- It is mouse operated.
- The operator can choose shapes from a menu which includes lines, circles, boxes, arcs and freehand drawing.
- Objects are positioned on the screen using a grid.
- MacDraw has a zoom control which allows the user to produce very detailed work.
- Objects created on the screen can be saved in a library.

A typical application for MacDraw is in drawing plans for a building – perhaps a house or an office. Standard shapes (doors, windows, chairs, tables, desks, lighting, power points and so on) can be saved in a library and used in drawing plans. This saves having to redraw these parts and increases the accuracy of the plan. MacDraw automatically calculates the sizes of any part of the plan and can print out the dimensions on the drawings.

MacDraw allows the drawing to be built up in layers, like the transparent film overlays used on an overhead projector. Each layer can include a particular detail – the basic outline may be on one layer, the electrical sockets on another, the furniture on the next and so on. The layers can be combined to give a whole drawing – see figure 11.6.

Drawing like this helps to avoid mistakes being made, and it simplifies the production of working drawings that are to be used by an electrician, plumber or joiner.

## Computer simulation

Designers are not just concerned with the way things look – a new car must look good but it must also be safe and efficient. When a new car is produced, dummies are strapped into the seats and the car is crashed against a wall to test how well protected the people inside would be in a car crash. This is very expensive and time consuming because the design has to be changed, a new car built and the whole process repeated if the design has any faults.

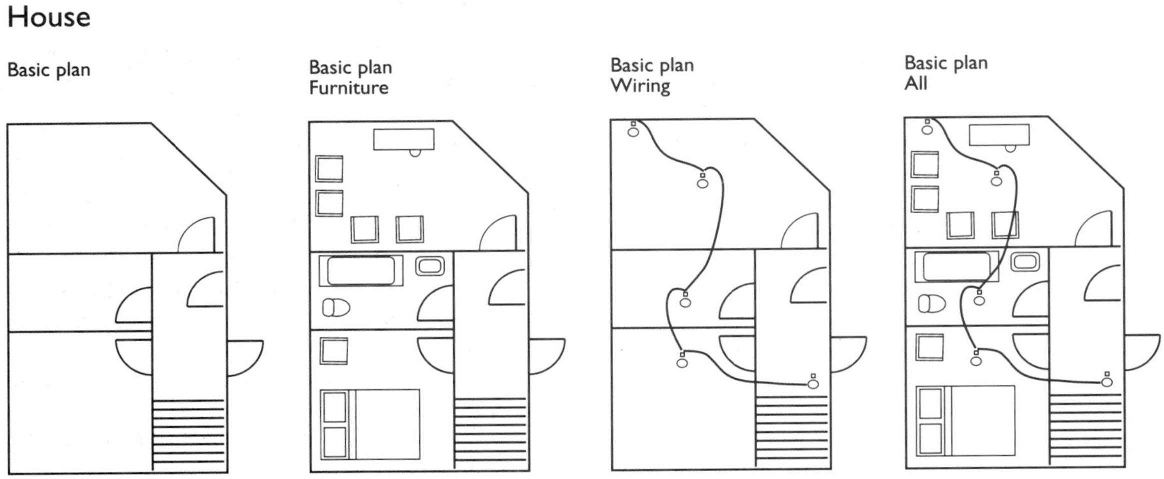


**FIGURE 11.6** *How layers are used in MacDraw. The basic plan of the house can have overlays added to help the electrician, the plumber or anyone else needing to do specialised work*

Using a computer the car can be designed and tested without spending any time or money on production. Once all the data about the new car has been input, the computer is programmed to 'crash ' the car. The effects of this pretend crash are measured and the design is changed as needed. Because all of this happens inside the computer no real cars need be produced and the design can be changed very quickly. This way of using computers to model something that happens in real life is called **simulation**.

Using computer simulation we try to predict what will happen in a real life situation from a **model** of that situation on the computer. A computer simulation program is a useful tool in providing answers to questions like these:

- An engineer would like to know the effects of various loading conditions on a bridge he's designing without actually having to build the bridge.
- An aircraft designer would like to know how changing the shape of the wings or the tail would affect the way the plane flies without having to build an aircraft specially.

There are also programs that will simulate the timing of traffic lights, or the effect that hunting will have on wildlife populations. In all of these (and lots of other) problems, computer simulations give you useful information which would have been difficult to obtain otherwise. Remember that the results depend heavily on the computer program used to model what will happen. The closer the computer program is to real life, the more reliable the results will be.

## TRAINING AIRCRAFT PILOTS

Computer simulation is used extensively for training. Perhaps one of the most well known applications of simulation is in training pilots to fly aircraft. You've probably seen flight simulators on television programmes like *The Krypton Factor*. Using simulators saves time and money when training pilots. Because a trainee isn't using a real plane, no fuel is wasted – and if he or she makes a mistake and crashes the plane no-one gets hurt! Aircraft simulators are more than just computer programs. They usually consist of a working model of the aircraft cockpit, with all the controls and indicators operating just as they would be in real life.

The main differences between a simulator and a real aircraft are

1. The windshield consists of computer monitors rather than being a view of the outside world.
2. The controls are linked to a computer running the simulation program, not to real wings or engines.
3. The model cockpit is mounted on a movable base which can simulate the movement of the aircraft during flight.

Normally a simulator is controlled by a human operator who monitors the trainee pilot's performance under different conditions, including emergency situations that are too dangerous to practice in a real aircraft.

## QUESTIONS

### Knowledge and understanding

1. What do these abbreviations mean?
   (a) CAD
   (b) CAM
   (c) CIM
   (d) CNC
   Write a sentence to explain each of these terms.
2. What is a simulation program used for?
3. Describe the stages involved in component production using computer integrated manufacture.
4. In computer aided design, what is nesting?

### Problem solving

1. What advantages does CAD/CAM bring
   (a) to a company?
   (b) to an employee?
2. What advantages are there in using a simulation program
   (a) to train pilots?
   (b) to plan a town?
   (c) to design a car?

### Practical activities

1. Use a CAD package
   (a) to draw a plan of one of the rooms in your house. Fill it with furniture.
   (b) to design a kitchen, gym or workshop.
   Save your work to disk and obtain a hard copy (on a plotter if one is available).
2. Find out what CAD packages are used in the technology department in your school.
3. Research some computer (games) magazines and find out details of any simulation programs which can run on the microcomputer systems you have in school or at home.

## KEY POINTS

- In computer aided design a computer is used to design the structure or appearance of an item on the screen
- A digitising tablet (graphics tablet) is often used as an input device in a commercial computer aided design system because it allows the operator to draw in a natural way
- Computer aided manufacture is when a computer is used to control the production process
- Computer aided manufacturing involves storing information about a product which can be changed or added to later
- Components produced using computer aided manufacture can be consistently produced very accurately
- In a flexible manufacturing system, the manufacturing process can easily be changed around to make completely different products
- In computer integrated manufacture computer aided design and computer aided manufacture are used from start to finish of a particular product with little or no human intervention
- Advantages of computer aided design and manufacturing:

  It is a faster, more accurate process than older methods

  The amount of waste can be minimised

  A single operator can see a complete job through from start to finish

  It is simpler to operate and demands less skill of the operator
- Computer simulation involves trying to predict what will happen in a real life situations from a model of that situation
- Computer simulation is used for training and in design work

# 12 Commercial data processing

## Computers in commercial data processing

**MAINFRAME COMPUTER SYSTEM**

a computer system that can carry out a very large amount of work at high speed. It usually occupies a whole large room

This chapter is about how large companies and other organisations use computers in their business. By large companies we mean supermarkets and chain stores with many branches throughout the country, banks, building societies, airlines, mail order companies and organisations like the police, income tax and the driver and vehicle licensing centre.

Large companies use computer systems because of the huge number of documents they need to deal with to run the company. It is much easier to process a customer's order or to answer enquiries about a customer's account with a computer than doing it manually. The computer searches through a large number of records much faster than a human can.

The important point to remember about commercial data processing is the huge amount of data that is being dealt with. Commercial data processing needs large **mainframe computer systems** which can process data very quickly and give the user **quick access** to data. These systems must be able to handle thousands of **repetitive tasks** that may be happening all at once. Microcomputers, regardless of their speed or processing capacity, are not able to cope with these tasks.

## *More to do*

On a manual system each piece of information (about each customer, for example) would be entered and stored by each department which needs it. This means that different departments hold many paper files, all containing much the same information (it could be names and addresses of customers). This unnecessary duplication can be avoided by using a computer to store the information. The information needs to be entered only once and held in a central computer. The different departments within a company can then make use of this information, by viewing it on their own terminals. This way of using information is called **single entry multiple use**.

Another reason why computers are used for commercial data processing is that it is easier to collect information for managers. A supermarket manager might want a report of total sales for each month, or breakdown of sales by type, or by area, which would take a very long while to collect by hand. Having a computer to help you speeds up the process.

## What is data?

We introduced data in Chapter 1. **Data** is a general term for numbers, characters and symbols which are accepted, stored and processed by a computer. When you know the structure or meaning of the data, the data becomes **information**.

Remember

*Information (for people) = data (for computers) with structure*

## The data processing cycle

The **data processing cycle** is the order that data is processed in. The data processing cycle is made up of four stages:

1 Data collection and preparation
2 Data input
3 Data processing and storage
4 Data output

Figure 12.1 illustrates how these stages are related in the data processing cycle.

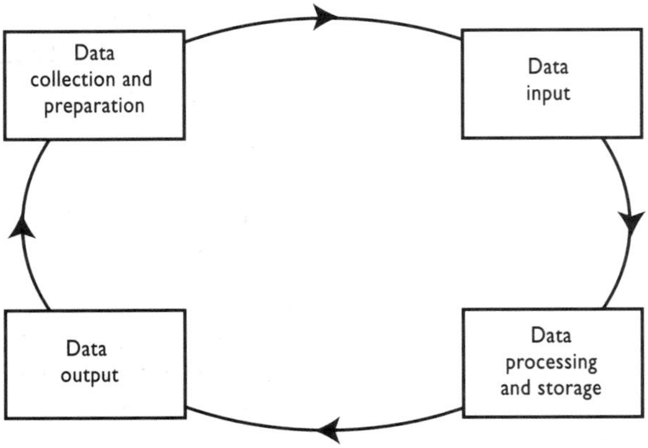


**FIGURE 12.1** *The data processing cycle*

# Data collection and preparation

The first stage in the data processing cycle is to collect and prepare data so that the computer can understand it. Data may be collected in many different ways (can you think of any?). If the data is written down or printed on a piece of paper, that paper is called a **source document**. An order form for a catalogue (like the one in figure 12.2) is an example of a source document. It is important that a source document is laid out clearly, so that people can fill it in without making mistakes.

**FIGURE 12.2** *A source document*

# Data input

The data must be input to the computer before it can be processed. Data may be input directly or indirectly to the computer system.

- If **indirect data input** is used the data is put onto a disk or tape that is not connected to the computer, or **off line**. The disk or tape is then used to put the data onto the mainframe computer system.
- **Direct data input** means that the device which takes in the information is connected directly to the mainframe computer system – it is **on line**.

The best method of inputting data is to do it directly because a human operator doesn't have to type the data in – it also means that fewer mistakes are likely to be made. Direct data input is much faster than indirect input because the data is being read directly into the computer rather than going through the preparation stages first.

**Here are some examples of indirect data input.**

### Punched cards and paper tape

Punched cards and paper tape were used in the early days of computing to input data. They are now being used much less because people prefer direct methods of data input. Punch cards and paper tape were handled in much the same ways. After the data had been keyed in, a device called a card punch was used to make a card with holes punched in it to represent the data (you can see one of these in figure 12.3) and then checked it for mistakes. The card was then read by a card reader and used to create an input file.

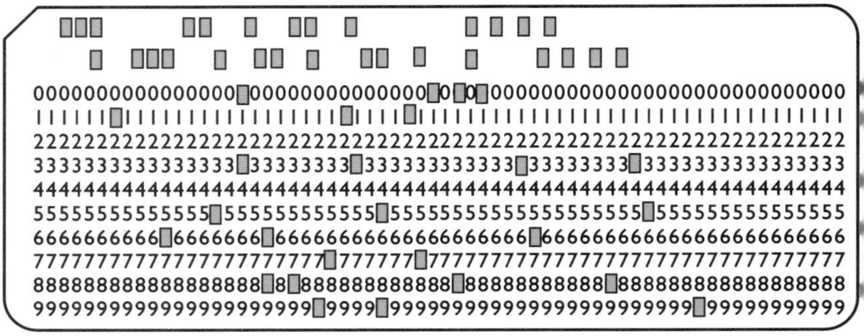

**FIGURE 12.3** *A punched card*

## Kimball tags

One type of punched card is still used today. This is the **Kimball tag**. A Kimball tag is a small piece of card with holes punched in it. It is usually attached to goods in a shop and is removed from the article when you pay for it. The sales staff collect the Kimball tags in the shop and send them back to head office where they are used as punched card input for a computer. One of these tags is shown in figure 12.4. Sometimes data is coded in a magnetic stripe on the tag instead of holes.

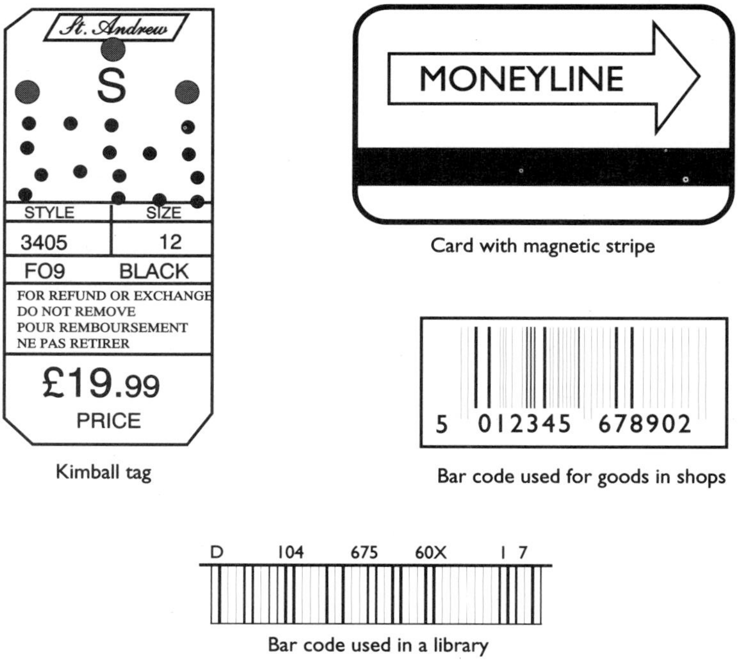


**FIGURE 12.4** *Data collection: Kimball tags, magnetic stripes and bar codes*

### Key to disk

A key to disk system consists of a keyboard, a monitor, and a disk drive. The keyboard is used to input the data, which appears on the monitor screen so it can be checked. One method of checking is for the data entry operator to enter the data twice – the data is accepted only if both versions match. (This is called verifying the data, which we looked at in Chapter 3). Accepted data is written to disk. When the time comes to process the data, the operator loads the disk into another disk drive on line to the mainframe computer. This allows the data to be input into the computer's memory for processing.

**And here are some examples of direct data input.**

### Bar codes

Most of you will be familiar with **bar codes**, because they appear on most products (from tins of beans to books and newspapers) you can buy. A bar code (you can see two examples in figure 12.4) is a set of lines of varying widths which can be read by passing a light pen or bar code reader across them. The example in figure 12.5 shows you how to understand the numbers on a bar code. The bar codes on household goods are made up of 30 lines, which gives a unique 13 digit code number to each product. Supermarkets use bar codes to keep track of their stock, as well as to save work in putting the price on every item – and then having to change it if the price changes. When the scanner at the checkout reads the bar code, the computer finds the price of the article from memory and reduces the stock number by one.

Below is a copy of the barcode for this book. The numbers at the bottom tell you quite a bit about it. 9 shows that it is a publication; 78 that it is a book; 0340 the publisher; 60556 the book title. The 1 is a computer generated check number.

ISBN 0-340-60556-1

9 780340 605561

**FIGURE 12.5** *How to read a bar code*

Library cards and library books sometimes have bar codes on them, though they have more lines than the ones used for household goods. Here the books borrowed during the day are recorded on tape using a bar code reader and the data is transferred to the computer at the end of the day.

Do you think the situation in figure 12.6 is ever likely to happen?

I THINK THEY"RE TRYING TO SELL YOU...
13
7
067432


**FIGURE 12.6**

### Magnetic stripe

A magnetic stripe is a narrow band of magnetic material on which data is held. You can see a magnetic stripe on the back of a credit card, cheque guarantee card, shop tag or train ticket. This strip can hold about 64 characters of data. This means that only a few details can be stored – the sorting codes and account numbers on bank cards, or product numbers on shop tags. A magnetic stripe on a bank card is shown in figure 12.4.

Magnetic stripes may also be used on personal identity cards. Some schools use a card with a magnetic stripe in a system of electronic registration. Every classroom has a magnetic card reader on the wall. Every time a teacher or a pupil enters the room, they pass their card through the reader. The information from each reader is sent to the school's registration computer, which can produce a period-by-period register for who was present each day.

## Character recognition

Although computer input devices can read bar codes and magnetic stripes, most people can only easily read characters. You can input characters into a computer by typing them on a keyboard but it would be much quicker if the computer could read written or printed characters. Two ways that computers can recognise characters which also make sense to people are **magnetic ink character recognition** (**MICR**) and **optical character recognition** (**OCR**).

## MICR

In this process characters are printed on forms in magnetic ink. The characters are easily read by humans so the forms can be sorted by hand. The characters are also easily recognised by a computer because they are made up of thick and thin lines.

*A cheque showing MICR characters*

The numbers along the bottom of a bank cheque are printed in magnetic ink (you can see one in the photograph). When a cheque is paid in or cashed at a bank other than the bank that issued it, the amount is typed onto the cheque in magnetic ink by the bank staff, and the cheque is sent to the clearing bank where a magnetic ink character reader is used to input the information to the computer system. There is a delay of around three days between paying in the cheque and the data reaching the computer because of the time it takes to process the vast number of cheques handled every day.

You might be familiar with the expression, 'waiting until a cheque is cleared' – now you know what it means. Magnetic ink is difficult to forge. It certainly can't be copied on a photocopier!

### *OCR*

A device called an optical character reader is able to recognise letters and numbers (like A B C or 1 2 3) and read them directly into a computer.

You must be careful if you are filling in forms that are going to be read by an OCR system, because the machine can't recognise letters or numbers that are badly formed. You wouldn't use OCR in situations where someone had to rush to fill in a form.

You can use a **scanner** with suitable OCR software to read in pages of text to a word processor, for example (more about this in Chapter 16).

**SCANNER**

an input device which allows printed text or graphics to be displayed on the screen. Usually used with OCR software

### Turnaround document

In some data processing systems, a document that is output from one process becomes the input to another. Such documents are known as **turnaround documents**.

Most gas, electricity, water and telephone bills are printed by computer. They include a tear off slip which you return with your payment. The slip has a row of OCR characters printed along the bottom. When you return the payment slip, additional characters may be typed on it, giving details of the payment made. The slip then becomes the input source document for the next stage in the process. Look at the gas bill in figure 12.7. Can you crack the code at the bottom?

## Making sure the data is correct

Data entered by the computer operator *must* be correct. The process of making sure the data is correct is called **error checking.**

### *Check digits*

One of the easiest ways of checking numbers is to add a **check digit** to the end of the number. A check digit is an extra digit which is calculated from the original number and put on the end of that number. As the number is entered, the computer calculates the check digit. If it doesn't come up with the same number as the one keyed in an error message is displayed and the computer won't accept the number.

This is very useful in making sure that the data has not been changed by being transferred from one computer to another, for example along the telephone line.

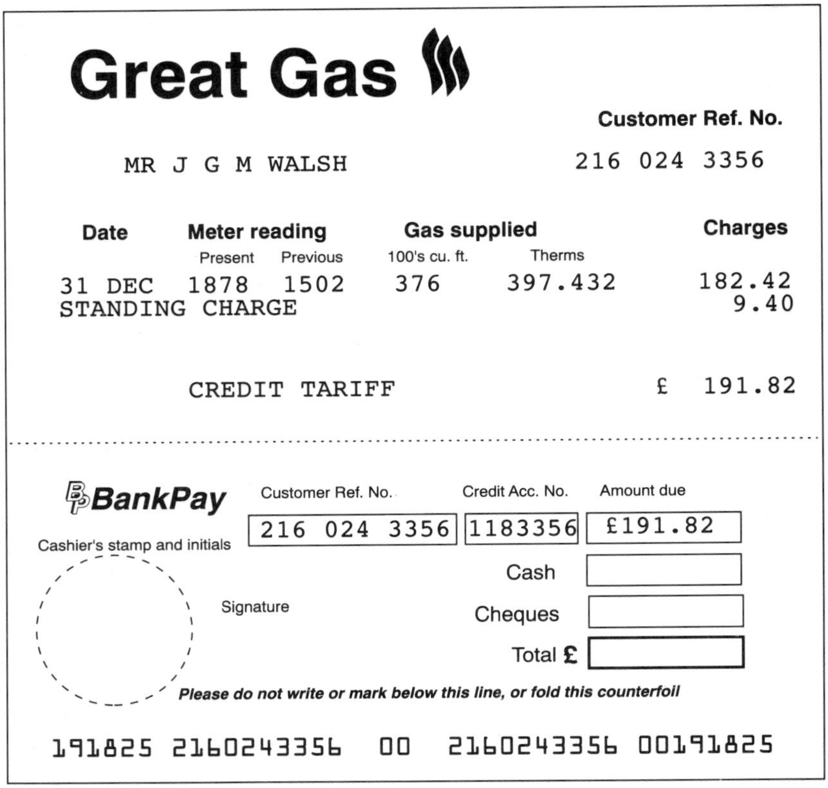

# Great Gas

**Customer Ref. No.**

MR J G M WALSH 216 024 3356

| **Date** | **Meter reading** Present | Previous | **Gas supplied** 100's cu. ft. | Therms | **Charges** |
|---|---|---|---|---|---|
| 31 DEC | 1878 | 1502 | 376 | 397.432 | 182.42 |
| STANDING CHARGE | | | | | 9.40 |

CREDIT TARIFF £ 191.82

**BankPay**

| Customer Ref. No. | Credit Acc. No. | Amount due |
|---|---|---|
| 216 024 3356 | 1183356 | £191.82 |

Cashier's stamp and initials

Signature

Cash

Cheques

Total £

*Please do not write or mark below this line, or fold this counterfoil*

191825 2160243356 00 2160243356 00191825

**FIGURE 12.7** *Here is a turnaround document with OCR characters at the bottom*

## *Calculating a check digit*

The number in a bar code also contains a check digit. If the bar code reader doesn't read the number correctly, the operator will be alerted by the computer to scan the bar code again.

One possible system for producing a check digit might be that the digits in a number must add up to a number that divides exactly by three.

> Suppose we want to make up a check digit for the number **2954**
> We add up the digits – 2 + 9 + 5 + 4 = 20
> To make the total divide exactly by three, we must add the number 1 at the end of the number to make the total 21, since 21 divides exactly by three.
> So the check digit is 1.
> Adding the check digit to the original number gives **29541**.

**VALIDATION**

checking that data is sensible. A range check is a way of validating data

### *Other checks*

Other checks which can be carried out involve checking the **number of characters** (numbers, letters and spaces) in a field. If the entry has more characters than will fit in the field, then an error message should appear.

A **range check** can be made against some fields which contain numbers (age, money or dates) to check that the number is sensible. This is called **validating** the data, and was discussed in Chapter 3. Examples would be

- an age of more than 100 or less than 0
- a total on a bill of £0.00
- a date of greater than 31 or less than 1.

One of the most reliable methods of checking that data is correct is to have the data entry operator type the data twice. This method (called verifying the data) was described earlier in the key to disk system, and in Chapter 3.

## QUESTIONS

**Knowledge and understanding**

1 Give three examples of companies or organisations which might use mainframe or large computers.
2 What is the data processing cycle? Name the stages involved.
3 Name one form of
   (a) direct data input
   (b) indirect data input
4 What is a key to disk system? How does it work?
5 What is a turnaround document? Give one example.

**Problem solving**

1 Give two reasons why companies use computers for commercial data processing.
2 Why is a bar code a more efficient method of data input than a Kimball tag?
3 Why does it take so long for a cheque to 'clear'?

## *More to do*

### *Remote data entry*

Data can be entered remotely from a **remote terminal** in another building – or even in another country, provided it is linked to the mainframe computer.

### *Mark sense cards*

**Mark sense cards** are cards divided into columns that allow spaces for marking with a pencil line. These marks can then be read electrically by a machine (a mark sense reader) linked to a computer or card punch. This is like optical scanning where the marks are read by a light

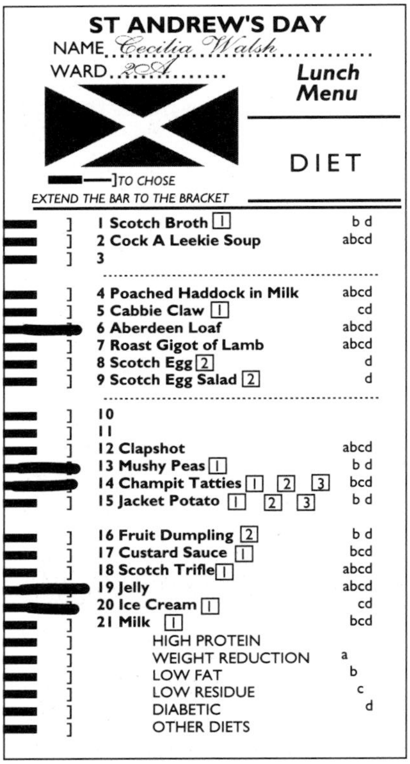

ST ANDREW'S DAY
NAME Cecilia Walsh
WARD 20A
Lunch Menu
DIET
]TO CHOSE
EXTEND THE BAR TO THE BRACKET

| | | |
|---|---|---|
| ] | 1 Scotch Broth [1] | b d |
| ] | 2 Cock A Leekie Soup | abcd |
| ] | 3 | |
| ] | 4 Poached Haddock in Milk | abcd |
| ] | 5 Cabbie Claw [1] | cd |
| | 6 Aberdeen Loaf | abcd |
| ] | 7 Roast Gigot of Lamb | abcd |
| ] | 8 Scotch Egg [2] | d |
| ] | 9 Scotch Egg Salad [2] | d |
| ] | 10 | |
| ] | 11 | |
| ] | 12 Clapshot | abcd |
| | 13 Mushy Peas [1] | b d |
| | 14 Champit Tatties [1] [2] [3] | bcd |
| ] | 15 Jacket Potato [1] [2] [3] | b d |
| ] | 16 Fruit Dumpling [2] | b d |
| ] | 17 Custard Sauce [1] | bcd |
| ] | 18 Scotch Trifle [1] | abcd |
| | 19 Jelly | abcd |
| | 20 Ice Cream [1] | cd |
| ] | 21 Milk [1] | bcd |
| ] | HIGH PROTEIN | |
| ] | WEIGHT REDUCTION | a |
| ] | LOW FAT | b |
| ] | LOW RESIDUE | c |
| ] | DIABETIC | d |
| ] | OTHER DIETS | |

**FIGURE 12.8** *A mark sense card*

sensor. Both methods of reading are useful for collecting data and analysing the responses to multiple-choice type questions. Figure 12.8 shows you a mark sense card used by patients to select their food while in hospital. Use of these cards is another example of direct data input.

## *More about error checking*

### Validation

Checking data to ensure that it is sensible and accurate is called validation. Validity checks do not eliminate mistakes, but they make it difficult for wrong data to get through to the computer or its peripherals.

All validity checks can be programmed into the computer so that it can automatically check the data input. Where checks for accuracy have to be made, there are several methods of generating a coded number that can be checked easily. A validation program will check the number each time it is used by duplicating the calculation, and if it fails to produce the same answer an error has been found.

### *Check digits*

One method of validating data is to use the check digit as described earlier. A common method of calculating check digits is to add each digit of the code number and take the least significant digit as the check digit.

Here is an example

| | |
|---|---|
| Code number | 13459 |
| Total of all the digits | 22 |
| Check digit | 2 |
| Number to be entered into computer | 134592 |

The most popular method of calculating a check digit is to use an extra stage of multiplying each digit of the number by a different factor, adding them together and dividing the total by 11. This method is called the **weight modulus 11 check digit**. It is supposed to be so reliable that it would be hundreds of years before a wrong entered number got through this check. Weighted modulus 11 is used to calculate International Standard Book Numbers (ISBN) and cheque account numbers.

For example:

Code number **13459**
Weighting values 65432
(the weighting values start at 2 and go up one at a time)

Now multiply each digit in the code number by its weighting value and add them together

(**1**[x]6) + (**3**[x]5) + (**4**[x]4) + (**5**[x]3) + (**9**[x]2) = 70

Now divide by this number by 11
70/11 = 6, remainder **4**

The check digit is calculated according to the following rules:

If the remainder is 0 then the check digit is 0
If the remainder is 1 then the check digit is X
Any other number gives a check digit of 11 – number
In this case the remainder is 4, so the check digit is 11 – 4 = **7**

So the number to be entered into computer is **134597**

### *Hash totals*

The **hash total** method of error checking involves adding together all the numbers that have been entered into the computer and entering this total. The computer adds up all the numbers that have been entered and checks the number it obtains against the total entered. If there is a difference, then a mistake has been made and the operator will have to enter the data again. Supposing the data preparation operator had to enter the numbers 12, 2, 8, 1. The total of these four numbers is 23. When using this method, the operator would enter 12, 2, 8, 1, 23.

### *Batch totals*

Using **batch totals** means counting the number of entries which are made and entering the number. For example 4, 3, 16, 17, 21 is five numbers in total, so 5 would be entered.

## Verification

The data preparation operator should type the data in accurately, but everyone can make mistakes. Verification ensures that errors don't get through. The usual method of verification is for the operator to type the data in twice. If the second set of data doen't match the first the operator is alerted to a mistake and has to type it in again.

# EXTRA QUESTIONS

**Knowledge and understanding**

**1** Explain the difference between validation and verification of data.

**2** What is
(a) a hash total?
(b) a batch total?

**Problem solving**

**1** What is a weighted check digit?

**2** Calculate the weighted modulus 11 check digit for this book's ISBN

**3** Read the following article and answer the questions

## *Postcode technology progresses*

New machines that will radically change the way mail is code marked are to be built for Royal Mail. These new machines incorporate three major new features. They include optical character recognition (OCR) computers that can 'read' an entire typewritten address. They can also 'read' the postcode for most hand-written addresses.

And if OCR cannot 'read' the address on one letter it can download an electronic image of the letter to a computer screen. A coding operator can then type in the postcode.

Paul Barton, head of automation development, said: 'These new machines will use similar technology to that developed for the American postal service – but they will be tailor-made for Royal Mail's operation.'

The first machine is expected to be installed in a sorting office by August 1992.

Dr Barton said: 'over the next few years they will replace all existing coding desks. In future coding operators will be coding letters that they see on computer screens. This means that instead of working in the main part of the sorting office the coding operators will be able to do their work in a special, quiet and well-furnished room.'

(a) What advantages will this new system have for the post office? For the postal workers?
(b) What happens if the OCR system can't read an address?
(c) Why is the OCR system expected to be able to read *entire* typewritten addresses yet only *most* handwritten addresses?

# Data processing and storage

## Files, records and fields

The names used in connection with computer files are the same as the ones used for manual filing. this was explained in Chapter 3, but here is a reminder:

- A **file** is an organised collection of data arranged according to a particular structure.
- The units of data which make up a file are called **records**. A record is like a single card in a card index.
- Each record contains a number of separate items of data called **fields**.
- A file is said to be **updated** when it is changed or new data is added to it to bring it up to date.

Two types of file are used in data processing:

1 The **master file** holds the latest version of the data. Files are copied from the master file for everyday use. The master file should always be used if a copy of a file is damaged, though it is normally only used when it is being updated.
2 A **transaction file** contains the data used to update the master file and holds everything that has been changed since the last time the master file was updated. This changed data is often recorded in a transaction file because it is received in no particular order and transferred by tape or disk at a later time. Since the data in the transaction file is usually not in any particular order, it must be **sorted** into the same order as the data in the master file before the master file can be updated. Figure 12.9 shows sorting a file.

**SORTING**

putting a list of items into order

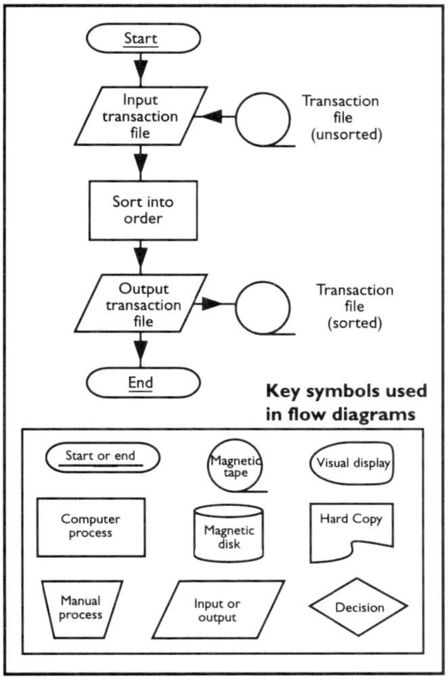


**FIGURE 12.9** *Sorting a file*

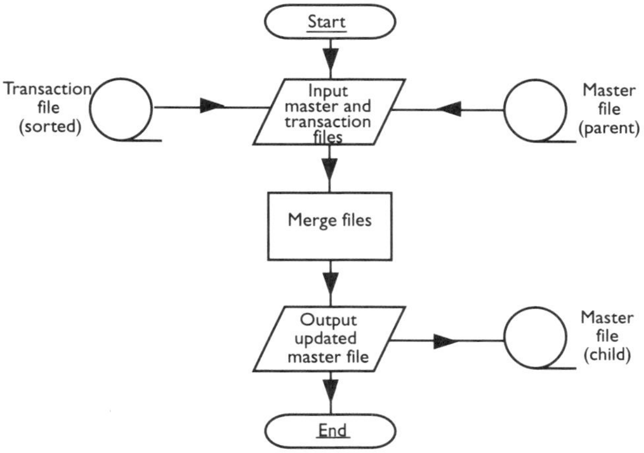


**FIGURE 12.10** *Updating a master file from a transaction file*

### Backing up

To make sure that valuable data is not lost if a file is damaged, you should always keep a spare copy of the file (a **backup**) in a safe place. Everyone should have at *least* one backup copy of their programs or data, though more than one is recommended.

### Information processing

A computer can process information in two ways.

1 **Batch processing** involves collecting all the different data that have been input together and putting them into a computer in one set or **batch**. This means that the operator only has to carry out one loading and running operation no matter how many programs are in the batch. The programs are processed as a single unit, which avoids wasting computer time to load each program.

Before computer facilities were introduced to schools, each pupil in a class could write a program on mark sense cards. These cards were taken and fed, as a batch, to a distant computer. There was usually some delay before the programs could be run and several days could pass before the output was returned.

2 **Interactive processing** is when data is processed or updated as the transaction is entered, and any enquiries are replied to immediately. This sort of system is used when it is important to have as much up-to-date information as possible, for example when booking seats in a cinema or on an aircraft.

## *More to do*

### *Reading data files*

There are two different ways of reading or accessing data files:

**1 SEQUENTIAL (SERIAL) ACCESS**

Data files stored in sequence can only be accessed in the same way. Magnetic tape is an example of a **sequential access** medium. To read a particular record stored on magnetic tape the users would have to go through all the records in sequence until they find it.

**2 RANDOM (DIRECT) ACCESS**

Data files stored by random access can be read directly without having to work through from the first one.

Magnetic disks and chips are two examples of **random access media.**

Because of these different access methods, it takes much longer to find a record on magnetic tape than on disk. Disk storage is normally used when speed is important – for example, during an interactive processing operation like a transaction at an automated telling machine.

### *File ancestry*

**File ancestry** involves keeping the previous version of a file that has been updated to reduce the effects of losing or damaging data. Three copies of a file should be kept. These are called **grandparent, parent** and **child** files. The disk or tape with the latest version is the child. The next time the files are used the user loads the child into the computer. The child becomes the parent at the end of the session and the updated file is saved as the new child. In the same session the parent becomes the grandparent and so on.

If one copy of the data is damaged you can work on the second copy knowing that there is still a third copy available. If there were only two copies and the first was damaged, then you should duplicate the second on to another disk before updating it – and there is a chance of losing the second copy while it's being copied. The third copy must *always* be stored separately from the first two. In practice, additional copies are usually stored over a period of time.

## *Data output*

After the data has been processed, the information can be output onto a computer screen. Generally output information for customers (like bills or statements) is output in printed form. Often businesses print the output on preprinted stationery. This reduces the amount of printing involved, and so is faster than printing out a complete bill on blank paper. By using preprinted stationery companies can use different colours of printing and include advertisements.

### Microfiche and microfilm

**Microfiche** slides are like photographic slides and are viewed using a special type of high-magnification projector. Many pages of print, diagrams and graphs are reduced in size and stored on microfiche. A microfiche slide 15 cm x 10 cm could hold up to 250 pages of A4. To reduce the amount of backing store needed, a company may transfer some of the files to microfiche. This also removes the need for a computer terminal to look at the records. Microfiche is used in libraries for holding catalogues of books. Microfiche is also sometimes used in car accessory shops, to help you find out the part number you need by showing diagrams of different areas of the car.

**Microfilm** is another way of reducing the pages of information but the pages are stored on a roll of film rather than on a slide. A roll of microfilm can hold about 2000 pages of A4.

## *More to do*

**File**

Instead of outputting data to a printer, to microfilm or displaying it on the screen it can be saved as a new file. This new file could be held on disk or magnetic tape. The advantage of keeping the data like this is that if it needs to be processed again later the information can simply be reloaded into the computer without having to be input all over again.

# *Hardware*

**HARDWARE**

the physical parts or devices which make up a computer system

**DEVICE**

a single item of computer hardware

The basic **hardware** required for commercial data processing usually consists of a **mainframe computer** system. A mainframe computer system is made up of separate **devices**. These usually include

- a central processing unit (or CPU), which carries out the data processing, holds the programs in its memory and coordinates the running of the whole computer system.
- input devices
- output devices, which can produce various different outputs, for example hard copy from line printers, page printers, or characters on the screen of a terminal.
- backing store. Common types of backing store are magnetic tape and magnetic disk. Backing store allows the computer access to large quantities of data, far more than can be stored in the main memory of the CPU at one time.
- terminals (these are used for data input to the computer. A terminal consists of a keyboard and screen)
- operator's console. The operator's console is connected directly to the CPU. It has a keyboard and screen like a terminal. The computer operator uses the console to communicate directly with the CPU.

A typical mainframe computer system is big enough to occupy a whole room (like a large classroom) and may cost millions of pounds. You can see a typical mainframe computer in this photograph.

*A mainframe computer system*

A terminal doesn't have to be in the same room – or even in the same building – as the mainframe computer it's attached to. In fact it could be connected to the computer via a telephone line. A terminal connected to a distant mainframe computer is called a **remote terminal**. The chapters on Viewdata and Electronic Mail give more examples of the use of remote terminals.

## Advantages of commercial data processing

Commercial data processing using computers has a number of advantages over a manual system.

- Orders can be processed much more quickly than with a manual system.
- Errors are less likely because of the checks built into the computer system.
- It is much easier for the company to keep in contact with and

**MAIL MERGE**

the process of automatically loading personal details from a separate mailing list and placing them into the correct places in a standard letter

hold information about a large number of customers.

- Very large lists of customers can be held on backing store.
- Lists held on backing store are easily kept up-to-date.
- Direct mailings to customers can be done automatically using a mail merge.

# *Staff in a data processing department*

The widespread introduction of computers has meant that many new types of jobs have been created which did not exist before. The staff in a data processing department of a large company would include systems analysts, programmers, data preparation operators, computer operators and librarians. A data processing manager is in charge of the department. The typical organisation of staff in a data processing department is shown in figure 12.11. Let us look at the jobs some of these people do.

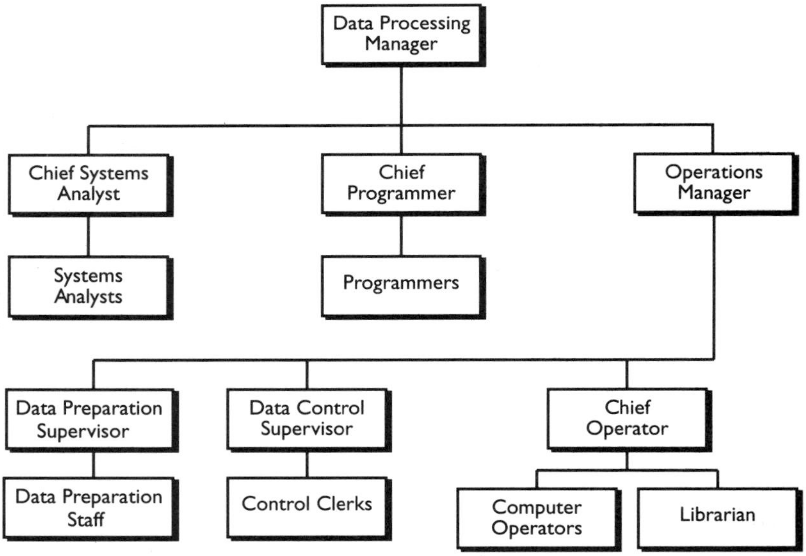


**FIGURE 12.11** *The organisation of staff in a data processing department*

## Data processing manager

The **data processing manager** is the person in charge of the whole data processing department. He or she will be responsible to the directors or owners of the company for all the computing activities which go on. The data processing manager will appoint new staff and must know about systems analysis, programming and operations.

Systems analyst

## Systems analyst

The job of the **systems analyst** is to plan exactly how a computer can be used to help the user. The systems analyst will look at all the jobs the company does manually and decide which ones can be done best by computer. This process is called **systems analysis**. The systems analyst spends a long time talking to the users of the manual system to help them decide what they need the computer system to be able to do. Each step of the task is carefully investigated and described and the systems analyst draws up a **systems flow diagram**. Figures 12.9, 12.10 and 12.12 are examples of systems flow diagrams.

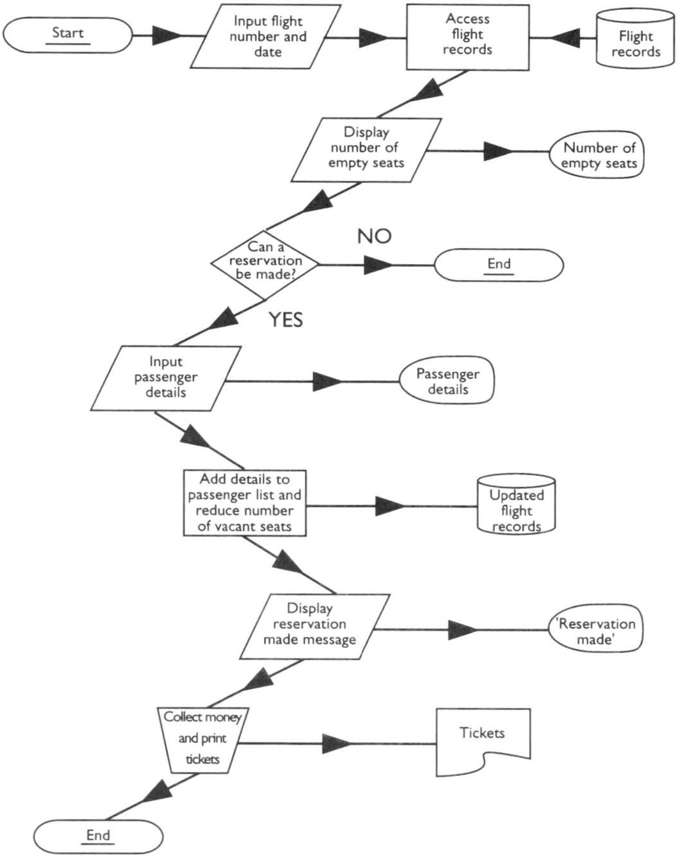


**FIGURE 12.12** *Airline seat reservations. Look back at figure 12.9 for an explanation of the symbols*

The systems analyst will also write a report which details the cost of installing and maintaining a computer system. The size of the computer system installed will depend on the size of the company and their plans for expansion. The systems analyst will usually advise a large company to buy a mainframe computer system.

After the computer has been installed and is working, the systems analyst looks for ways to improve the system and make it more efficient.

## Programmers

Programmer

The systems analyst will consult a **programmer** about the programs that the company needs and the programmer will write the programs or check whether there are some commercially available software applications to suit the company. Software which has already been written and which can be bought and used straight away without altering it to suit the particular company is called 'off the shelf'.

Usually the programmer will have to write completely new software, according to the systems flow diagram produced by the systems analyst. He might write large programs in several parts or **modules**. Sometimes each part is written by a different programmer and the parts are combined to make the whole program and have any mistakes taken out. The process of removing mistakes is called **debugging**.

The programmer also writes **documentation** for the project, which is a detailed explanation of how the program works so that other people can understand it.

## Data preparation operators

**Data preparation operators** type in programs and data, usually into devices which prepare media, such as disks or tape (this is called 'key to disk') so a computer operator can load them into the computer. Data preparation operators usually work from source documents (see page 155). Earlier in the book you were told that to make sure that the data has been entered correctly (to verify it) the data preparation operator should type the data twice. In fact data preparation operators usually work in pairs. Both people type in the same data, and the data is only accepted by the computer if both sets match. (See the section on data input for further details.) The **data preparation supervisor** watches over the operators and makes sure that they meet any deadlines.

Computer operator

## Computer operator

The **computer operator** is concerned with the day-to-day running of the computer system. He or she *may* use the keyboard to make small alterations to programs but their main task is to make sure the whole system operates properly. This will involve loading and running programs, changing magnetic tapes and disks, keeping printers supplied with paper, ribbons or toner and so on.

Librarian

Engineer

### Librarian

The **librarian** is responsible for storing, cataloguing and indexing all the computer software. He or she will make sure that it is put back in the correct place after use. The librarian may also make backups of files for data security and in case of loss or damage.

### Data control clerks

**Data control clerks** make sure that the right source documents are given to the right people at the right time and that this part of the operation works smoothly.

### Operations manager

The **operations manager** makes sure the jobs are done in the right order and that staff are available to get top priority work done on time.

### Engineers

New computer systems are installed and existing ones maintained by **engineers** who visit companies to repair and inspect computers. Maintenance is carried out on a regular basis and whenever there is a breakdown.

### Sales staff

Computer **sales staff** have the job of finding a system to suit the needs of any customer. They also arrange demonstrations of goods so that a potential customer can see a machine before he or she buys it. The salesperson may organise training courses for customers who need to learn to operate the particular computer system they're buying.

## QUESTIONS

### Knowledge and understanding

1 Describe some of the tasks performed by a
 (a) systems analyst
 (b) programmer
 (c) data preparation operator
 (d) computer operator
 in the data processing department of a large company

2 Explain the following terms
 (a) batch processing
 (b) interactive processing

### Problem solving

1 Why does data processing use both master files and transaction files?
 Why not just use the master file all of the time?

Why must a transaction file be sorted before it is used to update a master file?

2 Which type of data processing (batch or interactive) would be most appropriate in
   (a) a cash card machine?
   (b) stock control in a supermarket?
   (c) processing cheques?

3 Why is it important to keep backups of data files?

## EXTRA QUESTIONS

### Knowledge and understanding

1 What is the difference between sequential and random file access?

2 What is file ancestry?
Draw a systems flow diagram to explain the stages involved.

3 What is a remote terminal?

### Problem solving

1 Give one example of a data processing situation in which sequential access would be inappropriate.
Give a reason for your answer.

2 Why do data preparation operators work in pairs?

3 You are a data processing manager in a small company which sells seeds. The company sends out catalogues and customers buy the seeds by mail order. The managing director tells you that she can only afford to employ four people in your department. Which specialists would you employ? Why?

## *Computer crime*

Sometimes a person employed in a data processing department is untrustworthy and uses their position to commit crimes. It can be almost impossible to prevent computer crime, especially if the criminal is very clever.

Typical crimes involve damaging the computer system by destroying, **corrupting** or changing the data files. They may steal money by **computer fraud** (an employee who knows or can find out the security passwords to a computer system can steal money by transferring it from the company's account into one of their own). There are two very common ways of interfering with computer data – '**hacking**' and producing **viruses**. You first came across these in Chapter 1.

**CORRUPT**

to corrupt a file means to damage it so it can't be read

### Hacking

'Hacking' is gaining access to a computer system, usually illegally, and interfering with the data on it. It is possible for people to hack into a company's computer system from anywhere outside the company, using their own computer and a **modem** attached to a telephone line. So the 'intruder' does not have to be an employee with access to a terminal inside the company. If you are caught hacking you could be prosecuted.

People who tamper with computer systems in this way are called 'hackers', whether they are employed by the company whose system they're hacking or not. Companies can make hacking less easy by changing their security passwords regularly, and keeping them secure. One case reported in the newspapers involved a United States bank which was 'broken into' by hackers in March 1988 and again in October 1990. The bank hadn't even bothered to change its security passwords in over two and a half years!

Large companies (like banks) have been slow to appreciate the threat of computer crime. They won't believe that their security systems can be overcome so easily. Banks who have been victims of computer crime often bear the loss without telling the police because they are afraid that their customers will lose confidence in them and their ability to safeguard their money.

**FIGURE 12.13** *Computer crime*

## Computer viruses

A virus is a 'rogue' program that someone has deliberately created and written on to disk. A computer virus is able to make itself invisible to the computer until it passes into the memory of a host computer. Then the virus will reproduce itself on all the software being used by that machine until it is detected and eradicated (very much like 'real-life' viruses act, in fact). A virus can do nothing more serious than display a simple message (like 'Happy New Year') on the screen but sometimes, viruses cause a lot of damage by destroying and corrupting files.

In the early days of computing it wasn't easy to share data between computers, but floppy disks and networking have changed that. How often do you write a file to a floppy disk so you can use it at home, or later in another class? Computer viruses often originate as part of computer games which are exchanged and resold many times over. Here's how to prevent viruses spreading.

- *Don't* share disks.
- *Don't* copy software.
- *Do* check all your computer disks regularly with an anti-virus program.

In the figure below you can see some examples of the kinds of damage viruses can do.

## Michelangelo virus strikes - but its bark is worse than its byte

Thousands of computer owners lost data and software today when the mysterious Michelangelo virus was triggered in hard disks.

Businesses and industries around the world were hit by the computerised plague, and one US expert said as many as 10,000 computers could have been affected.

But no military or government data appeared to have been lost, and analysts agreed the effects could have been far worse.

Alan Solomon, who heads one of the world's leading computer anti-virus software suppliers, said he had heard of no more than three dozen virus attacks in Britain, and he regarded the Michelangelo scare as overblown.

"It's a massive fizzle...a storm in a tea-cup," he said. "It's scare-mongering by the Americans."

At least eight companies in Britain were affected by the virus. "The impact has been more severe then we thought," said Detective Inspector John Austen, head of Scotland Yard's computer crimes unit.

However, the Yard's advance warning about the virus, enabling computer users to detect it and "disinfect" their systems, had saved millions of pounds in Britain.

The Michelangelo virus - named after the artist born 517 years today - wipes out computer data by overwriting with gobbledygook.

It is thought to have been created by an Australian teenager and is believed to have been spread by a Taiwanese programme copying company.

Any computer compatible with the International Business Machines (IBM) standard was a potential target.

A Swedish engineer said the virus struck for the first time exactly one year ago, apparently on computers incorrectly set to its target date of March 6, 1992.

More than 1000 computers were affected in up to 500 companies in South Africa, most of them used by pharmacists likely to have infected each other's systems during their frequent communications.

Virus watchers reported 48 confirmed cases in Australia, including an airline in Melbourne, two mining and exploration companies in Perth and a car rental company in Adelaide.

The Federal Office for Computer Security (BSI) in Bonn said the worst case in Germany hit in the Ruhr industrial area, where one firm saw data on 75 computers wiped off on seconds.

But a BSI official said about 1000 Michelangelo viruses had been nipped in the bud by vaccines before the target date.

The virus itself is a simple instruction concealed on the floppy disk which tells any computer using it to destroy data on a given date, and to give the same order to any other computer with which it links up

"If the inventor was a very smart person it would have been about 20 minutes work," said Dutch computer fraud expert Loek Weerd.

In Japan, one architectural and civil engineering firm lost up to £17,000 worth of data, including architectural drawings stored on three personal computers.

—*The Herald 7/3/92*

**FIGURE 12.14** *What viruses can do*

The first time someone was convicted of using a virus to sabotage computer records was in the USA in 1988. They were ordered to pay damages of $11 800 to the company that employed them. By then, the Computer Virus Industry Association had documented 250 000 cases of virus sabotage.

In 1991 during the Gulf War it was rumoured that the United States intelligence agents disabled Iraq's air defence batteries by inserting a virus into the computers which controlled the entire system. The virus was smuggled into Baghdad in a microchip inside a printer, and had the effect of blanking the screen each time the operator tried to open a program.

# Electronic funds transfer

**Electronic funds transfer** (shortened to **EFT**) is a way you can pay for goods without actually using any money. When you decide to buy something the amount of money that you owe the shop is transferred automatically from your bank account into the shop's bank account. To pay for your goods this way you must have a special bank or building society card which supports this system. This card is called a debit card, and Switch and Delta are two examples. You will find out much more about EFT in Chapter 14.

**DIRECT DATA ENTRY**

when data is input straight into a computer system. Examples are bar codes, magnetic stripes

The place in a shop where the goods change hands is called the **point of sale** (**POS**) – when you pay at the till (the POS) the item becomes yours. Many shops now have computers at the POS so any record (for example the amount of goods in stock) can be changed as it happens. A POS terminal may have its own backing store or may be directly connected to a mainframe computer. POS terminals usually have some form of direct data entry (a bar code reader perhaps) built in to them. As the assistant passes the goods through, the information from the bar code is read into the terminal which will add up the total bill – and keep track of what's been sold for stock control.

The idea of electronic funds transfer can be combined with the POS terminal to give an **Electronic Funds Transfer at Point Of Sale** (**EFTPOS**) system. You will find out more about the EFTPOS system in Chapter 14.

# Costs of using computers for C.D.P.

### Initial costs

The costs of setting up a system are high – it costs a lot of money to buy the equipment needed to computerise a large business. You need to buy both hardware and software and the software may be more expensive than the hardware because of its complexity.

### Running costs

The larger a program is, the longer it takes to write. Hardware needs to be checked regularly and the software programs need to be checked and maintained. Maintaining hardware and software contributes to the running costs of a data processing department. What else would be part of the running costs?

Businesses introduce computer systems in order to increase their productivity, to sell to as many people as possible and to develop a mass market for their products. Mail order catalogue companies are a good example of how businesses can use computer systems to sell to a huge number of people all over the world.

## Security and privacy

**DATA PROTECTION ACT**

a law which regulates how personal data about individuals is kept on computer.

**PASSWORD**

a secret code that you use to access private information on a computer system or to log on to a network

All large companies hold data about their employees and customers on computer. Any information which a company holds must be registered under the terms of the Data Protection Act, and must be accurate and up to date. Companies must tell their customers if their details are to be stored on a computer system and must show its customers any information it holds about them if they ask for it. The Data Protection Act is explained in greater detail in Chapter 1.

Information held on computer files must be kept private. Information about how much credit someone was allowed or details about how much they earn must not be shown to anyone who doesn't need to know about it.

Information must also be kept secure. Files can be held in a safe place to which only certain members of staff have access, files can be protected by passwords, and the system can allow different levels of access for different users.

### AN ADVANTAGE OF COMPUTER FILES

A problem that many companies face is customers who don't pay their bills on time. How can a computer system help? A computer system can gather the files together on all the customers whose payments are overdue and print out a list. This will save someone having to search through all the records by hand.

### Sale of customer lists

**MAIL SHOT**

letters prepared by mail merge and sent out to individuals on a mailing list – also called direct mail or junk mail

In order to get back some of the money that they have had to spend in building up a data processing computer system, some companies sell their lists of customer's names and addresses to other companies. This is why we get so much 'junk mail' nowadays. People disagree whether it is right to sell lists like this.

Whole businesses have been set up around selling mailing lists. Some companies carefully study the area you live in, and group housing estates and roads into 'social classes'. Mail order companies can buy lists of names and addresses arranged like this. They then target a mail shot at people they think will buy particular products.

## *Customer lists and the law*

The Advertising Standards Authority has imposed strict regulations on the sale and transfer of mailing lists between companies since 1 January, 1992.

- The person must be told when their data is collected that it might be used for direct mail.
- The person must have the right to stop their name being used in this way.
- If anyone asks an advertiser to remove their name from this list, then the advertiser must do so.

Chapter 1 has more details about mail shots.

## QUESTIONS

### Knowledge and understanding

1 Here is an example of the data processing cycle in a DIY furniture store. Read it and then answer the questions.

### *Data collection and preparation*

The customer chooses something from the range of goods on display. Before she can buy the item, she has to fill in a 'personal selection form' (like the one in figure 12.15). This is the **source document** for the next stage in the data processing cycle.

**FIGURE 12.15** *An example of a completed source document*

# KNOW WHAT YOU WANT?

## SPEED YOUR SHOPPING WITH THIS PERSONAL SELECTION FORM

**Step 1** ***CHECK THE SELECTION NUMBER*** on the ticket of the item(s) you require. Enter the SELECTION NUMBER, THE QUANTITY REQUIRED AND THE UNIT PRICE

| SELECTION NUMBER | QUANTITY | UNIT PRICE |
|---|---|---|
| ALP 117 | 1 | 12.99 |
| | | |
| | | |
| | | |
| | | |
| | | |

**Step 2** ***TICK THE APPROPRIATE PAYMENT METHOD***

If paying by cheque, make payable to LNF Ltd, signed and dated. On the reverse side, please write your NAME, ADDRESS AND PHONE NO.

☑ CASH ☐ HOMEPLAN ☐ VISA
☐ DINERS ☐ CHEQUE ☐ ACCESS
☐ AMEX ☐ CONNECT ☐ OTHER

**Step 3** **ENTER YOUR NAME, ADDRESS AND TELEPHONE No.**

NAME *Mrs Walsh* TEL No.
ADDRESS POSTCODE

**Step 4** **HAND IN THE COMPLETED FORM AT THE PAYMENT DESK.**
Your details will be punched into the computer. Once your purchase has been confirmed, a sales slip/invoice will be issued so you can collect your purchase(s) at the PICK UP POINT

LNF

### *Data input*

The customer takes her completed form to the service point in the store. The sales assistant types in the details from the form into the computer terminal. The customer pays for the item and details of the payment are entered by the sales assistant into the terminal.

### *Data processing*

The terminal is linked to the company's stock control **master file** so the sales assistant can check the item is in stock before the transaction is completed. The details of the sale at the terminal are used to **update** the stock master file, reducing the stock of that item by one. This must be done in **real time,** so that the numbers of each item in stock are always correct.

### *Data output*

The terminal prints out a receipt containing all the transaction details and it is given to the customer. It could look like the one in figure 12.17. The customer takes the receipt to the pickup point in the store. At the same time the computer sends a message to the pickup point that this item has been sold and it is brought to the pickup point, ready for the customer to collect it.

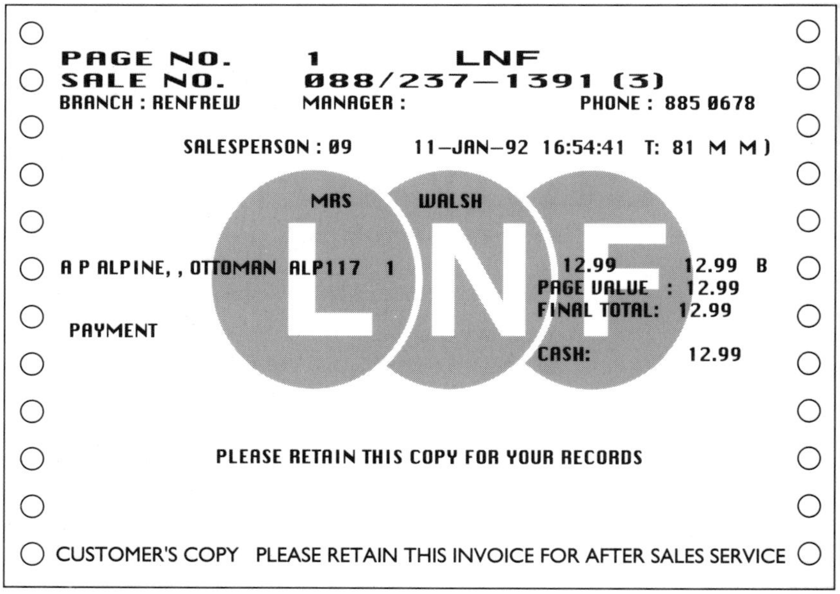
PAGE NO. 1 LNF
SALE NO. 088/237—1391 (3)
BRANCH : RENFREW MANAGER : PHONE : 885 0678
SALESPERSON : 09 11–JAN–92 16:54:41 T: 81 M M)
MRS WALSH
A P ALPINE, , OTTOMAN ALP117 1 12.99 12.99 B
PAGE VALUE : 12.99
FINAL TOTAL: 12.99
PAYMENT
CASH: 12.99
PLEASE RETAIN THIS COPY FOR YOUR RECORDS
CUSTOMER'S COPY PLEASE RETAIN THIS INVOICE FOR AFTER SALES SERVICE

**FIGURE 12.16** *A printed till receipt*

(a) What is meant by the words in **bold** in the text?

(b) What three data items are contained in the 'personal selection form'?

(c) Which of these must the sales assistant type into the terminal?
(d) What other information files are likely to be updated as a result of this transaction?

2 What is electronic funds transfer?

**Problem solving**

1 Why is it important that personal data which is held by companies should be accurate, secure and private?
By giving an example in each case, show what could happen if data was not accurate, secure and private.

## EXTRA QUESTIONS

**Knowledge and understanding**

1 What could happen if a company doesn't bother to take security measures with its data?
2 What regulations are in force concerning customer mailing lists?

**Problem solving**

1 What steps would be involved if the customer in the example above paid for the furniture with a debit card?
2 Discuss in class whether mailing lists should be sold from one company to another.

## KEY POINTS

- Commercial data processing involves very large amounts of data which are processed by mainframe computers
- The data processing cycle consists of
  data collection and preparation;
  data input;
  data processing and storage;
  data output
- Data must be collected and prepared in a form that the computer can understand
- Data input may be direct or indirect
- Examples of indirect data input include punched cards, Kimball tags, key to disk
- Examples of direct data input are bar codes, magnetic stripes, character recognition
- An optical character reader can recognise normal characters and read them directly into a computer

- All data input into a computer must be checked for errors
- Two ways of error checking are to use check digits and range checks
- Validation is checking that data is sensible and accurate (for example a range check)
- Verifying data is checking it has been accurately typed and transmitted
- A file is said to be updated when it is changed or has new data added to it
- A master file is the file that holds the latest version of the data
- A transaction file holds everything which has been changed since the last master file was updated
- A computer can process information by batch processing or by interactive processing
- Data files can be accessed by sequential (serial) access or random (direct) access
- The grandparent, parent and child system of keeping backups reduces the effects of losing or damaging data
- Data may be output in several ways – onto paper, on microfiche or to a file
- Staff who work in a data processing department include
  systems analyst
  programmer
  data preparation operator
  computer operator
  librarian
  data control clerk
  operations manager
  data processing manager
- Deliberately damaging a computer system, corrupting files or committing fraud are all examples of computer crime
- A virus is a rogue program which reproduces itself automatically and may cause damage or loss of valuable data
- Electronic funds transfer is a way of paying for goods without using money
- The point of sale is the place in the shop where goods change hands
- Information held on a computer system must be accurate, secure and private

# 13 Banking

Banks all over the world depend on computers and electronic communications for their everyday operations. The huge numbers of transactions, which involve millions of pounds would be impossible without computers.

## What do we expect of computers?

What do we expect of computers working for banks? We expect a very high standard of service from computers used by banks. We really expect four things.

- **SECURITY**
  We take it for granted that our money is **secure**, and that we can withdraw it when we want.
- **ACCURACY**
  Bank computers must be **accurate** – we expect the arithmetic on the accounts to be done correctly.
- **RELIABILITY**
  They must be **reliable** – for example, we expect **Automated Telling Machines** (you probably know them as cashcard machines) to work properly when we have to use them.
- **PRIVACY**
  They must be **private** – we expect the bank to keep our accounts secret.

## Bank accounts

**ON LINE**
connected to a computer system

Banks were some of the earliest users of computers. Most banks had a central computer centre where the data from the different branches was collected and processed. For example, the payment slips collected by all the branches during the day would be sent to the bank's computer centre when the branches closed for business. Customers' accounts would be updated, and a report sent to each branch to use on the next banking day.

Nowadays, the bank clerk will enter transactions directly using a terminal. The terminal is on line to the computer and can access the files of customer accounts so that they can be examined and updated in a few seconds. This makes things

*A bank clerk using a terminal*

much faster than the old manual system of looking through paper records.

You might still have a passbook for your account, but all the account details are visible on the terminal, so the clerk can copy the details of any transaction from the screen into the passbook. In some banks and building societies the details can be printed directly into the passbook. This is much quicker than waiting for someone writing in the information, and it reduces the chance of mistakes being made. (This is assuming that the computer has the correct information in the first place!)

## Clearing a cheque

When you pay a cheque into your bank account, it can take a few days for the money to go into your account. The reason for the delay is that it takes some time for all the information to be processed. This is **clearing** a cheque.

Suppose you are given a cheque which is drawn on the Midland Bank, Piccadilly, London and you pay it into your account in the Bank of Scotland, Ardrossan. Your cheque is processed in the local branch and is then sent (along with thousands of others) to the Clearing Department of the Bank of Scotland. At the Clearing Department, the amount the cheque is for is typed onto the cheque using magnetic ink and it is processed through a reader sorter (magnetic ink character reader), bundled with all the other Midland Bank cheques and then sent to the Midland Bank Clearing Centre. The cheques are passed through another reader sorter and sorted into piles for individual branches of the Midland Bank. Your cheque is sent to the Midland Bank, Piccadilly Branch, London.

**BATCH PROCESSING**

collecting together all the data to be processed and inputting it to the computer in one set or 'batch'

The final settlement is made between the banks by adding up all the cheques taken in and paid out each day and paying the difference between the totals.

You can see, then, why it can take several days before you can use the money that you've paid into your account!

Day 1 – Bank of Scotland, Ardrossan
Day 2 – Bank of Scotland Clearing Centre (processes)
Day 3 – Midland Bank Clearing Centre (processes)
Day 4 – Midland Bank, Piccadilly, London

This is an example of batch processing, since all of the cheques are processed in one go. A permanent record of all the cheques may be stored on microfiche.

## Know your cards!

Banks and building societies all give their customers cards so they can use their services. Most of these cards look pretty much the same (somewhat like the one in figure 13.1) and they do have quite a lot in common. They are all the same size and have a magnetic stripe on the back of the card with data on it so they can be used in card readers and automated telling machines. Look back at Chapter 12 for more about magnetic stripes. Banks normally issue their cards free to the customer but you may have to pay to use a credit card.

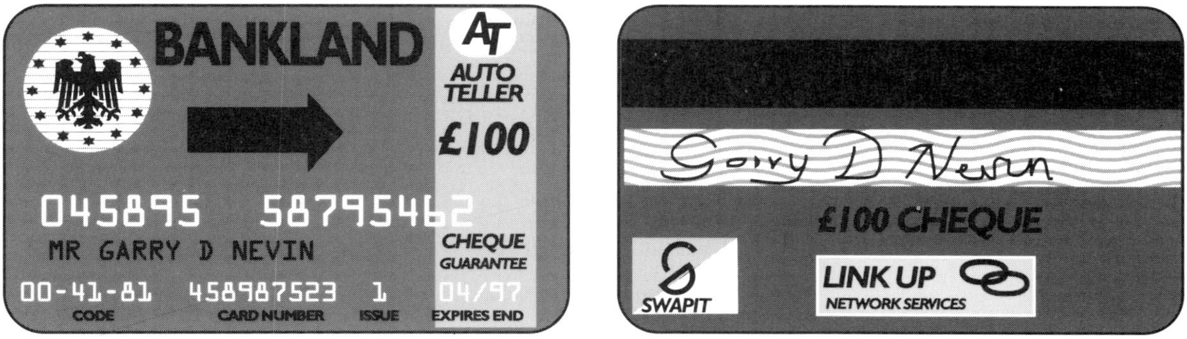


Front of card

Back of card showing magnetic stripe and security pattern under signature

**FIGURE 13.1** *A bank card. This card lets the user guarantee cheques, access an automated teller machine and use electronic funds transfer*

### Cheque guarantee cards

Whenever you write a cheque you give this card to the sales assistant to check your signature. It will guarantee that any cheque up to a certain limit (£50, £100, £250) will be paid by the bank.

### Credit cards

Credit cards (Visa and Mastercard are two examples) allow you to buy something without exchanging money. The amount is charged to the bank, which will send the customer details of the account every month. The customer can choose to settle the account in full each month, or they can pay in instalments. If you pay by instalment the bank will charge you interest on the outstanding balance.

**ELECTRONIC FUNDS TRANSFER**

automatically moving money from one account to another using a computer system. No cash changes hands

### Debit cards

Debit cards (like Switch and Delta) let you pay for purchases by electronic funds transfer directly from your bank account – but only if there's enough money in your account to pay for it.

### Cash cards

Cash cards (like Keycard and Cashline) let you withdraw cash from Automated Telling Machines. Most bank or building society accounts have cash cards and some banks use the cards to operate deposit accounts. A card reader inside the bank will let you use the cash card instead of a normal passbook.

### Multifunction cards

Cards often have more than one function – you can get cards that are combined cash and debit cards, which can also be used as a cheque guarantee card.

## Card security

If your cheque book or any of the cards just mentioned is lost or stolen, someone could use them to buy goods or get money from a cashcard machine. Some criminals still try to forge credit cards or cheque books. In 1991 these kinds of activities cost banks £150 million. To try to prevent this sort of fraud, the banks have incorporated security measures into their cards.

- Most cards have a special picture (called a hologram) which is impossible to forge.
- The surface of the card where you write your signature is made of a soft material and shows up any attempt to change the signature.
- Some cards have markings on them which only show up under ultraviolet light (for example the Visa card has a picture of a dove), which means they can't be forged.
- Some banks are now producing cards with the holder's photograph and an embedded laser engraved signature as extra security.

# Automated telling machines

You probably know these as cash dispensers or cashcard machines. You will usually find one of these machines built into the outside wall of a bank or building society (like the one in the photograph). You can carry out quite a few transactions with these machines, such as

1 take out cash
2 get a brief statement
3 find out the balance
4 order a cheque book
5 deposit money
6 pay bills
7 transfer money between accounts.

Each automated telling machine is part of a wide area network and is linked to the bank's main computer.

*An automated telling machine*

## How these machines work

To operate an automated telling machine, the customer must first insert the right card. A bank card stores information about the customer in the magnetic stripe on the card (look back at Chapter 12). The information is usually the customer's account number and bank or branch number.

The machine reads the stripe on the card to confirm that it *is* a bank card (not some other card like a phone card). If it is the right type the customer is asked to enter their **personal identification number** (usually shortened to **PIN**). The PIN

**WIDE AREA NETWORK (WAN)**

a network which covers a large geographical area like a country. Used for long-distance communication via satellite, radio or telephone line should be a secret between the customer and the bank's computer – it is the customer's password to the computer system. When you type in the right PIN a menu of the services available to you comes up on the screen.

The automated telling machines outside many banks will accept cards that are for accounts not at that bank. For instance, you can use a Bank of Scotland card in a Royal Bank of Scotland automated telling machine. Usually though, if you're using another bank's machine you won't be able to use the full range of options that the bank's own customers can use – you can withdraw cash but you probably won't be able to order a cheque book or a printed statement, although some systems might allow you to check your balance.

## Credit cards

Some automated telling machines let you get cash using your credit card. In this case the money is not taken directly from your bank account, but will appear as an item on your monthly statement from the credit card company. A credit card has its own PIN, so you have to remember another number if you use credit cards as well as cash cards.

## Advantages of automated telling machines

1 The automated telling machine makes you (the customer) do the work normally done by a clerk. This means the bank has to employ fewer people.
2 There is less paperwork involved with these transactions, so banks can increase business and offer more services without having to spend extra money on systems to handle large amounts of paper.
3 Since the customer communicates directly with the bank's computer in real time, there is no time delay involved (as there is with clearing a cheque) and the information is used to update the customer's account immediately.
4 The customer can choose when he or she wants to use the bank and can withdraw money even when the bank is closed, for example on a Sunday.
5 Customers can use any machine belonging to their own bank or one which is on the same network. For instance, Bank of Scotland customers can use their cards in machines belonging to Barclays, Lloyd's, the Royal Bank of Scotland or any of the thirty-five banks or building societies belonging to the LINK network.
6 People don't need to carry around large amounts of cash, since they can withdraw what they need at any time.

**NETWORK**

two or more computers joined together so that data can be transferred between them

## Take care of your PIN!

When you are given a bank card, you are told *never* to let anyone else (not even a member of the bank staff) find out your PIN. You should *never* write down your PIN, *always* memorise it.

Some people keep their PIN in their wallet with their bank card, which is not a good idea (why?) If you forget your PIN, you should write to the bank and they will send you a new one.

When you are issued with a PIN, you must first acknowledge its receipt in writing. Once the bank receives your letter they will activate the PIN so you can use the card.

Banks will not accept claims that funds have been withdrawn from someone's account without their knowledge because it is impossible without the PIN and the card. Most cases of so called 'phantom' withdrawals are caused by the person being careless with their PIN and someone else is using it. If you lose your card or think that someone else knows your PIN you should telephone your bank at once. The computer operator will tell the bank's computer not to accept your card, so that no-one (not even you!) can use it. In a very few cases, people have been able to convince the bank that they have not allowed anyone to know their PIN, and have had their money refunded. In these cases the withdrawals were caused by mistakes in the system.

To help you keep track of the transactions you make, every time you use an automated telling machine it issues you with a short statement which shows the date and exact time when the machine was used. Even so, mistakes *will* happen. You should always check any statements you receive very carefully.

Very occasionally money could be paid into your account by the bank in error. If you don't notice this, and spend the money without realising it wasn't yours to spend you could have a very nasty shock. You can guarantee that the bank will discover the mistake and insist that every penny is paid back with interest! This happened to the woman described in figure 13.2.

### £8m overdraft floors Alison

Pretty nurse Alison Caseby was recovering from shock last night - after discovering she had a £8m overdraft.

But her huge debt - almost enough to launch her own health service and much more than she could ever earn - was thankfully a mistake.

The bombshell dropped on 21 year - old Alison, who works in Aberdeen's Woodlands Hospital, when she went to check her own bank account at an autoteller, after drawing out £5.

She said : "I almost died of shock when I saw the overdraft of £8,000,008.

"Even if I worked for the rest of my life and beyond, I'd never pay that off."

"What was really worrying me were the bank charges."

But after the penny dropped, the Royal Bank of Scotland told Alison, of Counterswell Crescent, Aberdeen, that she is still a valued customer - and certainly does not owe £8m.

"They have been very nice about it and apologised," she said.

The mistake is believed to be due to a combination of human error and a bank computer.

*—Donald Stewart,*
*Scottish Daily Express 8/6/88*

**FIGURE 13.2**

# *Home banking*

The idea behind home banking is that you don't have to go into your bank or building society – you use the telephone to carry out any business. Because home banking uses the telephone, it is sometimes called **tele-banking**.
Here are some examples of home banking systems.

- In one system you dial the number of the bank's computer and talk to the computer itself.
- In another system you use a tone-dialler to send sounds along the telephone line which the bank's computer can understand.

**LOG ON**

the way of identifying the user to the network system

- A third way of home banking is to use a Viewdata terminal (we talked about Viewdata in Chapter 8) to communicate with the bank's computer.

The system that was started by the Royal Bank of Scotland in 1988 uses voice recognition technology developed by British Telecom to allow customers to speak directly to the bank's computer. It is called Phoneline.

Before they are allowed to use the system, customers have to send a tape-recording of their voice to the bank. The bank's computer uses this tape-recording to 'learn' the pattern of the customer's voice. When a customer wants to log on to the computer he or she speaks the PIN and a password. If the computer recognises the voice and password are right it logs you on. Using this service you can check your account balances, order cheque books and statements, listen to a 'mini-statement' of the last six transactions, pay bills and transfer money between accounts. The computer repeats any figures which the customer gives it so that he can check they're right.

This system is cheap, simple to use and secure, and the customer doesn't need any special hardware to use the system. You can also access the system from anywhere that has a clear telephone line.

## USING A VIEWDATA TERMINAL FOR HOME BANKING

**MODEM**

a device used to connect a computer system to a telephone line. Modem is short for **mo**dulator–**dem**odulator

The first Viewdata home banking service in the United Kingdom was the Bank of Scotland's Home and Office Banking Service (HOBS™), which they introduced in 1985. You can see what a home banking terminal looks like in the photograph.

To use HOBS™ you must have either a dedicated Viewdata terminal or a home computer and a modem. You must pay a subscription to the HOBS™ service and you pay the normal telephone call charges when you are on line.

*A home banking terminal*

If you use HOBS™ you can

1 check your account details and statement index
2 keep track of your cash flow (if you have a business account)
3 examine details of all your standing orders and direct, debits and details of bills which have been entered for payment via HOBS™
4 change your password
5 ask for a printed statement or new cheque book
6 pay bills up to 30 days in advance by specifying the amount and future date of payment (and of course the company you're paying!)
7 transfer money between your accounts.

Before you can use this system you log on to the bank network, and then type in your bank account number, your PIN and your password (which you should change regularly). The first time you log on the only thing the computer will let you do is change the password. You must write to the bank, telling them that the password has been changed. Once they receive your letter, the bank will activate the service.

HOBS™ lets you see much more detailed information about your account on the screen than you can get over the telephone. You are less likely to make mistakes, since all your account details are displayed before and after you've carried out a transaction.

Customers can move their money between different bank accounts using HOBS™, which means that they can keep their money in the account with the highest interest and only transfer it when they need to pay a bill.

## *Effects of computer banking on employment*

Computers haven't really had much effect on jobs in banks. On one hand, by using computers very large numbers of transactions can be handled by small numbers of people, but on the other hand, computers have helped banks to grow very quickly. These two factors more or less balance each other.

All levels of bank staff have had to be trained in new technology and whole new levels of organisation have been needed so all the credit, debit and cash cards can be dealt with efficiently.

## QUESTIONS

### Knowledge and understanding

1 What is an automated telling machine? What services are normally available from an automated telling machine?
2 What is the difference between a cash card and a debit card?
3 What is tele-banking? What systems of tele-banking are offered by banks?

**Problem solving**

1 When you operate an automated telling machine, you are usually given only three chances to type your PIN correctly.
(a) Why?
(b) What happens after the third wrong entry?
(c) Why can't you withdraw exactly £14 from an Automated Telling Machine?
(d) Why do most automated telling machines have a limit on the amount you can withdraw each day?
(e) What would happen if you took out the maximum you were allowed from one machine and then went to another machine somewhere else and tried to get more?
(f) A British Telecom Phonecard is the same size as a cash card. Why can't you use it to with draw cash from an automated telling machine?

2 Why should you always check your bank statements, even if your account is fully computerised?

3 What advantages do automated telling machines have
(a) for the bank?
(b) for the customer?

## *More to do*

### *More about automated telling machines*

The automated telling machine is on line to the bank's main computer through a wide area network. This allows access to the customers' records. When the customer puts their card into the machine, it reads the card number and account number from the magnetic stripe and asks the customer to type in her PIN. As soon as she types her PIN the computer changes it into a secret code. This is called **encryption**, and the message is **encrypted**. The customer is then asked which service she would like to use. Suppose she wants to withdraw £100. The automated telling machine then sends out an encrypted message – 'the person who holds card number xxxxxx for account number yyyyyy says that her PIN is nnnn and she wants to withdraw £100. Should I pay out the money?'

This message goes first to a computer called a branch controller, which handles several automated telling machines, and then on to the central mainframe computer. An application program in the mainframe computer compares the encrypted PIN with a copy of it held on a database stored on magnetic disk. If they match, and if the account has enough money in it, the program sends a message back to the automated telling machine instructing it to pay the customer.

The message is passed back to the automated telling machine via the branch controller. When the automated telling machine gets the message, it pays out money and

**MAINFRAME COMPUTER SYSTEM**

a computer system that can carry out a very large amount of work. It usually occupies a whole large room

**DATABASE**

a structured collection of similar information which can be searched

> **INTERACTION**
> the operator's instructions are processed continuously by the computer – like a conversation

sends another message back to the mainframe computer to let it know it has paid out. An application program updates the customer's records and debits £100 from her account. This whole process takes less than thirty seconds.

Using an automated telling machine is an example of **interactive processing,** since the questions asked by the program are answered by the user, and the application program in the mainframe computer system responds straight away.

All the customers' accounts are updated by the computer overnight to show the money that has been withdrawn and the most up-to-date balance. This is an example of batch processing, since all the transactions in one day are stored and then processed as a single unit.

## *Smart cards*

In the future, bank cards are likely to be **smart cards**. A smart card will have its own microprocessor, and will be able to store much more information than fits on a magnetic stripe. A smart card will probably look like the one in the photograph. A smart card could be programmed with a small amount of cash to allow you to buy small items like newspapers. This feature is called an **electronic purse**. The details of someone's signature could also be stored on a smart card, which could help in defeating cheque fraud – this is explained in the newspaper article in figure 13.3.

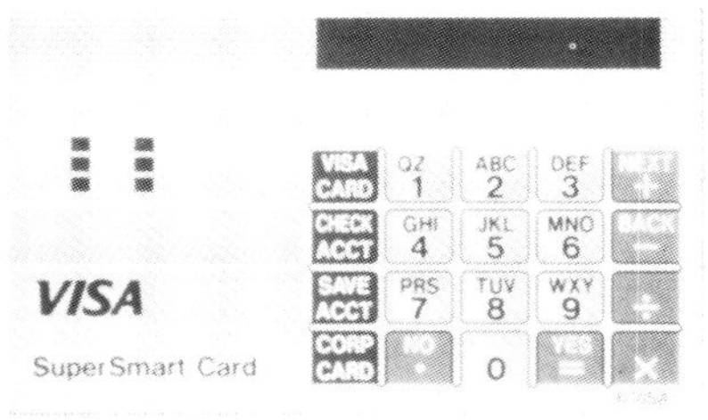


*A computerised credit card. This card has a microprocessor, a memory, a keypad and a display. It identifies its user during transactions and could be reprogrammed as a personal representative for spending digital money*

# SIGNATURE TEST COULD HELP CUT CHEQUE FRAUD

**An amazing new cheque card that will help put an end to stolen cheque fraud could soon be in widespread use in Britain.**

The smart card has a built-in micro-chip that stores the account holder's signature in its memory bank and automatically checks it against the signature of the card user each time.

The card is passed through a machine which compares the signature on the card to the user's in the shop.
If the machine concludes you are not who you say you are it issues a bleep.

**Compares Time**

"It's a new system that will eliminate fraud with regards to stolen cheque books and cards," said Alan Leibert of Alan Leibert Associates, the company behind the new card.

"A person's signature is unique because it is written by means of an unconscious interaction between the brain and the hand."

It matches things as obvious as the number of loops, to more complex things like the exact time it takes the person to write the signature.

Ninety-nine percent of the time the card can say for certain if the signature is genuine or fraudulent, and 1 percent of the time it is unsure.

"Previous attempts at such a system have been frowned on by banks because they worried that occasionally a genuine customer could sign badly on the day and be confronted by security officers," explained Mr Leibert. "This system gets around that in two ways.

"Firstly, every time that you sign a cheque the card updates your signature, because in time people's signatures do change.

**Further proof**

"Secondly, for the 1 percent where the machine is uncertain, it uses all the tests to state just how confident it feels about the signature. The shop assistant can then discreetly ask a customer for further proof of identity if the degree of uncertainty warrants it."

The new system has already received praise from the police stolen cheque squads and is now being looked at by the major banks.

—*The Weekly News,*
*© D. C. Thompson & Co*

FIGURE 13.3

Smart cards can be used as a security system to keep track of staff in a building. All the workers are given smart cards with details special to them. A central computer linked to detectors controls the doors in the building. The employee keeps the smart card in his pocket and as soon as he comes within range of a smart card detector, the smart card transmits his identity to the main computer which logs the employee's location, and opens and closes doors as required. The system can alert security staff if someone tries to enter an area they're not allowed into. It will *not* open the door. Since the system operates automatically, the employee's hours of working are recorded and linked into the payroll computer. If an employee works overtime, or sneaks off home a little early, then the computer will know about it.

## *More on EFT*

Large amounts of money are now transferred between different banks by direct computer links. The bank terminals are linked in a wide area network, with central computers which act as exchanges between different banks. These allow different types of bank computers which work in different ways to be connected together. The biggest network is the Society for Worldwide Inter-bank Financial Telecommunications network (SWIFT for short). SWIFT is owned by 900 banks and is used in 39 countries.

The Bankers' Automated Clearing Service (BACS) is a form of EFT. It is used for regular payments like standing orders, direct debits, salaries and dividends, between banks in the United Kingdom. BACS is not used to process paper cheques. (We explain EFT further in Chapter 14.)

# EXTRA QUESTIONS

### Knowledge and understanding

1 What type of data processing is involved in
   (a) using an Automated Telling Machine
   (b) clearing a cheque
2 Read this passage from PRESTEL MICRONET and answer the questions.

## *French Credit Card Scam*

One of Europe's biggest credit card forgery rings was broken up last weekend, following several months of intensive investigation by the French and Spanish police. France leads the world in its use of smart card technology – the use of computer chips on the credit card itself, in a bid to reduce fraud and customer overdrawings. More than 40 people were arrested in simultaneous raids which took place in Paris and Marseilles in France, as well as several locations in Spain. The group are said to have netted as much as 80 million francs (about £6 m) from their frauds over recent months.

Details of legitimate cards, including name, account number and expiration date, were extracted by examining credit card voucher carbons thrown out by retail establishments throughout France. These details were then relayed to the crook's colleagues in Spain, who embossed them onto the face of the card, as well as programming them into the smart card's memory. As a result of the investigation, Carte Bleu, the major Visa credit card company in France, is rewriting the software in its smart cards, which will ultimately be adopted as the European standard for Visa cards. Carte Bleu remain tight-lipped on how the crooks beat their security system, but sources suggest that on line authorisations on French smart cards are carried out whenever a programmed credit limit is exceeded using the card. By programming a high credit limit into the cards, it is thought that the crooks were able to make large purchases.

(a) What is a 'smart card'?
(b) How did the criminals beat the security system?
(c) What is the Carte Bleu company doing to stop the fraud?

**Problem solving**

1 Look at figure 13.4, which shows a systems flow diagram for an automated telling machine transaction.
(a) What transaction is involved?
(b) What changes would you make to this diagram if the transaction was cash withdrawal?
(c) Redraw the diagram to show cash withdrawal.

2 Cheques which have been processed are often photographed and stored on microfiche. What advantages does this bring to
(a) the bank?
(b) the customers?

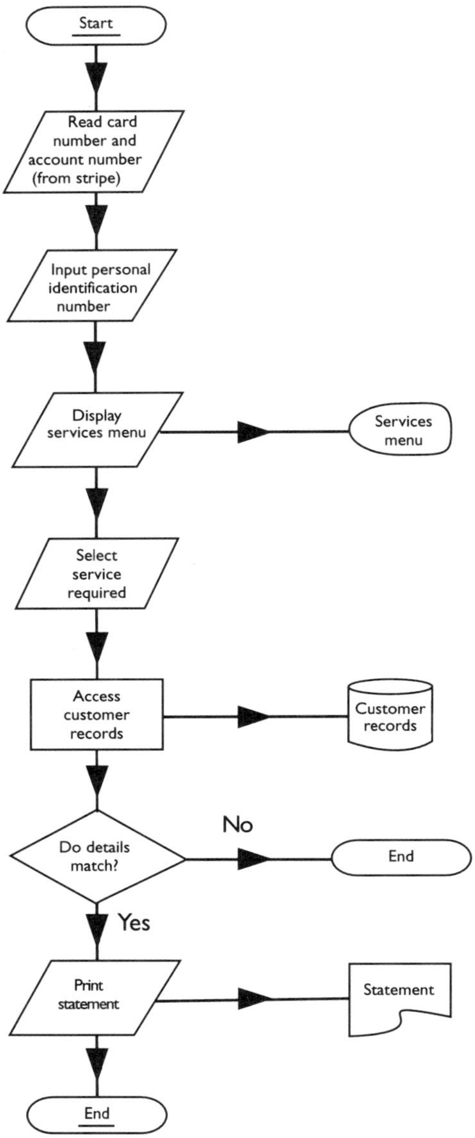


**FIGURE 13.4** *A transaction on an automated telling machine. The user is asking for a statement of their account. Look back at figure 12.9 for an explanation of what the symbols mean*

## KEY POINTS

- Information stored in bank computers must be accurate, reliable, secure and private
- When you visit the bank, the clerk enters transactions directly onto a computer terminal
- The clerk's terminal is on line to the main computer, which can access the files of customer accounts
- When you write a cheque, it takes a few days before the money is cleared in your account

- Cheques are processed by batch processing
- Banks may issue various types of card to allow customers to make use of their services
- Bank cards contain security devices (like holograms) to help prevent fraud
- Automated telling machines form part of a wide area network and are linked to their bank's main computer
- Using an automated telling machine is an example of interactive processing
- Automated telling machines allow customers to choose their banking hours
- Keeping your personal identification number secure can prevent your card being misused
- Home banking (or tele-banking) allows customers to carry out their banking over the telephone
- To carry out home banking you may use a tone-dialler, a Viewdata terminal or talk to a computer over the telephone
- Smart cards are bank cards which contain a microprocessor
- Smart cards can store much more information than a card with a magnetic stripe
- Electronic funds transfer between banks is now done by direct computer links in a wide area network

# 14 Electronic point of sale

## Why are computers used in shops?

Computers already play an important part in shopping. Big shops, especially chain stores with branches all over the country, have to deal with huge amounts of information which would take humans a lot of time and effort to cope with.

- They have to keep the shelves well stocked with goods for customers to buy.
- They need to reorder stock that is low.
- Someone must decide which things are selling well so they can decide whether to do a special promotion.
- The price has to be right.

Computers are very good at keeping track of this type of information. This is why many shops have installed **electronic point of sale** (**EPOS**) systems.

## What is an electronic point of sale system?

**DIRECT DATA ENTRY**

when data is input straight into a computer system. Examples are bar codes, magnetic stripes

We first mentioned electronic point of sale (EPOS) in Chapter 12. EPOS is the name given to a computerised system which collects data automatically from the checkout (this is called the point of sale, or POS) as the customer buys the goods. EPOS is an example of direct data input to a computer system.

### Shopping without an EPOS system

In a shop without an EPOS system, the customers take their goods to a checkout operator who reads the price on each item and then types the price into the till. The till calculates the total, the customer pays and is given a receipt with a list of prices and the total. In this system, every item has to be labelled with a price ticket. If an item hasn't got a price ticket, someone has to look up the price, which usually takes some time – and the queue builds up!

At the end of the working day the cash in the till and the till roll receipt are collected by the manager and the cash is taken to the bank's night safe. The information on the till roll receipt is transferred to a book and the shelves are restocked.

This system has quite a few disadvantages.

1 If the retailer wants to change any of the prices on the goods, the price tickets on all the goods have to be changed. This is a very slow, laborious task and it's easy to make mistakes.
2 The checkout operator could type the wrong prices into the till by mistake. The customer might not spot the mistakes afterwards because the till receipt only gives the prices and not the names of the items.
3 Stock control is difficult, because there is no way of recording the stock level as purchases are made.
4 Theft of stock is often undetected.

### Shopping with an EPOS system

Many of the problems mentioned above can be overcome by an EPOS system like the one shown in the photograph on the left.

In a shop which uses EPOS, each item is marked with a bar code unique to it. You can see some labels with bar codes in the photograph on the right. The bar code is put on by the manufacturer, so the retailer does not have to employ someone to go around putting prices on each item. The prices only need to be displayed on the edge of the shelves where the goods are stacked so the customer can see them.

*An EPOS checkout*

*Product labels with bar codes*

Customers choose their goods and take them to the checkout. At the checkout the bar code is read by a scanner. The scanner might be built into the checkout (like the one in figure 14.1) or it might be held by the operator. Scanners may use laser beams or light pens to read the bar code.

The scanner reads the data from the bar code and sends the product code to the till. The computer connected to the till is programmed to recognise the product codes for all of the items

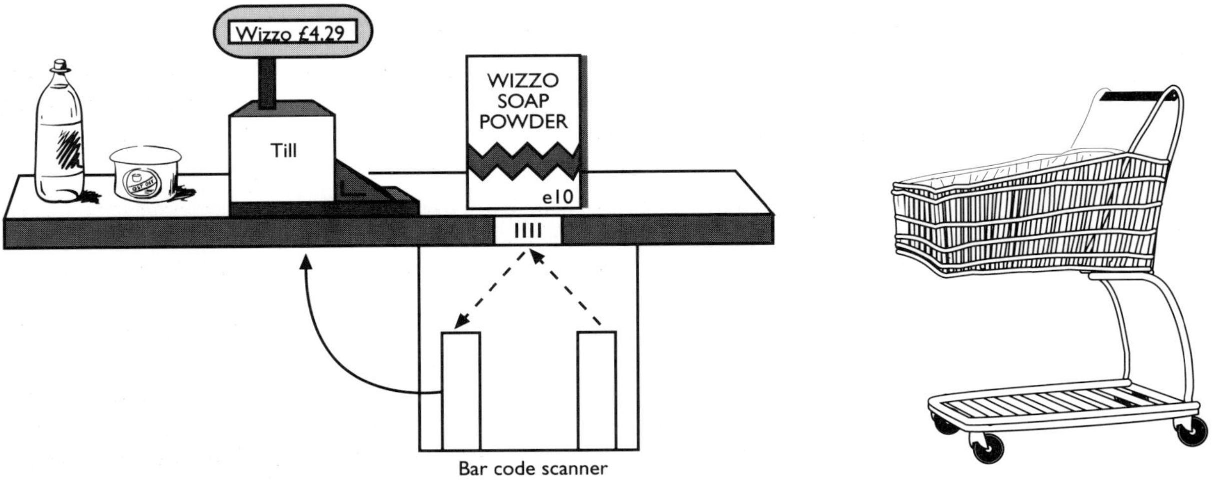


**FIGURE 14.1** *EPOS at the checkout*

on sale in the shop. The till displays the name and price of each item as it is scanned and prints this information on an itemised receipt. You are probably very used to seeing itemised receipts like the ones in figure 14.2. Sometimes the itemised receipt also has the name of the checkout operator on it.

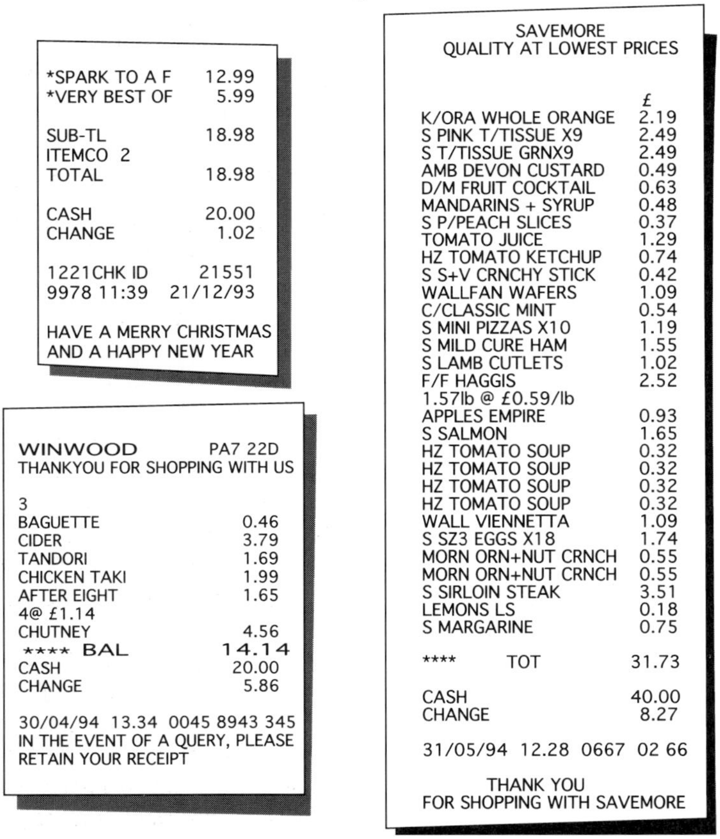

*SPARK TO A F 12.99
*VERY BEST OF 5.99

SUB-TL 18.98
ITEMCO 2
TOTAL 18.98

CASH 20.00
CHANGE 1.02

1221CHK ID 21551
9978 11:39 21/12/93

HAVE A MERRY CHRISTMAS
AND A HAPPY NEW YEAR

WINWOOD PA7 22D
THANKYOU FOR SHOPPING WITH US

3
BAGUETTE 0.46
CIDER 3.79
TANDORI 1.69
CHICKEN TAKI 1.99
AFTER EIGHT 1.65
4@ £1.14
CHUTNEY 4.56
**** BAL 14.14
CASH 20.00
CHANGE 5.86

30/04/94 13.34 0045 8943 345
IN THE EVENT OF A QUERY, PLEASE
RETAIN YOUR RECEIPT

SAVEMORE
QUALITY AT LOWEST PRICES

| | £ |
|---|---|
| K/ORA WHOLE ORANGE | 2.19 |
| S PINK T/TISSUE X9 | 2.49 |
| S T/TISSUE GRNX9 | 2.49 |
| AMB DEVON CUSTARD | 0.49 |
| D/M FRUIT COCKTAIL | 0.63 |
| MANDARINS + SYRUP | 0.48 |
| S P/PEACH SLICES | 0.37 |
| TOMATO JUICE | 1.29 |
| HZ TOMATO KETCHUP | 0.74 |
| S S+V CRNCHY STICK | 0.42 |
| WALLFAN WAFERS | 1.09 |
| C/CLASSIC MINT | 0.54 |
| S MINI PIZZAS X10 | 1.19 |
| S MILD CURE HAM | 1.55 |
| S LAMB CUTLETS | 1.02 |
| F/F HAGGIS | 2.52 |
| 1.57lb @ £0.59/lb | |
| APPLES EMPIRE | 0.93 |
| S SALMON | 1.65 |
| HZ TOMATO SOUP | 0.32 |
| HZ TOMATO SOUP | 0.32 |
| HZ TOMATO SOUP | 0.32 |
| HZ TOMATO SOUP | 0.32 |
| WALL VIENNETTA | 1.09 |
| S SZ3 EGGS X18 | 1.74 |
| MORN ORN+NUT CRNCH | 0.55 |
| MORN ORN+NUT CRNCH | 0.55 |
| S SIRLOIN STEAK | 3.51 |
| LEMONS LS | 0.18 |
| S MARGARINE | 0.75 |
| **** TOT | 31.73 |
| CASH | 40.00 |
| CHANGE | 8.27 |

31/05/94 12.28 0667 02 66

THANK YOU
FOR SHOPPING WITH SAVEMORE

**FIGURE 14.2** *Itemised receipts printed at the POS*

**FIGURE 14.3** *A bar code – what the numbers mean*

## The structure of a bar code

We mentioned bar codes in Chapter 12. A bar code is a series of lines which code for information. If you look at the bar code in figure 14.3 you will see that it also has numbers on it.
A typical bar code has 13 digits.

- The first two stand for the country the product came from.
- The next five digits are the code for the manufacturer.
- The next five digits code for the name (and size) of the product.
- The last digit is a special number – the check digit. The check digit is there to make sure the scanner has read the bar code properly. If the bar code is not scanned correctly the checkout operator is alerted by the computer, usually by a warning sound, to scan the product again. If the bar code on the item is damaged and the scanner can't read it the operator can type the number under the bar code directly into the till and the computer recognises the product.

Not all EPOS systems use bar codes. In some shops each item has a label with an individual code number which the checkout operator has to type into the till. This system is often used in clothes shops, and you will see the number printed on the label inside the garments. This system isn't as fast as automatically scanning bar codes, but still has all the other advantages of EPOS.

## Advantages and disadvantages of EPOS systems

1. Using an EPOS system can make shopping quicker and easier, because shoppers can go through the checkout quicker. The operator doesn't have to type prices into the till – and you don't have to wait for someone to go and find the price of something because the price label has fallen off.
2. The customer is given an itemised receipt, which gives the name of each item, the price and the date of purchase. This makes it easy for you to check that your bill is correct. It also means that if someone brings an item back the retailer will know if it was bought recently.
3. The retailer can order fresh supplies quickly and accurately, so the shop is less likely to run out of popular goods.
4. The shop's computer keeps a record of exactly how much of each item is sold. The retailer can therefore see which goods sell fast, and which ones are not popular. He can tell how much to reorder at the end of each day so the shop is always well stocked. He can decide to advertise slow selling goods or give them a special price to encourage people to buy them.
5. Retailers can easily organise special prices for some goods, or arrange a price cut if you buy several of the same item (you've

probably all seen advertisements like 'buy two, get one free') or goods which could go together (like tea and biscuits). Instead of changing the price label on each item, they only have to tell the computer what the special price is for the bar codes on those goods, and change the price label on the shelf edge.

6 It is much more difficult for criminals to tamper with receipts. It also means that dishonest employees stealing from stock or the till can be caught.
7 Because none of the items have price labels on them fewer staff are needed. This means the retailer has to pay out less wages and can keep their prices down.
8 The checkout operator doesn't need to type in prices and doesn't need to remember the prices of items.
9 Management can check up on how fast the checkout operators are working.

But EPOS has its disadvantages too:

1 If the computer in the shop has been programmed with the wrong price then you could be overcharged without knowing it. When each item had its own price ticket, the shopper could keep an eye on the checkout operator as he typed in each price and could have any mistakes corrected straight away. But with an EPOS system, the price is only displayed on the shelf. To prove a mistake has been made you'd have to go back to the shelf to find out the displayed price and compare it with your receipt.
2 Each item has its own bar code, and multipack of items must have a separate bar code to make sure the scanner can recognise them as new items. If this isn't done properly, the individual bar code may be scanned by mistake and the customer could be charged only for one item instead of a six-pack, for example (you might not think this is a disadvantage but the retailer would!).

In figure 14.4 you can see what would happen if an EPOS system breaks down.

**FIGURE 14.4**

## So you might get a real bargain at the supermarket!

**Shopping has** never been easier at the supermarket, thanks to EPOS.

It stands for Electronic Point Of Sale, the hi-tech tills which have been in operation for a couple of years.

The check-out girl simply passes the goods over a scanner and they are automatically recorded from a bar code.

It means stores have been able to do away with price stickers on tins of beans and the like. But what happens if EPOS breaks down? Imagine the chaos as dozens of shoppers queued with filled trolleys—and not a price on any item.

Well, most stores have a back-up computer. But in the unlikely event that goes down as well, there's an amazing—and secret—plan of action.

First, they shut all the doors and ask the shoppers to wait at the tills. Then the manager comes round and asks you how much you think that the goods in your trolley are worth.

If the manager disagrees, you have to haggle over the goods until there's an agreement on a price!

If you like a good argument, chances are you can come away with a bargain.

The whole palaver has to be repeated until the store is cleared and everyone is happy.

The big stores, including Safeway and Sains-bury, tell us it's the only thing they can do.

It would take too long to go through the trolley, list each item and tot up the total on the back of an envelope!

And after all, they're in the business of selling. So they can hardly say,"Sorry folks, the computer isn't working, would you mind putting your shopping back on the shelves!"

—*Sunday Post 23.2.92*

*© D. C. Thompson & Co.*

# Electronic Funds Transfer at Point of Sale

We discussed electronic funds transfer (or EFT) in the last chapter. **Electronic funds transfer at point of sale** (usually shortened to **EFTPOS**) is when money is authorised to be debited from a customer's bank account at the checkout terminal. EFTPOS uses a plastic card (called a debit card) which has a magnetic stripe with the user's bank account number stored on it. Two examples of debit cards are Switch and Delta. Look back at Chapter 13 to remind yourself about how debit cards work.

## How EFTPOS works

At the POS terminal, the assistant passes (or **swipes**) the debit card through a card reader which reads the information on the magnetic stripe on the card. The terminal first checks that the card is not on file as a stolen card – if it is it rejects the card and warns the operator. If the total amount is below a set limit (known as the '**floor limit**'), the computer authorises the transaction. If the total amount is above the 'floor limit' the checkout operator has to contact the bank before the sale can go ahead. Depending on the shop either the operator telephones the bank and is given an authorisation number for the transaction (this is called **voice authorisation**) or the terminal itself dials the bank's computer and gets **automatic authorisation**.

## Note

**BATCH PROCESSING**

collecting together all the data to be processed and inputting it to the computer in one set or 'batch'

Although the card used in an EFTPOS system is called a debit card, the customer's account is *not* debited immediately the purchase is made because the shop's computer is not always on line to the bank's computer (imagine the phone bill if it was!). During the night the bank's computer telephones the shop's computer and the details of that day's transactions are uploaded for batch processing.

## Advantages and disadvantages of EFTPOS

These systems are becoming very popular for several reasons:

1 Payment into the shop's bank is guaranteed by the system as long as the transactions are properly authorised or are below the floor limit.
2 There is less paperwork (no cheques or cash to process) when goods are paid for using EFTPOS, so less staff are needed.
3 EFTPOS transactions are usually quicker than writing a cheque, so the queues at the checkout move quicker.

4 If the bank account where the money is to be placed attracts interest, then the quicker the money is deposited in the account, the more interest it will earn for the retailer.
5 The shop collects less cash so there is less chance of theft. A thief can't make much use of a pile of EFTPOS receipts!
6 Fewer administration staff are needed in the shop.
7 The person holding a debit card gets an itemised bank statement showing the name of the retailer, instead of just the number of the cheques they have written. This helps you to keep track of your finances.
8 The money is debited quickly from your account so the balance displayed on an automated teller machine is always up to date.

But EFTPOS has some disadvantages too:

1 The systems are expensive to install (but they are getting cheaper).
2 The customer's account is debited within two days, slightly quicker than if a cheque was being used, so you have to keep careful track of your spending.

## QUESTIONS

### Knowledge and understanding

1 Read this article and answer the questions which follow

> The SellQuick supermarket chain recently announced record profits and a big performance lead over its rivals. Use of computerised stock control linked to laser reading checkouts was attributed to its success. SellQuick's technology lead looks set to continue with the announcement they are to start EFTPOS trials. In conjunction with Mainland Bank, two branches in Musselburgh and Buckie will have EFTPOS terminals, enabling electronic payment of grocery bills.

(a) What has caused SellQuick's 'record profits'?
(b) What does a 'laser reading checkout' read?
(c) What is EFTPOS?
(d) Explain how you can use EFTPOS to pay for your groceries at SellQuick.

### Problem solving

1 Give two advantages and two disadvantages of
(a) an EPOS system
(b) an EFTPOS system.

2 One of the advantages of EPOS to the shop's management is that they can check up on the work rate of the till operators. Discuss in class how you would feel about this if you were
(a) the employer
(b) an employee.

### Practical activities

1 Go on a Scavenger Hunt – collect bar code labels from products and fill in the table.
Manufacturer's code number
Safeway _____
Tesco _____
Asda _____
Co-op _____
Heinz 00157
Batchelors _____
Kellog's 00127
2 The code number on a bar code for the United Kingdom is 50. Find out the code numbers for three other countries.
3 Find out how some libraries use bar codes

## More to do

**BACKING STORE**

a system for permanently holding the contents of memory on media such as disk or tape

**BACKUP**

a copy of a program or data made in case the original is lost or destroyed

### THE HARDWARE USED FOR AN EPOS SYSTEM IN A LARGE DEPARTMENT STORE

A large department store could have fifty or more terminals (tills) connected to two terminal controllers (like the system shown in figure 14.5). The controllers are connected to each other by a high-speed link. During normal operation, one controller acts as the master and the other acts as a standby, ready to take over if the master controller fails. The tills in the store are connected to the main computer through these controllers. Each till has a backing store on magnetic tape, which will act as a backup if any of the connections to the main computer fail.

There are also some computer terminals in the main office of the shop. These are used by the management to access information such as detailed reports of sales in each department or sales of a particular item. The management might also use them to find out the number of customers that have used each till and the percentage of the takings that were cash, credit, cheque or by EFT.

At the end of a day's trading the sales information is sent to the computer in the head office. This information is used for stock control, so the store doesn't run out of any item.

**FIGURE 14.5** *Data communication at EPOS*

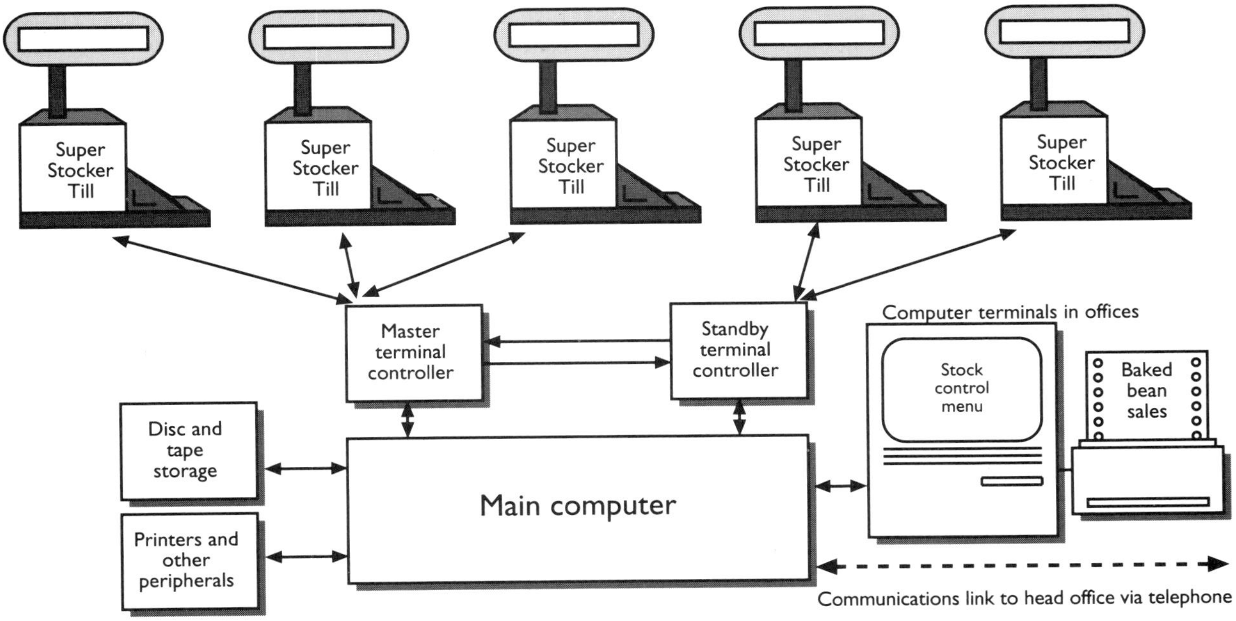

## *More about bar codes and stock control*

When goods are delivered to the shop the information about them is put into the file of product records in the shop's computer.

Here is an example of a product record

Product code 00157 00297
HEINZ Tomato soup 800g (00157 means HEINZ and 00297 means Tomato soup 800g)
Price 0.62
Number in stock 123

You can see this in the photograph.

What happens when something is sold at an EPOS terminal?

You can follow what happens in figure 14.6:

1 The bar code on the packet is scanned.
2 The product code is sent to the till.
3 The file of product records on backing storage is searched for a record which matches the code.
4 The product record is stored in the till's memory. The price and name of the item are displayed on the screen and printed on the receipt.
5 The number of these items in stock on the record in the till memory is reduced by one, since one packet has been sold.

**FIGURE 14.6** *Processing a bar code*

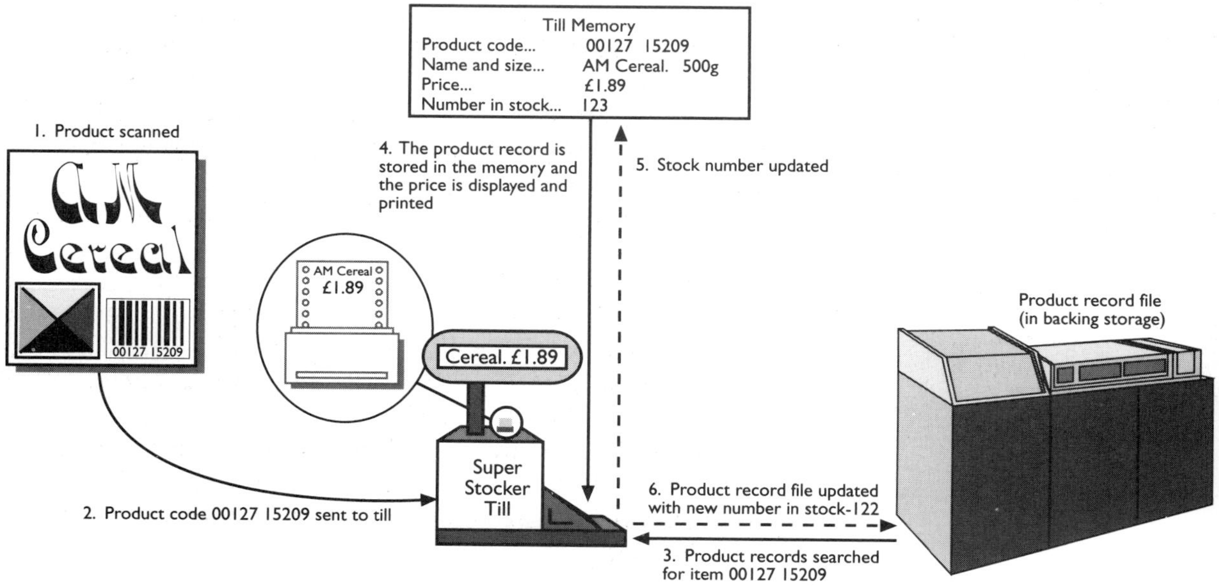
Till Memory
Product code... 00127 15209
Name and size... AM Cereal. 500g
Price... £1.89
Number in stock... 123
1. Product scanned
AM Cereal
00127 15209
4. The product record is stored in the memory and the price is displayed and printed
5. Stock number updated
AM Cereal £1.89
Cereal. £1.89
Product record file (in backing storage)
Super Stocker Till
2. Product code 00127 15209 sent to till
6. Product record file updated with new number in stock-122
3. Product records searched for item 00127 15209

6 Finally, the product record in the till memory is used to update the file on backing storage with the new stock number.
7 On some EPOS systems, if the stock number falls below a certain level, it is automatically re-ordered.
8 Note that the bar code itself doesn't have the price on it. The price of each item must be fetched from the file which is held on disk.

## *ShopperTrak*

ShopperTrak is a system that tells the retailer about the ways customers are moving around the store. ShopperTrak uses scanners in the ceiling to record the numbers of customers going into and leaving the store, and how many people are in one place at one time. So it can warn the manager that she needs to send more staff to a particularly busy department or to open more checkout lanes. The system displays information on a terminal in front of the store so the personnel can see it easily and act quickly. ShopperTrak can also help retailers predict the number of staff they will need in the store at different times of day.

## *Point of sale information systems*

A POS information system is a dedicated computer system which is linked to a backing storage device like a hard disk or **video disc**. Systems where video players are linked to computer systems like this are called **multimedia** systems – more about multimedia in Chapter 16. You will see POS information systems in shops, banks, exhibitions and museums. You can use them to find out where certain exhibits in a museum are, for example, or the range of goods a shop has to offer.

Here are some examples of POS information systems.

- **SAFEWAYS 'COOKBOOK'**
  The 'cookbook' system has a lot of recipes stored on it. You can choose a recipe, find out how to cook it, what you should eat with it, how to adapt it to the social occasion and then get a printout of the list of ingredients you need. Each unit records which recipes have been called up, so the manager can adjust the shop's stocks according to the shopper's need, fashion and seasonal differences.

**VIDEO DISC**

an optical storage medium similar to compact disc (CD-ROM), which holds video (TV programmes or films)

**MULTIMEDIA**

when devices such as video, hi-fi and compact discs are linked to a computer and operated by a computer program

- **THE ZANUSSI 'FACTFILE'**
  Zanussi's 'factfile' (shown in the photograph on this page) holds detailed information on the whole range of Zanussi's domestic products – including prices. Customers choose the products they want to know about and the system takes them through a menu of the products available and how they function. Customers can get a printout of all the information they need.
- **THE NATWEST 'INFORMATION POINT'**
  This system tells customers about the services the bank offers. The user touches the screen to bring up the main menu and a video is displayed, taking the customer through the options that are available. The user can look through pages of information simply by touching a button. You can get a printout of the services you need, including contact names.

*A POS information system – Zanussi's 'factfile'*

# EXTRA QUESTIONS

**Knowledge and understanding**

1 Why does a bar code have a check digit?
2 What is a point of sale information system?
How is it different from a point of sale system?
3 What is ShopperTrak?
How does ShopperTrak help the customer?
4 Name three types of information management can get from an EPOS system.

**Problem solving**

1 When electronic funds transfer was first introduced some people thought that it would lead to a 'cashless society'. Has the 'cashless society' arrived? Discuss this in class.
2 If the bar code doesn't have the price of goods on it, explain how the till can display the price when a bar code is scanned at the checkout.
3 How does an EPOS system keep track of stock?
4 Suppose an unscrupulous retailer used an EFTPOS system to make a database about his customers which linked their names with the items they buy in his store.
   (a) What could he do with this information?
   (b) What is to prevent this from happening today?

## KEY POINTS

- Electronic point of sale (EPOS) is a system which collects sales data automatically as a customer buys goods
- EPOS is an example of direct data input to a computer system
- In a shop which uses EPOS, all the items are marked with a bar code
- EPOS systems help the shopper and the retailer
  Shopping can be quicker for shoppers to go through the checkout
  The shopper is given an itemised receipt
  The retailer can reorder fresh supplies quickly and accurately
  The shop's computer keeps records of exactly how much of each item is sold
  It is easier for retailers to organise special prices for certain goods
  There is less chance of fraud
  Fewer staff are needed since it is not necessary to attach a price to each item
  Less skill is needed by the checkout operator
  Management can check up on the rate of work of the checkout operators
- Electronic funds transfer at point of sale (EFTPOS) is when a customer's bank account is authorised to be debited at the checkout terminal

- Advantages of using EFTPOS
  Payment is guaranteed by the system
  There is less paperwork
  Transactions are quicker than writing a cheque.
  There is less chance of theft because there is less cash in the shop
  Less staff are required for administration in the shop
- A point of sale information system is a dedicated computer system linked to a backing storage device like a hard disk or a video disc

# 15 Airline reservations

## *What is an airline reservations system?*

Travel agencies display holiday brochures and other advertising material for airlines and tour operators. They take bookings and offer advice on the different aspects of each holiday that they advertise.

Before computers, the only way the travel agent could book your holidays was by telephoning or writing to the holiday company. They would check the availability of the holiday you wanted then come back to you with the information. This was a very slow process. It also meant that several travel agents could be trying to book the same holidays and double bookings often happened. Nowadays travel agents use an on line computer system like FASTRAK or PRESTEL (we talked about PRESTEL in Chapter 9) to find out the availability of a holiday, and to book it straight away.

**ON LINE**

connected to a computer system

By using computers the travel agent can book a holiday more quickly – and double bookings are much less likely.

Using a computer to book your holiday means that the chances of making a mistake are less when the travel agent, the airline, the tour operator and the hotel are accessing the same information from the same computer database.

**MODEM**

a device used to connect a computer system to a telephone line. Modem is short for **mo**dulator–**dem**odulator

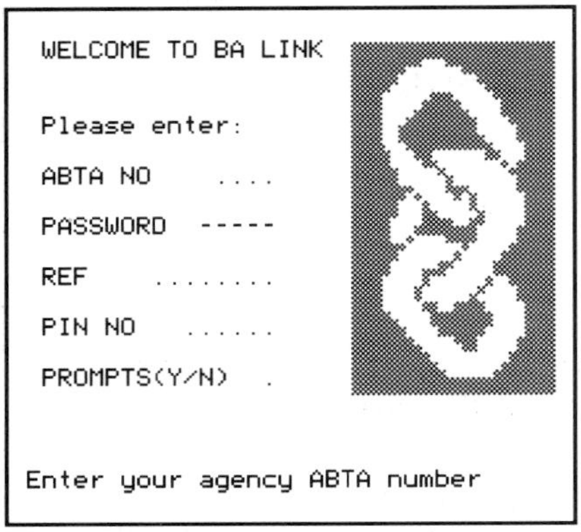


**FIGURE 15.1**
*A typical log on screen you will see at a travel agent*

**LOG ON**
the way of identifying the user to the network system

**ACCESS**
to gain entry to a computer system

To access an on line system, the travel agent connects to the remote computer by dialling the telephone number (this is usually done automatically by the software and the modem). The travel agent then has to log on to the system by typing in their user identity and password(s). The user identity includes the travel agent's ABTA number. In figure 15.1 you can see the type of screen a travel agent would see. Once they're logged on the travel agent can find out information and book a holiday.

These reservations systems are called **multi-access systems** because many users can be on line at one time. A multi-access system is shown in figure 15.2. By using these systems travel agents can access the databases run by the airlines and tour operators. To access the database the user needs a **terminal** consisting of a keyboard, monitor and modem. Usually a printer is attached so the travel agent can give the customer a copy of their travel details (the **itinerary**). You can see an example of the kind of printout you'd get on the next page.

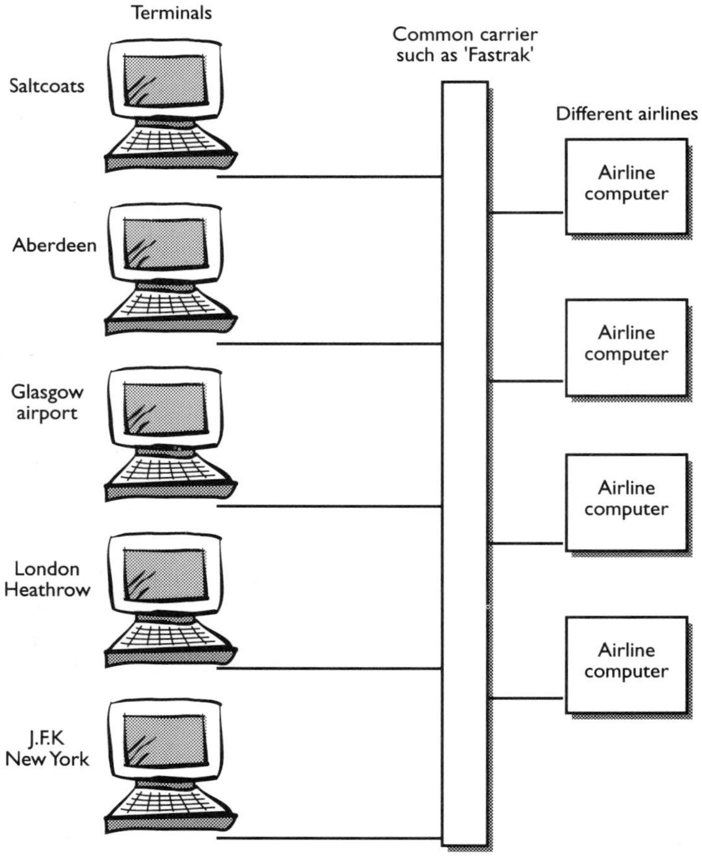


**FIGURE 15.2** *A multi-access system*

## A SAMPLE ITINERARY FOR A TRIP AROUND THE WORLD

WONDERTOURS WORLDWIDE TRAVEL AGENTS ABTA IATA
MR. J SCOTT, 54 NANSEN CRESCENT, KILMARNOCK, KA13RG

| DATE | FLIGHT |
|---|---|
| 24 NOVEMBER | LONDON-HEATHROW to MOSCOW<br>ECONOMY CLASS FLIGHT: SU581 (AEROFLOT)<br>CONFIRMED DEPART: 1125 ARRIVE: 1645 |
| 24 NOVEMBER | MOSCOW to DELHI<br>ECONOMY CLASS FLIGHT: SU557 (AEROFLOT)<br>CONFIRMED DEPART: 2125 ARRIVE: 0905 (1 DAY LATER) |
| 01 JANUARY | DELHI to BANGKOK<br>ECONOMY CLASS FLIGHT: SU553 (AEROFLOT)<br>CONFIRMED DEPART: 1100 ARRIVE: 1605<br>SURFACE |
| 01 FEBRUARY | SINGAPORE to JAKARTA<br>ECONOMY CLASS FLIGHT: GA865 (GARUDA INDONESIA)<br>CONFIRMED DEPART: 1535 ARRIVE: 1610 |
| 08 FEBRUARY | JAKARTA TO DENPASAR (BALI)<br>ECONOMY CLASS FLIGHT: GA668 (GARUDA INDONESIA)<br>CONFIRMED DEPART: 1200 ARRIVE: 1445 |
| 15 FEBRUARY | DENPASAR (BALI) to SYDNEY<br>ECONOMY CLASS FLIGHT: GA898 (GARUDA INDONESIA)<br>CONFIRMED DEPART: 2230 ARRIVE: 0700 (1 DAY LATER) |
| 26 JUNE | SYDNEY to AUCKLAND<br>ECONOMY CLASS FLIGHT: CO015 (CONTINENTAL AIRLINES)<br>CONFIRMED DEPART: 0730 ARRIVE: 1220 |
| 26 JULY | AUCKLAND to HONOLULU<br>ECONOMY CLASS FLIGHT: CO016 (CONTINENTAL AIRLINES)<br>CONFIRMED DEPART: 1335 ARRIVE: 0555 |
| 02 AUGUST | HONOLULU to LOS ANGELES<br>ECONOMY CLASS FLIGHT: CO002 (CONTINENTAL AIRLINES)<br>CONFIRMED DEPART: 0800 ARRIVE: 1610 |
| 04 AUGUST | LOS ANGELES to NEW YORK (NEWARK)<br>ECONOMY CLASS FLIGHT: CO556 (CONTINENTAL AIRLINES)<br>CONFIRMED DEPART: 0805 ARRIVE: 1620 |
| 05 AUGUST | NEW YORK (NEWARK) to LONDON (GATWICK)<br>ECONOMY CLASS FLIGHT: CO028 (CONTINENTAL AIRLINES)<br>CONFIRMED DEPART: 2000 ARRIVE: 0800 (1 DAY LATER) |
| CHECK-IN: | Please check-in at LONDON-HEATHROW AIRPORT TERMINAL 2 THREE HOURS prior to departure. |
| VISAS REQUIRED: | INDIA THAI/AUSTRALIA |
| IMMUNISATION: | HEPATITIS CHOLERA TYPHOID POLIO MALARIA TETANUS |

**May we take the opportunity of wishing you a most enjoyable trip**

# *Booking a holiday*

**MENU**

a list on screen for the user to choose from

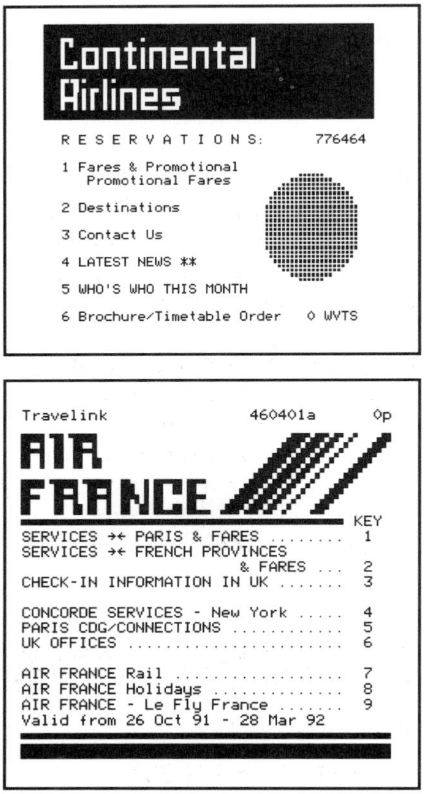


**FIGURE 15.3** *A selection of airline menu pages*

When you book a holiday, the first thing that usually happens is that your flight is booked. Let us look at how a travel agent books your holiday.

1 The travel agent logs on to the airline's system and will see a menu like the one in figure 15.3.
2 To book a flight the travel agent types in the customer's preferred airport, destination and date they want to travel to check if the flight is available. On the database every airport is coded for by three letters.

## EXAMPLE

Suppose you wanted to travel from Glasgow to Kingston (in Jamaica) on 10th December. The travel agent would type in 10DEC GLA KIN. Their computer is linked to all the different airlines and will find out about the flights available.
This is what the computer database could come up with:

10 DEC TUE
1 GLA KIN 1030 1925 R7 BA 156 SSC
2 GLA KIN 1500 0005 F7J5 AA 123 747
3 GLA KIN 1800 0335 F6M5 BA 169 707

This means that

- Flight 1 leaves Glasgow at 10.30 in the morning and arrives in Jamaica at 7.25 in the evening. It is a British Airways flight on Concorde and there are seven seats available.
- Flight 2 (an American Airlines Boeing 747) leaves Glasgow at 3.00 in the afternoon and arrives at 12.05 in the morning. On this flight there are seven first class and five club class seats.
- Flight 3 is a British Airways Boeing 707. It leaves at 6.00 in the evening and arrives at 3.35 in the morning. There are six first class seats and five economy class seats available on this flight.

The times may look a bit odd, but they are always quoted as local times. You could find yourself arriving an hour after you've left after a flight that lasts for four hours!
Can you crack the code that's been used?

**REAL TIME**

interacting with a computer program and receiving the output immediately

3 Once the availability of the flights has been checked, the travel agent can book the flight the customer wants by choosing from the menu on the screen.
4 The information is instantly passed to the airline's database so that no-one else can book that particular seat. The booking system is a **real-time system** because the computer

must be able to keep up with a situation that's always changing.

5 The travel agent will also type in the name of each passenger and the ages of any children going. Any special requirements the passengers have – for example if they're disabled passengers – are also entered. These details are sent to the hotel's and the airline's database systems.

6 The database will reserve the hotel rooms and arrange for the tickets to be printed.

7 The computer will also print out the unpleasant part of the holiday – the bill!

**RECORD**

a data structure with one or more fields of information

**FIELD**

a single item of data stored in a record

### Passenger records

Each booking is stored in a passenger name record which can be called up on screen if it is needed. This record has details of all parts of the journey. It includes ticket and fare details, contact addresses or telephone numbers and any special requirements the passengers have – such as vegetarian meal, wheelchair or medical assistance.

The computer database holds a lot more information than is usually displayed on the screen. For example, it could hold prices, hotel bookings, details of hotel rooms and rates of exchange. But so far, one detail you can't call up on screen is a picture of the hotel or holiday resort. For this, you still have to look at the brochure. Travel agents' computer systems might be able to display pictures on their screens in the future, but most people prefer to look through places in a brochure before choosing a resort at their leisure.

## QUESTIONS

### Knowledge and understanding

1 List four types of information held in a tour operator's database.

2 What hardware does a travel agent need?

3 What must the travel agent do before he can access the database system? Why?

4 What is a passenger name record? What is it used for?

### Problem solving

1 Why is it important for the computer database to be updated once a flight has been booked?

2 List the steps involved in booking a holiday
(a) if the travel agent is using a computer system
(b) before computers were introduced to travel agents

3 Here are three airline messages

1 KIN GLA 0525 2230 F1J2 AF 146 707
2 LHR JFK 1500 1835 R6 BA 105 SSC
3 AMS GLA 2000 2105 F2M3 BA 235 747
(KIN = Kingston (Jamaica); JFK = John F Kennedy (New York); GLA = Glasgow; AMS =Amsterdam.
Class codes R= Concorde; F =First Class; J = Club Class; M= Economy).

What does each message mean?

4 Why do people still need holiday brochures?

5 Before they can book a flight, the travel agent must search the database on three fields. One field is the departure date. What are the other two fields?

## *More to do*

### *Other ways that airlines use computers*

Airlines use computers for many different purposes as well as flight reservation:

- passenger check-in
- aircraft load distribution and cargo control
- simulation and planning
- preparing flight plans
- flight operations control
- accounting
- personnel, crew support and workload forecasting.

Let's look at a few of these in more detail.

**DYNAMIC LINKAGE**

a change to the information in one file will automatically be carried over to the same information in another file

#### Passenger check-in

The check-in clerk uses a terminal to pass the passenger's details to the airline's booking computer. The system can be used to keep a count of the passengers who have checked in. It can also be linked to the booking computer to make sure that only the passengers with a recorded reservation are accepted. To do this, the system keeps a dynamic link with the booking computer so that all passenger names and booking levels are kept up to date by comparing that particular flight with the passenger lists for other flights currently open for check-in. Passengers who haven't booked in advance are often allowed to buy any vacant seats so the aircraft is used as efficiently as possible.

Once everyone has checked in for their flight the final passenger list will include any special arrangements that were made when the flight was booked – like special meals. This information is used to create a catering order so the right number and type of meals is loaded onto the plane.

#### Aircraft load distribution and cargo control

To make sure they're used efficiently, many passenger-carrying planes also carry cargo (items that don't belong to the passengers).

If the plane isn't loaded properly, it won't be able to take off or fly safely. Careful attention must be paid to the total weight of passengers, cargo and fuel on board and how all this weight is distributed in the plane. Distribution of the load is fully automated. At a preset time before departure, the system calculates the weight of the passengers and their luggage, taking into account any changes that are likely to happen at stop-off points. If there is any free space on board, the computer tells the cargo centre and any cargo will be sent to the plane. The computer controls the amount of load that will be accepted, and plans the distribution on the aircraft so the plane is safely balanced for take-off.

Requests for cargo reservations are input to the computer system. The computer allocates the cargo to a particular flight depending on the space and load available on each aircraft. A list of the cargo going on the flight is sent with the shipment and this list is stored within the system so that it can be read from a terminal at the destination airport. When the flight lands the system is updated to show that the cargo has arrived. Microfiche is used to provide a permanent record of all cargo carried. Some airports provide a printout of the cargo on board each aircraft for Customs and Excise.

**MICROFICHE**

a tiny photograph or slide which can be viewed using a projector

### Simulation and planning systems

Computers are also used by airlines to model (simulate) the operation of the airline. Planners enter details about the types and numbers of aircraft the airline has and the possible routes they could take into the computer system. A simulation program will then show how the airline would operate in real life. The planner can find out how altering the number of aircraft on a particular route will affect how the system would operate, and can work out the most efficient way of working. The program is **interactive** – it lets the planner hold a 'conversation' with the computer about problems and possible solutions that couldn't be done in real life because a mistake could cause chaos or even loss of life. In Chapter 10 we talked about other ways that airlines use simulation.

**SIMULATION**

a computer program used to model a real-life situation

**INTERACTION**

the operator's instructions are processed continuously by the computer – like a conversation

### Preparing flight plans

The computer system is used to prepare a **flight plan** which takes into account the total weight of passengers, luggage and cargo. The person planning the flight may choose the route, flying height and cruise speed or she may ask the system to recommend a flight plan. The computer can prepare a flight plan because the system stores details of all the major airports in the world, especially the routes usually used by the airline. It also keeps detailed

**WIDE AREA NETWORK (WAN)**

a network which covers a large geographical area like a country. Used for long-distance communication via satellite, radio or telephone line

information on how each aircraft performs so changes in weight and so on to may be taken into account. Weather forecast data is also sent to the airline computer directly from the Meteorological Office computer.

When the plan is finalised, the planner sends it through the wide area network for printing at the departure airport.

### Flight operations

The **flight operations control system** is a database for operations, maintenance and crew purposes. Flight schedules, crew shifts and flight plans are entered into the system and used to prepare a daily plan for the airline. During the day, the progress of flights is recorded and the system alerts the control centre to situations that need their attention. Information displays help controllers to solve problems, to produce network messages which track aircraft operations and to warn passengers of likely delays. The Flight Operations Control system is linked to sales and information points worldwide, to information display systems in the airports and other information services such as PRESTEL and CEEFAX. You can see an airport information display in the photograph.

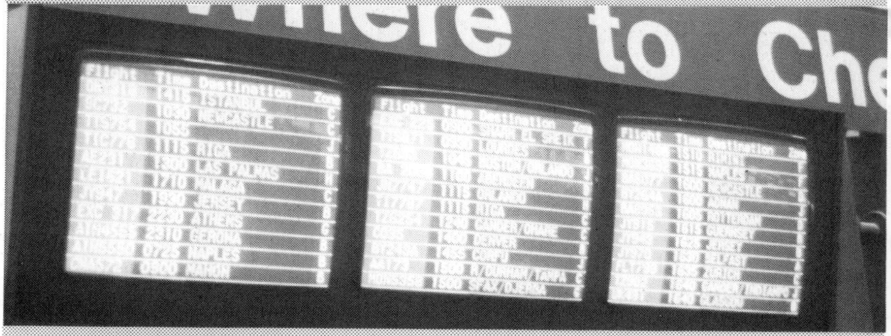


*The sort of information display you'd see at an airport*

### Accounting

A set of computer programs controls all the aspects of accounting for an airline. Flight documents are processed daily to work out the income earned from transporting passengers, cargo and mail. Bills to agents and other airlines are calculated, and incoming bills are checked. The accounts programs can also provide statistical data for planning, budgeting and market research.

### Forecasting personnel, crew support and workload

The information on payroll, staff needed and pensions is output from a single database. As well as the normal

**OUTPUT**

data passed out of a computer system

payroll calculations for staff and payments to pensioners and their families, the system produces regular reports. In particular, overtime payments are analysed and sick leave is monitored. Staff records are maintained, updated and used for general enquiries. All this confidential information is protected by a security system.

Maintenance of the aircraft on the ground is carried out by specialised technicians (these are called the ground crew). If the schedule of work is input, the computer will produce a list of the jobs that each member of the ground crew has to do. The computer is in control of scheduling the ground crew from the moment a schedule is agreed to the calculation of pay. The computer translates the schedule into work patterns for individual crew members, changes the planned schedules and follows the crew through the actual operation. The computer helps the airline to produce a work schedule for each member of the ground crew so the most work is done at the lowest cost to the airline. The computer can also be used to forecast the total work load of staff, and how ground facilities (like aircraft stands) are likely to be used.

## Real time and batch processing

Each application described in this chapter is carried out by a different computer program. These programs run on mainframe and minicomputer systems. Mainframes and minicomputers are not only physically larger than microcomputers, they run faster and can deal with much more data than a microcomputer can. They have large amounts of random access memory and use very large hard disks and magnetic tapes as backing store. They can run many different programs at once (this is called **multi-programming**) and they can be accessed by many users at the same time (they are multi-access systems – you saw an example of one of these in figure 15.2) because they are run by specialised **operating systems**.

Not all of the jobs of an airline computer need a speedy response. Tasks like analysing ticket sales and calculating wages can be handled as batch jobs when the system isn't fully occupied in dealing with user requests. A system where both batch and interactive processing are happening is called a **mixed system**. It is also called a **foreground/background system**, since some jobs are being processed in real time (they are in the *foreground*) while the batch jobs are run in between (in the *background*).

**MAINFRAME COMPUTER SYSTEM**

a computer system that can carry out a very large amount of work. It usually occupies a whole large room

**RANDOM ACCESS MEMORY (RAM)**

a microchip that stores data temporarily. The data is lost when the machine is switched off

**OPERATING SYSTEM**

programs which control the operation of a computer system. Part of the systems software

## EXTRA QUESTIONS

### Knowledge and understanding

1 Make a list of the applications for which airlines may use computers (other than travel reservations)
2 Holiday reservations, fare quotation and ticketing are described as real-time applications of an airline's computer system. What do we mean by real-time?
3 Explain how an airline's computer system can help the airline to get the best value for money from its staff.
4 Give one example of the airline computer being used to
   (a) help management make decisions?
   (b) carry out routine calculations?
   (c) obtain immediate and up-to-date access to information?

### Problem solving and practical activities

1 How does the computer system help the airline to fill as many seats as possible up to the last moment of departure without over booking?
2 If you have access to PRESTEL ask your teacher to demonstrate the Airline pages.
   Alternatively you could examine one of the Teletext services.
3 Simulation allows planners to use the computer to experiment with how to operate the airline as efficiently as possible. Why don't the airline's planners experiment in real life?
4 Why is the confidential personnel information held on computer protected by a security system?
5 Why does foreground and background operation increase the efficiency of the airlines computer systems?
6 Look back at the itinerary for a trip around the world you saw at the beginning of the chapter.
   (a) How many different airlines are involved?
   (b) How long does the whole journey take?
   How long would the total travelling time be if there were no stop-overs between flights (assume that travelling from Bangkok to Singapore takes one day)
   (c) What code should the travel agent type to search for the flight on 24 November?
   Give one line that would appear on the screen as a response to this search.
   (d) What other information appears on the itinerary apart from dates and flight information? Where must this information have come from?
   (e) Write down what the travel agent would have had to do to organise this trip before computers were introduced.

## KEY POINTS

- Travel agents use an on line computer system to book holidays for customers
- These systems are called multi-access systems because many users can be connected to them at the same time
- The booking system must work in real time because the computer needs to keep up with a constantly changing situation
- Each booking is recorded in a passenger name record
- Using computers to book holidays means that there is less chance of mistakes being made since all the people involved are using the same database
- Airlines use computers for other purposes too:
  passenger check-in
  aircraft load distribution and cargo control
  simulation and planning systems
  preparing flight plans
  flight operations
  accounting
  personnel, crew support and workload forecasting
- The programs used by airlines run on mainframe and minicomputers because of the huge amount of information they have to process quickly

# 16 Hardware

## What is hardware?

**DESKTOP COMPUTER**

a microcomputer consisting of a CPU, keyboard and monitor which is normally operated sitting at a desk

All the physical parts of a computer system (the bits you can see and touch, not the programs) are called the **hardware**. A single item of hardware is called a **device**. A computer system is made up of a central processing unit and main memory together with **input**, **output** and **backing storage devices**.

A typical computer system might include a central processing unit, a monitor, a keyboard, a printer and one or more disk drives. Can you identify these in the computer system in this photograph?

*A desktop computer system*

You can see examples of the types of device in figure 16.1. Let's look at some of them more closely.

## The central processing unit or CPU

This is the part of the computer where all the sorting, searching, calculating and decision-making goes on. In a lot of computers nowadays all these processes are carried by a single **chip**. A chip is a specially treated piece of silicon and is very small, only a few millimetres across. Because it is so small a CPU stored on a chip is called a **microprocessor**, and computers that have microprocessors as their CPUs are called

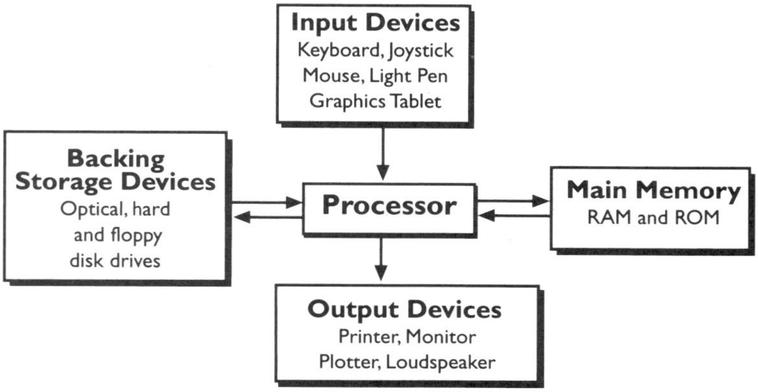


**FIGURE 16.1** *A block diagram of a computer system*

**DATA**

a general term for numbers, characters and symbols which are accepted and processed by a computer system

**microcomputers**. You can see a chip in the photo on the next page. A computer can carry out any process if it is given a set of instructions to tell it what to do. The instructions that control how a computer works is called a **program**. Another name for computer programs is **software**. It may help you to think of the CPU as the 'brain' of the computer system – but it isn't like a real brain because a computer can't think or act for itself. It can only carry out the instructions programmed into it. Computers can carry out instructions very quickly because the CPU can process millions of instructions every second. (More about software in the next chapter.)

## Main memory

The **main memory** or **main store** of a computer is used to store programs and data. A computer *must* have a memory. The CPU can't store a whole program at one time so the computer needs its memory to store the parts of a program and data it's not using at any particular moment. Programs stored in the main memory can be accessed straight away and because of this the main memory of a computer is sometimes called the **immediate access store**.

**STORAGE LOCATION**

a place in a computer's memory where an item of data may be held

The amount of information that can be stored in the memory of a computer depends on the number of **storage locations** that are available. A single storage location can hold one byte of information. One byte is the amount of space needed to store one character, for example the letter B takes up one byte of

**BIT**

a binary digit, either 1 or 0

**BYTE**

a group of eight bits

storage. You will find more information on bytes in Chapter 19.

The main memory of a computer system is made up of a set of memory chips. There are two types of memory chip. Each type of memory chip is used for a different purpose in a computer system.

1 **RANDOM ACCESS MEMORY (RAM) CHIPS**
RAM is also called read/write memory. RAM is used to store programs and data temporarily because anything stored in RAM is *lost* when the computer is switched off.

2 **READ ONLY MEMORY (ROM) CHIPS**
ROM can be used to store programs and data permanently. ROM's contents are *not* lost when you switch the computer off.

**APPLICATIONS PACKAGE**

a piece of software (together with its accompanying disks and manuals) that performs a particular task

ROM chips are used on some computers to store the programs that control how the computer works from the moment it is switched on. These programs are called operating systems programs. Operating systems are explained further in Chapter 18.

ROM chips are also used to store many other types of programs – applications programs and computer languages. The BBC model B and Master computers and the Cambridge Z88 use ROM chips in this way.

*A silicon chip*

**FIGURE 16.2** *A microprocessor chip. The 'legs' allow the chip to be plugged into a socket in the computer*

## QUESTIONS

### Knowledge and understanding

What is
(a) hardware?
(b) software?

2 Where are programs and data held inside a computer system?

3 How much information can a single storage location hold?

### Problem solving

Mary has been given a pocket computer game for her birthday. She has two different games which are stored on plug-in cartridges. Her sister Sarah is doing Computing Studies at school. Sarah says the cartridge that plugs into Mary's game is a ROM cartridge.

(a) What is ROM?
(b) Why are the games stored on ROM cartridges and not RAM cartridges?

2 A computer is sometimes described as 'a very fast idiot'. Why is this a good description?

### Practical activities

1 Find out which of the computer systems in your school have any of these stored on ROM chips
(a) their operating system or filing system
(b) applications programs
(c) computer programming languages
Give one example of each.

2 Find out how much RAM and ROM one of the computer systems in your school has.

## *More to do*

**CIRCUIT BOARD**

a thin board on which chips and other components are fixed by solder

### *More about chips*

Look back at the photograph of a silicon chip. The chips inside a computer are held on a **printed circuit board** and they are connected to the other parts of the system (like the screen and the keyboard). The chip is made up of thousands of tiny components and circuits all squeezed into a space only a few millimetres square.

The small size of chips means that:

- They take up less space and so lots of them can be fitted inside a machine, increasing the processing power or memory
- They work faster because the electricity has only a very short journey to flow round a very small circuit
- Thousands of them are produced at a time, so they are very cheap to make.

### *Types of chip*

There are many different types of chip, not just microprocessors and memory chips. Different chips are designed to do different things. A telephone might have three chips – one to turn the incoming analogue signals

**LAPTOP COMPUTER**

a portable computer which folds and has a screen and keyboard in a single unit. It is powered from batteries and may be operated while travelling. A laptop computer usually has an LCD screen

*A laptop computer*

**PALMTOP COMPUTER**

a hand-held computer. A palmtop computer usually has an LCD screen but may or may not have a keyboard

into digital data, a control chip to carry out functions like automatic dialling and a memory chip to store telephone numbers. Chips are programmed to perform these tasks when they are made and can't change what they do – so you couldn't take the control chip out of a dishwasher and make it work a computer.

## *Effect of changes in technology*

Each year, the number of storage locations and circuits (connections) that can be placed on a single chip gets bigger. This has affected computer systems because

- The price of memory chips has gone down
- Memory size of computers (ROM and RAM) has gone up
- Chips work faster and can handle more data in a single operation
- Many more functions can be stored on a single chip – an extra processor (or **co-processor**) to speed up arithmetical calculations is now included in a single chip
- Complete computers can be produced on a single chip, which holds both the CPU and the memory
- Powerful computers can now be made very small. You will have noticed how many palmtop and laptop (or 'notebook') computers there are on the market – and many other related devices too, like cellular telephones and radio pagers.

Manufacturers have to work very hard to keep pace with the advances in chip technology and computer design. The computer user now expects more and more features from her machine. The latest, fastest and most powerful computer system is now outdated in less than a year as competition forces manufacturers to make new models with extra features to keep up with the opposition.

# EXTRA QUESTIONS

**Knowledge and understanding**

1 What effects are advances in technology having on the microprocessor chip?

**Problem solving**

1 Why do computer systems need a main memory when programs and data can be loaded from disk?

2 What can you do to stop a program stored in RAM from being lost when you switch your computer off?

**Practical activities**

1 Find out how a chip is made.

# Backing storage media

**Backing storage** is a way of permanently storing programs and data. Backing storage is needed by computers because data in the main memory is lost when the computer is switched off. Magnetic tape, floppy disks and hard disks are all examples of backing storage **media** and the hardware that uses or holds the media is known as a **backing storage device**. Be careful not to confuse the terms media and software.

*Remember: software means programs not disks!*

| Backing storage devices | Backing storage media |
|---|---|
| Tape drive/tape recorder | Magnetic tape/cassette tape |
| Floppy disk drive | Floppy disk |
| Hard disk drive | Hard disk |
| CD ROM drive | CD ROM |

Let's look at a few of these devices and media.

## Magnetic tape

**MAINFRAME COMPUTER SYSTEM**

a computer system that can carry out a very large amount of work at high speed. It usually occupies a whole large room

**Magnetic tape** is usually used in two forms for backing storage – large open reels and in small cassette tapes. You are more likely to see large reels of magnetic tape as backing storage devices on mainframe computers.

## Cassettes

Cassette tapes (the same as the ones you use to tape music) are used as backing storage for some microcomputer systems. In the early 1980s many microcomputers used cassette tape for backing storage because floppy disk drives were much more expensive than they are today. As disk drives get cheaper, cassette tapes are getting less popular.

Some microcomputers with hard disk drives still use cassettes to back up all the information on the hard disk. This is done using a device called a **tape streamer**. It uses specially made tape cassettes, which are smaller than standard audio cassettes.

Loading and saving programs on magnetic tape takes much

longer than from floppy or hard disks, so magnetic tape isn't used where speed of access to data is important. For instance, a program that might take five minutes to load from tape can usually be loaded in five seconds from a floppy disk.

## Floppy disks

**BACKUP**
a copy of a program or data made in case the original is lost or destroyed

A **floppy disk** is a plastic disk coated with magnetic material and enclosed in a square or rectangular cover of cardboard or hard plastic. The inside of the cover is coated with tissue paper which cleans the disk as it spins around in the disk drive. Floppy disks are called 'floppy' because the disk is made of a thin flexible material. They are easily damaged and you must be careful when using them. If the disk is damaged you could lose all the data it contains. This is one good reason why you should *always* keep a backup copy of anything you have on a floppy disk.

### *Sizes of disks*

Floppy disks come in different sizes. The ones you're most likely to see nowadays are $5^{1}/_{4}$" disks and $3^{1}/_{2}$" disks. You can see some of the features of these disks in figure 16.3.

**FIGURE 16.3** *Floppy disks*

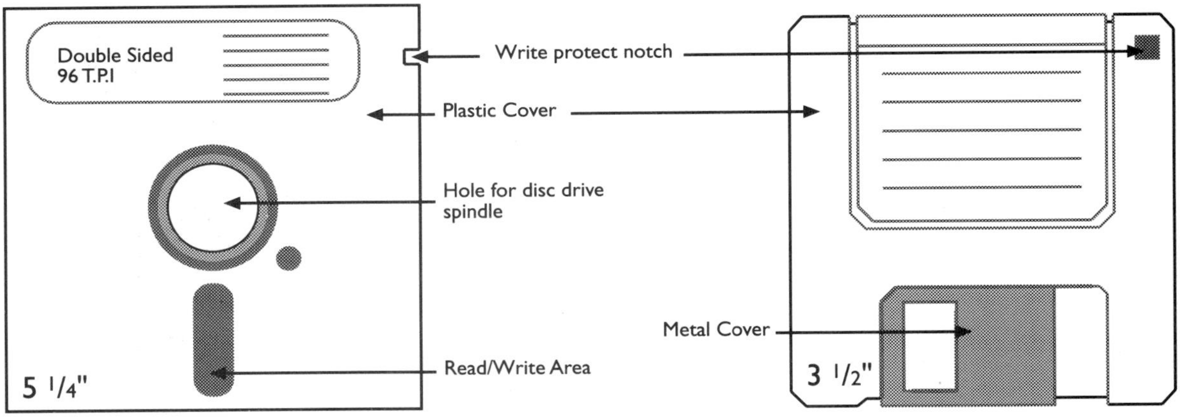


### *Handling disks*

When you're handling floppy disks

1 Always keep the disk in its envelope when you're not using it
2 Never touch the surface of the disk itself – always hold a disk by the label
3 Do not bend or crease the disk
4 Always write the label before sticking it onto the disk
5 Keep disks away from dust (like chalk or talcum powder) and liquids (like tea and coffee)

**FIGURE 16.4** *Always hold a floppy disk by the label side*

6 Keep disks away from direct heat
7 Do not put disks on top of electrical equipment or anything that has a magnet in it (like a monitor)

The smaller ($3\frac{1}{2}$") disks have a hard plastic cover and a metal flap which covers the read/write area, so you don't need to keep them in a paper envelope when not in use like you do the $5\frac{1}{4}$" disks. They are less likely to get damaged than the $5\frac{1}{4}$" disks. The $3\frac{1}{2}$" disks are sometimes called **microfloppy** disks.

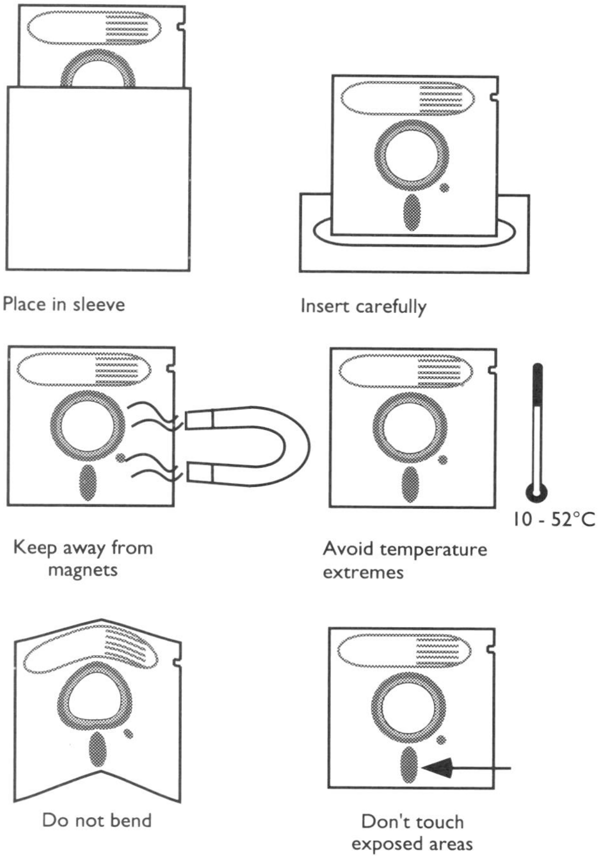
Place in sleeve
Insert carefully
Keep away from magnets
Avoid temperature extremes
10 - 52°C
Do not bend
Don't touch exposed areas

**FIGURE 16.5** *Precautions you should take when handling floppy disks*

## *Formatting floppy disks*

Before you can use a floppy disk in your computer it must be prepared in a special way. This process is called **formatting**. Formatting produces invisible circles (called **tracks**) and lines (called **sectors**) of magnetism on the surface of the disk. These are explained in figure 16.6. A disk doesn't look any different after it has been formatted – you can't see the tracks or tell by looking at it. But if you try to use an unformatted disk you won't be able to save any data.

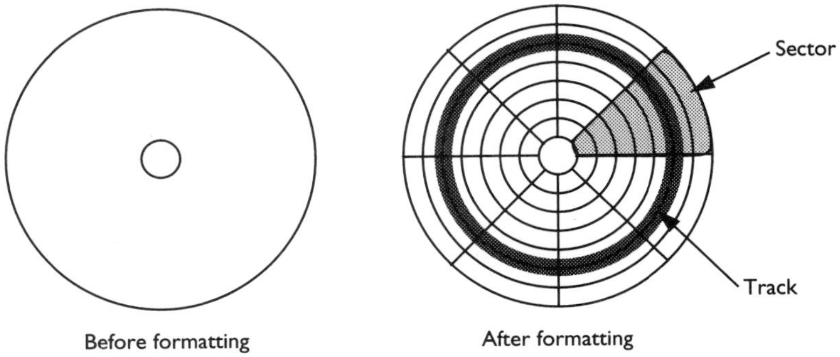


**FIGURE 16.6** *Formatting a floppy disk. You can't see the lines and circles on the disk, because they're lines of magnetism*

### *Write protection*

If you format a disk that already has data on it you will lose all that data. To stop accidents like this from happening, floppy disks have a 'write protect' notch. These notches work differently depending on the type of disk.

A $5^{1}/_{4}$" disk can be formatted or used to save data when the notch is open. When you buy a box of blank disks you are given a set of small sticky tabs which you can use to cover this notch. When the notch is covered, the disk is **write protected** or **read only** – you can't write anything to that disk.

On the $3^{1}/_{2}$" disks the hard plastic case has a slider in it which you can use to open or close the notch as you want. When the notch on a $3^{1}/_{2}$" disk is open the disk is write protected.

## Hard disks

A **hard disk** is a circular metal disk coated with magnetic material. Hard disks for microcomputers are usually sealed inside a hard disk drive and cannot be removed, though you can buy removable hard disks. Some hard disks used on mainframe computers are also removable. They are called **exchangeable disk packs.**

Hard disks are used because you can store much more data on them and access it more quickly than with floppy disks.

### *How a hard disk works*

A hard disk drive normally contains several disks, stacked on top of each other with a gap between them – you can see how in figure 16.7. The gaps are needed so the read/write heads on the disk drive can move across the disk surface and reach the tracks nearest the centre of the disk.

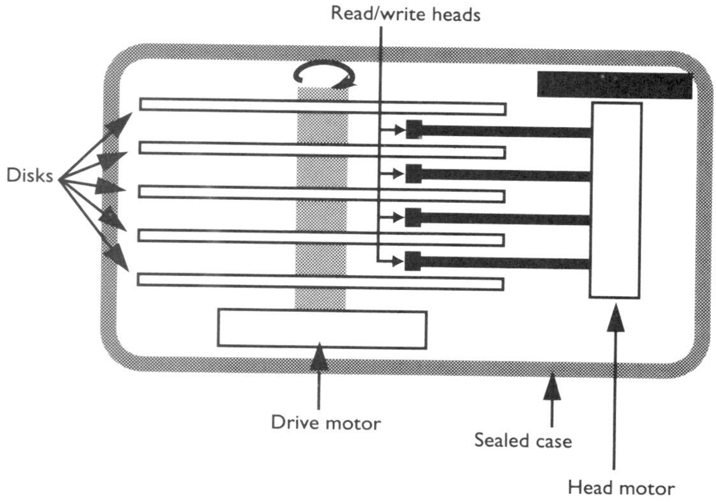


**FIGURE 16.7** *A hard disk drive*

Hard disks rotate very fast and the gap between the read/write heads and the surface of the metal disk is tiny. If you bump or drop the hard disk drive while it is switched on or switch it off without shutting it down properly the heads could collide with the surface of the disk. This is called **crashing** – it usually results in all the data on the disk being lost. The disk itself could be permanently damaged. If you treat a hard disk properly it is generally much more reliable than a floppy disk.

### Compact disc read only memory

This is usually shortened to CD ROM. A CD ROM looks just like an audio compact disc. CD ROMs can store a huge amount of information, about six hundred times the amount that you can get onto a $3^1/_2$" magnetic floppy disk. A CD ROM disc (one of these is shown in figure 16.8) comes with information already stored on it so it doesn't need to be formatted. A CD ROM disc is read only, so you can't erase the data on it.

Many titles have been produced on CD ROM. Because of their large storage capacity, CD ROMs are ideal for storing material in archives. Many newspapers are available on CD ROM, and you can buy complete databases such as ECCTIS and various other reference works like encyclopaedias and dictionaries on CD ROM.

### Laservision discs

Laservision discs are the same size as long-playing records (12") and were originally designed to store television programmes (like video recorders do nowadays). But they never really caught on – the BBC's Domesday Book system linked to the BBC

*A selection of CD ROM titles*

**DATABASE**

a structured collection of similar information which can be searched

Master computer was one of the few successful computer databases produced using Laservision. There are still some Laservision discs being produced and used for applications such as training.

### Write once read many

This is usually shortened to **WORM**. A WORM disc works like a CD ROM except that you can write to it as well as read from it. This gets over one of the limitations of a read-only medium such as CD ROM. However, you can only write data to any part of a WORM disc once. Once you have filled that part of the disc with data, you can't use that part again. This is why they're called write *once*, read *many*.

To save to a WORM disc you must write the program to a new part of the disc. When a WORM disc is full it will behave like a CD ROM, since you can no longer write on it, only read from it. A Kodak PhotoCD is an example of a WORM disc.

**MEGABYTE**

1024 kilobytes

### Re-writable optical discs

You can now get rewritable optical discs which you can use in the same way as floppy disks. These rewritable discs can hold much more data, usually about a hundred times more than will fit on a $3^1/_2$" magnetic disk. There is still a lot of work going on about rewritable optical discs, and disc capacities are constantly increasing. In 1993 two manufacturers produced rewritable optical discs ($5^1/_4$") that could hold up to 1500 **megabytes** of data.

## QUESTIONS

### Knowledge and understanding

1 Write down the precautions you should take when handling floppy disks.
2 Approximately how many times faster at accessing data is a floppy disk than a cassette tape?
3 What is a tape streamer used for?
4 What is the purpose of a disk's write protect notch?
5 Why must floppy disks be formatted before they can store data?
6 What is the difference between a CD ROM and a WORM disc?

### Problem solving

1 Write down instructions for your system on how to
(a) back up one floppy disk onto another floppy disk
(b) copy a single file from one disk to another
(c) format a floppy disk for use.
2 Which type of computer system (micro or main frame) might use
(a) audio cassettes
(b) open reel tapes
as backing storage media?
3 A large mainframe computer system may have both hard disk and magnetic tape.
Suggest a use for each type of medium.

## *More to do*

### *Sequential and random (direct) access devices*

Suppose you have a music centre at home with a cassette tape recorder and a compact disc player. If you want to find a particular song on the tape, you have to play the tape from the beginning and listen to all the songs until you find the one you want. You can speed things up by fast forwarding or rewinding the tape to the position where you think the song will be, but it is still quite slow.

It is much quicker to find a song on a disc than on a tape. You can send the player directly to any track and it will start playing the song immediately.

Computer tapes and disks store data in the same sort of way. Finding data on a tape is slow because you can only get the data back in the same order you recorded it onto the tape. Tape gives **sequential access** to data because the data can only be read back in sequence. A tape recorder is a **sequential access device** because it reads and writes data in sequence.

Disks can access data **directly** because the read/write head on the disk drive can go straight to the track where the data is stored, without having to read all the data in

**SEQUENTIAL ACCESS**

reading a set of records or storage locations in the same order as they were originally stored

**RANDOM/DIRECT ACCESS**

being able to locate a data item straight away, wherever it is stored

between. Direct access is also called **random access** because you can read the data on the disk in any order, not just the order it was written in. A disk drive is called a **random access device** because the disk drive head can read data in any order.

## *A comparison of backing storage media*

- How much you can store on a floppy disk depends not so much on the size of the disk but on how it is formatted.

**EXAMPLE**

A 5¼" floppy disk used with the BBC model B microcomputer formatted with forty tracks can hold a total of 100 kilobytes of data on one side of the disk. If you use both sides of the disk and format the disk to eighty tracks you can store 200 kilobytes on each side – making a total of 400 kilobytes. If you format the same disk to its full capacity on a BBC Master computer it can hold 640 kilobytes. You can store more than a megabyte of data on a 3½" disk depending on how you format it.

- Hard disks can load and save programs faster than floppy disks. It takes a second or two for the disk drive to start spinning the floppy disk around before the read/write head can move to the right track but a hard disk drive is spinning all the time and much faster than a floppy disk, so there is no delay before the read/write head can reach the correct track.
- Hard disks can store more data than magnetic floppy disks. You can store more on a hard disk than on a floppy disk because the read/write head in a hard disk drive is very small and close to the surface of the disk and the tracks can be packed together closely when the disk is formatted. The gap between the disk and the read/write head is larger in a floppy disk drive so a floppy disk can't be formatted with as many tracks as a hard disk and so can't store as much data.
- Not all backing storage media use magnetism to store the data on their surfaces. When a CD ROM (or an audio CD) is made, the data is moulded into tiny holes (these are called 'pits') on the clear plastic disc. The plastic disc is then coated with a reflective metal layer and then a protective lacquer. The data is read by focusing a laser beam through the clear plastic onto the

**BINARY**

having only two states (on and off), counting using only two digits

tracks. When the laser light strikes the area between the pits (these areas are called 'lands') it is reflected into a photodetector and registers as a 1, and light which hits a pit is scattered and absorbed, registering as a 0, to give you the binary information. You can see a section of a compact disc, greatly magnified, in figure 16.8.

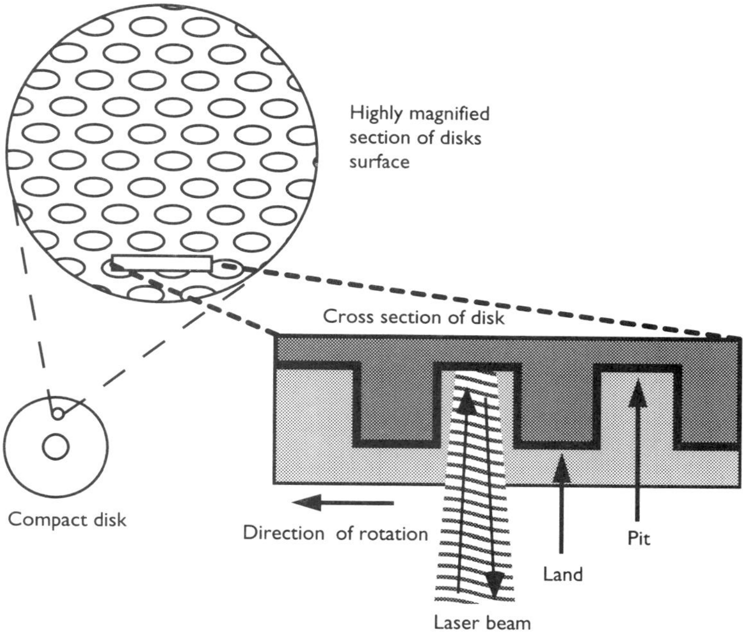


**FIGURE 16.8** *A section of a compact disk greatly magnified*

- Read/write heads on a CD ROM drive are faster than ordinary CD players. One important difference between an audio CD player and a CD ROM drive is that the read/write head in a CD ROM drive *must* move faster than in an audio CD player because the CD ROM drive must be able to access the different tracks on the CD ROM in a random fashion. It's not so important when you're playing music to be able to leap randomly from track to track.
- CD ROM drives also need extensive error correction features. This is not as important in an audio CD where if a single bit is read wrongly you probably won't notice. A single bit wrong in a computer program or data file could have disastrous results. The reverse is not the case, though – a CD ROM drive makes an excellent audio CD player!

- Loading a program from a CD ROM is about as fast as loading from a floppy disk.

## *Effect of technology on backing storage*

Continual progress is being made in backing storage technology. The table on the next page shows you roughly the capacities and relative speeds of different backing storage media and the devices available. Some of the disks seem quite expensive, but you must compare the cost per megabyte of storage. You can see a rough comparison in figure 16.9.

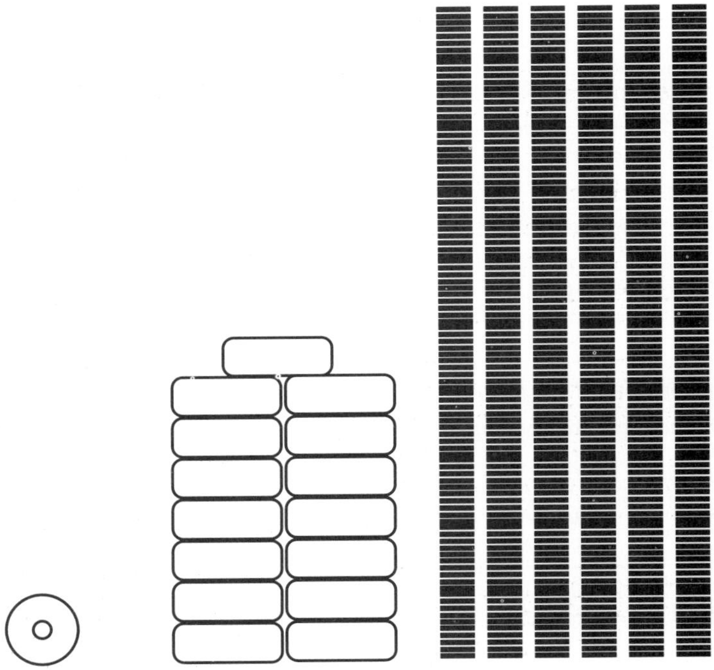


**FIGURE 16.9** *Capacity of backing store*

## *Multimedia*

When video players, compact disks, tape recorders and so on are connected to a computer system and are operated together by a program you get **multimedia** (many media are being used). The user of a multimedia system can see high-quality images on the screen and listen to hi-fi sound, all brought together on a computer system.

| MEDIUM | CAPACITY | COST (March 1993) | SPEED OF ACCESS |
|---|---|---|---|
| **Magnetic media** | | | |
| Tape reel (2400 feet) | 50 Megabytes | £20 | Slow |
| Cassette (tape streamer) | 20 kilobytes to 100 megabytes | £30 | Slow |
| Floppy disk (5¼") | 100 to 800 kilobytes | 20 p | Medium |
| Floppy disk (3½") | 400 kilobytes to 1.6 megabytes | 40 p | Medium |
| Hard disk (drive) | 20 to 600 megabytes | £100–£2000 | Fast |
| Hard disk (exchangeable) | 44 to 88 megabytes | £50–£80 | Fast |
| **Optical media** | | | |
| CD ROM | 660 Megabytes | £30 | Medium to fast |
| Rewritable 3½" | 128 Megabytes | £60 | Medium to fast |

**USER-FRIENDLY**

an interactive computer system which helps the user by giving clear prompts, menus and help screens when needed

**HUMAN COMPUTER INTERFACE**

the way the computer and its user communicate

**TOUCH-SENSITIVE SCREEN**

a screen with sensitive areas on it. The user presses particular areas to input into the computer or operate a program

Specialised software has been produced to operate multimedia systems and to give them a user-friendly human computer interface. Here are some examples of software which can be used:

- Hypercard
- Supercard
- Genesis
- Storybook
- Magpie.

Multimedia systems often use a touch-sensitive screen to make them even more user friendly.

## *One problem with multimedia*

High-quality pictures and sound take up a great deal of space on backing store. An 80 Mbyte hard disk can only hold a few minutes of video. Multimedia developers and computer manufacturers are trying to get over this problem by compressing files on backing storage so that they take up less space without losing quality. In Chapter 14 we described some of the uses of multimedia.

## EXTRA QUESTIONS

**Knowledge and understanding**

1 What determines the capacity of a magnetic floppy disk?
2 Explain how data is stored on a CD ROM.

3 Give two ways that a CD ROM drive and an audio CD player are different, and one way they're the same.
4 What is multimedia?

**Problem solving**

1 Why is a sequential access medium slower than a direct access medium?

**Practical activities**

1 Use catalogues and/or computer magazines to find out how much a 100 megabyte magnetic hard disk drive would cost. Compare this with the prices of a magnetic floppy disk and a rewritable optical disk (and find out their capacity). Which one offers the best value for money? Discuss the advantages and disadvantages offered by each storage method.

# *Input devices*

You saw in figure 16.1 the types of devices you can use to input data.

## Keyboard

The input device used most often with a computer system is a **keyboard**. Each key on a keyboard has a switch under it. When you press the key, the switch beneath it is closed and a signal is sent to the computer. The keyboard is wired so that each key switch sends a different code number into the computer. This code is called the **American Standard Code for Information Interchange** (shortened to **ASCII**). You will find more about ASCII in Chapter 19. The keys on a computer keyboard are normally arranged in the same way as they are on a typewriter, so a standard computer keyboard is sometimes called a QWERTY keyboard (from the top row of a typewriter, where the keys are QWERTYUIOP).

Many computer keyboards also have function keys, and on some computers you can program these keys. Other keys have built-in functions (like 'print' or 'clear screen'). A software package which uses the **function keys** will often have an overlay that you put over the function keys to label the keys. This is called a **function keystrip**. Some keyboards also have a small key pad to the side of the main keyboard which has numbers on it (it is the **numeric keypad**). This can speed up your work if you have to enter a lot of numbers.

### *Concept keyboards*

A '**concept' keyboard** is a flat board which contains a grid of key switches. You can program each switch or group of switches like you would program a function key. By placing a paper overlay on the concept keyboard and loading the appropriate software you can operate the program from the concept keyboard. This is especially useful for very young children or for people who find using an ordinary keyboard difficult.

### Graphics tablets

A **graphics tablet** is a flat pressure-sensitive board with a pen or pointer connected to it. By pressing on the graphics tablet with the pen, the pen's position is sent to a computer. Often the pointer has a small window with a fine cross-hair marked on it. This helps the user to position the pointer accurately on the board. By using a graphics tablet the user can draw or trace a shape which will appear on the computer screen. A graphics tablet is often used for computer aided design (CAD) applications. (These were explained in Chapter 11.)

### Touch-sensitive screens

On a touch-sensitive screen there is an invisible infrared grid across the front of an ordinary screen. When you touch the screen with your finger you 'break' the grid, and a message is sent to the computer to give the position of the finger.

A touch-sensitive screen can be used in many ways:

- Like a concept keyboard to help very young children or disabled people to use a computer
- In dedicated systems like a holiday resort guide in a tourist information office
- As a guide in a museum where it is easier to make choices by pointing at a screen than using a keyboard.

**DEDICATED**

a computer or machine which can only perform one particular task

### Mouse

A **mouse** is a device with a ball underneath it and one or more buttons on top (like the one in figure 16.10) When you move the mouse on your desk, a signal is sent back to the computer, giving the position of the mouse and indicating whether you've pressed a button. The computer uses this information to move a pointer and to select items on the screen. You can use a mouse to cut down on the number of keyboard instructions you use when operating the computer, especially if you're using a WIMP environment.

**WIMP**

Windows, Icons, Menu (or Mouse), Pointer (or Pull down menu)

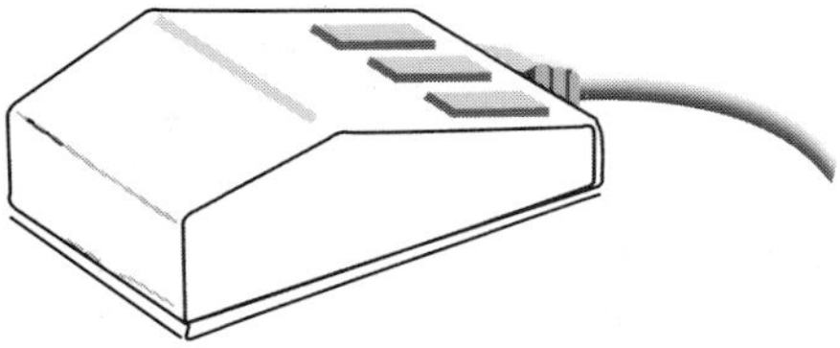

FIGURE 16.10 *A mouse*

## Trackball

A **trackball** (sometimes called a **tracker ball**) works exactly the same way as a mouse, except that the ball is on top. You can see one of these in figure 16.11. The user rolls the ball around with her hand to operate it. If you use a trackball you don't need any extra space on your desk to move it around (like you do with a mouse). Trackballs are often used on small portable computers and on some video games machines where it wouldn't be practical to operate a mouse.

FIGURE 16.11 *A trackball*

## Joystick

A **joystick** is another input device you can connect to a computer system. The joystick is able to move in eight directions. Joysticks are mostly used in computer games to control the way a picture on the screen moves. Sometimes two joysticks are connected to a computer so two people can play the game at once. You can see a joystick in figure 16.12.

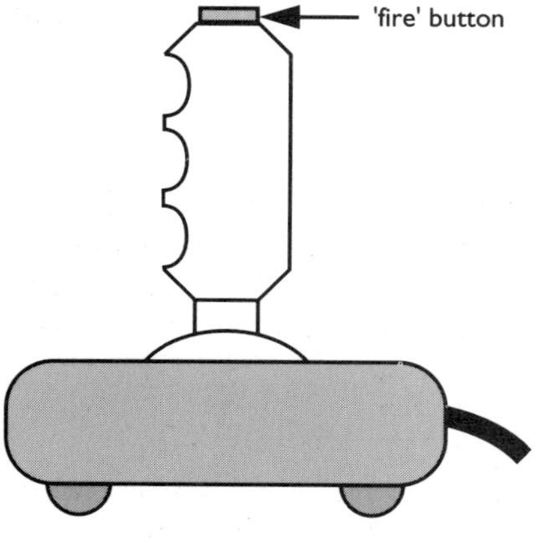


FIGURE 16.12 *A joystick*

## Light pens

A **light pen** can be used to draw pictures directly onto a computer screen or to read the pattern on a bar code (look back at Chapter 14 for details about bar codes). A light pen that draws on the screen works by detecting the brightness of the screen and sending its position as a signal into the computer. A light pen that can read bar codes detects the difference between the light reflected from a black bar code line and its lighter background. Light pens are used in computer aided design systems and in some shops at electronic point of sale (EPOS) terminals (we discussed these in Chapter 14).

**FIGURE 16.13** *Using a light pen*

> **OPTICAL CHARACTER RECOGNITION**
>
> characters can be read in to the computer automatically from a page of text

### Scanner

Using a **scanner** you can input printed drawings, photographs or text directly into a computer. A scanner works like a photocopier – a light is shone on the material and the scanner detects the reflected light. You can use a scanner with optical character recognition (OCR) software to input the scanned text into a word processing package.

### Voice recognition

Speech can be input to a computer system using voice recognition. To use this system, the computer must be fitted with a microphone and **voice recognition software**. To use voice recognition the user must speak slowly and clearly and the system usually understands only a limited number of words. The user usually has to 'teach' the computer to recognise his voice by repeating certain words or phrases. Voice recognition is used in one form of tele-banking, which we looked at in Chapter 13.

> **PALMTOP COMPUTER**
>
> a hand-held computer. A palmtop computer usually has an LCD screen but may or may not have a keyboard

### Handwriting recognition

Some computers can read your writing and turn it into print. This is called **handwriting recognition**. The user writes in her normal handwriting on a pressure-sensitive tablet connected to a computer system. The computer reads the shape of the writing and decodes it into a command or text that goes into a word processor. Like voice recognition, handwriting recognition takes a great deal of computer processing power. Also like voice recognition, you have to 'teach' the computer your handwriting. The new generation of palmtop computers (like the Apple Newton Message Pad in the photograph overleaf) use handwriting recognition as one of their main selling points.

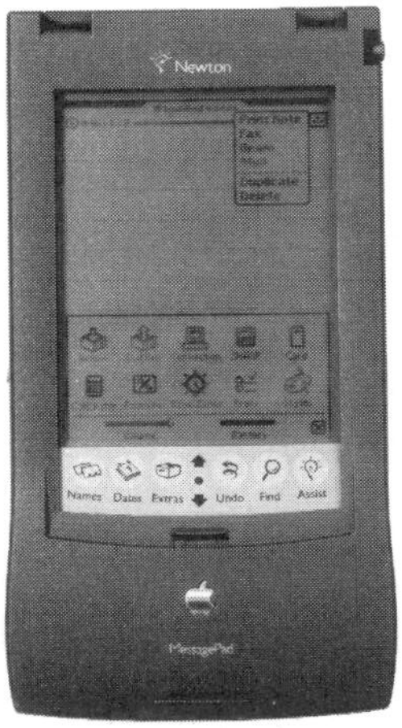

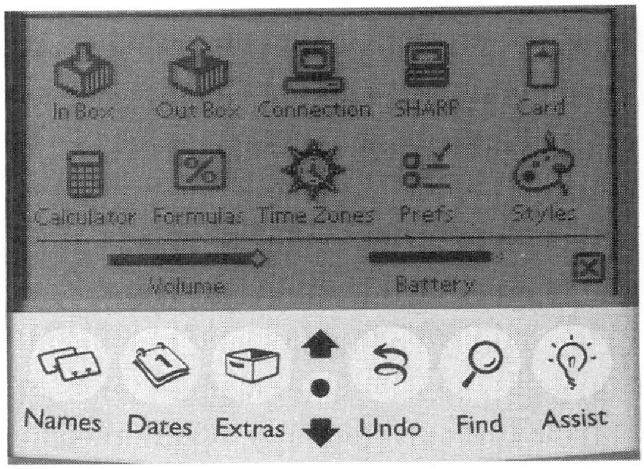


*A palmtop computer (Apple Newton Message Pad)*

# Output devices

## Monitors and VDUs

A **monitor** is an output device which accepts a video signal directly from a computer. A **visual display unit** (or **VDU**) consists of a monitor and a keyboard. The **screen** is the part of a monitor or VDU which displays the graphics or text.

Here are some of the most important features of monitors:

- A monitor gives a better output than you would get by connecting your computer to your TV set.
- Monitors are available in black and white and full colour.
- You can get monitors with different resolutions. A high-resolution monitor will show much finer details on the screen than a low-resolution monitor can.
- You should choose a monitor of a resolution suitable for its use, to avoid eye strain, especially if you're using an application which displays a lot of text on the screen.
- A monitor doesn't usually have a tuner (unlike a TV set), so you can't receive TV broadcasts on your monitor.
- A monitor may have one or more loudspeakers which can output sound.

**LIQUID CRYSTAL DISPLAY (LCD)**

a type of flat screen display which is used in calculators, palmtop and laptop computers because of its low power consumption. It may be monochrome (black and white) or colour

**RESOLUTION**

the amount of detail which can be shown on a screen (or a hard copy)

## Printers

A **printer** is a device that you use to produce a printout (or hard copy) of the output from a computer.

Various types of printer are used with microcomputers:

- Dot matrix
- Daisy wheel
- Laser
- Inkjet.

**HARD COPY**

a printed copy of your work, usually on paper

All of these printers print onto paper and some can print directly onto transparent film. Some printers can print in colour. Let's look at the printers most often used.

## *Dot matrix printers*

A **dot matrix printer** forms its characters on the paper by producing a pattern of dots. A typical dot matrix print head has nine pins arranged one above the other (look at the one in figure 16.14). The print head moves across the paper, and different pins are pushed out of the print head to hit the paper through the inked ribbon. This leaves a column of dots. By arranging these columns in particular ways a single character can be formed.

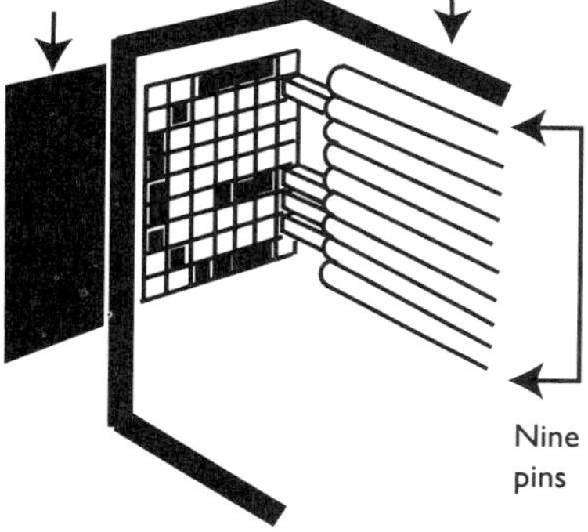


**FIGURE 16.14** *A dot matrix print head*

Dot matrix printers can print about 200 characters per second but the printout you get at this speed is poor quality. If the printer prints more slowly (about 50 characters per second) then you get **near letter quality** printout. To get this kind of quality each character has to be printed twice, slightly offset from one another. This makes it harder to see the individual dots which make up each character. Another way of making the print look better is to use a different printer with more pins in the print head. A print head with twenty-four pins will produce a much clearer output than one with only nine pins.

Dot matrix printers can produce different styles, sizes and weights of print (like **bold** or *italic*). They can also produce a few different typefaces (usually only two or three) and can be used to print graphics. Dot matrix printers are quite noisy while operating. A colour dot matrix printer uses a special ribbon with four separate colours along its length.

## *Daisy wheel printers*

A **daisy wheel printer** has a print head made up of a plastic wheel with spokes arranged like the petals on a daisy flower (that's why it's called a 'daisy wheel'). At the end of each spoke there are two characters, one for capitals and one for lower case letters. To print a character, the wheel turns until the right character is in place then a hammer hits the back of the character and pushes it through a ribbon. This leaves an imprint of the character on the paper.

Daisy wheel printers are quite slow (they print about 20 characters per second) and are very noisy. They produce a very clear print, but you can't use them to print graphics. Also, one daisy wheel only has one set of characters on it – if you want to use a different typeface you have to change the daisy wheel. Daisy wheels are therefore less versatile than dot matrix printers.

You can produce carbon copies of your document by using both dot matrix and daisy wheel printers. They are sometimes called **impact printers** because they actually strike the paper. The printers we'll discuss next (laser printers and inkjet printers) don't strike the paper. They are examples of **non-impact printers.**

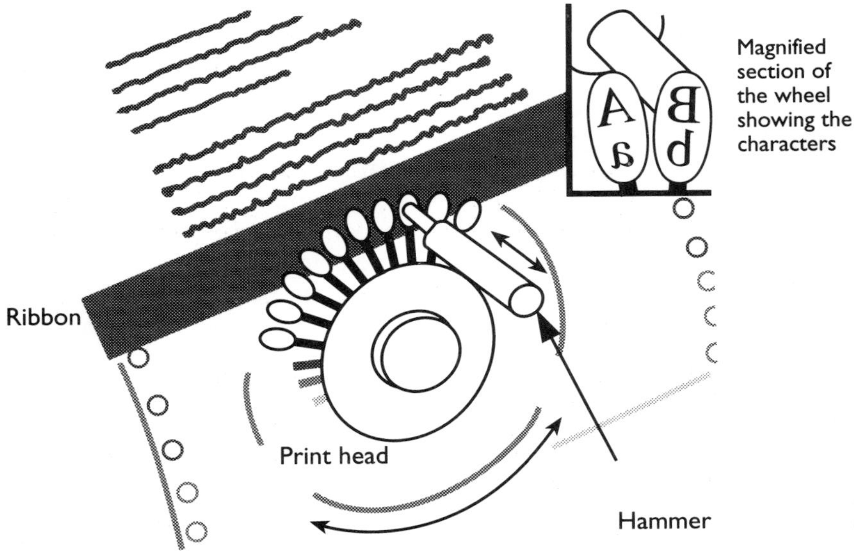


**FIGURE 16.15** *The print head on a daisy wheel printer*

### *Laser printers*

From its name, you might think that a **laser printer** produces an image by 'burning' the paper with a laser beam, but it doesn't. Laser printers work like photocopiers. They use a powder (which is called toner) to produce an image on the paper. The laser in a laser printer is only used to project the image of the page onto a drum. The toner sticks to the parts of the drum with the image projected on them and it is transferred to the paper. The paper is passed between heated rollers which seal the toner onto the paper. You can see what a laser printer looks like in figure 16.16. Laser printers print a whole page at once and produce between four and twelve pages a minute. Because of this they are also called page printers. With a laser printer you can produce very high quality printing of both text and graphics – quietly! There are colour printers on the market but these are still quite expensive to buy and use. A laser printer is often used as part of a desktop publishing system (we discussed this in Chapter 7).

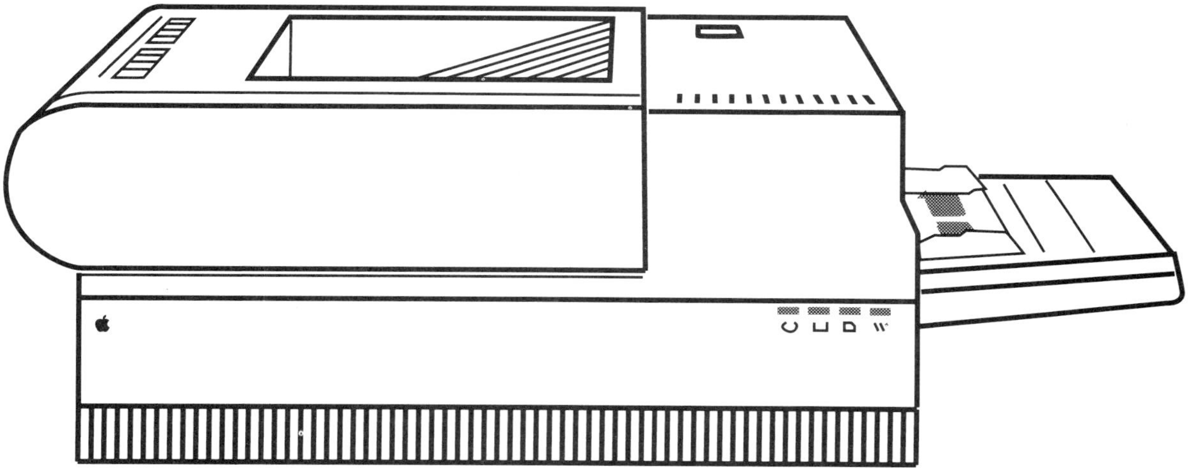

**FIGURE 16.16** *A laser printer*

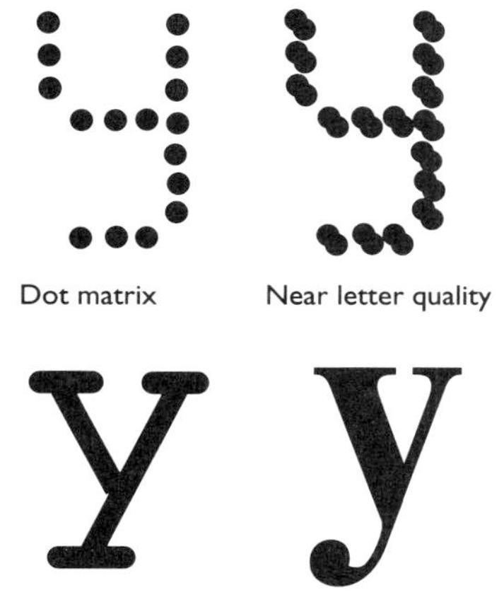


**FIGURE 16.17** *Comparing print quality of dot matrix, daisy wheel and laser printers (each is greatly enlarged)*

### *Inkjet printers*

**Inkjet printers** work like dot matrix printers because the characters they produce are made up of dots. But they are different from dot matrix printers because the print head has a set of tiny holes rather than pins. As the print head moves across the paper, a jet of ink is forced out of the holes to form the letters.

Inkjet printers are very quiet to operate and can produce a good printout of both graphics and text. They are especially good at producing cheap colour graphics and can print on many different surfaces – for instance, inkjet printers are used to print 'sell by' dates on the bottom of drink cans.

An inkjet printer can achieve a print quality similar to a laser printer. In figure 16.17 you can see how the print quality of dot matrix, daisy wheel and laser printers compare.

**SUMMARY OF PRINTERS**

| NAME | SPEED | NOISE OF OPERATION | PRINT QUALITY | PRINTS GRAPHICS? |
|---|---|---|---|---|
| Nine pin dot matrix | 200 characters per second | Noisy | Low | Yes |
| Twenty-four pin dot matrix | 200 characters per second | Noisy | High | Yes |
| Daisy wheel | 20 characters per second | Very noisy | High | No |
| Laser | 4-12 pages per minute | Quiet | High | Yes |
| Inkjet | 150 characters per second | Quiet | High | Yes |

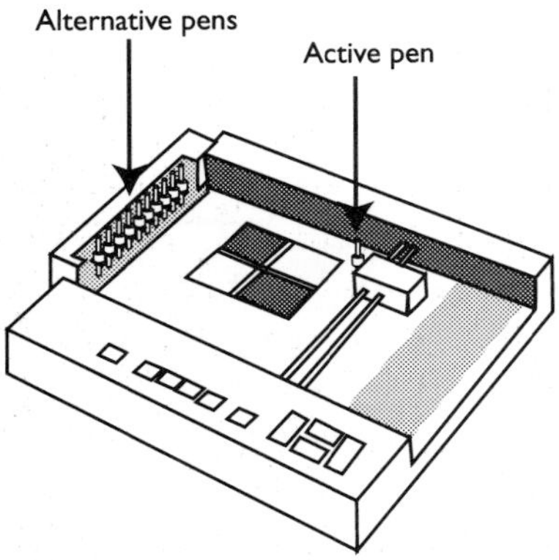


**FIGURE 16.18** *A flat bed plotter*

## Plotters

A **plotter** is another device for producing hard copy of the output from a computer. The difference between a printer and a plotter is that a plotter uses a pen to draw the computer output onto paper. There are three types of plotter.

1 On a **flat bed plotter** (like the one in figure 16.18) the paper is fixed and the pen moves in two dimensions (up and across).
2 On a **drum plotter** the pen moves in one dimension and the paper is moved in the other dimension by the rotation of the drum.
3 A third type of plotter works like a motorised buggy or turtle and moves over the paper carrying its pen.

By using several different coloured pens you can get colour output from plotters. Plotters are capable of producing very accurate drawings and are often used in computer aided design.

## Voice output

Most microcomputers have a built-in loudspeaker or can be connected to a loudspeaker. If they also have software that will produce speech then the computer can produce **voice output**. When a computer produces the speech (this is also called **speech synthesis**) on its own you can usually easily recognise that it has been produced by a computer. By saving real speech onto backing store and telling the computer to play it back at the appropriate time you will get real speech output. Voice output is especially useful for visually impaired and disabled users.

## QUESTIONS

### Knowledge and understanding

1 Make a list of all the
(a) input devices
(b) output devices
(c) backing storage devices
described in this chapter
How many of the devices in your list are available in your school?

### Problem solving/practical activities

1 Find out which types of printers are available in your school and the speed they print text.
Discuss in class how you could test the speed of a printer.
Carry out the test you decide upon.
What did you find out?
Is your printer as fast at printing text as it is supposed to be?
What difference does it make to the speed of printing if you print graphics?

## More to do

**SPECIALISED INPUT DEVICE**

an input device which is adapted for a particular purpose, such as use by a disabled person or for virtual reality

**SPECIALISED OUTPUT DEVICE**

an output device which is adapted for a particular purpose, such as use by a disabled person or for virtual reality

### *Specialised user interfaces*

People who are disabled in some way can often be helped to use a computer by having a **specialised user interface** with a computer system. For example, visually impaired users can use spreadsheets and word processors linked to voice output devices and Braille keyboards.

#### 'TOUCH TALKER' – A SPECIALISED INPUT DEVICE

The photograph shows a 'touch talker' – this is a device that Debbie uses to communicate with her parents and fellow pupils at school. Debbie can communicate by touching a picture on the 'touch talker' which contains a speech synthesiser.

*Debbie McMullan and her 'Touch Talker'*

#### COMBAT AIRCRAFT – THE USE OF A SPECIALISED OUTPUT DEVICE

Computers can be used to prevent the pilot of a military aircraft from being overloaded with information during combat. Using a specialised output device built into the helmet's visor the computer can alert the pilot to situations that require immediate attention without being distracted by irrelevant details.

**VIRTUAL REALITY**

a method of reproducing the outside world digitally within a computer system and displaying it to the user in such a way that allows them to interact with a wide range of situations. To take part in virtual reality, the user may need to wear a special headset and gloves rather than use a keyboard and monitor

## EXTRA QUESTION

**Practical activities**

Find out some other ways that specialised input and output devices on computer systems can be used to help people with disabilities.

## KEY POINTS

- All the physical parts that make up a computer system are known as the hardware
- A single item of hardware is called a device
- A computer system is made up of a central processing unit and main memory together with input, output and backing storage devices
- A typical computer system has a central processing unit, a monitor, a keyboard, a printer and one or more disk drives
- A keyboard allows information to be entered into the computer. It is an input device
- Both a printer and a monitor allow information to be passed out from the computer. They are output devices
- A disk drive is used for storing information on a disk. It is a backing storage device
- A microprocessor is a central processing unit stored on a single chip
- Chips used in computers are made of silicon and are only a few millimetres across
- A computer that has a microprocessor as its central processing unit is called a microcomputer
- A set of instructions that control the operation of a computer is called a program
- The main memory or main store of a computer is used to store programs and data
- A single storage location can hold one byte of information
- One byte is the space on a disk needed to store one character
- There are two types of memory chip: random access memory (RAM) chips and read-only memory (ROM) chips
- The contents of random access memory are lost when the computer is switched off
- The contents of a read-only memory chip are not lost when the computer is switched off
- Backing storage is used as permanent storage for programs and data
- Disks must be formatted before they can be used to store programs
- Formatting produces invisible tracks and sectors on the surface of the disk

- A CD ROM disc doesn't need to be formatted and it can't be accidentally erased since it is a read-only disk
- A WORM disc works like a CD ROM except that it can be written to as well as read from
- WORM discs have now been replaced by rewritable optical discs
- Magnetic tape gives sequential access to data because the data can only be read back in the order it was written
- Disks give you direct access because the data on a disk can be read in any order, not just the order in which it was written
- The capacity of a floppy disk (how much data it can hold) depends on how it is formatted
- Multimedia is the use of video players, compact disks and so on connected to a computer system and being operated by a program
- Examples of input devices:
  keyboard
  graphics tablet
  touch-sensitive screen
  mouse
  trackball
  joystick
  light pen
  scanner
  microphone
- Examples of output devices:
  monitor
  printer (dot matrix, daisy wheel, laser or inkjet)
  plotter
  loudspeaker
- People who are disabled in some way can often be helped by using specialised input and output devices with a computer system.

# 17 Systems software

## Giving instructions to a computer

If you want a computer to do something, you must give it a set of instructions. What do you think would happen if you gave these instructions to the computer?

'Get my new super program'
'Get the program I wrote last lesson'
'Print it out over there'

The computer probably wouldn't understand instructions like this. You'd have a better chance of getting the computer to do what you wanted if you had told it to

'Load super program'
'Switch printer on'
'List program'
'Switch printer off'

The important difference between these two sets of instructions is that one set makes sense to a computer system and one doesn't (which is which?). When you want a computer to do what you ask, you must give it instructions in a way it will understand them.

FIGURE 17.1

**PROGRAM**

a list of instructions which tell the central processing unit what to do

A set of instructions that a computer can understand is called a **program**. Programs are written in computer languages. Here are two programs, each written in a different computer language:

| Program 1 | Program 2 |
|---|---|
| PRINT 'HELLO' | 1000 1101 |
| PRINT 'PLEASE TELL ME YOUR NAME' | 1110 0011 |
| INPUT YOUR NAME | 1000 1101 |

Which one is easier for you to understand? Program 1 is written in a language very like English. A computer language that uses normal or everyday language is called a **high level language**.

The second example is not at all easy for most people to understand. This is because it is written in the computer's own language. The computer's own language is called **machine code**. Machine code is an example of a **low level language**.

### Translation

When you give an instruction to a computer in a high level language (like this: PRINT 'Hi There!') the computer changes the high level language into machine code so it can understand it before it can carry out the instruction. The instruction 'PRINT' in the example becomes '11110001' inside the computer. Only once the computer changes the instruction into machine code will it be able to carry out the instructions.

Like changing a sentence from Gaelic into English, changing a program from one computer language into another computer language is called **translation**. Programs that carry out translations are called **translator programs**. Using a translator program means that if you want to use a different computer language, you only have to change the translator program and the computer will be able to understand you.

## *High level languages*

The computer language BASIC is a high level language. The name BASIC is made up from the initial letters of the words **B**eginner's **A**ll-purpose **S**ymbolic **I**nstruction **C**ode. BASIC was invented at Dartmouth College in the United States by Thomas Kurtz and John Kemeny in 1964. BASIC was originally designed as a computer language to help beginners learn to program. BASIC is a very popular language and most microcomputers are supplied with a version of BASIC.

Here are some other high level languages:

ALGOL
COMAL

COBOL
FORTRAN
SMALLTALK
C
LOGO
HYPERTALK
SQL
ADA
LISP
PROLOG
PASCAL
MODULA2

Which languages in this list have you heard of? Have you used any of them? Find out more about one language you haven't used. You should try and answer questions like

When was it invented?
Who invented it?
What was it invented to do?
Can it run on the computers in your school?
How much does it cost?

### Common features of high level languages

High level languages have a number of features in common.

1. High level language programs are much easier to read and to write than programs in a low level language because the program's instructions are like instructions written in everyday language.
2. Programs written in a high level language must be translated into machine code before they can be run.
3. High level languages should help the programmer solve problems. In the same way as someone who drives a car doesn't care about how every part of the car works while they're driving, a person who programs in a high level language doesn't care about what happens inside the computer when she tells it PRINT 'HELLO'. She is more worried about the result – whether the machine does what she wants it to do.
4. High level language programs are easy to change so they can be run on different computer systems.

## QUESTIONS

### Knowledge and understanding

1 What is
  (a) a high level language?
  (b) a low level language?

2 Give two features that the various high level languages have in common.

## More to do

**HARDWARE**

the physical parts or devices which make up a computer system

### Translator programs

A translator program changes program instructions into machine code. Translator programs are used because writing programs directly in machine code is very difficult. It is much easier for the programmer to write the program in a high level language and then have it changed into machine code by the translator program in the computer.

Translator programs are part of the systems software of the computer. The **systems software** is a collection of programs that help the computer hardware to work properly. Other programs that are part of the system software are the **operating system** and the **filing system**. These two programs will be explained further in the next chapter.

There are three types of translator programs. They are called **compilers, assemblers** and **interpreters**.

Let's look at them in more detail.

### Compilers

A **compiler** is a program that can translate a high level language program into machine code in a single operation. The original high level language program is called the **source code** and the machine code program produced by the translation is called the **object code**.

The compiler changes each high level language instruction into several machine code instructions. The object code runs very fast because it is in the computer's own language, machine code.

The source code in the high level language isn't needed once it has been compiled and the object code can be saved and run on its own. However, you should keep the source code in case you want to change or update the program in the future.

The programming language PASCAL is a language which is normally compiled before it can be run.

### Assemblers

An **assembler** is a program which translates a low level language called **assembly language** into machine code. Assemblers take the whole of the assembly language (the source code) and translate it into machine code (the object code) in one operation. A compiler and an assembler are compared in figure 17.2.

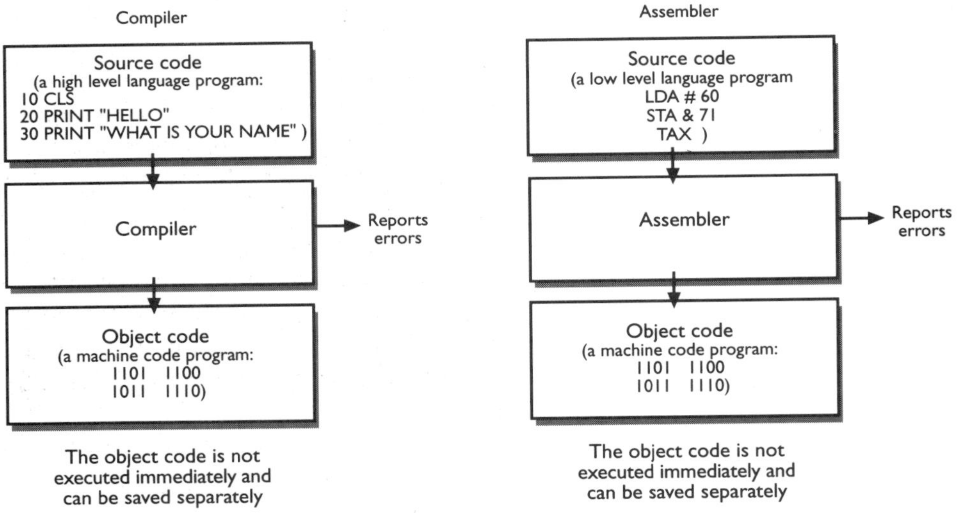


**FIGURE 17.2** *Comparing a compiler and an assembler*

Because assembly language is a low level language it is easy to translate into machine code. Unlike an instruction in a high level language, one instruction in assembly language usually corresponds to a single instruction in machine code.

## COMPARING HIGH LEVEL, ASSEMBLY LANGUAGE AND MACHINE CODE

Here is the same program instruction written in a high level language, assembly language and machine code for comparison.

| High level language | Assembly language | Machine code |
|---|---|---|
| number = number + 1 | LDA &71 | 10100101 01110001 |
| | CLC | 00011000 |
| | ADC #&01 | 01101001 00000001 |
| | STA &71 | 10000101 01110001 |

You can see that part of each assembly language instruction is made up of letters. These are called mnemonics. A **mnemonic** is a shortened word or abbreviation (just like we might say CPU when we mean central processing unit), so LDA means load, CLC means clear, ADC means add and STA means store. Using mnemonics makes it easier for programmers working in assembly language to remember what they're doing. (You don't need to know any assembly language instructions for your Standard Grade course. They're only included here to help with the explanation.)

Machine code has no mnemonics to help the programmer. It's very easy to make mistakes when programming directly in machine code.

### Interpreters

An **interpreter** is a translator program which changes a high level language into machine code one instruction at a time. Interpreted programs run much more slowly than compiled or assembled programs because the interpreter must translate each instruction every time the program is run. Unlike assemblers and compilers, you can't save the object code produced by an interpreter. You can see what happens when an interpreter works in figure 17.3.

The programming language BASIC normally uses an interpreter.

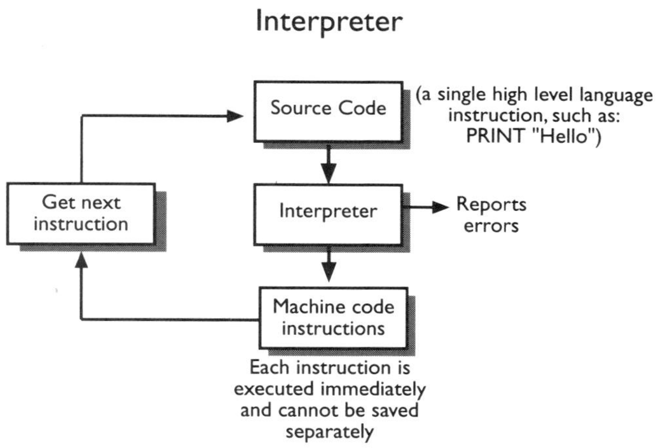


**IGURE 17.3** *An interpreter rogram*

## *Which language?*

Each computer language has good and bad points.

- A program written in an interpreted language will run more slowly than a similar program which is compiled.
- Interpreted languages report any mistakes as soon as they are entered into the computer.
- A programmer using a compiled language has to wait until the compilation stage before the system will report any errors in the program.
- A program written in assembly language will run very

**INTERFACE**

part of a computer system that lets different devices to communicate with the processor by compensating for any differences in their operation

quickly, but is more difficult for people to understand than a high level language.

- It's not easy to find mistakes in an assembly language program and they may take a long time to correct.

## *Special-purpose languages*

A **special-purpose language** performs a particular function, in the same way a special-purpose (or dedicated) computer is built to do a specific task.

### CONTROL LOGO

Control Logo is a special-purpose language dedicated to interfacing and control. Suppose a lamp was connected to an interface on a microcomputer and this program was run

```
REPEAT 10 [TURNON 1 WAIT 50 TURNOFF 1 WAIT 50]
```

What would this program do?

## *Software portability*

The **portability** of a program is whether or not you can run a computer program that you write on one computer system on a different computer system without altering it. The more easily it can be used on different systems, the more portable the program is. For example, if this BASIC program was typed into a number of different computers which had a BASIC interpreter, it would probably work without any changes.

```
10 CLS
20 PRINT "This program is portable"
30 END
```

Programs written in a low level language like assembly language are related directly to the hardware of a particular computer system and aren't usually as portable as the example above. Since different computers may have different processors, changing a low level language program from one computer system to another usually means having to rewrite the whole program.

High level language programs are more likely to be portable than low level language programs.

Portability is very important for software companies. Imagine a company which has spent a long time and a lot of money to develop a game for an Atari computer. If they could easily change their game to run on a different type of computer, the sales of the program would go up.

Portability is also important to individuals or organisations who own a number of different computers because a portable program would be able to run on all of their systems.

## EXTRA QUESTIONS

**Knowledge and understanding**

1 What is
   (a) an assembler?
   (b) an interpreter?
   (c) a compiler?
2 What is meant by software portability?

**Problem solving**

1 A programmer has to write a program that will run fast, but will be easy to edit. Which type of translator software should she choose?

## KEY POINTS

- A set of instructions which a computer can understand is called a program
- Programs are written in computer languages
- The computer's own language is called machine code
- Machine code is a low level language
- Changing a program from one computer language to another is called translation
- Translation is done by a translator program
- The computer language BASIC is a high level language
- High level languages
  - Are like everyday language
  - Must be translated before they can be run
  - Are intended to help the programmer to solve problems
  - Are easy to change
- A translator program is used to change program instructions into machine code
- Translator programs are part of the systems software of the computer

- The three types of translator programs are compilers, interpreters and assemblers
- A compiler translates a complete high level language program into machine code
- An interpreter translates a high level language program into machine code one instruction at a time
- An assembler translates a complete low level language (assembly language) program into machine code
- Portability means whether or not a computer program can be run on different computer systems without being altered

# 18 Operating and filing systems

## What does an operating system do?

**DEVICE**

a single item of computer hardware

**CENTRAL PROCESSING UNIT (CPU)**

the part of the computer which processes the information

Most people probably don't realise that there is a program running in a computer from the moment it is switched on. This program is called the **operating system**. The operating system is part of the systems software of the computer. An operating system program is needed to control how the computer works and to control any **devices** attached to the computer.

The central processing unit (or CPU) of a computer works much faster than the devices (such as a keyboard or a printer) attached to it. The operating system coordinates the activities of the other parts of the computer system so the CPU is used efficiently.

## Standard functions of an operating system

Let's look at how the operating system helps a user who is using a word processing application on a computer system.

1 The user loads the word processing program into the computer.
2 The operating system retrieves the program from backing storage and puts it in the right place in the computer's memory.
3 The user then starts a new document
4 Each time the user presses a key on the keyboard, the operating system checks to see which key he has pressed and if necessary displays that character on the screen.
5 When the document is finished, the user saves it to disk. The operating system asks the user to name the file and then saves the document to backing storage.
6 If the user wants to print the document, the operating system sends the data to the printer.

**BACKING STORE**

a system for permanently holding the contents of memory on media such as disk or tape

**NETWORK**

two or more computers joined together so that data can be transferred between them

If you are using a terminal on a network, you may have to type in your user identity and password before you're allowed on to the system. This process (called logging on) is also controlled by the operating system.

**OUTPUT**

data passed out of a computer system

**MAIN MEMORY**

the memory in a computer system. It is linked to the central processing unit

### What does the operating system do?

- It checks input devices like the keyboard and mouse
- It manages the sending of data to output devices like the screen and the printer
- It controls where programs and data are placed in the main memory of the computer
- It manages the filing system
- In some network systems it controls the security of the system.

## *Interactive, batch and real-time systems*

### Interactive systems

Most microcomputers operate using an **interactive system**. In an interactive system the user and the computer communicate (they interact), and the computer program responds immediately to commands. In an interactive system, the user can type in a program and ask the computer to run it, or can load and run a program from backing store. If she finds any mistakes in the program or in the data she has entered, then she can make changes at once (and so interact with the program while it is being processed).

**PRESTEL** is an example of an interactive system. The user selects which pages are to be viewed and the system fetches those pages from backing storage and displays them on the screen.

### Batch systems

**MAINFRAME COMPUTER SYSTEM**

a computer system that can carry out a very large amount of work. It usually occupies a whole large room

Some computers are not always interactive. Their operating systems allow you to input the data that needs to be processed in one set or **batch**. The computer operator only has to load and run once, no matter how big a batch is. The data are processed as a single unit, making efficient use of processor time. This type of system is known as a **batch system**. Batch systems are used in large data processing operations on a mainframe computer system, like clearing cheques, calculating payroll and billing.

### Real-time systems

A batch system is not suitable for all situations. For example, if you are booking a seat on an aircraft, the reservations program must give you an accurate, up to date picture of the seats available on a particular flight at any time. If the program isn't

**UPDATE**

adding new data. A transaction file may be used to update a master file

up to date more than one person could book the same seat on the aircraft. To stop mistakes like this happening the program must reserve your seat by updating the passenger list at the moment your booking is made. It must work in **real time**. Systems like this are called **real-time systems**.

A program that controls a robot vehicle moving around a factory floor (like the ones we discussed in Chapter 10) is a real-time system. If the vehicle bumps into an obstruction it must be able to stop instantly. Real-time systems are also used in military applications such as missile guidance systems.

## QUESTIONS

**Knowledge and understanding**

1 What is an operating system?
2 Name four tasks that an operating system may perform while you are using a computer.
3 What is meant by
(a) a batch system?
(b) a real-time system?
(c) an interactive system?

**Problem solving**

1 Here is a list of applications. For each one, state whether it would use a batch, interactive or real-time system.
(a) airline reservations
(b) payroll
(c) word processing
(d) air traffic control
(e) cheque clearing
(f) preparing a gas bill
(g) entering a PASCAL program into a terminal.

## *More to do*

### *Other functions of operating systems*

Think about a mainframe computer system linked to a number of terminals in a data processing department. Some terminals are being used to type in the weekly wage details from employee clock cards. One terminal is being used to run a program which keeps track of the work rate of the data preparation operators. Another is being used to monitor how the system is being used. The remaining terminals are being used to print out program listings.

The fact that so many people can use the same computer system at the same time and for different tasks is due to the operating system. The operating system on this computer has to carry out

- **MULTI-ACCESS**
  This means that many users can be on line to the mainframe computer simultaneously.

- **MULTI-PROGRAMMING**
  This means that a number of different programs are running at the same time on a single computer.
- **RESOURCE ALLOCATION**
  In this system some users are saving data to disk, others are entering data to be processed, others are using the printers attached to the mainframe computer. This is an example of resource allocation.

**FIGURE 18.1** *Resource allocation*

## *More about interactive systems*

Suppose you are using a word processing program on a microcomputer and have just finished typing a document. You save your document to disk and print it out. You've now got another document to type, but have to wait for the printer to finish printing before you can get on with it.

It would be much more useful if the operating system of your computer allowed you to print the first document while you were typing the second document because you wouldn't have to waste time waiting for the printer before you could continue with your work.

In fact, many microcomputers *do* allow you to do this. They have interactive operating systems which let tasks like printing go on 'in the background' while you're working. The tasks that go on like this are called **background jobs**.

This is another example of the way the operating system always tries to use the processor's time efficiently. A fast CPU in an interactive processing situation (such as word

**READ ONLY MEMORY (ROM) SOFTWARE**

software distributed on read-only memory chip

processing) spends a lot of time (for the computer) waiting for the user to press a key – even the fastest typist can't type as fast as the computer can accept the data. The operating system uses these gaps to share out the processor time between word processing and background printing. Because the processor is operating so quickly, the user thinks the tasks are happening at the same time.

## *Types of operating system*

Some computers (like the IBM PC, the RM Nimbus and the Apple Macintosh) have their operating system stored on disk. Other machines have their operating system stored permanently on ROM chips inside the computer. Examples of these are the Sinclair Spectrum computer, A3020 and Acorn Archimedes.

Each method has its advantages.

- Storing your operating system on disk means that if a new version of the operating system comes out the new version can be put in very easily. All you need is a copy of the new program on disk.
- Storing the operating system on ROM means you don't have to load from disk every time you switch the computer on. A ROM-based operating system is there all the time.
- If the computer has only one disk drive then a ROM-based operating system means the disk with the operating system doesn't fill up the only disk drive. This means the disk drive is free to be used with other applications. Most computers have at least two disk drives, a floppy disk drive and a hard disk drive. The operating system is normally stored on the hard disk drive, and is loaded into the computer automatically when it is switched on.

### MS DOS

The most widely used operating system is the **Microsoft Disk Operating System** or **MS DOS,** which is used to operate IBM and Nimbus computers. MS DOS is a command-driven operating system. People who use MS DOS have to know a list of command words in order to operate the computer – for instance, to run a program the user must type in the name of the program.

**COMMAND-DRIVEN SOFTWARE**

software that needs commands from the user to work

**MENU-DRIVEN SOFTWARE**

software which needs the user to choose from a menu to make it work

**WIMP**

Windows, Icons, Menu (or Mouse), Pointer (or Pull down menu)

**USER-FRIENDLY**

an interactive computer system which helps the user by giving clear prompts, menus and help screens when needed

### RISC OS

The BBC A3020 and Archimedes computers use **RISC OS**, which is a menu-driven operating system. The Apple Macintosh series of computers also uses its own type of menu-driven operating system. The menu-driven system which is in use on these computers is known as a **WIMP** system. Operating a computer which uses a WIMP system is easy because all the commands are presented on the screen as a series of menus and you choose the command you require with a screen pointer, operated by moving a mouse. WIMP systems are explained in Chapter 1.

Because WIMP systems are generally more user-friendly than command-driven systems, a lot of manufacturers have used them on their MS DOS computers. One of the most popular programs of this kind is **Microsoft Windows**.

## EXTRA QUESTIONS

### Knowledge and understanding

1 What is meant by
   (a) multi-access?
   (b) multi-programming?

### Problem solving

1 The ability to process a background task is one way of improving the efficiency of the use of the CPU of a computer.
   (a) How does the operating system do this?
   (b) Why does it improve the efficiency of the CPU?
   (c) What name is given to the way the operating system makes efficient use of the devices attached to the computer?

2 Why are some command-driven operating systems being replaced with menu-driven operating systems?

### Practical activities

Find out what operating systems are in use on the computers in your school.
Are they loaded from disk or stored on ROM?
If they are stored on ROM, how are they updated if a new version is produced?
Can any of the operating systems carry out background tasks?

# Filing systems

A very important function the operating system carries out is managing your files on backing storage. The part of the operating system which deals with files on backing storage is called the **filing system**.

## How does the filing system work?

**DATABASE**

a structured collection of similar information which can be searched

Think about what happens when you are using a database of your friends' names and telephone numbers. You make up the database by entering the data into the program and then save your work to disk. To store the file on disk you must give it a name. Suppose you call your file 'Telephone'. The file 'Telephone' is called a **data file** because it contains the list of names and numbers which you entered.

Next day in class you are doing some programming using the language COMAL. You wrote out the program for homework the night before. You type your program into the computer and run it to make sure that it is working correctly. You save your program on your disk, using the name 'Salaries'. 'Salaries' is a COMAL **program** because it contains a list of instructions in the COMAL language.

If you want to load 'Telephone' later, you must first run the database program, since 'Telephone' is a data file, not a program. If you want to load 'Salaries', you must first select the COMAL language, since 'Salaries' is a COMAL program, not a data file.

If you want to see what files you have on your disk you must put your disk in the disk drive and type the command for your computer which gives you a list of the file names.

```
*CAT
Cecilia's disk(6entries)
Cafe          Hotel
Numbers       Salaries
Telephone     Triangle
```

The box to the left shows what you might see on the screen if you were using a BBC Model B computer.

An area where files are stored is called a **directory** and a list of files is called a **catalogue**.

## QUESTIONS

### Knowledge and understanding

1 Explain the difference between a data file and a program.

2 What is the name for

(a) the part of the operating system which deals with files on backing storage?

(b) an area in which files are stored?

(c) a list of file names?

### Problem solving

1 What steps would you take to load the files 'Numbers' and 'Triangle' from Cecilia's disk into the computer, if 'Numbers' is a spreadsheet document and 'Triangle' is a program written in BASIC?

# More to do

## More about filing systems

### Flat filing systems

Look back at the directory on Cecilia's disk we looked at earlier. The directory contains six files. When Cecilia gets a list of file names, she can see all the files on the disk. A filing system like this, which has a single directory containing all the files on a disk is called a **single level** or **flat filing system**.

A flat filing system is used on many microcomputers, but it has some disadvantages.

- If there are so many files on the directory that their names won't fit on one screen it can be difficult to find the particular file you want.
- Each file on a flat filing system must have a different name. If you give two files the same name the most recent one will overwrite the first file – which you will lose.

### Hierarchical filing systems

A filing system has been developed to get round these problems. It is called a **hierarchical filing system.** Instead of a single directory which contains only files, the entries in a directory may be other directories. These are called **sub-directories**. Each sub-directory may have other sub-directories in it, and so on. In figure 18.2 you can see a comparison between a flat filing system and a hierarchical filing system.

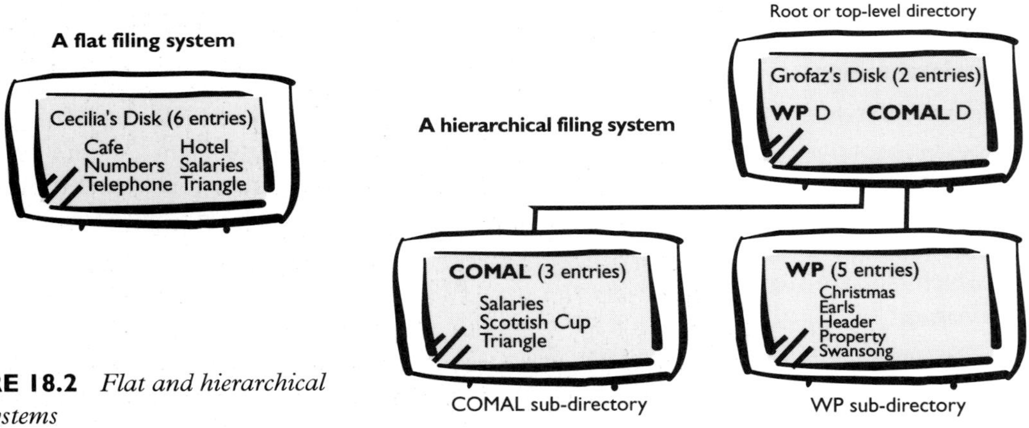


**FIGURE 18.2** *Flat and hierarchical filing systems*

*Imagine that a filing system is like the roots of a tree. The directory at the top level is called the* ***root directory*** *and all the other directories in the filing system are sub-directories of the root.*

A hierarchical filing system allows you to create sub-directories to keep groups of related files. In a hierarchical filing system the directory of the disk might look like this:

```
Grofaz's disk (2 entries)
WP D    COMAL D
```

The 'D' after the names shows that WP and COMAL are sub-directories, not files. Grofaz has grouped together all his COMAL programs and his word processing files. If Grofaz had any spreadsheet files, he could create a new sub-directory to store them in. It is sensible to group related files like this, because it's much easier to find a file - especially when a single disk can hold a hundred or more files.

In a hierarchical filing system you are much less likely to give two files in a directory the same name. Each directory will also have fewer files in it, so it's easier to view the complete directory catalogue on screen at one time. Examples of hierarchical filing systems are

MS DOS
RISC OS
the Macintosh operating system.

## *Sequential and random (direct) access to data*

Suppose you have a music centre at home with a cassette tape recorder and a compact disc player. If you want to find a particular song on the tape you have to play the tape from the beginning and iisten to all the songs until you find the one you want. You can speed things up by fast forwarding or rewinding the tape to the position where you think the song will be, but it is still quite slow.

It is much quicker to find a song on a disc than on a tape. You can send the player directly to any track and it will start playing the song immediately.

Finding data on a tape is slow because you can only get the data back in the same order you recorded it onto the tape. Tape gives sequential access to data because the data can only be read back in sequence.

Disks can access data **directly** because the read/write head on the disk drive can go straight to the track where the data is stored, without having to read all the data in between. Direct access is also called **random access** because you can read the data on the disk in any order, not just the order it was written in.

## EXTRA QUESTIONS

### Knowledge and understanding

**1** What is
(a) a flat filing system?
(b) a hierarchical filing system?

**2** Why is it quicker to find a program stored on disk than a program stored on tape?

### Problem solving

**1** What advantages does a hierarchical filing system have over a flat filing system?

**2** A disk is a direct access medium used in a computer system. Name one other direct access medium.

**3** What type of access do you think would be used on
(a) the PRESTEL computer?
(b) an airline reservations computer?
(c) the police national computer?
(d) the electricity board billing computer?

### Practical activities

**1** Find out whether the filing system used on the computers in your school is flat or hierarchical.

**2** If your school has a network with a hierarchical filing system, find out what is meant by 'owner access' and 'public access' to files and directories on the network

## KEY POINTS

- The operating system is part of the systems software of the computer
- The operating system controls the operation of the computer and any devices attached to it

- The operating system does the following things
  - checks input devices
  - manages the sending of data to output devices
  - controls where programs and data are placed in memory
  - manages the filing system
  - controls the security of the system
- Most microcomputers use an interactive operating system
- In an interactive system the user and the computer communicate and the computer program responds directly to commands
- Some computers allow you to input data to be processed in one set or batch
- Batch systems are used a lot in commercial data processing
- Systems which are constantly updated are called real-time systems.
- Real-time systems are used for airline reservations
- Operating systems also have to perform certain specialised tasks, such as
  - multi-access (many users on line simultaneously)
  - multi-programming (a number of different programs run simultaneously)
  - allocate peripherals to different users
  - print a document as a background job
- The operating system of a microcomputer may be stored on disk or read-only memory
- Operating systems may be command-driven or menu-driven
- The part of the operating system which deals with files on backing storage is the filing system.
- An area where files are stored is called a directory and a list of files is called a catalogue
- A filing system with only one directory containing all the files on a disk is called a single level or flat filing system
- In a hierarchical filing system, entries in a directory may be other directories
- Magnetic tape gives sequential access to data because the data can only be read back in the order it was written
- Disks give you direct access because the data on a disk can be read in any order, not just the order in which it was written

# 19 Low level machine

## *Input, process and output*

Most jobs that you do can be split up into three main stages:

- input
- process
- output.

This system is usually shortened to **IPO**.

Here are some examples of how different tasks can be broken into these three stages.

**1 BOILING A KETTLE**
Input – electricity + cold water
Process – heating
Output – boiling water

**2 WASHING CLOTHES**
Input – dirty clothes + soap + clean water
Process – washing
Output – clean clothes + dirty water

**3 MAKING TOAST**
Input – bread + electricity
Process – toasting
Output – toast

**4 PLAYING A CD**
Input – compact disc + electricity
Process – playing
Output – music

You find the words **input, process** and **output** used all through this book because computer systems also work in this way. Like a washing machine a computer accepts input (which might be a list of names), processes the input (the list could be sorted), and gives output (a new list in alphabetical order).

**DEVICE**

a single item of computer hardware

### Input and output

To work through the stages of IPO the computer system needs input and output devices. For example, to get the names into the computer in the first place, you could type them in using an input device like a keyboard. The new list which is the output can be displayed on a monitor or printed on a printer (these are both output devices). We looked at input and output devices in Chapter 16. Some of the input and output devices used in a computer system are shown in figure 19.1.

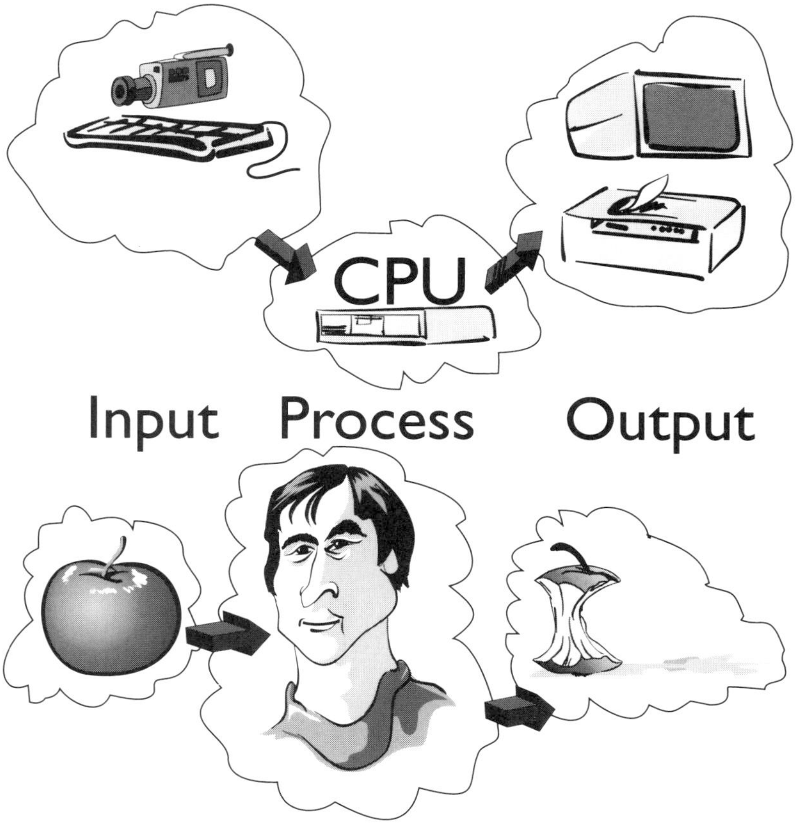


**FIGURE 19.1** *Input, process, output*

### Processing

The part of the computer which carries out the actual process is known as the **central processing unit** or **CPU**. The CPU can carry out a process only when it is given a set of instructions called a **program**. By changing the program which is stored or held in the computer's memory, a computer can carry out a completely different process.

You could think of the CPU as the 'brain' or 'nerve centre' of the computer system. But the CPU isn't like a real brain because a computer can't think or act for itself – it can only carry out the instructions it's given. Computers can carry out instructions very quickly because the CPU can process millions of instructions every second.

**PROGRAM**

a list of instructions which tell the central processing unit what to do

## More to do

### Inside the CPU

The CPU has three main parts. These are

- **THE CONTROL UNIT**

  The control unit makes the computer carry out each instruction of a program in the right order and controls the other parts of the CPU.

- **THE ARITHMETIC AND LOGIC UNIT**

  The arithmetic and logic unit (usually shortened to **ALU**) does all the calculating (arithmetic) and performs the logical operations (it makes decisions).

- **THE MAIN MEMORY.**

  The main memory is used to hold the programs and data being used. It is also called the **immediate access store** because the memory is instantly accessible. You can see the main parts of the central processing unit and how data is passed between them in figure 19.2.

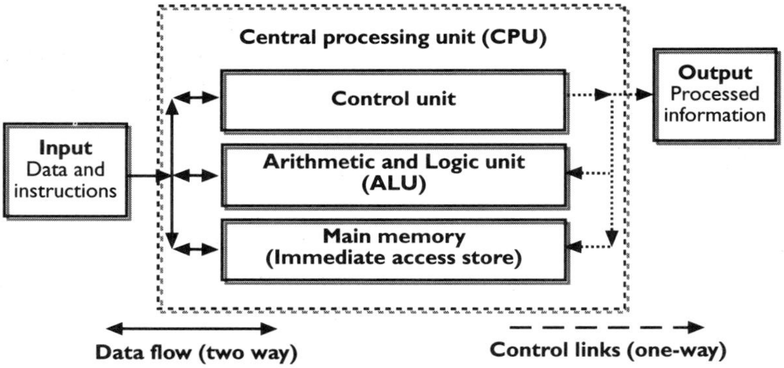


**FIGURE 19.2** *The parts of the CPU*

# How data is stored in a computer

The processing and storage devices of a computer system have one feature in common – they can exist in one of two states, 'on' and 'off'. They are called **two-state systems**. You can see some examples of other two-state systems in figure 19.3. All the codes which represent data in a computer use only two numbers – 0 and 1. This number system is called **binary** because the word binary means 'two states'. Just as a light bulb can have two states ('on' or 'off') a **binary number** has two values, 1 or 0 ('on' or 'off').

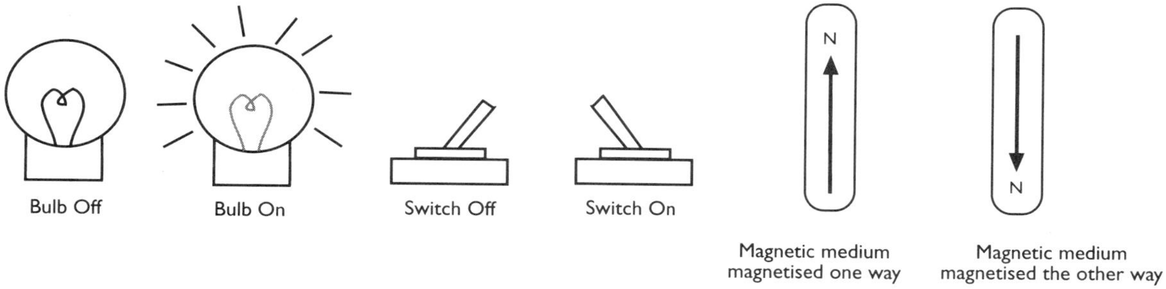


**FIGURE 19.3** *Some examples of two-state systems*

# Representing numbers

Computers need some way to store data. In the binary system the two states 'on' and 'off' inside a computer represent the number 1 (for 'on') or 0 (for 'off') inside the memory of the computer.

A single unit in binary is called a **bit**. The word bit is made up from the two words **b**inary dig**it**.

## Counting in decimal

Humans usually count in units, followed by tens, hundreds (ten × ten), thousands (ten × ten × ten) and so on. This is called the decimal system, from the Latin word for 'ten'.

For example, the number 5430 is made up like this

| | | | |
|---|---|---|---|
| 1000 | 100 | 10 | 1 – these are the **place values** |
| 5 | 4 | 3 | 0 – these are the **digits** |

This means 5 × 1000 + 4 × 100 + 3 × 10 + 0 × 1. We are all familiar with the decimal system and find counting like this easy to understand. By thinking about place values we will be able to understand the binary system.

## Counting in binary

We count in binary like we count in decimal, except that place values in binary go up in twos, so instead of having place values of units, tens, hundreds we have units, twos, fours (two × two), eights (two × two × two) and so on.
Let's look at a binary number made up of four bits

| | | | |
|---|---|---|---|
| 8 | 4 | 2 | 1 – these are the place values |
| 1 | 1 | 0 | 1 – these are the bits |

This binary number is 1101. This means

1 × 8 + 1 × 4 + 0 × 2 + 1 × 1, which is 13 in decimal.

## Practice with binary

Work out the decimal values of these binary numbers

(a) 1001
(b) 1000
(c) 1010
(d) 0011
(e) 0000

Now change these decimal numbers into binary numbers

(a) 4
(b) 6
(c) 15
(d) 11

## Bytes

A binary number which is made up of eight bits (for instance 1101 0110) is called a **byte**. What is the largest number a byte can be?

Let's work it out. A byte is made of eight bits, and the biggest value of each bit is 1. If every bit in a byte had the value 1, you would get 1111 1111.

Now let's look at the place values for eight bits.

| | | | | | | | | |
|---|---|---|---|---|---|---|---|---|
| Place values | 128 | 64 | 32 | 16 | 8 | 4 | 2 | 1 |
| Bits | 1 | 1 | 1 | 1 | 1 | 1 | 1 | 1 |

So the value of this byte is 128 + 64 + 32 + 16 + 8 + 4 + 2 + 1, which is 255 in decimal.

Of course, a byte can have the value zero, so the smallest number a byte will have is zero (0000 0000). So a byte can hold a range of values from zero (0000 0000) to 255 (1111 1111), making a total of 256 different numbers.

## QUESTIONS

### Knowledge and understanding

1 Describe the input, process, and output involved in
 (a) making a cup of tea
 (b) formatting a disk.
2 What is a program?
3 Where is a computer program stored while it is being processed?
4 What is
 (a) a bit?
 (b) a byte?
5 What range of values can be held in a byte?

### Problem solving

1 Why isn't the CPU of a computer like your brain?

## EXTRA QUESTIONS

### Knowledge and understanding

1 Name the three parts of a CPU and describe what each part does.

### Problem solving

1 Why do computers use the binary system and not the decimal system to represent numbers?

# *Representing text*

A computer stores characters in its memory in bytes – one byte for each character. What do we mean by 'character'? A character is a symbol or letter on the computer keyboard. Characters include the digits 0 to 9 (these are the **numeric** characters), letters (these are **alphabetic** characters) and punctuation marks (these are the **special** characters). The numeric and alphabetic characters together are called **alphanumeric** characters. a, b, c, A, B, C, 0, 1, 2, 9, &, £, * are all characters. We worked out earlier that bytes have a range of values. Each value could stand for one character. How many different characters can we represent by using one byte?

The computer must be able to represent all the characters we might want to use. A list of all the characters which a computer can process and store is called the computer's **character set**. Different types of computer have slightly different character sets. So that a computer can represent all the characters it needs to, every character has a different code number in binary.

**CHECK DIGIT**
A figure that's calculated from the digits of a number and placed at the end of a number. Used to check the number has been input correctly.

### ASCII

The code that is most used is called the **American Standard Code for Information Interchange** – this is shortened to **ASCII**. ASCII is a code made up of seven bits. The eighth bit is used as a **check digit**. Many different computers use ASCII to represent text. This makes it easier for text to be transferred between different computer systems. On the next page you can see some characters with the ASCII codes for them.

### *Control characters*

There are some characters in the ASCII code that don't print on the screen in the normal way. These characters control certain operations of the computer system and they are called **control characters**. If you have used the BBC

| CHARACTER | BINARY | DECIMAL |
|---|---|---|
| Space | 0010 0000 | 32 |
| ! | 0010 0001 | 33 |
| ‘ | 0010 0010 | 34 |
| 0 | 0011 0000 | 48 |
| 1 | 0011 0001 | 49 |
| 2 | 0011 0010 | 50 |
| 3 | 0011 0011 | 51 |
| ? | 0011 1111 | 63 |
| @ | 0100 0000 | 64 |
| A | 0100 0001 | 65 |
| B | 0100 0010 | 66 |
| C | 0100 0011 | 67 |
| D | 0100 0100 | 68 |
| E | 0100 0101 | 69 |
| F | 0100 0110 | 70 |
| G | 0100 0111 | 71 |
| H | 0100 1000 | 72 |
| I | 0100 1001 | 73 |
| J | 0100 1010 | 74 |
| K | 0100 1011 | 75 |
| L | 0100 1100 | 76 |
| M | 0100 1101 | 77 |
| N | 0100 1110 | 78 |
| O | 0100 1111 | 79 |
| P | 0101 0000 | 80 |
| Q | 0101 0001 | 81 |
| R | 0101 0010 | 82 |
| S | 0101 0011 | 83 |
| T | 0101 0100 | 84 |
| U | 0101 0101 | 85 |
| V | 0101 0110 | 86 |
| W | 0101 0111 | 87 |
| X | 0101 1000 | 88 |
| Y | 0101 1001 | 89 |
| Z | 0101 1010 | 90 |
| a | 0110 0001 | 97 |
| b | 0110 0010 | 98 |

model B or Master computers then you probably know the ‘CONTROL-B’ and ‘CONTROL-C’ keyboard commands which you use to enable and disable the printer.

The ASCII codes from 0 to 31 (binary 00000 to 11111) are used as control characters. Here are some control characters and the effects they have.

| BINARY | DECIMAL | EFFECT |
|---|---|---|
| 0010 | 2 | Enable printer |
| 0011 | 3 | Disable printer |
| 0111 | 7 | Bell |
| 1010 | 10 | Cursor down |
| 1011 | 11 | Cursor up |
| 1100 | 12 | Clear screen |
| 1101 | 13 | Return (new line) |

# Representing graphics

You will remember from Chapter 5 that graphics (pictures) on the computer screen are made up from tiny dots called **pixels**. Imagine the whole of the computer screen being made up of thousands of pixels. Each pixel may be 'on' or 'off' depending on whether the value of the pixel in memory is 1 (on – so you can see it) or 0 (off – so you can't see it).

Look at figure 19.4, which shows how graphics are stored in the computer's memory. The picture is drawn on a grid 16 pixels across and 16 down. Grid squares which are 'on' are represented by a 1 and grid squares which are off are represented by a 0. The amount of memory needed to store this picture would be $16 \times 16$ bits – which is 256 bits.

The picture would be more clearly defined (less rough) if we

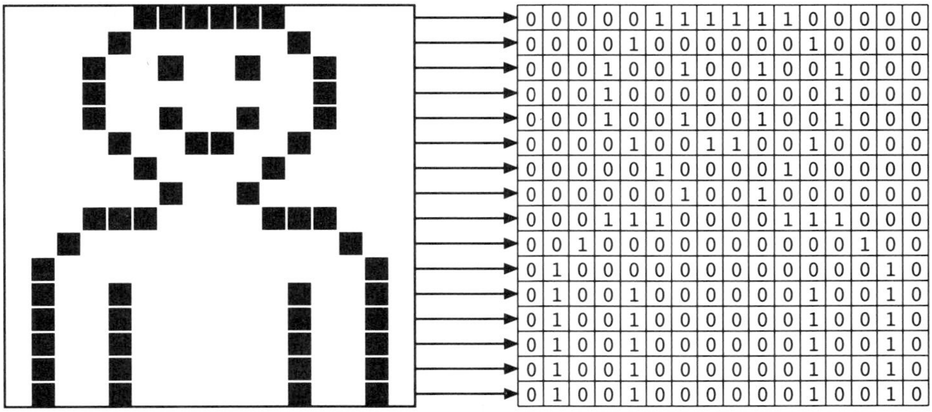


Picture displayed on screen

How the same picture is stored in the computer's memory

**FIGURE 19.4** *How graphics are stored*

used more, smaller, pixels to make it up. You can see how reducing the size and increasing the number of pixels affects a picture. By doing this we can put more detail into the picture.

This is called increasing the **resolution** of the graphics.

Think about the amount of memory used to store the picture on the right in figure 19.5. Suppose that to get this resolution each pixel has to be one-tenth of the size it was in the left-hand picture. How will this affect the amount of memory needed to show it? How does this compare to the memory required for the original (low resolution) graphic?

**FIGURE 19.5** *Resolution of graphics*

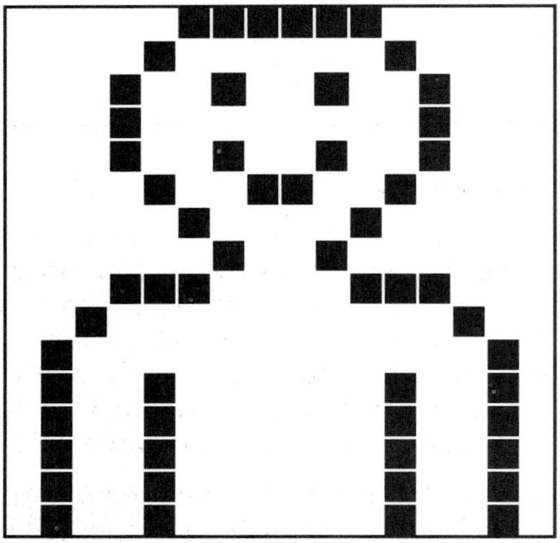

Low resolution picture
(few pixels)

High resolution picture
(many pixels)

# Adding more bytes

In the decimal system we use the prefix kilo to mean 1000 ($10 \times 10 \times 10$, or $10^3$). We use kilo in computing as well, but it doesn't mean 1000. One **kilobyte** is 1024 bytes. The reason why it is 1024 and not 1000 is because 1 kilobyte is $2^{10}$ (or $2 \times 2 \times 2 \times 2 \times 2 \times 2 \times 2 \times 2 \times 2 \times 2 = 1024$) – remember computers work in binary. We usually write a kilobyte shorthand as the letter k. One kilobyte is 1 k. A **megabyte** (which we write as 1 Mb) is 1024 kilobytes ($1024 \times 1024$ bytes) and one **gigabyte** (we write this as 1 Gb) is 1024 megabytes ($1024 \times 1024 \times 1024$ bytes).

## Computer memory

We usually measure the **size of the main memory** of a computer in kilobytes or megabytes because it is large. Here are some different computer systems and their main memory sizes.

**MAIN MEMORY SIZE**

the number of storage locations available in a computer system

| COMPUTER | MAIN MEMORY SIZE |
|---|---|
| BBC model B | 32 k |
| BBC Master | 128 k |
| BBC A3020 | 1 Mb |
| BBC A5000 | 4 Mb |
| Commodore Amiga | 1 Mb |
| Macintosh Plus | 1 Mb |
| Macintosh Classic | 4 Mb |
| Macintosh LC II | 4 Mb |
| IBM PS/1 | 1 Mb |

**BACKING STORE**

a system for permanently holding the contents of memory on media such as disk or tape

### Changing memory size

In many cases the main memory of a computer is not fixed. You can buy extra memory and add it to some computer systems so you can use larger programs and keep more data in memory rather than have to use backing storage all the time. This makes the computer system work faster because it is quicker to access data from main memory than from disk. One reason for adding extra memory is so you can use high-resolution colour graphics.

## QUESTIONS

### Knowledge and understanding

1 What is
  (a) a character?
  (b) a character set?
  (c) ASCII?
  (d) a pixel?
2 Arrange these terms in order of size, from smallest to largest
  Byte, Gigabyte, Bit, Megabyte, Kilobyte

### Problem solving

1 What advantage will adding extra main memory to a computer have for the user?
2 Why may it be an advantage if your computer uses the ASCII code to store text?
3 If someone sent you this message in ASCII, what would you send in reply?
  72, 69, 76, 76, 79, 32, 72, 79, 87, 32, 65, 82, 69, 32, 89, 79, 85, 63
4 Draw a 8 × 8 grid on squared paper. Use it to decode the following bit patterns.
  (a) 11111111 01000010 00100100 00011000
  00011000 00100100 01000010 11111111
  (b) 00111100 01000010 01000010 01000010
  00111100 00100100 01000010 10000001

(Looking back at figure 19.4 might help you work it out.)

## *More to do*

### *More about storage in memory*

Do you have a good memory? Having a poor memory may be inconvenient or embarrassing for a person, but for a computer a poor memory would be a disaster. If it doesn't have a perfect memory the computer can't work properly, since it needs its memory to store programs and data before and after processing. A single error in memory would mean that the program wouldn't work.

The place where each item is stored in a computer's memory is important because the computer has to be able to find any given item of data. An item is stored in memory in a **storage location**. Just as your home has an address, each storage location has its own address in the computer's main memory. If you look at figure 19.6 you will see how a computer can use an address to find a particular storage location. The method it uses to identify storage locations is called its **addressability**.

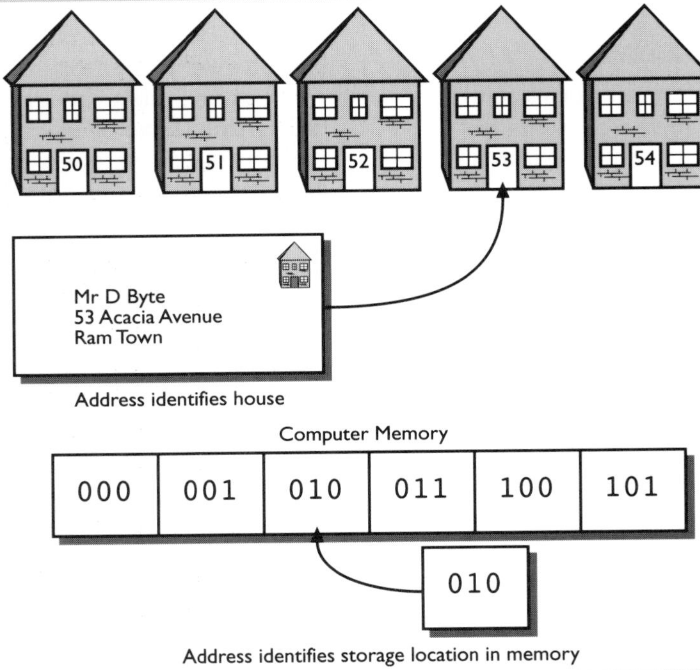


**FIGURE 19.6** *Addressing memory*

Suppose you were only allowed one digit to identify every house in the street where you live. In the decimal system you could have numbers from zero to nine – you could only identify ten houses. If you were allowed to use two digits you could have a hundred houses (0–99).

The number of storage locations in the computer's memory that a CPU can identify depends on the number of bits in the address (in binary). A **one-bit address** only has two values – 0 and 1 – so a one-bit address could only identify two storage locations, one at address 0 and one at address 1. With a **two-bit address** you could identify four locations (00, 01, 10 and 11) and so on.

Here are some more examples.

| NUMBER OF BITS IN ADDRESS | NUMBER OF STORAGE LOCATIONS THAT CAN BE IDENTIFIED |
|---|---|
| 1 | 2 |
| 2 | 4 |
| 3 | 8 |
| 4 | 16 |
| 5 | 32 |
| 10 | 1024 (1 k) |
| 16 | 65536 (64 k) |
| 20 | 1048576 (1 Mb) |

Each storage location in a computer's memory can hold a single unit of storage, which is called a word. A **word** is the number of bits that the CPU can process *in a single operation*. A word can store one or more characters, or a complete number, or an instruction to the computer.

Some microcomputers, like the Spectrum, process data in groups of eight bits, so the word size for a Spectrum is eight bits. More powerful microcomputers like the Macintosh Classic use words that are sixteen bits long, and the BBC A3020 uses words of thirty-two bits. This is why microcomputers are sometimes called 8-bit, 16-bit or 32-bit machines.

## *How large numbers are stored in a computer*

Let's start by looking at some large numbers in decimal. We can write any decimal number with the decimal point in a fixed position and a multiplier which is a power of 10.

Here are some examples of what we mean:

$1\ 000\ 000 = 0.10 \times 10\ 000\ 000 = 0.10 \times 10^7$
$93\ 000\ 000 = 0.93 \times 100\ 000\ 000 = 0.93 \times 10^8$
$18\ 500\ 000 = 0.185 \times 10\ 000\ 000 = 0.185 \times 10^8$
$201\ 000\ 000 = 0.201 \times 1\ 000\ 000\ 000 = 0.201 \times 10^9$

All these numbers are in powers of ten. Ten is the base. Any number can be represented in any number base like this:

$$m \times \text{base}^e$$

Where m is called the mantissa and e is the exponent.

The exponent is the power the base is raised to. An example of this in binary (or base two) would be

$$11100.0101 = 0.111000101 \times 2^{0101}$$

If we always keep the position of the point the same and if the number base is always two, all we have to store are the **mantissa** and the **exponent**. From the above example

11100.0101

can be stored as

| 111000101 | 0101 |
|---|---|
| Mantissa | Exponent |

Any number can be stored in a computer's memory as two binary numbers. This way of representing numbers is called **floating point representation**.

## EXTRA QUESTIONS

**Knowledge and understanding**

**1** What is
(a) a control character?
(b) a word?
(c) a storage location?

**2** How do we
(a) store large numbers in a computer system?
(b) find a particular storage location in the memory of a computer?

**Problem solving**

**1** How many bits are needed to identify 128 storage locations?

**2** Prabhu says that his 16-bit computer system is faster than his friend Ravinder's 8-bit computer. Ravinder says that his is faster because it has an extra megabyte of memory.
(a) What is an 8-bit computer?
(b) What advantage does Ravinder's extra megabyte provide?
(c) Who do you think is right?

**3** Find out what is meant by user-defined graphics .

**Practical activities**

**1** Find out if any of the computer systems in your school provide user defined graphics, sprites or icons. Find out how to make your own graphics like this and try to get a hard copy of the result.

## KEY POINTS

- Most tasks can be split up into three stages – input, process and output
- The part of the computer which carries out the process is the central processing unit (CPU)
- A program is a set of instructions which controls the operation of the central processing unit.
- The central processing unit is made up of three main parts – the control unit, the arithmetic and logic unit (ALU) and the main memory.
- The processing and storage devices in a computer have only two states – on or off
- All the codes which represent data on a computer use only two digits, 0 and 1. This is the binary system
- A single unit in binary is called a bit
- A binary number which is made up of eight bits is a byte
- A byte can hold 256 different values
- A byte is the space in memory which is used to hold one character.
- A list of all the characters a computer uses is its character set
- Control characters control certain operations the computer carries out
- Graphics on the computer screen are made up from tiny dots called pixels
- The graphics resolution may be increased by having a large number of small pixels
- One kilobyte (k) is 1024 bytes
- One megabyte (Mb) is 1024 kilobytes
- One gigabyte (Gb) is 1024 megabytes
- The place in memory where an item of data is stored is a storage location
- Each storage location has a unique address
- A word is the number of bits which can be processed by the central processing unit in a single operation
- Floating point is a way of representing numbers using a mantissa and an exponent

# 20 Programming

**PROGRAM**

a list of instructions which tells the central processing unit what to do

This chapter is not a programming manual! It is an outline of how to solve problems by writing programs that are readable, easy to develop and easy to maintain. The information in this chapter applies to any programming language, but where we give examples, they are in COMAL or BASIC.

## *Readability and programming style*

Which of these program listings do you find easier to understand?

```
100 INPUT a
110 INPUT b
120 c = 2 * a * b
130 PRINT c
140 END
```

```
100 // area1 – a program to calculate the area of a rectangle
110 // by Cecilia
120 // 19.10.95
130 //
140 //
150 PRINT "Please enter the length of the rectangle (Type a whole number between 1 & 50)"
160 INPUT length
170 PRINT "Please enter the breadth of the rectangle (Type a whole number between 1 & 50)"
180 INPUT breadth
190 area := length * breadth * 2
200 PRINT "The area of the rectangle is"; area
210 END
```

You probably find the second program listing easier to understand because

1 It uses ordinary words like 'length' and 'breadth' instead of 'a' and 'b' for the names of the variables.
When writing your code, *always* use ordinary words rather than single letters as far as possible. This is called using **meaningful variable and procedure names**.

**PROMPT**

a character which appears on screen to tell the user that the computer wants you to do something

2 It makes use of **comment lines**. In this language these are shown by //. We use comment lines to give information about a program, but they don't have an effect when the program is run.
Including comments in your program listings helps to show anyone reading it what each part of your program is doing. Put comment lines at the top of the program to identify it: you should put the name of the program, your name and the date.
3 It contains questions or **prompts** for the user, which make it clear what keys should be pressed.

If you can, give the user an example of what they should enter. Telling them

'Please enter a whole number between 1 and 20'

is much more helpful than

'Please enter a number'

If you follow these three points when you're writing a program they will be more **readable** and easier to **maintain**. Any programs you write should

- be easy for yourself and for others to read
- have a clear purpose and structure
- be easy to maintain (change or expand later on).

# *Testing your program*

To make sure that your program actually solves the problem it is supposed to you have to test it. To carry out a proper test on a program you need to use a set of data, called **test data**. There are three different types of test data

- normal
- extreme and
- exceptional.

The best way to use test data is to calculate what the answer will be if your program works properly before you run the program. Then run the program with the test data. If the results from the program match the answers you got from your first calculation, the program's probably right.

Another way of testing a program is to get someone else to do it for you! By the time you've finished writing your program, you're usually so familiar with the code you've written you can't see any mistakes. Someone else looking at it might be able to pick up mistakes that you've missed.

**FIGURE 20.1** *Testing a program*

## *More to do*

### *Testing a program*

Let's look at part of a program which will help us to understand what we mean by normal, extreme and exceptional test data.

```
100 // date3 – a program to check that a date has been entered
correctly
110 // by Siobhan
120 // 20.7.99
130 //
140 REPEAT
150 CLS
160 PRINT "Please enter the day (1–31)"
170 INPUT day
180 PRINT "Please enter the month (1–12)"
190 INPUT month
200 PRINT "Please input the year (1954–1999)"
210 INPUT year
220 check_date
230 UNTIL correct
240 PRINT "Your date is correct – Thank You"
250 END
```

This program allows you to enter a date. It then uses the check_date procedure to check if you have put the date in correctly. The check_date procedure makes sure that

- the year is in the range 1954–1999
- the month number is in the range 1–12
- the number of days entered is within the range for the month (February 29 is only allowed in a leap year).

## Using test data

Here are appropriate test data for this program

**Normal – the program should accept this data**

| | |
|---|---|
| 2.2.1989 | (2 February 1989) |
| 3.3.1954 | (3 March 1954) |
| 24.7.1980 | (24 July 1980) |

Normal data is data which is well within the limits that your program should be able to deal with.

**Extreme – the program should accept this data**

| | |
|---|---|
| 1.1.1992 | (1 January 1992) |
| 31.12.1999 | (31 December 1999) |
| 29.2.1996 | (29 February 1996) |

Extreme data is data which is at the ends of this range – on the limit.

**Exceptional – the program should reject this data**

| | |
|---|---|
| 29.2.1993 | (29 February 1993) |
| 31.11.1994 | (31 November 1994) |
| 1.4.2000 | (1 April 2000) |

Exceptional data is data which is wrong. A well written program should be able to detect exceptional data, warn the user of the error, and give them a chance to enter the data again.

Some commercial programs are so large and complicated that it is impossible to test them and be sure that you've got rid all the errors. Some people criticised the Strategic Defense Initiative 'Star Wars' mostly because the control program needed to run it would be so large and so complex that you could never be sure that it will work properly. The programs used in some aircraft which have computerised controls are also so big they can't be tested properly. Any mistakes in this program could be very dangerous.

Any programs you'll be asked to write in your computing course will be quite short and should pass all the tests that you can think up. You should try to write programs that are as free from errors as you can make them.

Depending on the problem you've been asked to solve, you might be given a set of test data to use, or might make up your own. If you have to make up your own test data, you should try to choose a set of data which includes normal, extreme and exceptional data.

If your program doesn't produce the results you expect, you'll have to check through each line of the code. Sometimes it is useful to put extra statements into the program which will print out the values of certain variables at different stages of the run. This is called **printing a snapshot of selected variables**. It can help you find out where the program goes wrong.

# *Types of error*

**PERIPHERAL**

any device that may be attached to a computer system for input, output or backing storage

There are three types of error:

- System errors
- Syntax errors
- Logic errors.

Let's have a look at them.

## System errors

**System errors** affect the computer or its peripherals. You might have written a program which needs access to a printer. If there is no printer present when you run the program the computer will produce a system error message. Sometimes a system error makes the computer stop working altogether and you will have to restart the computer.

A sensible way of avoiding system errors is to write code to check that a printer is present *before* any data is sent to it. Then the computer would warn you by a simple message on the screen, like 'printer is not ready or available', so you can turn the printer on before you try to do any more.

**FIGURE 20.2** *System error*

## Syntax errors

A **syntax error** is a mistake in the programming language (like typing PRNIT instead of PRINT). Syntax errors cause the program to fail.

## More to do

**HIGH LEVEL LANGUAGE**

a computer language with instructions written in normal or everyday language

**INTERPRETER**

a translator program which is part of the systems software of a computer. An interpreter changes a high level language into machine code one instruction at a time

**COMPILER**

a translator program which is part of the systems software of a computer. A compiler changes a high level language into machine code

High level language interpreters and compilers (we talked about these in Chapter 17) normally have a syntax checker built in to them. Some translator programs won't accept any line that has syntax errors. Some only report a syntax error when they run the program. Some languages also contain special commands such as *debug*, which will report structural errors in a program (like forgetting to put ENDPROC at the end of a procedure definition). The programming manual for the particular language you're using will give details of error messages and what each message means.

### Logic errors

A **logic error** is much more difficult to detect than a syntax error. This is because a program containing logic errors will run, but won't work properly. For example, you might write a program to clear the screen and then print 'hello'. Here is the code for this

```
10 // Message
20 PRINT "Hello"
30 CLS
40 END
```

This code has a logic error in it, but the syntax is right so it will run. Can you see what the error is? What do you think will happen if you run this program?

## More to do

Logic errors often occur when you are testing a condition before branching or exiting from a loop.

**PROGRAM 1**

```
10 // Logic error 1
20 FOR times:=2 TO 10
30 IF times=1 THEN PRINT "HELLO"
40 NEXT times
50 END
```

In this program the value of times *never* reaches 1 so 'HELLO' will never be printed.

**PROGRAM 2**

```
10   // Logic error 2
20 total:=0
30 REPEAT
40 total:=total+1
50 UNTIL total=0
60 END
```

In this program the value of total will *always* be more than 0 and so the program will go on for ever. This is called an **infinite loop**.

You can get rid of logic errors from simple programs by 'Hand-testing' them, which means working through each line of the program on paper to make sure it does what you want it to do. You should do this long before you type in the code. Testing your program on paper first is also known as doing a 'dry run'.

## *User interface*

**HUMAN COMPUTER INTERFACE**

the way the computer and its user communicate

**PROBLEM STATEMENT**

the problem you are given to solve, e.g. display your name on the centre of the screen

A program's **user interface** is the way your program looks to the person who is using it. (This is part of the human computer interface of the program. We looked at this in Chapter 1.) The screen layout, the prompts or instructions which appear and the way it checks the input are all parts of the user interface. Let's examine these in more detail.

### Screen layout

The way your program looks on the screen is important. If it is clearly laid out the user will find it easier to follow. A problem statement may well include a description of the way your screen must look to the user during input or output or while the program is running.

### Prompts to user

A sensible programmer will always make sure they tell the user about what keys to press to operate the program, or what type of input to give.

**EXAMPLE**

```
PROC input
CLS
INPUT cost
........
```

```
PROC input
CLS
PRINT 'Please type the cost and press RETURN'
PRINT 'Use whole numbers from 1 to 20 only'
INPUT cost
.......
```

If you run the program on the left you will see a blank screen and a question mark and you won't be told what you should type. The program on the right gives you the information you need to put in the right numbers.

### *Input validation*

In any situation where the user can choose what they input, the program must check the input to see that it is what it needs (text or a number). If a number has been put in the program has to check the number is in the right range. These checks are called validating the data. If they are not done, even the most carefully written program will fail to work as it should or might stop altogether (this is called 'crashing'). A well written program will either not respond if the wrong keys are pressed or it will print a message on the screen and give the user a second chance to enter the data.

**VALIDATION**

checking that data is sensible. A range check is a way of validating data

## *Documentation*

Documentation can be of two types

- **USER DOCUMENTATION**
  User documentation (this is often called the user guide) gives the instructions on how to use a program.
- **TECHNICAL DOCUMENTATION**
  Technical documentation explains what each part of the program code does. This would be useful to another programmer or to the person who wrote the program, if they decide to make changes to it later. Comment lines and test data are part of the technical documentation.

## *Structure diagrams*

Computer programs used in business and industry are often thousands of lines long. You're not likely to understand one of these programs just by looking at the printed listing. The programmer needs some way of describing the overall way the program looks (its structure) so it's easier to understand. One way of describing the structure of a program is to use a **structure diagram**. Structure diagrams use specially shaped boxes to show loops, decisions, procedures or single steps. Common symbols used in structure diagrams are shown in figure 20.3. These boxes are usually joined together by lines to form a diagram. The example program in figure 20.4 shows how a programmer can link these boxes to describe the structure of a program.

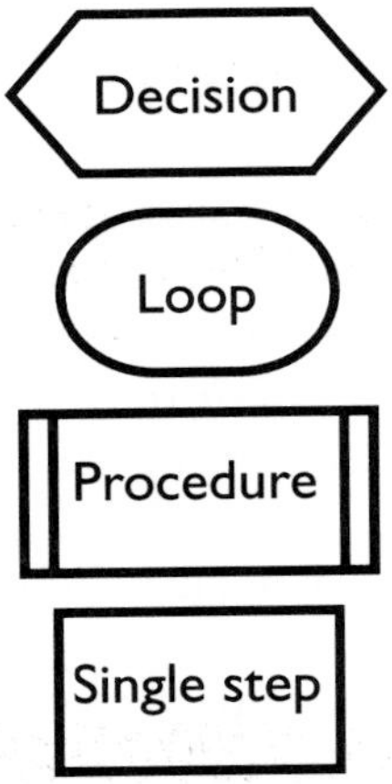


**FIGURE 20.3** *Common symbols used in structure diagrams*

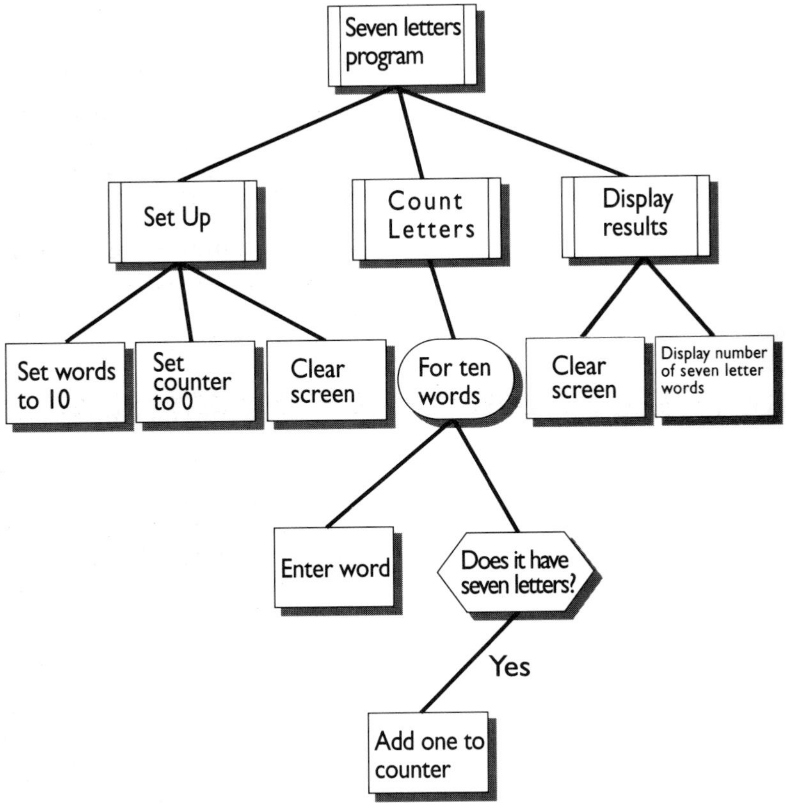


**FIGURE 20.4** *A structure diagram for the seven letters problem on the next page*

## *Libraries*

Professional programmers usually work in teams on a project, with each person writing different blocks of code (these blocks are called **procedures**). When all the procedures have been written, they are joined together to make up the finished program.

Sometimes programmers can buy already written procedures to put into the program to do certain things, like sort a list of names and addresses. These procedures are available from **program libraries**, and they are called **library procedures**. If you write a program using procedures you can easily add library procedures to it. This saves time when you're writing a large program, since a lot of the work has already been done for you.

Here are a few examples of the sort of things library procedures could do:

1 Take in a set of words and numbers
2 Sort in order a set of words and numbers
3 Display a set of words and numbers on the screen
4 Draw a picture on the screen.

In the computer language COMAL library procedures are called DEMONS (which comes from DEMONStration procedures). The examples that you have just seen would look like this in COMAL

1 sort_numbers_and_words
2 take_in_words_and_numbers
3 display_words_and_numbers
4 draw_graphic

## An approach to problem solving

The title of this chapter should really be 'problem solving', since people write computer programs so they can solve problems. But writing programs is not always the best way to solve a problem. Let's look at an example problem which you may be asked to solve. We will work through the stages together.

> **Problem statement**
>
> *The computer must take in a list of ten words, one word at a time and count the number of words with seven letters. The result should be displayed on the screen.*

The first thing you must do is think carefully about the problem. Here are some suggestions to help you.

1 Decide what the problem is. Read the question carefully. Sometimes writing the problem in your own words helps you to understand it.
2 Ask yourself if using a computer is the best way to solve this problem. Can it be solved more easily in any other way?
3 If you decide to use a computer to solve the problem, what information does the problem contain which you must enter into the computer? What must the computer do to this information? What must the output from the computer be? Write down the headings INPUT, PROCESS and OUTPUT and write the answer to these questions under the appropriate headings.

**FIGURE 20.5** *An approach to problem solving*

> ***Input***
> *ten words*
> ***Process***
> *count the words*
> ***Output***
> *the number of words with seven letters*

4 What software do you have to help you solve the problem? Can a general purpose package like a spreadsheet or database help? If you decide to use a package instead of writing your own program, does the package have the features you need already built in? Can you program the package (for example using its special language) to solve the problem?

> *If you think you can use a general purpose package to solve the problem, you must decide what properties you need the package to have. The package must be able to handle text, to count and should be able to tell you about the length of each word. One type of package that might be able to do this is a spreadsheet. In figure 20.6 you can see a sample solution for this problem using Microsoft Excel (a spreadsheet). Let's assume for the moment that you don't have access to a suitable spreadsheet. So what now?*

**FIGURE 20.6** *Using a spreadsheet to solve the seven letter problem*

| | A | B | C | D |
|---|---|---|---|---|
| 1 | | | | |
| 2 | | | | |
| 3 | **Spreadsheet** | **Solution for Seven Letters Problem** | | |
| 4 | | | | |
| 5 | Please enter | word 1 | | =IF(LEN(C5)=7,1,0) |
| 6 | Please enter | word 2 | | =IF(LEN(C6)=7,1,0) |
| 7 | Please enter | word 3 | | =IF(LEN(C7)=7,1,0) |
| 8 | Please enter | word 4 | | =IF(LEN(C8)=7,1,0) |
| 9 | Please enter | word 5 | | =IF(LEN(C9)=7,1,0) |
| 10 | Please enter | word 6 | | =IF(LEN(C10)=7,1,0) |
| 11 | Please enter | word 7 | | =IF(LEN(C11)=7,1,0) |
| 12 | Please enter | word 8 | | =IF(LEN(C12)=7,1,0) |
| 13 | Please enter | word 9 | | =IF(LEN(C13)=7,1,0) |
| 14 | Please enter | word 10 | | =IF(LEN(C14)=7,1,0) |
| 15 | | | | |
| 16 | Total number | of words with 7 letters is | | **=SUM(D5:D14)** |

| | A | B | C | D |
|---|---|---|---|---|
| 1 | | | | |
| 2 | | | | |
| 3 | **Spreadsheet** | **Solution for Seven Letters Problem** | | |
| 4 | | | | |
| 5 | Please enter | word 1 | Hello | 0 |
| 6 | Please enter | word 2 | there | 0 |
| 7 | Please enter | word 3 | I | 0 |
| 8 | Please enter | word 4 | am | 0 |
| 9 | Please enter | word 5 | looking | 1 |
| 10 | Please enter | word 6 | for | 0 |
| 11 | Please enter | word 7 | words | 0 |
| 12 | Please enter | word 8 | with | 0 |
| 13 | Please enter | word 9 | seven | 0 |
| 14 | Please enter | word 10 | letters | 1 |
| 15 | | | | |
| 16 | Total number | of words with 7 letters is | | **2** |

5 If none of the application packages have the features you need, you may have to write a program in a high level programming language like BASIC, PASCAL, COMAL, PROLOG or LOGO.

6 Can you use any of the programs (or parts of programs) you've written to help solve the problem? If the problem involves steps like sorting words or numbers you might be able to find a library procedure to help you.

7 Break the problem down into its main steps and write them out in a list. If you are using a programming language which allows you to write procedures, then make the main steps into the procedure names. Use plain language that you can understand instead of programming keywords. Language used like this is called **pseudocode**.

> ***List of main steps for seven letters problem***
>
> *1 Set up*
> *2 Count letters*
> *3 Display results*

Keep breaking down these steps into smaller ones.

> ***More steps in problem***
>
> *1.1 Set counter to zero*
> *1.2 Set number of words to zero*
> *1.3 Clear the screen*
>
> *2.1 Loop*
> *2.2 Take in a word*
> *2.3 Does it have seven letters?*
> *2.4 If so, add one to counter*
> *2.5 If not, do nothing*
> *2.6 End loop*
>
> *3.1 Clear the screen*
> *3.2 Display the total number of seven-letter words*

9 When you can't break the steps down any further, you need to change each step into instructions in your chosen programming language. This is called coding, and you can see an example of coding in figure 20.7.

10 At this point you might find a structure diagram (like the one in figure 20.4) more helpful than breaking the problem down into lots of steps.

On the next page you can see the final program, which has been written in COMAL.

11 Now you have coded your program on paper, and it is time to make up test data. You can see one set on the next page, under the program, but you should use several sets of test data to thoroughly test your program.

**FIGURE 20.7** *Program coding*

***Program for seven letters problem***

```
100   // Filename : Seven
110   // Seven Letters Program
120   // by Elizabeth Mary
130   // June 1993
140   //
150   set_up
160   count_letters
170   display_results
180   END
190   //
1000  PROC set_up
1010  number_of_words :=10
1020  counter :=0
1030  CLS
1040  END PROC set_up
1050  //
2000  PROC count_letters
2010  FOR times:=1 TO number_of_words DO
2020  INPUT "Please type in a word":word$
2030  // if the word has seven characters, then add 1 to counter
2040  IF LEN(word$) = 7 THEN counter:=counter+1
2050  NEXT times
2060  END PROC count_letters
2070  //
3000  PROC display_results
3010  CLS
3020  PRINT "You typed in"; counter ; "seven letter words"
3030  END PROC display_results
```

***Suitable test data***

*Hello, there, I, am, looking, for, text, with, seven, letters*

*You would expect the output using this test data to be*
*You typed in 2 seven letter words*

**12** After you have typed your program into the computer, correct any mistakes and get the program working. Save your program. Run the program a number of times using different test data as input. Check that your program produces the expected results when you enter the test data.

**13** Print a listing of your program code. If you can, print a sample run of your program using your test data as well.

**14** You might be asked to write a set of instructions to tell someone else how to use your program. This is the **user guide** and is part of the program's **documentation**. Write some **technical documentation** for your program for some one who wants to know how your program works.

> ***User guide***
>
> *Start the program by typing RUN SEVEN. Follow the instructions on the screen. The program will print out the number of words with seven characters that you have entered. To run the program again when it is finished, type RUN.*
>
> ***Technical documentation***
>
> *The program is written in COMAL.*
> *It was written on a BBC model B computer.*
> *The number of words that can be taken in is set in line 1010.*
> *The variable 'counter' is used to count the number of words with seven letters.*
> *The value '7' in line 2040 controls the length of the words which are counted by the program.*

**15** Finally, **evaluate** your solution. Does your program solve the problem as you wrote it out in step 1? Is it easy for others to use? Make a list of anything that could make your program better. List any problems you had in doing the task.

> ***Evaluation***
>
> *When the program is run, it works as expected and gives the correct output from the test data.*
> *The program has clear instructions and is easy to use.*
> *I could have improved the program by*
>
> - *allowing the user to enter the number of words*
> - *allowing the user to enter the length of the word to be counted*
> - *adding colour to produce a more attractive screen display.*
>
> ***Problems***
>
> *When I started I didn't know how to find the length of a word.*
> *I solved this problem by looking up the keyword 'LEN' in the COMAL programming manual.*

**16** Depending on the problem, you might not have to complete all of these stages to produce a fully documented solution. If you are doing a coursework task or a programming project, you will usually have to produce a solution with all of these stages in it.

***Summary of the steps involved in problem solving***

- *Read the question carefully*
- *Is using a computer the best way to solve this problem?*
- *What information does the problem contain which must be input?*
- *What must the computer do to this information?*
- *What must the output be?*
- *Can you use a general purpose package or must you write a program?*
- *Can any of the programs you have already written help?*
- *Break the problem down into its main steps*
- *Keep breaking down the steps into smaller steps until you can't break them down any more*
- *Write out your program code*
- *Make up test data*
- *Write the documentation*
- *Type your program into the computer, correct any mistakes and get the program working*
- *Save your program*
- *Run the program several using your test data as input*
- *Print a listing of your program code*
- *Print a sample run of your program using your test data*
- *Evaluate your solution.*

Depending on the type of the problem, you might not have to do all of these steps, or you might have to do some of them more than once. You should at least consider all of the steps for each problem.

## QUESTIONS

**Knowledge and understanding**

1 Name one way of describing the structure of a program.
2 Describe two ways you can make your program code easier for other people to read.
3 Why should a program be tested?
4 What can the programmer do to avoid system errors occurring when the program is run?
5 How can library procedures help the programmer?
6 What is program documentation for?

## EXTRA QUESTIONS

**Knowledge and understanding**

1 Describe the three categories of test data
2 Why are logical errors in program code much more difficult to find than syntax errors?
3 Why do you need to validate input?
4 What is pseudocode?

**Practical activities**

Here are some programming ideas for you to try. Begin by thinking about how to solve the problem using the approach we have just described.

1 Write a quiz program which asks ten questions and gives a score at the end. The program should ask for the user's name at the start, and display a suitable message depending on the score.

2 Write a program to calculate the number of days between any two dates in a single year. Use the day and month only as input.

3 Write a program which will ask the user for two numbers and give their sum, product and quotient.

4 Write a program which will take in a list of words until the word 'stop' is entered and print the list in the reverse order to the way it was entered.

5 Write a program which will count the number of words in any sentence that is input (up to a maximum of twenty words).

6 Write a program that will calculate how fast a runner is moving (in kilometres per hour) if you input the time they take to run100 metres.

7 Write a program which will take in a word of up to fifteen letters and display it on the screen backwards.

8 Write a program to test a person's reaction time from the time a word appears on the screen until they press the space bar. The word should appear at random intervals each time the program is run.

## KEY POINTS

- Programs can be made more readable and easier to maintain by using
  - meaningful variable and procedure names
  - comment lines in the code
  - prompts for the user
- Testing a program makes sure that the program solves the problem which was set
- Test data may be of three types:
  - normal
  - extreme
  - exceptional
- Program errors may be of three types:
  - system errors, which affect the computer or its peripherals

syntax errors, where mistakes have been made in the programming language
logic errors, where the programs seem to run, but don't work the way you meant them to

- The user interface is the way a program appears to the person using it
- All user input to a program should be validated as far as possible
- One way of describing the structure of a program is to use a structure diagram
- Another way of describing a program's structure is to use plain language or pseudocode
- Library procedures may save you time when writing programs
- Documentation can be of two types:
  user documentation
  technical documentation
- There are 18 steps involved in problem solving:
  **1** Read the question carefully
  **2** Is using a computer the best way to solve this problem?
  **3** What information does the problem contain which must be entered into the computer?
  **4** What must the computer do to this information?
  **5** What must the output from the computer be?
  **6** Can you use a general purpose package or must you write a program?
  **7** Can any of the programs you already have written help?
  **8** Break the problem down into its main steps
  **9** Keep breaking down these steps into smaller ones until you can't break them down further
  **10** Write out your program code
  **11** Make up test data
  **12** Write documentation
  **13** Type your program into the computer, correct any mistakes and get the program working
  **14** Save your program
  **15** Run the program a number of times using your test data as input
  **16** Print a listing of your program code
  **17** Print a sample run of your program using your test data
  **18** Evaluate your solution

# Appendix 1

## Glossary of terms used in the book

**Access** to gain entry to a computer system

**Addressability** a way of identifying storage locations in main memory using a number called an address

**Analogue** a signal (like temperature or speed) which changes continuously rather than in definite steps

**Analogue to digital converter** equipment (usually a chip) which can accept an analogue signal and change it into a digital signal (usually in binary)

**Applications package** a piece of software (together with its accompanying disks and manuals) that performs a particular task

**Arithmetic logic unit (ALU)** the part of the central processing unit of a computer system which does the calculations and makes the decisions

**ASCII** this stands for American Standard Code for Information Interchange

**Assembler** a translator program which is part of the systems software of a computer. An assembler changes assembly language into machine code

**Background job** a secondary task or program which runs in a computer system at the same time as an interactive program

**Backing store** a system for permanently holding the contents of memory on media such as disk or tape

**Backup** a copy of a program or data made in case the original is lost or destroyed

**Batch processing** collecting together all the data to be processed and inputting it to the computer in one set or 'batch'

**Batch system** the system which carries out batch processing, like clearing cheques, gas and electricity billing

**Binary** having only two states (on and off), counting using only two digits

**Bit** a binary digit, either 1 or 0

**Byte** a group of eight bits

**Catalogue** a list of all the files or programs stored in a directory

**CD ROM** stands for Compact Disc Read Only Memory. It is a high-capacity optical disc

**Cell** a box on a spreadsheet that can contain text, numbers or formulas

**Central processing unit (CPU)** the part of the computer which processes the information

**Character set** a list of all the characters, symbols and numbers stored by the computer

**Charting** drawing a graph from a set of numerical data, usually from a spreadsheet program

**Check digit** a figure that's calculated from the digits of a number and placed at the end of a number. Used to check that the number has been input correctly

**Chip** a small piece of silicon used to make an integrated circuit

**Circuit board** a thin board on which chips and other components are fixed by solder

**Closed loop system** a (control) system which uses feedback

**Command-driven software** software that needs commands from the user to work

**Compiler** a translator program which is part of the systems software of a computer. A compiler changes a high level language into machine code

**Computer aided design (CAD)** using a computer system to help design something

**Computer aided manufacture (CAM)** using a computer system to help manufacture something

**Computer crime** using a computer for criminal purposes. 'Hacking' is a computer crime

**Computer integrated manufacture (CIM)** The maximum use of CAD/CAM systems from start to finish of a particular product

**Computer Misuse Act** a law which allows computer criminals (like hackers) to be prosecuted

**Computer numerical control (CNC)** automatically controlling a machine like a lathe according to instructions or feedback from sensors

**Computer operator** a person who controls the day-to-day operation of a mainframe computer system using a terminal

**Control characters** non-printing characters which control the way the computer system works

**Control language** a special language designed to control a device such as a robot or a robot arm

**Control unit** part of the central processing unit which controls the running of a program

**Corrupt** to corrupt a file means to damage it so it can't be read

**Daisy wheel** a printer with a print head that looks like a flower with characters on the end of the 'petals'

**Data** a general term for numbers, characters and symbols which are accepted and processed by a computer system

**Data collection** gathering data. May involve source documents

**Data file** a file containing data on backing storage or in memory. Normally organised as a set of records

**Data input** when data is put into the computer system. May be direct or indirect

**Data output** data sent out

**Data preparation** data is made ready for input

**Data preparation operator** person who inputs data into the computer system

**Data processing cycle** a cycle of events beginning with data collection and preparation and ending with data output

**Data Protection Act** a law which regulates how personal data about individuals is kept on computer

**Data storage** transferring data to backing storage

**Database** a structured collection of similar information which can be searched

**Dedicated** a computer or machine which can only perform one particular task

**Degrees of freedom** the number of independent axes of movement, for example of a robot arm

**Desktop computer** a microcomputer consisting of a CPU, keyboard and monitor which is normally operated sitting at a desk

**Desktop publishing (DTP)** producing professional looking publications on a microcomputer and its peripherals

**Device** a single item of computer hardware

**Digital** a signal which changes in steps and not continuously like an analogue signal

**Digital to analogue converter** equipment (usually a chip) which can accept a digital signal (usually in binary) and change it into an analogue signal

**Digitise** converting an analogue quantity to a digital one. Digitising a picture breaks it into dots and each dot is given a digital value for brightness and colour

**Digitiser** a device which takes the image from a video (camera) and puts it on a computer screen

**Direct data entry** when data is input straight into a computer system. Examples are bar codes, magnetic stripes

**Directory** an area on backing storage where files are stored (this is called a folder on some systems)

**Documentation** a detailed explanation of how a program works

**Dot matrix** a printer which forms characters using a series of dots produced by pins in the print head

**Dynamic linkage** a change to the data in one file will automatically be carried over to the same data in another file

**Electronic funds transfer (EFT)** automatically moving money from one account to another using a computer system. No cash changes hands

**Encryption** processing a message so that it can't be understood by anyone who is not authorised to use it

**End effector** the part on the end of a robot arm which carries out a particular task, like spraying paint

**Engineer** a person who maintains and repairs a computer system

**Facsimile (fax) machine** a machine that scans a document and changes it into a signal that can be sent along a telephone line. The document is printed on another fax machine somewhere else

**Feedback** the output from a process which is used to control the input of the same process

**Field** a single item of data stored in a record

**File ancestry** a system for keeping backups of files using 'generations' of files like grandparent, parent and child

**File** information held on backing storage or in memory. Files may hold data, programs, text or any other information

**File server** a station on a local area network which holds files that can be accessed by the users

**Flat filing system** a filing system where there is only a single directory which everyone can access

**Floating point** using the mantissa and exponent to store numbers in a computer system

**Floppy disk** a plastic disk coated with magnetic material used as a backing storage medium

**Formatting** laying down tracks and sectors on a disk. It is also called initialising

**Formula** a calculation involving one or more cell references

**Gateway** a link between two different host computers

**Gigabyte** 1024 megabytes (1024 × 1024 × 1024 bytes)

**GIGO** stands for Garbage In Garbage Out – if you make a mistake in your input, your output will also have mistakes in it

**Graphical user interface** an interface which lets the user work with icons and a mouse rather than text

**Graphics** pictures or charts on a computer screen

**Graphics package** a piece of software used for producing or editing graphics

**Graphics tablet** an input device which allows you to draw freehand using a hand-held pointer on a board

**Hacking** interfering with information stored on a computer system. It is usually illegal

**Handwriting recognition** a system that turns handwriting on a special screen using a pen into print on a computer

**Hard copy** a printed copy of your work, usually on paper

**Hard disk** a backing storage device made up of metal disks coated with a magnetic material. It is usually sealed against dust and dirt

**Hardware** the physical parts or devices which make up a computer system

**Hierarchical filing system** a filing system with many directories. Not every user can access every directory

**High level language** a computer language with instructions written in normal or everyday language

**Human computer interface (HCI)** the way the computer and its user communicate

**Icon** a symbol or picture on a screen – part of a graphical user interface

**Import** to bring in data from one file into another, sometimes between two different types of package

**Inkjet** a printer which forms dots produced by tiny jets of ink

**Input** to enter data that needs to be processed

**Input device** a device which allows data to be entered, like a keyboard or a graphics tablet

**Integer** a whole number, with no fractional part or decimal point

**Integrated package** software made up of separate parts which can share data. All the parts have a similar HCI

**Interaction** the operator's instructions are processed continuously by the computer – like a conversation

**Interface** part of a computer system that allows different devices to communicate with the processor by compensating for any differences in their operation

**Interpreter** a translator program which is part of the systems software of a computer. An interpreter changes a high level language into machine code one instruction at a time

**IPO** input, process, output

**Justification** a way of arranging text on screen or on hard copy

**Key field** a field used to identify a particular piece of information in a database

**Key to disk** a method of indirect data entry used off line

**Keyboard** an input device consisting of a set of buttons or keys marked with characters

**Keyword** a word which is used to search for an item in a database

**Kilobyte (k)** 1024 bytes

**Knowledge system** a system which contains rules and data about a particular topic

**Laptop computer** a portable computer which folds and has a screen and keyboard in a single unit. It is powered from batteries and may be operated while travelling. A laptop computer usually has an LCD screen

**Laser printer** a printer which produces a high-quality image of text and graphics using a laser

**Light guide** a line painted on a factory floor that an autonomous guided vehicle can follow

**Light pen** an input device used to scan bar codes or to input data to a screen

**Liquid Crystal Display (LCD)** A type of flat screen display which is used in calculators, palmtop and laptop computers because of its low power consumption. It may be monochrome (black and white) or colour

**Local area network (LAN)** a network confined to a single room or building

**Log on** the way of identifying the user to the network system

**Logic error** a mistake whch causes your program to produce an unexpected result

**Low level language** a computer language which is similar to the computer's own language (machine code)

**Machine code** the computer's own language. It is made up of binary numbers (0 and 1 only)

**Magnetic guide** a cable buried in a factory floor for an autonomous guided vehicle to follow

**Magnetic ink character recognition (MICR)** an input device which can read characters written in magnetic ink. It is used for direct data input

**Magnetic tape** plastic tape coated with a magnetic material used as a backing storage medium

**Mail merge** the process of automatically loading personal details from a separate mailing list and placing them into the correct places in a standard letter

**Mail shot** letters prepared by mail merge and sent out to individuals on a mailing list – also called direct mail or junk mail

**Main memory** the memory in a computer system. It is linked to the central processing unit

**Main memory size** the number of storage locations available in a computer system

**Mainframe computer system** a computer system that can carry out a very large amount of work at high speed. It usually occupies a whole large room

**Mark sense card** a card with lines drawn on it to indicate one or more choices. It is used for direct data input

**Master file** a file which holds the latest version of your data

**Megabyte** 1024 kilobytes

**Menu** a list on screen for the user to choose from

**Menu-driven software** software which needs the user to choose from a menu to make it work

**Microfiche** a tiny photograph or slide which can be viewed using a projector

**Microprocessor** the central processing unit of a microcomputer

**Modem** a device used to connect a computer system to a telephone line. Modem is short for **mod**ulator–**dem**odulator

**Mouse** an input device (with a ball underneath and one or more buttons on top) used to control a pointer on screen

**Multi-access** more than one person using a computer system at once

**Multimedia** when devices such as video, hi-fi and compact discs are linked to a computer and operated by a computer program

**Multi-programming** more than one program running on a computer system at once

**Network** two or more computers joined together so that data can be transferred between them

**Numeric** data consisting of numbers which may have fractions or a decimal point

**Off line** not connected to a computer system

**On line** connected to a computer system

**On-line help** help in the form of information screens available when using a computer program

**On-line tutorial** help in the form of guided lessons available when using a computer program

**Open loop system** a control system which does not involve feedback

**Operating system** programs which control the operation of a computer system. Part of the system software

**Optical character recognition (OCR)** characters can be read in to the computer automatically from a page of text

**Optical storage** a form of non-magnetic storage, like CD ROM

**Output** data passed out of a computer system

**Output device** a device which displays data from a computer system, such as a monitor or a printer

**Palmtop computer** a hand-held computer. A palmtop computer usually has an LCD screen but may or may not have a keyboard

**Password** a secret code that you use to access private information on a computer system or to log on to a network

**Peripheral** any device that may be attached to a computer system for input, output or backing storage

**Pixel** stands for 'picture element'. A tiny dot used to make up a picture on a screen

**Plotter** an output device which draws on paper using pens. Used mainly for CAD

**Point of sale (POS)** a computer terminal or 'till' in a shop where the goods and money change hands

**Pointer** a shape displayed on screen which is used to select from a menu. It is usually controlled by a mouse

**Portability** programs written on one computer system can be used on a different computer system without alteration

**Printer** an output device which produces hard copy usually on paper. Examples are dot matrix, inkjet, laser

**Problem statement** the problem you are given to solve, e.g. display your name on the centre of the screen

**Procedure** part of a computer program which is identified by name (like TAKE_IN_WORDS or MOVE_BUGGY)

**Program** a list of instructions which tell the central processing unit what to do

**Program listing** a hard copy or a screen display of the instructions making up a computer program

**Programmer** a person who writes computer programs

**Prompt** a character which appears on screen to tell the user that the computer wants you to do something

**Pseudocode** a way of describing a problem using ordinary language rather than a particular computer language

**Pull-down menu** a menu on a WIMP system which can be operated by using a mouse pointer and button

**Random access memory (RAM)** a microchip that stores data temporarily. The data is lost when the machine is switched off

**Random/direct access** being able to locate a data item straight away, wherever it is stored

**Read only memory (ROM)** a microchip that stores data permanently. The data is not lost when the computer is switched off

**Read only memory (ROM) software** software distributed on read only memory chip

**Real time** interacting with a computer program and receiving the output immediately

**Record** a data structure with one or more fields of information

**Remote data entry** when data is input from a terminal at some distance from the host computer

**Resolution** the amount of detail which can be shown on a screen (or a hard copy)

**Resource allocation** when the operating system allows a program to have access to a particular piece of hardware

**Re-writeable optical disc** a type of non-magnetic storage which may be used in the same way as a floppy disc

**Robot** a device which can carry out repetitive tasks under the control of a computer program

**Routine** a programming instruction which carries out a particular task

**Scanner** an input device which allows printed text or graphics to be displayed on the screen. Usually used with OCR software

**Screen layout** the way a program looks on a monitor screen

**Scrolling** moving the display on the screen, usually by using the cursor keys or the mouse

**Searching** looking for an item using a database program and perhaps one or more keywords

**Sensor** a device which detects something and provides input to a computer system. A bump sensor is an example

**Sequence** the order in which a set of instructions is carried out or the order in which a set of data is stored on backing storage

**Sequential access** reading a set of records or storage locations in the same order as they were originally stored

**Simulation** a computer program used to model a real-life situation

**Software** the programs that the hardware of the computer runs

**Sorting** putting a list of items into order, for example numeric or alphabetic

**Special-purpose language** a language (such as a control language), which is to do a certain task

**Specialised input devices** an input device which is adapted for a particular purpose, such as use by a disabled person or for virtual reality

**Specialised output devices** an output device which is adapted for a particular purpose, such as use by a disabled person or for virtual reality

**Specialised user interface** an input device controlled by software. It is designed for a particular situation – perhaps to be used by a disabled user

**Spreadsheet** a program which divides the screen into rows and columns. Cells in a spreadsheet can contain text, numbers or formulae

**Standard letter** a general letter with spaces for personal details (such as a person's name). Used in mail shots

**Standard paragraph** a piece of text that you can combine with others like it to make up a complete document

**Static linkage** a change to the data in one file will not affect the same data in other files

**Storage location** a place in a computer's memory where an item of data may be held

**Stored program** a set of instructions which is held in a computer's memory

**Structure diagram** a diagram made up of different-shaped boxes containing text and linked by lines. It is usually used to explain the structure of a computer program

**Syntax error** a mistake in a programming instruction – for example typing PTRIN instead of PRINT

**System error** a mistake in the computer's operating system program which may stop the computer working

**Systems analysis** examining a method of working

**Systems analyst** a person who examines a method of working and decides the best way of doing it using a computer system

**Systems software** a set of programs which controls the operation of a computer system

**Teletext** pages of information transmitted with a television signal which may be received by a suitable television set or a computer and adapter. A one-way system only

**Terminal** a piece of hardware consisting of a keyboard and a screen or a keyboard and a printer. Used to communicate with a computer system. A 'dumb' terminal does not have a central processing unit

**Test data** data used to test a computer program to find out if it works the way the programmer wants it to

**Text** characters or symbols displayed on a screen or printed as hard copy on a printer

**Touch-sensitive screen** a screen with sensitive areas on it. The user presses particular areas to input into the computer or operate a program

**Trackball** an input device consisting of a ball which is turned by hand, moving a cursor on the screen around. Works like an upside-down mouse

**Transaction file** a file which holds new information to update a master file

**Translation** changing a program from one computer language into another, usually from a high level language into a low level language

**Turnaround document** a document like a cheque or order form which is received and then sent back into the system to complete a transaction

**Update** adding new data. A transaction file may be used to update a master file

**User identity** your name or a code which identifies you to a network. Usually used with a password

**User-friendly** an interactive computer system which helps the user by giving clear prompts, menus and help screens when needed

**Utility** a program which helps you to perform a task, such as delete a file or format a disk

**Validation** checking that data is sensible. A range check is a way of validating data

**Verification** checking that data has been entered correctly

**Video disc** an optical storage medium similar to compact disc (CD ROM), which holds video (TV programmes or films)

**Virtual reality** a method of reproducing the outside world digitally within a computer system and displaying it to the user in such a way that allows them to interact with a wide range of situations. To take part in virtual reality, the user may need to wear a special headset and gloves rather than use a keyboard and monitor

**Virus** a 'rogue' program which can spread through computer systems and may damage files

**Visual display unit (VDU)** an output device consisting of a monitor and usually a keyboard. May be used as a terminal

**Voice output** speech produced by a computer system usually by special software and a loudspeaker

**Voice recognition** software which can recognise spoken input

**Wide area network (WAN)** a network which covers a large geographical area like a country. Used for long-distance communication via satellite, radio or telephone line

**WIMP** **W**indows, **I**cons, **M**enu (or **M**ouse), **P**ointer (or **P**ull down menu)

**Window** an area of the screen set aside for a particular purpose

**Word processor** a program used for writing and editing text

**Word** the number of bits a computer can process in a single operation

**Wordwrap** text formatting used in a word processor which stops words at the end of one line being split over two lines

**WORM** stands for write once read many (times). It is a large capacity optical backing storage device

**WYSIWYG** stands for 'what you see is what you get'. When what you see on a screen is exactly the same as the way it will be printed

# Appendix 2

## History of computers

This chapter is a very brief history of computers. In it we look at some of the people and inventions involved in the evolution of the computer. This is not part of the Standard Grade syllabus, but some background knowledge of the history of computing is useful, and it will help you to appreciate the developments that are still happening. You will see how the modern computer has developed from early calculating machines

### Abacus

The abacus is a device consisting of rods with beads that can be moved up and down them. It has been around for about 5000 years and is still used in Japan and China. Someone who is very skilled at using an abacus can usually work out calculations quicker than someone using an electronic calculator.

### Napier's Bones

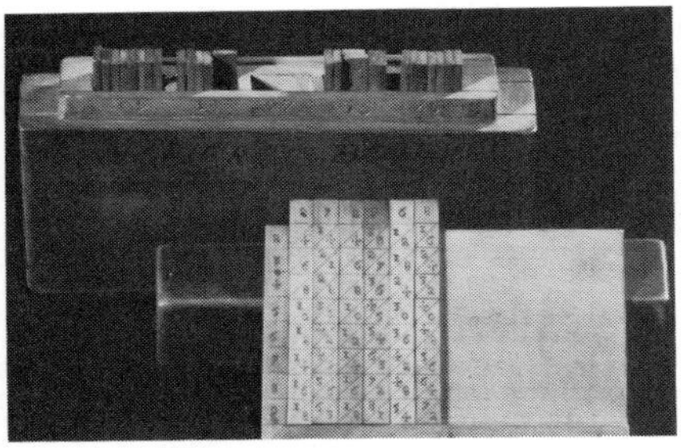

*Napier's Bones*

In 1617, John Napier invented a calculating aid made of sliding rods. This is known as Napier's Bones. Napier is more famous for inventing logarithms, which are tables of numbers for working out multiplication and division simply by addition and subtraction. You can see a set of Napier's Bones in the top photograph.

### Slide rule

Napier's Bones and his logarithms inspired William Oughtred to invent the slide rule in 1621. The slide rule was the equivalent of the pocket calculator of today and was used for calculations until the late 1970s, when pocket calculators became more popular.

### Pascaline

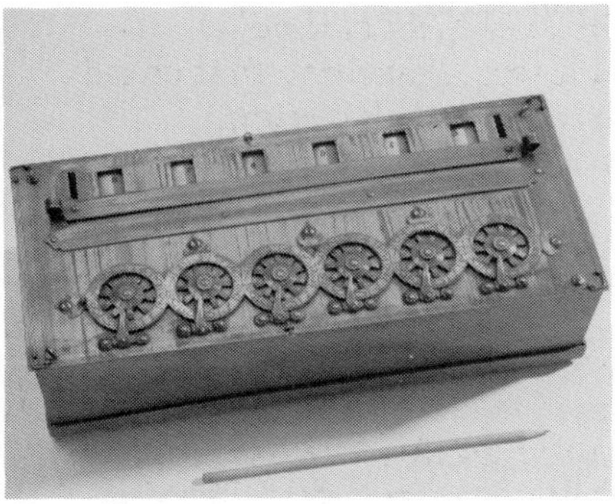

*Pascaline*

The Pascaline was invented by Blaise Pascal in 1642 to help his father who was a tax collector. The Pascaline could be used to add and subtract. You will already know the name Pascal because a high level language was named after him. The Pascaline is shown in the bottom photograph.

### Leibnitz calculator

In 1671 Gottfried von Leibnitz produced the Leibnitz calculator. This was based on the Pascaline, but it was able to multiply and divide as well as add and subtract. Leibnitz also investigated the binary number system that is used in modern computers.

Up to now, the machines we have looked at don't look much like the modern computer. In all of these inventions, numbers were represented as physical states by beads, bones or gear wheels. The last two had dials to set (input devices), gears to do the calculations, and dials showing the results (the output). But there was no memory, no internal decision-making unit and the devices couldn't be programmed for different uses.

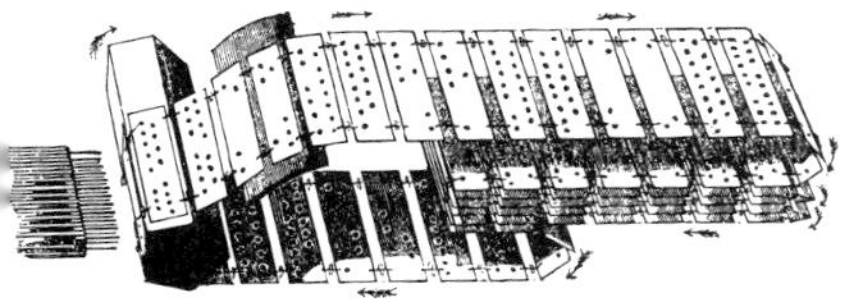
*Jacquard cards in action*

### Jacquard's loom

In 1801, Joseph Marie Jacquard, a French textile manufacturer, invented a punch card system for controlling looms. The holes in the wooden cards controlled the pattern of the weave. You can see how the cards worked in the illustration. Different patterns could be produced by changing the cards. Paisley mills invested in this new technology, which made them very successful, as you can see by how popular Paisley patterns still are. The development of these cards inspired both Babbage and Hollerith.

### Babbage's Difference Engine

Charles Babbage was a mathematician at Cambridge University. In 1822 Babbage invented a machine which he called the Difference Engine. This machine was designed to make up more accurate tables of logarithms. He spent £17 000 (a very large sum of money for the time) on the Difference Engine, but only a model of it was made. The project stopped when Babbage's funds ran out.

In 1991, two hundred years after Babbage was born (26 December 1791) his difference engine was actually built for an exhibition at the Science Museum in London. It cost £295 000, is made from bronze and steel and weighs three tonnes.

### Babbage's Analytical Engine

*Charles Babbage*

In 1834 Babbage invented his Analytical Engine, a calculating machine which could be programmed to solve particular problems. Charles Babbage is regarded as the 'Father of Computing' because although the analytical engine was too complicated to build at the time, it was a machine that could follow a program, rather than do just one calculation.

Babbage's analytical engine was like modern computers because

- one part was dedicated to performing calculations (like the arithmetic logic unit)
- one part made sure the instructions were carried out in sequence (like the control unit)
- a series of cogs made sure that the numbers weren't presented until they were ready to be used in a calculation (like the memory)

*Augusta Ada Byron, Countess of Lovelace*

- different parts of the machine were recognisable as input and output
- its programming included the equivalent of IF ... THEN and FOR ... NEXT loops.

Babbage was helped in his work by Lord Byron's daughter Augusta Ada, the Countess of Lovelace, who helped to program the analytical engine. Since the machine was not built, her programs were never tested, but she was really the world's first computer programmer. The high-level programming language Ada was named after her.

### Herman Hollerith

In 1887 the United States government was still working through the census returns for 1880. A competition was held for improving the recording and counting to help speed up processing the results from the next census (1890). The competition was won by Herman Hollerith's Pantograph Punch and Electrical Tabulator. The information obtained from completed census forms (these were the source documents) was transferred to punch cards using Hollerith's punch. The cards were then put through the tabulator which sorted and processed the information much faster than could be done by hand. The company which Hollerith founded became part of International Business Machines (IBM) in 1911.

### Automatic Sequence Controlled Calculator

The Automatic Sequence Controlled Calculator (usually shortened to ASCC) was built at Harvard University in 1944 by Howard Aiken, working on an IBM scholarship. He based it on an electromechanical switch called a relay. The IBM Harvard Mark I was the first machine with the capability of Babbage's Analytical Engine.

### First-generation computers (the 1940s)

#### *Valves*

The first generation of modern electronic computers was developed in the 1940s using electronic valves. Valves worked much faster than relays but used huge amounts of energy. World War II provided a stimulus to the development of these computer systems.

#### *Colossus*

The Colossus computer was built in 1943. It was used during the war to crack the top secret Enigma code used by the German high command. By the end of the war ten computers were being used. Each computer had 1500 valves and could input and process 25 000 characters every second. The

*An Enigma machine*

ENIAC

Colossus computers decoded nearly every message passed out from the German high command within a few hours of receiving them. Nowadays people think that the computers were important in bringing about the eventual Allied victory.

### *Electronic Numerical Integrator And Computer (ENIAC)*

ENIAC was built in 1946 using 18 000 valves. It need a large hall to store it, but could work very fast – for example it could do the calculation

$$93\,367 \times 93\,367 \times 93\,367 \times 93\,367 \times 93\,367$$

in half a second.

ENIAC could be programmed by connecting a large number of wires and was used to calculate the path a rocket would take. It was the first computer that was fully electronic. It used no gears or wheels.

### *John von Neumann*

In 1946 John von Neumann stated that

- Computers should have data and instructions coded as binary digits and stored together in the computer memory. The hardware should treat the data and instructions identically.
- A computer should process both data and instructions

This led to the idea of having a stored program inside a computer.

Many other computers were built using valves, like the Lyons Electronic Office (LEO). LEO was the first computer built and used by a company for office work in Britain. The tea shop firm of J.M. Lyons founded LEO computers, which eventually merged with other companies to become International Computers (ICL).

## Second-generation computers (the 1950s)

### *Transistors*

The transistor was invented in 1948. It could do the same things as a valve as far as computers were concerned, but transistors are cheaper, smaller, more reliable and used less power.

### *Core storage*

Another development was core storage, which was made from small ring-shaped magnets. Core storage was used for the computer's internal memory.

### *Backing store*

There were also developments in backing storage. As more storage was required, ways of storing information outside the central processing unit were investigated. Magnetic disks, drums and tape were developed.

### *Modular systems*

Computer manufacturers started to build computer systems in the form of separate modules. Each module would perform a different function. Different modules could be combined to meet a customer's needs and the system could be expanded if necessary by adding more modules.

## Third-generation computers: integrated circuits (the 1960s)

Transistors and other components were joined together on a single piece of silicon to become an integrated circuit or a silicon chip. One of the first successful third-generation computers was the IBM 360 series.

## Fourth-generation computers: large-scale integrated circuits and very large-scale integrated circuits (1970s onwards)

First hundreds, then thousands, then tens of thousands and hundreds of thousands of individual units could be placed on a single silicon chip. These are called large-scale integrated circuits and very large-scale integrated circuits. The first computer processor on a single chip (a microprocessor) was produced by Intel in 1972. Microprocessors and the large memory chips used with them are very large scale integrated circuits. As you will know if you have read this book, microprocessors form the basis of thousands of electronic devices, from hand-held games to washing machines, televisions and computers. The computers we use today are fourth-generation computers.

## Fifth-generation computers: 'intelligent' computers (started 1981)

There is a lot of work going on into developing fifth-generation computers. Fifth-generation computers will be able to learn and reason in a way which fourth-generation computers can't. They will have a natural language interface. The user should be able to describe a problem to the computer and the computer should be able to solve it without being programmed in the normal way. If we can produce the fifth-generation computer then there will be even more new and exciting developments in computing just around the corner.

# Index


. to D and D to A converters 130
bacus 308
ctuator 130
ddressability 280
.irline reservations 211
lphanumeric 275
.merican Standard Code for
Information Interchange
(ASCII) 275, 238
nalogue 130
nalogue input / output 130
.nalytical Engine 309
pplications packages 2
.rithmetic/Logic Unit
(ALU) 272
rtificial intelligence 48
.SCII 275, 238
ssembler 253, 254
ssembly language 253, 254
ssembly line 121
.ugusta Ada Byron 310
utomated systems 120
- accuracy 124
- adaptability 124
- efficiency 124
- hazardous environment 123
- repetitive tasks 123
- speed 123
utomated telling machine 187
.utomatic Sequence Controlled
Calculator (ASCC) 310

abbage 309
acking store 227
- capacity 234, 235, 237
- non-magnetic 231, 234, 235
ackup 15, 166
anker's Automated Clearing
Service (BACS) 194
anking 183
ar codes 156, 157, 201, 206
ase 281
ASIC 136
atch processing 166, 219
atch system 260
atch total 163
aud 93, 98
BC Buggy 135
inary 272, 273
it 130, 273
yte 274

CAD packages 148
CAD/CAM 141
cash card 186, 185, 156
cassette tapes 227
catalogue 265
CD ROM 231, 234, 235
CEEFAX 88
central processing unit
(CPU) 222, 271, 272
character 275
character recognition 158
character set 275
check digit 159, 160, 162, 275
chip 222, 224, 225
CIM 145
closed loop control system 124
CNC 146, 147
Colossus 310
command-driven 7
comment lines 285
commercial data processing 153
- basic hardware 168
- economic implications 177
- job types and careers 170
- mainframe computer
system 153
- management information 154
- remote terminals 169
- repetitive tasks 153
- security and privacy 178
- social implications 178
- speed of access 153
- speed of processing 153
- technical implications 177
- terminals 168, 212
- volume of documents 153
compiler 253
computer 222
computer aided design
(CAD) 141
computer aided manufacture
(CAM) 144
computer crime, fraud 174
computer integrated
manufacture (CIM) 146
Computer Misuse Act 18
computer numerical control
(CNC) 146, 147
computer operator 172
concept keyboard 239
conferencing 113

control characters 275, 276, 277
control language 136
control unit 272
core storage 311
corrupt (a file) 174, 176
crashing 231

data 1, 154
data input 155
data link - reliability of 24
data output 167
- file 168
- microfiche 167
- paper 167
- pre-printed stationery 167
- screen 167
data preparation 155
data preparation operator 172
data processing and storage 165
data processing cycle 154
Data Protection 15
Data Protection Act 17
data subject 17
data user 17
data, storage of 14
data, types of - graphics 1
data, types of - numbers 1
data, types of - text 1
database 39
- add record 41
- alter output format 45
- alter record format 41
- alter screen input format 45
- computed field 44
- create fields 41
- key field 46
- keywords 45
- search 41
- sort 42
debug 289, 172
dedicated system 3, 28
degrees of freedom 132
desktop computer 222
desktop publishing (DTP) 80
- banner headlines 83
- columns 83
- drop capitals 84
- style sheets 85
- templates 84
- text flow 84
- typefaces 85

device 222, 168
Difference Engine 309
digital 130
digitiser 131
direct data entry 155
direct data input 155
directory 265
diskfax 110
documentation
- technical 291
- user 291

ECCTIS 117
economic implications - automated systems 126
electronic communication 22
Electronic Data Interchange 114
electronic funds transfer (EFT) 177, 194
electronic funds transfer at point of sale (EFTPOS) 177, 203
electronic mail 103
Electronic Numerical Integrator and Computer (ENIAC) 311
electronic point of sale (EPOS) 198
Electronic Yellow Pages 100
encryption 192
end effector 129
engineer 173
Enigma 310
errors
- logical 289
- syntax 288
- system 288
evaluation 297
expert system shell 48
expert systems 47, 136
explanatory interface 48
exponent 282

facsimile (fax) 26, 110
feedback 124
field 39
file 39
file ancestry 167
file server 23
file, types of
- data 265
- program 265
filing system 265
- flat 266
- hierarchical 266
Fischer Technik 135
flexible manufacturing system 145
floating point 282
floppy disk 228
footer 10
formatting 229
function key 238

gateway 98
general purpose packages 2, 4
- accuracy of information 16
- advantages 20
- alter page length 29
- basic hardware 3
- change text appearance 5
- common features 5
- copy/move 5
- handling large quantities of information 3
- insert/amend/delete 5
- new 4
- open/load file 4
- print file 4
- printer quality 33
- run/open application 4
- save file 4
- social implications 19
gigabyte 278
grammar checking 32
grandparent, parent and child 167
graphical user interface 8
graphics 65
- alter tool attributes 67
- animation 71
- draw graphic 66
- draw package 69
- enter text 66
- paint package 69
- resolution 70, 278
- rotate graphic 68
- scale graphic 68
- select tool 67
graphics tablet 141, 239
guides - magnetic and light 133

hacking 18, 174
handwriting recognition 241
hard copy 28
hard disk 230
hardware 222
hash total 163
header 10
Herman Hollerith 310
high level languages 251
- common features 252
- need for translation 251
- purpose 251
Home and Office Banking Service (HOBS™) 190
human computer interface (HCI) 6

IBM 310
icon 8, 9
immediate access store 223, 272
import and export of text 37
indirect data input 155
industrial and commercial applications
- automated systems 120
- commercial data processing 153
inference engine 48
information 1, 154
input validation 291
input, process, output (IPO) 120, 270
integrated circuit 312
integrated package 73, 11
integrated software - see software
integration 11
interactive processing 166, 193
interactive system 262, 217
interactive systems with background job capability 219
interface 130
interpreter 255

Jacquard's loom 309
John von Neumann 311
joystick 240
junk mail 21-2

key to disk 157
keyboard 238
keypad 238
kilobyte 278
Kimball tags 156
knowledge base 48
knowledge engineer 48
knowledge systems 47, 48

laptop computer 226
lands (CD ROM) 235

Laservision Disc 231, 207
LCD 242
Lego Technic 135
Leibnitz 308
librarian 173
light pen 240
Liquid Crystal Display (LCD) 242
local area network 22, 23
Lyons Electronic Office 311

machine code 251, 254
magnetic ink character recognition (MICR) 158
magnetic stripes 156, 157
magnetic tape 227
mail merge 35
mail reference file 111
mail shot 21
mailbox 97, 109
main memory size 278, 279
main steps 295
main store/memory 223, 272
maintainability 285
mantissa 282
mark sense cards 161
master file 165
meaningful variable and procedure names 284
media 227
megabyte 278
menu 9
menu-driven 7
microcomputer 223
microfiche 167
microfilm 168
microprocessor 222, 224
mimic controller 123
mnemonic 254
modem 24, 114, 115
monitor 242
mouse 239, 240
MS DOS 263
multi-access 261, 212
multi-access (communication) 25
multi-programming 262, 219
multimedia 207, 208, 236, 237

Napier's Bones 308
near letter quality (NLQ) 243, 245
networks 22

object code 253, 254
off line 107, 155
on line 107, 155
on-line help 7, 108
on-line tutorial 7
open loop control system 124
operating system 259, 219
- specialised functions 261
- standard functions 259
optical character recognition (OCR) 159
optical disc 232

palmtop computer 241, 242
Pascaline 308
peripheral - see device
personal identification number 187, 189
Phonebase 99
Phoneline 190
Photo CD - see WORM
pitch 132
pits (CD ROM) 234, 235
pixel 65, 277
place value 273
plotter 246
point of sale (POS) 198
pointer 9
portability of software 256
PRESTEL 95, 107
printer 242
- daisy wheel 243
- dot matrix 243
- inkjet 245
- laser 244
printer drivers 36
procedure 136, 292
program 223, 251, 265
program libraries 292
program listing 136
programmer 172
programming by example 131
prompts to user 285, 290
pseudocode 295
pull-down menu 8

quality control 126

random access memory (RAM) 224
random/direct access
- devices 233
- to data 166, 268
read only memory (ROM) 224
readability 285
real-time 219
real-time systems 133, 260
record 39
remote data entry 161
representation of
- graphics 277
- large numbers 281
- non-negative integers 281
- number 273
- text 275
resource allocation 262
retraining - GPPs 19, 20
re-writeable optical disc 232
right of access to personal data 16, 17
RISC OS 264
robotics 129
robots 129
- anatomy 129
- motor 130
- programmable 131
- stationary/mobile 130, 133, 134, 135
roll 132
ROM 224
ROM software 10, 132
root directory 266
routine 136

scanner 241
screen 242
screen layout 290
sector 229
security and privacy
- Commercial data processing 178
- General Purpose Packages 15, 24
selection of packages 12, 13, 14
sensors 124
sequential access
- devices 233
- to data 166, 267
serial (sequential) access devices 233
serial (sequential) access to data 166
Shoppertrak 207
signal converters 130

simulation 52, 149, 217
single entry multiple use 153
single purpose packages 2
smart cards 193
social implications
- automated systems 125
- commercial data processing 178
- general purpose packages 19
software 223
software integration 11, 77
- common HCI 11, 73
- ease of transfer 11, 74
- links between tasks 12, 74
- static / dynamic linkage 12, 74, 75
software portability 256
source code 253, 254, 255
source document 155
special purpose languages 256
specialised input devices 247
specialised output devices 247
specialised user interfaces 247
speech synthesis 246
spreadsheet 51
- absolute reference 58
- alter cell attributes 54
- calculation 56
- cell protection 59
- cells 51
- charting 56, 75
- columns 51
- formula 51, 53, 58
- insert column 55
- insert row 55
- relative reference 58
- replicate 55
- rows 51
- text 51
- values 51
storage
- electronic 14
- manual 14
storage location 223, 280
storage, magnitude of 234, 15
stored program - see program
structure diagram 291
sub-directory 266
systems analysis 128, 171
systems analyst 171
systems software 250

tabulation 30
tape streamer 227
technical implications - automated systems 126
tele-banking 189
teleshopping 100
telesoftware 93
Teleworking 103
Teletext 88
- frame 90
- page 89
- speed 93
Teletext adapters 89, 93
Teletext editor 91
test data 285, 287
thesaurus 32
touch sensitive screen 239
Touch talker 247
track 229
trackball (tracker ball) 240
transaction file 165
transducer 131
transistors 311
translation 251
translator - types of 253
Trekker 135
turnaround document 159
turtle 134
types of check 159, 160, 161

update 165
user guide 296, 297
user identity 23
user-interface 290
user-friendly 6
utility 8

validation 47, 161, 162
valves 310
VDU 242
verification 47, 163
video disc 207, 231
Viewdata 94, 190
- closed user group (CUG) 98
- frame 95
- host computer 98
- page 95
- speed 98
virtual reality 247
virus 18, 175
visual display unit (VDU) 242
voice output 246
voice recognition 241

wide area network 22
WIMP environment 8, 264
Window 8
word 281
word processing 28
- alter line length 29
- centre text 30
- enter text 28
- justify text 30
- search and replace 30,31
- spelling check 31
- standard letters 21, 34
- standard paragraph 32
- wordwrap 29
WORM (write once read many times) 232
write protection 230

yaw 132